A Supplement to
Distribution and Taxonomy of
Birds of the World

A Supplement to
Distribution and Taxonomy of
Birds of the World

Charles G. Sibley and Burt L. Monroe, Jr.

Yale University Press

New Haven and London

Printed in the United States of America.

International standard book number: 0-300-05549-8
Library of Congress catalog card number: 93-60154

A catalogue record for this book is available from the British Library.

The paper in this book meets the guidelines for permanence and durability of the committee on Production Guidelines for Book Longevity of the Council on Library Resources.

10 9 8 7 6 5 4 3 2 1

INTRODUCTION

This supplement includes changes in distribution and taxonomy, and corrections to the original text, of Sibley and Monroe's *Distribution and Taxonomy of Birds of the World* (1990, Yale University Press), compiled from published references or information received by us through 30 September 1992.

The *Supplement* consists of two parts:

Part 1—The first 13 pages are a summary of *changes in systematics* that affect classification, scientific name changes (including those in "groups" within species accounts), English name changes, or changes in the sequence of species. Thus changes in taxonomic matters may be noted without reference to the specific entries in the second part. Refer to the pertinent entries in Part 2 for reasons for the changes.

Part 2—Pages 14-108 list *changes in text*, including the table of contents, list of world numbers, gazeteer, index, and changes in systematics mentioned in Part 1.

Some locality names have been changed to the names used in recent bird books. These include Burkina Faso (for Upper Volta), Bioko (for Fernando Po) and Pagalu (for Annobón) in Africa, as well as Senegambia for the combined region of Senegal and Gambia, to conform to the *Birds of Africa* volumes. In the New Guinea region, change Rooke I. to Umboi and Vuatom to Watom, and in the Marianas, change Aguijan to Agiguan. *These changes should be made everywhere in the original text.*

Few English names have been changed because a Committee of the International Ornithological Congress is currently producing a list of standardized English names for the I.O.C. in 1994. In some instances where our policy was not followed in the original text (e.g., use of BOREAL PEWEE for the well-established OLIVE-SIDED FLYCATCHER, *Contopus borealis*), or where the change was clearly in error (e.g., "GABOON" WOODPECKER, COUCAL, BOUBOU and HELMETSHRIKE have been changed to "GABON" because in each case the modifier pertains to the country rather than to the mahogany-colored wood or tree), the original name has been restored. We have restored the word "ISLAND" or "ISLANDS" to some English names, and have changed "TAIWAN" to "FORMOSAN" to conform to usage in that region. The names of birds in Madagascar have been changed to conform to the *Guide to the Birds of Madagascar,* by Olivier Langrand (1990, Yale University Press), according to policy as outlined in the original book.

Special effort has been made to improve accounts for some of the more complex avian genera, notably *Collocalia* and *Otus*. Changes in *Otus* are based on suggestions provided by Joe T. Marshall and Ben King, who have made additional studies on most of the species since their suggestions for the original text. Sequence changes have been made in two other large genera *(Francolinus, Anas),* based on recently published studies.

We have added references, including those for all new species names proposed since 1950, and pertinent taxonomic articles since 1989, as well as older articles now deemed relevant or missed in the earlier text.

The response to our request for suggestions and corrections for the present supplement has been extensive and gratifying. We request that suggestions and corrections continue to be sent to Burt L. Monroe, Jr., Dept. of Biology, Univ. of Louisville, Louisville, KY 40292, USA. Taxonomic opinions are welcome, but we ask that they be accompanied by reasons why a change should be made and by a complete citation for publications or articles in press.

How to use this supplement.—Both parts have an initial page number entry that refers to the account in Sibley and Monroe (1990). Changes in the accounts should be made in their entirety *before* a sequence change is made, because the page numbers refer to those in Sibley and Monroe (1990). In Part 1, following a change, the original form is included parenthetically after the word "not."

Part 2 is more complex. The original species accounts consist of four parts: *heading* (consisting of **genus**, *[superspecies]* if appropriate, **species**, author, year of publication of original description, ENGLISH NAME, and [World Number]); *habitat* (up to first period in initial paragraph of account following heading); *range* (remainder of initial paragraph); and *comments* (optional final paragraph). Changes in accounts are noted as to the appropriate section; if no section is specified, the change pertains to the *range* section.

Inclusion of an ellipsis "..." in a changed account means that the original wording in that section between the word preceding the ellipsis and that following it remains unchanged. If a species has been split into two or more accounts, or if a new species has been added, the pertinent accounts are reproduced in their entirety.

In the section on updated world numbers (pages 80-83 herein, pages 785-848 in the original book), entries are listed by world number. If the world number of the entry already exists in the original book, then the updated version should replace the old one. If the number is new, it should be inserted in the appropriate place.

In the sections on the gazeteer (pages 83-84 herein, pages 875-906 in the original book) and index (pages 90-108 herein, pages 940-1111 in the original book), if the entry already exists, the updated version should replace the old one. If the entry is new, where it is to be placed alphabetically in the sequence will be indicated.

In the section of references (pages 84-90), entries should be changed or inserted as indicated.

An updated world list (scientific and English names, including those of groups, plus abbreviated geographical distributions), *World List of Birds* (Monroe and Sibley), will be published by Yale University Press in 1993. Systematic treatment in this list will correspond to the updated material included herein.

Acknowledgments.—We thank the following persons who have provided suggestions and corrections for this supplement: Per Alström, Richard C. Banks, Mark Beaman, Bruce M. Beehler, M. Ralph Browning, P. A. Clancey, William S. Clark, James F. Clements, Paul R. Clyne, Mike Crosby, Normand David, Paul DeBenedictis, Edward C. Dickinson, R. J. Dowsett, C. Craig Farquhar, Gary M. Fellers, L.D.C. Fishpool, Asbjørn Folvik, James Hancock, Melanie Heath, Graham Higman, Steve N.G. Howell, Tim Inskipp, Mort Isler, Phyllis Isler, Alan C. Kemp, Ben King, Lars Larsson, Ian Lewis, S. M. Lister, Richard Liversidge, Adrian Long, Ian McAllan, Linda R. Macaulay, Glenn R. Mahler, Joe T. Marshall, Krister Mild, Urban Olsson, Kenneth C. Parkes, Robert B. Payne, William S. Peckover, Alan P. Peterson, Missy Peterson, H. Douglas Pratt, Robert S. Ridgely, J.T.R. Sharrock, Hadoram Shirihai, Fred C. Sibley, Alfred E. Smalley, Phoebe Snetsinger, Alison Stattersfield, James R. Stewart, J. Denis Summers-Smith, Y. Swaab, and Don A. Turner. The World Numbers used in the original text and this update have been adopted and extended with permission from the "Bird Master Data File (BMDF)," © 1985 by P. William Smith.

Sibley and Monroe (1990), *Distribution and Taxonomy of Birds of the World*, Yale Univ. Press.
SUPPLEMENT, Part 1—Scientific or English name, or classification [changes through 30 September 1992]

page #

[*Listed in "Errata" sheet published with book]

2 —Family **Tinamidae** (not **Tinamiidae**)
5 —Order **CRACIFORMES** (not **GALLIFORMES**)
6 —*Ortalis [poliocephala] wagleri*, RUFOUS-BELLIED CHACHALACA (not WAGLER'S)
10 —*Megapodius [freycinet] layardi*, VANUATU SCRUBFOWL (not NEW HEBRIDES)
10 —*Megapodius pritchardii*, NIAUFOOU SCRUBFOWL (not POLYNESIAN)
12-14 Sequence species of *Francolinus* as follows: *francolinus, pictus, pintadeanus, pondicerianus, gularis, coqui, albogularis, schlegelii, lathami, sephaena, streptophorus, finschi, africanus, levaillantii, psilolaemus, shelleyi, levaillantoides, nahani, hartlaubi, bicalcaratus, clappertoni, icterorhynchus, harwoodi, adspersus, capensis, hildebrandti, natalensis, ahantensis, squamatus, griseostriatus, leucoscepus, rufopictus, afer, swainsonii, erckelii, ochropectus, castaneicollis, nobilis, jacksoni, camerunensis* and *swierstrai*
15 —*Perdix dauurica* (not *dauuricae*)
15 —*Coturnix [coromandelica]* has priority over *C. [delegorguei]* for superspecies name
16 —*Arborophila crudigularis*, FORMOSAN PARTRIDGE (not TAIWAN)
17 —*Arborophila [javanica] hyperythra* (add to superspecies and sequence before *A. gingica*); add groups ¶*hyperythra*, RED-BREASTED PARTRIDGE; and ¶*erythrophrys*, KINABALU PARTRIDGE
*17 —*Rollulus rouloul* (not *roulroul*)
*19 —*Lophura [inornata] hoogerwerfi* (not *hoogerswerfi*)
19 —*Lophura erythrophthalma* (not *erythropthalma*)
19 —*Lophura hatinhensis* (not *haitensis*), VIETNAMESE PHEASANT (not FIREBACK); sequence after *L. edwardsi*
21 —*Argusianus argus*, remove superspecies
21 —Delete *Argusianus bipunctatus* entry
23 —*Tympanuchus [cupido] cupido* and *T. [cupido] pallidicinctus* (both PRAIRIE-CHICKEN, not PRAIRIE-CHICKEN); superspecies [PRAIRIE-CHICKEN] (not [PRAIRIE CHICKEN])
28 —Under Oxyurinae after *Biziura lobata*, insert *Heteronetta atricapilla* from p. 42
29 —*Anser [fabalis] fabalis*, add groups ¶*fabalis*, FOREST BEAN-GOOSE; and ¶*serrirostris*, TUNDRA BEAN-GOOSE
34-38 —Sequence species of *Anas* as follows: *specularioides, specularis, capensis, strepera, falcata, penelope, americana, sibilatrix, sparsa, rubripes, fulvigula, platyrhynchos, wyvilliana, laysanensis, poecilorhyncha, luzonica, superciliosa, undulata, melleri, discors, cyanoptera, smithii, platalea, rhynchotis, clypeata, bernieri, gibberifrons, gracilis, castanea, aucklandica, bahamensis, erythrorhyncha, flavirostris, acuta, eatoni, georgica, querquedula, formosa, crecca, puna, versicolor* and *hottentota*
34 —*Anas crecca* and *Anas flavirostris* (delete superspecies)
35 —*Anas bernieri*, BERNIER'S TEAL (not MADAGASCAR)
35 —*Anas laysanensis* and *Anas fulvigula* (delete superspecies)
36 —*Anas [superciliosa] poecilorhyncha*, add groups ¶*zonorhyncha*, EASTERN SPOT-BILLED DUCK; and ¶*poecilorhyncha*, INDIAN SPOT-BILLED DUCK
*36 —*Anas specularioides* (not *specularoides*)
*38 —*Netta peposaca* (not *peposeaca*)
41 —*Melanitta fusca*, change English names of ¶*stejnegeri* to ASIATIC SCOTER and ¶*deglandi* to WHITE-WINGED SCOTER
42 —*Mergus australis*, AUCKLAND ISLANDS MERGANSER (not AUCKLAND MERGANSER)
42 —*Heteronetta atricapilla*, move to Oxyurinae (p. 28) and sequence after *Biziura lobata*
46 —*Picumnus [cirratus] dorbygnianus* (not *dorbygianus*)
46 —*Picumnus fuscus*, sequence after *P. exilis* on p. 45
50 —*Campethera [maculosa] maculosa*, LITTLE GREEN WOODPECKER (not LITLE)
51 —*Dendropicos [gabonensis] gabonensis*, GABON WOODPECKER (not GABOON)
53 —*Dendrocopos leucotos*, add groups ¶*leucotos*, WHITE-BACKED WOODPECKER; and ¶*lilfordi*, LILFORD'S WOODPECKER

60 —Split *Picus viridis* into **Picus [viridis] viridis**, EURASIAN GREEN WOODPECKER, and **Picus [viridis] vaillantii**, LEVAILLANT'S WOODPECKER; retain [EURASIAN GREEN WOODPECKER] for superspecies

60 —*Picus [viridis] viridis*, add groups ¶*viridis*, EURASIAN GREEN WOODPECKER; and ¶*sharpei*, IBERIAN WOODPECKER

63 —*Megalaima corvina*, BROWN-THROATED BARBET (not BROWN-THRAOTED)

63 —*Megalaima [armillaris] armillaris*, FLAME-FRONTED BARBET (not ORANGE-FRONTED)

64 —*Pogoniulus [simplex] coryphaeus*, WESTERN TINKERBIRD (not WESTERN GREEN-TINKERBIRD)

65 —*Pogoniulus [simplex] leucomystax*, MOUSTACHED TINKERBIRD (not MOUSTACHED GREEN-TINKERBIRD)

65 —*Pogoniulus [simplex] simplex*, GREEN TINKERBIRD (not AFRICAN GREEN-TINKERBIRD)

66 —*Lybius [leucocephalus] leucocephalus*, add group at end of others ¶*leucogaster*, WHITE-BELLIED BARBET

71 —Order **GALBULIFORMES** (not **GABULIFORMES**)

73 —*Jacamerops aureus* (not *aurea*)

77 —*Penelopides [panini] manillae* (not *manilloe*)

78 —*Aceros [undulatus] narcondami*, NARCONDAM HORNBILL (not NARCODAM)

79 —*Bucorvus leadbeateri* (not *cafer*)

79 —*Upupa [epops] africana*, add groups ¶*africana*, AFRICAN HOOPOE; and ¶*marginata*, MADAGASCAR HOOPOE

80 —Apalodermatinae, *not* Apaloderminae

81 —Sequence *Trogon [viridis] bairdii* before *T. [viridis] viridis*

84 —*Brachypteracias squamigera*, SCALY GROUND-ROLLER (not SCALED)

84 —*Atelornis crossleyi*, RUFOUS-HEADED GROUND-ROLLER (not CROSSLEY'S)

85 —*Leptosomus discolor*, CUCKOO ROLLER (not COUROL)

86 —*Alcedo [meninting] quadribrachys*, SHINING-BLUE KINGFISHER (not SHINING BLUE)

87 —*Alcedo [cyanopecta] cyanopecta*, INDIGO-BANDED KINGFISHER (not DWARF RIVER)

87 —Split *Alcedo [cristata] cristata* into **Alcedo [cristata] cristata**, MALACHITE KINGFISHER, and **Alcedo [cristata] vintsioides**, MALAGASY KINGFISHER; retain [MALACHITE KINGFISHER] for superspecies

88 —HALCYONOIDEA and **Halcyonidae** (not DACELONOIDEA and **Dacelonidae**)

90 —*Todirhamphus cinnamominus*, change groups to ¶*miyakoensis*, RYUKYU KINGFISHER; ¶*cinnamominus*, GUAM KINGFISHER; and ¶*reichenbachii*, CAROLINE ISLANDS KINGFISHER

91 —*Todirhamphus australasia*, CINNAMON-BANDED KINGFISHER (not CINNAMON-BACKED)

92 —*Tanysiptera sylvia*, add groups ¶*sylvia*, BUFF-BREASTED PARADISE-KINGFISHER; ¶*nigriceps*, BLACK-HEADED PARADISE-KINGFISHER

94 —*Merops hirundineus* (not *hirundinaceus*)

97 —*Cuculus fugax*, add groups ¶*hyperythrus*, NORTHERN HAWK-CUCKOO; ¶*fugax*, HODGSON'S HAWK-CUCKOO; and ¶*pectoralis*, PHILIPPINE HAWK-CUCKOO

102 —*Coua delalandei*, SNAIL-EATING COUA (not DELALANDE'S)

102 —*Coua reynaudii*, RED-FRONTED COUA (not REYNAUD'S)

102 —*Coua ruficeps*, RED-CAPPED COUA (not OLIVE-CAPPED)

104 —*Centropus [leucogaster] anselli*, GABON COUCAL (not GABOON)

105 —*Coccyzus euleri* (not *julieni*)

106 —*Hyetornis rufigularis*, BAY-BREASTED CUCKOO (not RUFOUS-BREASTED); sequence after *H. pluvialis*

106 —*Saurothera merlini*, GREAT LIZARD-CUCKOO (not CUBAN)

110 —*Vini stepheni*, STEPHEN'S LORIKEET (not STEPHENS'S)

110 —*Vini peruviana*, BLUE LORIKEET (not TAHITIAN)

113 —*Nestor [meridionalis] productus*, NORFOLK ISLAND KAKA (not NORFOLK KAKA)

113 —*Nestor [meridionalis] meridionalis*, NEW ZEALAND KAKA (not COMMON)

114 —*Prioniturus [platenae] montanus*, MONTANE RACQUET-TAIL (not LUZON)

117 —*Cyanoramphus cookii*, NORFOLK ISLAND PARAKEET (not NORFOLK PARAKEET)

117 —*Cyanoramphus novaezelandiae*, ¶*subflavescens*, LORD HOWE ISLAND PARAKEET (not LORD HOWE PARAKEET)

117 —*Cyanoramphus ulietanus*, RAIATEA PARAKEET (not SOCIETY PARAKEET)

118 —*Geopsittacus occidentalis* (not *Pezoporus*)

118 —*Strigops habroptilus* (not *hapbroptilus*)

120 —*Loriculus philippensis*, add groups ¶*philippensis*, COLASISI; and ¶*bonapartei*, BLACK-BILLED HANGING-PARROT

123 —*Aratinga holochlora*, after ¶*holochlora*, add ¶*brevipes*, SOCORRO PARAKEET

128 —*Nannopsittaca [panychlora] panychlora*, add superspecies

128 —After *Nannopsittaca [panychlora] panychlora*, add ***Nannopsittaca [panychlora] dachilleae***, AMAZONIAN PARROTLET

132 —After *Amazona farinosa*, add ***Amazona kawalli***, KAWALL'S PARROT

133 —After *Cypseloides cherriei*, add ***Cypseloides [cryptus] storeri***, WHITE-FRONTED SWIFT

133 —*Cypseloides [cryptus] cryptus*, add superspecies; retain [WHITE-CHINNED SWIFT] for superspecies

134 —*Collocalia esculenta* (delete superspecies); add group ¶*marginata*, GREY-RUMPED SWIFTLET after ¶*affinis*

134 —Delete *Collocalia marginata* entry

135 —Before *Collocalia [spodiopygius] infuscata*, insert *Collocalia [spodiopygius] mearnsi* from p. 136

135 —After *Collocalia [vanikorensis] palawanensis*, insert *Collocalia [vanikorensis] amelis* from p. 136

136 —*Collocalia [spodiopygius] mearnsi* (not *[vanikorensis]*), move to p. 135, and sequence before *Collocalia infuscata*

136 —Delete *Collocalia bartschi* entry

136 —*Collocalia [vanikorensis] inquieta*, MICRONESIAN SWIFTLET (not CAROLINE); add groups ¶*bartschi*, MARIANA SWIFTLET; and ¶*inquieta*, CAROLINE ISLANDS SWIFTLET

136 —*Collocalia [leucophaeus] sawtelli*, ATIU SWIFTLET (not SAWTELL'S)

136 —Split *Collocalia [leucophaeus] leucophaeus* into ***Collocalia [leucophaeus] leucophaeus***, TAHITI SWIFTLET, and ***Collocalia [leucophaeus] ocista***, MARQUESAN SWIFTLET; retain [POLYNESIAN SWIFTLET] for superspecies

136 —*Collocalia [vanikorensis] amelis* (not *[fuciphaga]*), move to p. 135, and sequence after *Collocalia palawanensis*

137 —*Zoonavena grandidieri*, MALAGASY SPINETAIL (not MADAGASCAR)

137 —*Telacanthura ussheri* and *melanopygia* (not *Telecanthura*)

142 —*Threnetes [leucurus]* superspecies and reverse sequence: *T. [leucurus] ruckeri* and *T. [leucurus] leucurus*

143 —*Phaethornis superciliosus*, add groups ¶*griseoventer*, JALISCO HERMIT; ¶*mexicanus*, HARTERT'S HERMIT; ¶*longirostris*, LONG-TAILED HERMIT; and ¶*superciliosus*, RUSTY-BREASTED HERMIT

144 —*Phaethornis [longuemareus] longuemareus*, add groups ¶*adolphi*, BOUCARD'S HERMIT; ¶*striigularis*, STRIPE-THROATED HERMIT; and ¶*longuemareus*, LITTLE HERMIT

*145 —*Doryfera ludovicae* (not *ludoviciae*)

148 —Split *Lophornis delattrei* into ***Lophornis [delattrei] brachylopha***, SHORT-CRESTED COQUETTE, and ***Lophornis [delattrei] delattrei***, RUFOUS-CRESTED COQUETTE; retain [RUFOUS-CRESTED COQUETTE] for superspecies

149 —*Chlorostilbon [mellisugus] canivetii*, add groups ¶*auriceps*, GOLDEN-CROWNED EMERALD; ¶*forficatus*, COZUMEL EMERALD; ¶*canivetii*, CANIVET'S EMERALD; and ¶*salvini*, SALVIN'S EMERALD

150 —Split *Thalurania [furcata] colombica* into ***Thalurania [furcata] ridgwayi***, MEXICAN WOODNYMPH; ***Thalurania [furcata] colombica***, BLUE-CROWNED WOODNYMPH (with groups ¶*townsendi* and ¶*colombica*); and ***Thalurania [furcata] fannyi***, GREEN-CROWNED WOODNYMPH (with groups ¶*fannyi* and ¶*hypochlora*)

152 —*Trochilus polytmus*, ¶*polytmus*, RED-BILLED STREAMERTAIL (not WESTERN); and ¶*scitulus*, BLACK-BILLED STREAMERTAIL (not EASTERN)

155 —*Amazilia viridifrons*, add groups ¶*viridifrons*, GREEN-FRONTED HUMMINGBIRD; and ¶*wagneri*, CINNAMON-SIDED HUMMINGBIRD

156 —*Aphantochroa* (not *Aphanotochroa*)

161 —*Polyonymus* (not *Polyonomus*)

167 —*Corythaixoides [personatus] concolor* and *C. [personatus] personatus* (genus masculine)

168 —Sequence *Tyto [tenebricosa] tenebricosa* before *T. [tenebricosa] multipunctata*

168 —*Tyto soumagnei*, MADAGASCAR RED OWL (not SOUMAGNE'S)

169-174 —Sequence species of *Otus* as follows: *sagittatus, rufescens, icterorhynchus, ireneae, balli, spilocephalus, umbra, angelinae, manadensis, longicornis, mindorensis, mirus, hartlaubi, brucei, flammeolus, scops, elegans, mantananensis, magicus, rutilus, pauliani, brookii, bakkamoena, mentawi, fuliginosus, megalotis, silvicola, leucotis, kennicottii, asio, trichopsis, choliba, koepckeae, roboratus, clarkii, barbarus, ingens, marshalli, watsonii, atricapillus, vermiculatus, sanctaecatarinae, lawrencii, nudipes, podarginus, albogularis*

170 —*Otus spilocephalus*, remove superspecies; change groups to ¶*spilocephalus* MOUNTAIN SCOPS-OWL; ¶*hambroecki* FORMOSAN SCOPS-OWL; ¶*vandewateri*, VANDEWATER'S SCOPS-OWL; and ¶*luciae*, BORNEAN SCOPS-OWL

170 —*Otus [manadensis] mirus*, change superspecies to *[manadensis]* (not *[spilocephalus]*)

170 —*Otus scops*, COMMON SCOPS-OWL (not EURASIAN); remove superspecies; add groups ¶*scops*, EURASIAN SCOPS-OWL; ¶*sunia*, ORIENTAL SCOPS-OWL; and ¶*senegalensis*, AFRICAN SCOPS-OWL

170 —Delete *Otus senegalensis* and *O. sunia* entries

171 —*Otus [manadensis]* superspecies: *O. [manadensis] umbra*, *O. [manadensis] angelinae*, *O. [manadensis] manadensis*, *O. [manadensis] longicornis*, *O. [manadensis] mindorensis* and *O. [manadensis] mirus*

171 —Delete *Otus alfredi* entry

171 —*Otus [magicus] magicus*, change groups to ¶*insularis*, SEYCHELLES SCOPS-OWL; ¶*enganensis*, ENGGANO SCOPS-OWL; ¶*magicus*, MOLUCCAN SCOPS-OWL; ¶*albiventris*, FLORES SCOPS-OWL; and ¶*beccarii*, PAPUAN SCOPS-OWL

171 —Delete *Otus [magicus] enganensis* entry

171 —*Otus [rutilus] rutilus*, MALAGASY SCOPS-OWL (not MADAGASCAR); change groups to ¶*pembaensis*, PEMBA SCOPS-OWL; ¶*capnodes*, ANJOUAN SCOPS-OWL; and ¶*rutilus*, MADAGASCAR SCOPS-OWL; retain [MALAGASY SCOPS-OWL] for superspecies

171 —After *Otus [rutilus] rutilus*, add **Otus [rutilus] pauliani**, COMORO SCOPS-OWL

171 —*Otus [bakkamoena] bakkamoena*, COLLARED SCOPS-OWL (not INDIAN); add groups ¶*bakkamoena*, INDIAN SCOPS-OWL; ¶*lempiji*, COLLARED SCOPS-OWL; and ¶*semitorques*, JAPANESE SCOPS-OWL; remove English name for superspecies

171 —Delete *Otus [bakkamoena] lempiji* entry

172 —*Otus [bakkamoena] megalotis*, add groups ¶*megalotis*, PHILIPPINE SCREECH-OWL; ¶*nigrorum*, NEGROS SCREECH-OWL; and ¶*everetti*, EVERETT'S SCREECH-OWL

172 —*Otus [asio] kennicottii*, change groups to ¶*kennicottii*, WESTERN SCREECH-OWL; ¶*vinaceus*, VINACEOUS SCREECH-OWL; ¶*seductus*, BALSAS SCREECH-OWL; ¶*lambi*, OAXACA SCREECH-OWL; and ¶*cooperi*, PACIFIC SCREECH-OWL

172 —Delete *Otus seductus* and *O. cooperi* entries

173 —*Otus roboratus*, add groups ¶*pacificus*, COASTAL SCREECH-OWL; and ¶*roboratus*, WEST PERUVIAN SCREECH-OWL

173 —*Otus barbarus*, SANTA BARBARA SCREECH-OWL (not BRIDLED)

173 —*Otus [atricapillus] vermiculatus*, add superspecies

173 —After *Otus [atricapillus] vermiculatus*, add **Otus [atricapillus] sanctaecatarinae**, LONG-TUFTED SCOPS-OWL

173 —*Otus [atricapillus] atricapillus*, add superspecies; delete group ¶*sanctaecatarinae*; add English name for superspecies [VARIABLE SCREECH-OWL]

173 —*Otus watsonii*, delete superspecies; add groups ¶*watsonii*, TAWNY-BELLIED SCREECH-OWL; and ¶*usta*, AUSTRAL SCREECH-OWL; delete English name for superspecies

172 —Delete *Otus usta* and *O. petersoni* entries

173 —*Otus marshalli*, delete superspecies; add groups ¶*petersoni*, CINNAMON SCREECH-OWL; and ¶*marshalli*, CLOUD-FOREST SCREECH-OWL

174 —*Otus [nudipes] lawrencii* and *O. [nudipes] nudipes*, add superspecies and reverse to this sequence

174 —*Otus podarginus*, PALAU OWL (not SCOPS-OWL)

174 —*Mimizuku gurneyi*, LESSER EAGLE-OWL (not GIANT SCOPS-OWL)

174 —Split *Bubo poensis* into **Bubo [poensis] poensis**, FRASER'S EAGLE-OWL, and **Bubo [poensis] vosseleri**, USAMBARA EAGLE-OWL (not NDUK); retain [FRASER'S EAGLE-OWL] for superspecies

177 —*Pulsatrix [melanota] melanota*, change name of superspecies *P. [melanota]* to [WHITE-CHINNED OWL]

178 —*Glaucidium minutissimum* add **Glaucidium [passerinum] hardyi**, HARDY'S PYGMY-OWL

178 —Split *Glaucidium brasilianum* into **Glaucidium [brasilianum] brasilianum**, FERRUGINOUS PYGMY-OWL, **Glaucidium [brasilianum] peruanum**, PERUVIAN PYGMY-OWL, and **Glaucidium [brasilianum] nanum**, AUSTRAL PYGMY-OWL

179 —*Glaucidium [passerinum] jardinii*, add superspecies and sequence after *G. [passerinum] gnoma*; also split into **Glaucidium [passerinum] jardinii**, ANDEAN PYGMY-OWL, and **Glaucidium [passerinum] bolivianum**, YUNGAS PYGMY-OWL

179 —*Glaucidium [radiatum] castanonotum* (not *castanonotus*)

179-180 —*Athene [noctua] noctua* and *Athene [noctua] brama*, add superspecies

180 —Merge *Aegolius acadicus* and *A. ridgwayi* as groups under *Aegolius acadicus* (SAW-WHET OWL): ¶*acadicus*, NORTHERN SAW-WHET OWL, and ¶*ridgwayi*, UNSPOTTED SAW-WHET OWL; remove English name for superspecies

180 —Delete *Aegolius ridgwayi* entry

180 —*Aegolius harrisii*, delete superspecies

181 —*Ninox [novaeseelandiae] rudolfi*, not *N. rudolphi*

181 —*Ninox [novaeseelandiae] novaeseelandiae*, ¶*albaria*, LORD HOWE ISLAND BOOBOOK (not LORD HOWE BOOBOOK); ¶*undulata*, NORFOLK ISLAND BOOBOOK (not NORFOLK BOOBOOK)

181 —*Ninox scutulata*, add groups ¶*scutulata*, BROWN HAWK-OWL; and ¶*obscura*, HUME'S HAWK-OWL

181 —*Ninox superciliaris*, WHITE-BROWED HAWK-OWL (not MADAGASCAR HAWK-OWL)

181 —*Ninox squamipila*, ¶*natalis*, CHRISTMAS ISLAND HAWK-OWL (not CHRISTMAS HAWK-OWL)

182 —*Ninox jacquinoti*, SOLOMON ISLANDS HAWK-OWL(not SOLOMON HAWK-OWL)

184 —*Batrachostomus [javensis] javensis*, change English name of superspecies to [HORSFIELD'S FROGMOUTH]

186 —Split *Lurocalis semitorquatus* into **Lurocalis [semitorquatus] semitorquatus**, SHORT-TAILED NIGHTHAWK, and **Lurocalis [semitorquatus] rufiventris**, RUFOUS-BELLIED NIGHTHAWK; groups in *L. semitorquatus* remain ¶*semitorquatus* and ¶*nattereri*

188 —*Caprimulgus [vociferus] saturatus* (add to superspecies)

189 —*Caprimulgus [parvulus] anthonyi*, SCRUB NIGHTJAR (not ANTHONY'S)

190 —Split *Caprimulgus [macrurus] manillensis* into **Caprimulgus [macrurus] manillensis**, PHILIPPINE NIGHTJAR, and **Caprimulgus [macrurus] celebensis**, SULAWESI NIGHTJAR

191 —After *Caprimulgus [pectoralis] pectoralis*, add **Caprimulgus prigoginei**, ITOMBWE NIGHTJAR

197 —*Streptopelia [lugens] hypopyrrha*, ADAMAWA TURTLE-DOVE (not ANDAMAWA)

203 —*Claravis [godefrida]* superspecies: *C. [godefrida] mondetoura* and *C. [godefrida] godefrida*, and reverse sequence; retain [MAROON-CHESTED GROUND-DOVE] for superspecies

206 —*Gallicolumba kubaryi*, CAROLINE ISLANDS GROUND-DOVE (not CAROLINE GROUND-DOVE)

208 —Split *Treron [australis] australis* into **Treron [australis] pembaensis**, PEMBA GREEN-PIGEON, and **Treron [australis] australis**, MADAGASCAR GREEN-PIGEON

210 —*Ptilinopus porphyraceus*, ¶*ponapensis*, PURPLE-CAPPED FRUIT-DOVE (not POHNPEI)

210 —*Ptilinopus rarotongensis*, COOK ISLANDS FRUIT-DOVE (not RAROTONGAN)

211 —*Ptilinopus [purpuratus] chalcurus*, MAKATEA FRUIT-DOVE (not MAHATEA)

211 —*Ptilinopus [purpuratus] insularis*, HENDERSON ISLAND FRUIT-DOVE (not HENDERSON FRUIT-DOVE); and add to superspecies

212 —*Ptilinopus [luteovirens] layardi*, WHISTLING DOVE (not VELVET)

213 —*Ducula [rosacea] whartoni*, CHRISTMAS ISLAND IMPERIAL-PIGEON (not CHRISTMAS IMPERIAL-PIGEON)

213 —*Ducula pinon*, PINON IMPERIAL-PIGEON (not PINYON)

214 —*Ducula [bicolor]* superspecies: *D. [bicolor] bicolor*, *D. [bicolor] luctuosa* and *D. [bicolor] spilorrhoa*, in that sequence; after *spilorrhoa*, add **Ducula [bicolor] constans**, KIMBERLEY IMPERIAL-PIGEON, and **Ducula [bicolor] subflavescens**, YELLOW-TINTED IMPERIAL-PIGEON

214 —*Hemiphaga novaeseelandiae*, ¶*spadicea*, NORFOLK ISLAND PIGEON (not NORFOLK PIGEON)

219 —FAMILY **Aramidae** (not **Heliornithidae**)

219 —Delete Tribe Aramini

219 —Family **Heliornithidae** (not Tribe Heliornithini)

219 —*Rhynochetos jubatus* (not *Rhynochetus jubata*)

220 —*Sarothrura watersi*, SLENDER-BILLED FLUFFTAIL (not WATERS'S)

223 —*Gallirallus [lafresnayanus] sylvestris*, LORD HOWE ISLAND RAIL (not LORD HOWE RAIL)

223 —*Gallirallus conditicius* (not *conditicus*)

223 —After *Gallirallus [philippensis] philippensis*, add **Gallirallus [philippensis] rovianae**, ROVIANA RAIL

223 —*Gallirallus [philippensis] wakensis*, WAKE ISLAND RAIL (not WAKE RAIL)

223 —*Gallirallus [philippensis] modestus*, CHATHAM ISLANDS RAIL (not CHATHAM RAIL)

225 —*Lewinia [pectoralis] muelleri*, AUCKLAND ISLANDS RAIL (not AUCKLAND RAIL)

225 —*Dryolimnas cuvieri*, WHITE-THROATED RAIL (not CUVIER'S)

225 —*Atlantisia rogersi*, INACCESSIBLE ISLAND RAIL (not INACCESSIBLE RAIL)

226 —*Amaurornis [olivaceus] isabellinus*, ISABELLINE WATERHEN (not BUSH-HEN); sequence after *A. olivaceus*
226 —*Amaurornis [olivaceus] olivaceus*, BUSH-HEN (not PLAIN BUSH-HEN); sequence before *A. isabellinus*
226 —*Amaurornis [olivaceus] moluccanus*, RUFOUS-TAILED WATERHEN (not BUSH-HEN)
226 —*Amaurornis [flavirostra] olivieri*, SAKALAVA RAIL (not OLIVIER'S CRAKE)
228 —*Porzana [tabuensis] atra*, HENDERSON ISLAND CRAKE (not HENDERSON CRAKE)
229 —*Porphyrio [albus] albus*, LORD HOWE ISLAND SWAMPHEN (not LORD HOWE SWAMPHEN)
231 —*Mesitornis variegata*, WHITE-BREASTED MESITE (not ROATELO)
232 —*Mesitornis unicolor*, BROWN MESITE (not ROATELO)
232 —*Monias benschi*, SUBDESERT MESITE (not MONIAS)
232 —*Pterocles personatus*, MADAGASCAR SANDGROUSE (not MASKED)
235 —*Coenocorypha [aucklandica] pusilla*, CHATHAM ISLANDS SNIPE (not CHATHAM SNIPE)
238 —*Tringa [hypoleucos] hypoleucos* and *Tringa [hypoleucos] macularia* (add superspecies)
243 —CHIONOIDEA and **Chionidae**, *not* CHIONIDOIDEA and **Chionididae**
243 —After *Chionis minor* entry, add Family **Pluvianellidae** with species account of *Pluvianellus socialis* from p. 250
244 —*Haematopus [ostralegus] meadewaldoi*, CANARY ISLANDS OYSTERCATCHER (not CANARY OYSTERCATCHER)
244 —*Haematopus [ostralegus] unicolor*, ¶*chathamensis*, CHATHAM ISLANDS OYSTERCATCHER (not CHATHAM OYSTERCATCHER)
247 —*Charadrius thoracicus*, MADAGASCAR PLOVER (not BLACK-BANDED)
249 —Change *Charadrius novaeseelandiae* to *Thinornis novaeseelandiae*
250 —Move *Pluvianellus socialis* to p. 243 under Family **Pluvianellidae** following *Chionis minor* account
256 —*Larus [argentatus] argentatus*, add groups ¶*argentatus*, HERRING GULL; ¶*heuglini*, HEUGLIN'S GULL; and ¶*vegae*, VEGA GULL
257 —*Larus cachinnans*, remove from superspecies; add groups ¶*atlantis*, ATLANTIC ISLANDS GULL; and ¶*cachinnans*, YELLOW-LEGGED GULL; sequence after *L. schistisagus*
257 —*Larus fuscus*, add groups ¶*graellsi*, DARK-BACKED GULL; and ¶*fuscus*, LESSER BLACK-BACKED GULL
263 —Merge *Procelsterna cerulea* and *P. albivitta* as groups under *Procelsterna cerulea* (BLUE-GREY NODDY): ¶*cerulea*, BLUE NODDY; and ¶*albivitta*, GREY NODDY
263 —Delete *Procelsterna albivitta* entry
269 —*Milvus [migrans] migrans*, add groups ¶*migrans*, BLACK KITE; and ¶*aegyptius*, YELLOW-BILLED KITE
270 —*Haliaeetus [leucogaster] sanfordi*, SANFORD'S FISH-EAGLE (not SOLOMON)
273 —*Spilornis [cheela] cheela*, after ¶*cheela*, add ¶*perplexus*, RYUKYU SERPENT-EAGLE
275 —*Micronisus gabar* (not *Melierax*)
283 —*Buteo [albicaudatus] polyosoma* (add to superspecies)
284 —*Buteo [albicaudatus] poecilochrous* (add to superspecies)
286 —*Aquila rapax*, TAWNY EAGLE (delete superspecies), add groups ¶*rapax*, AFRICAN TAWNY-EAGLE; and ¶*vindhiana*, ASIAN TAWNY-EAGLE
286 —Delete *Aquila vindhiana* entry
286 —*Aquila nipalensis*, STEPPE EAGLE (delete superspecies), add groups ¶*orientalis*, WESTERN STEPPE-EAGLE; and ¶*nipalensis*, EASTERN STEPPE-EAGLE
286 —*Aquila wahlbergi*, sequence after *A. verreauxii* on p. 287
*287 —*Lophaetus* (not *Lophoaetus*)
288 —*Sagittarius serpentarius*, SECRETARYBIRD (not SECRETARY-BIRD)
291 —*Falco [tinnunculus] newtoni*, MADAGASCAR KESTREL (not NEWTON'S)
292 —*Falco zoniventris*, BANDED KESTREL (not BARRED)
293 —*Falco [subbuteo] cuvierii* (not *cuvieri*)
293 —*Falco novaeseelandiae* (not *novaezeelandiae*)
294 —Delete *Falco altaicus* entry
295 —After *Tachybaptus [ruficollis] novaehollandiae*, add **Tachybaptus rufolavatus**, ALAOTRA GREBE
299 —*Phalacrocorax [pygmeus] pygmeus* and *Phalacrocorax [pygmeus] niger* (not *pygmaeus*)
300 —*Phalacrocorax [carbo] carbo*, add groups ¶*carbo*, GREAT CORMORANT; and ¶*lucidus*, WHITE-BREASTED CORMORANT; delete English name for superspecies
300 —Delete *Phalacrocorax lucidus* entry

301 —*Phalacrocorax campbelli*, CAMPBELL ISLAND SHAG (not CAMPBELL SHAG)

301 —*Phalacrocorax [carunculatus] onslowi*, CHATHAM ISLANDS SHAG (not CHATHAM SHAG)

301 —*Phalacrocorax colensoi*, AUCKLAND ISLANDS SHAG (not AUCKLAND SHAG)

301 —*Phalacrocorax ranfurlyi*, BOUNTY ISLANDS SHAG (not BOUNTY SHAG)

302 —*Phalacrocorax [punctatus] featherstoni*, PITT ISLAND SHAG (not PITT SHAG)

303 —*Egretta [garzetta] dimorpha*, DIMORPHIC EGRET (not MASCARENE REEF-EGRET)

304 —*Ardea [cinerea] cinerea*, add groups ¶*cinerea*, GREY HERON; and ¶*monicae*, MAURITANIAN HERON

304 —*Ardea [melanocephala] humbloti*, HUMBLOT'S HERON (not MADAGASCAR)

305 —*Casmerodius albus*, add groups ¶*albus*, GREAT EGRET; and ¶*egretta*, AMERICAN EGRET

305 —*Mesophoyx intermedia*, add groups ¶*brachyrhyncha*, YELLOW-BILLED EGRET; ¶*intermedia*, LESSER EGRET; and ¶*plumifera*, PLUMED EGRET

308 —*Cochlearius cochlearia* (not *Cochlearius cochlearius*)

310 —*Dupetor flavicollis* (not *Ixobrychus*)

313 —Merge *Threskiornis bernieri* and *T. aethiopicus* as groups under *T. [aethiopicus] aethiopicus* (SACRED IBIS): ¶*aethiopicus*, SACRED IBIS; and ¶*bernieri*, MADAGASCAR IBIS

318 —*Fregata andrewsi*, CHRISTMAS ISLAND FRIGATEBIRD (not CHRISTMAS FRIGATEBIRD)

321 —Merge *Pagodroma nivea* and *P. confusa* as groups under *Pagodroma nivea* (SNOW PETREL): ¶*nivea*, LESSER SNOW-PETREL; and ¶*confusa*, GREATER SNOW-PETREL; delete superspecies

321 —*Pterodroma brevirostris* (not *Lugensa*)

321 —*Pseudobulweria [rostrata]* superspecies, change all four species to *Pterodroma* (not *Pseudobulweria*); change English name of *macgillivrayi* to FIJI PETREL (not MACGILLIVRAY'S)

321 —*Pterodroma axillaris*, CHATHAM ISLANDS PETREL (not CHATHAM PETREL)

322 —Merge *Pterodroma heraldica* and *P. arminjoniana* as groups under *Pterodroma arminjoniana* (HERALD PETREL): ¶*heraldica*, HERALD PETREL; and ¶*arminjoniana*, TRINDADE PETREL; delete superspecies

323 —Split *Pterodroma phaeopygia* into **Pterodroma [phaeopygia] sandwichensis**, HAWAIIAN PETREL, and **Pterodroma [phaeopygia] phaeopygia**, GALAPAGOS PETREL; retain [DARK-RUMPED PETREL] for superspecies

325 —*Calonectris diomedea*, add groups ¶*diomedea*, CORY'S SHEARWATER; and ¶*edwardsii*, CAPE VERDE SHEARWATER

326 —*Puffinus nativitatis*, CHRISTMAS ISLAND SHEARWATER (not CHRISTMAS SHEARWATER)

326 —*Puffinus yelkouan*, MEDITERRANEAN SHEARWATER (not YELKOUAN)

327 —*Diomedea [exulans] amsterdamensis*, AMSTERDAM ISLAND ALBATROSS (not AMSTERDAM ALBATROSS)

328 —*Diomedea cauta*, ¶*eremita*, CHATHAM ISLANDS ALBATROSS (not CHATHAM ALBATROSS)

330 —*Xenicus lyalli*, STEPHENS ISLAND WREN (not STEPHENS WREN)

331 —*Pitta superba*, SUPERB PITTA (not BLACK-BACKED)

334 —*Neodrepanis coruscans*, SUNBIRD ASITY (not WATTLED)

334 —*Neodrepanis hypoxantha*, YELLOW-BELLIED ASITY (not *hypoxanthus* or SMALL-BILLED)

334 —*Mionectes macconnelli*, MACCONNELL'S FLYCATCHER (not MCCONNELL'S)

338 —*Phyllomyias reiseri*, add groups ¶*urichi*, URICH'S TYRANNULET; and ¶*reiseri*, REISER'S TYRANNULET; sequence *reiseri* before *virescens*

339 —*Zimmerius vilissimus*, add groups ¶*vilissimus*, PALTRY TYRANNULET; and ¶*parvus*, MISTLETOE TYRANNULET

340 —*Phaeomyias murina*, add groups ¶*murina*, MOUSE-COLORED TYRANNULET; and ¶*tumbezana*, TUMBES TYRANNULET

340-341 —Split *Sublegatus [modestus] modestus* into **Sublegatus [modestus] obscurior**, AMAZONIAN SCRUB-FLYCATCHER; and **Sublegatus [modestus] modestus**, SOUTHERN SCRUB-FLYCATCHER

345 —Change *Anairetes [agilis] agilis* and *A. [agilis] agraphia* to *Uromyias [agilis] agilis* and *U. [agilis] agraphia*; sequence before *A. alpinus*

348 —Move *Ramphotrigon megacephala*, *R. fuscicauda* and *R. ruficauda* to p. 364 and sequence after *Deltarhynchus flammulatus*

350 —*Onychorhynchus coronatus*, add group after others: ¶*swainsoni*, SWAINSON'S ROYAL-FLYCATCHER

350 —*Myiophobus fasciatus* and *M. cryptoxanthus*, delete superspecies

352 —*Lathrotriccus euleri*, change ¶*lawrencei* to ¶*flaviventris*

352 —*Contopus borealis*, OLIVE-SIDED FLYCATCHER (not BOREAL PEWEE)

353 —Change *Empidonax griseipectus* to *Lathrotriccus griseipectus* and move to p. 352 following *L. euleri*

364 —After *Deltarhynchus flammulatus*, sequence *Ramphotrigon* spp. from p. 348

376 —Split *Pipra [serena] serena* into **Pipra [serena] suavissima**, TEPUI MANAKIN, and **Pipra [serena] serena**, WHITE-FRONTED MANAKIN

382 —*Clytoctantes [alixii] alixii* (add superspecies); after *C. alixii* add **Clytoctantes [alixii] atrogularis**, RONDONIA BUSHBIRD

383 —*Dysithamnus occidentalis*, BICOLORED ANTBIRD (not WESTERN)

387 —Split *Formicivora melanogaster* into **Formicivora [melanogaster] melanogaster**, BLACK-BELLIED ANTWREN, and **Formicivora [melanogaster] serrana**, SERRA ANTWREN; retain [BLACK-BELLIED ANTWREN] for superspecies

389 —After *Cercomacra carbonaria* add **Cercomacra manu**, MANU ANTBIRD

390 —*Myrmeciza berlepschi*, not *Sipia*

390 —Delete *Sipia rosenbergi* entry

391 —Split *Myrmeciza laemosticta* into **Myrmeciza [laemosticta] laemosticta**, DULL-MANTLED ANTBIRD, and **Myrmeciza [laemosticta] nigricauda**, ESMERALDAS ANTBIRD; retain [DULL-MANTLED ANTBIRD] for superspecies

392 —*Myrmeciza atrothorax* (delete superspecies)

392 —Delete *Myrmeciza [atrothorax] stictothorax* entry

393 —*Geobates poecilopterus* (not *poeciloptera*)

402 —After *Asthenes modesta* add **Asthenes luizae**, CIPO CANASTERO

403 —*Asthenes [anthoides] punensis*, add group after others: ¶*sclateri*, CORDOBA CANASTERO

403 —Delete *Asthenes [anthoides] sclateri* entry

404 —*Phacellodomus erythrophthalmus*, add groups ¶*erythrophthalmus*, RED-EYED THORNBIRD; and ¶*ferrugineigula*, ORANGE-EYED THORNBIRD

406 —*Pseudocolaptes lawrencii*, add groups ¶*lawrencii*, BUFFY TUFTEDCHEEK; and ¶*johnsoni*, PACIFIC TUFTEDCHEEK

407 —After *Syndactyla rufosuperciliata*, insert *Syndactyla ruficollis* from p. 409

409 —Change *Automolus ruficollis* to *Syndactyla ruficollis* and sequence on p. 407 after *S. rufosuperciliata*

411 —*Dendrocincla merula*, add groups ¶*castanoptera*, BLUE-EYED WOODCREEPER; and ¶*merula*, WHITE-CHINNED WOODCREEPER

412 —*Glyphorynchus spirurus* (not *Glyphorhynchus*)

412 —*Hylexetastes perrotii*, add groups ¶*perrotii*, RED-BILLED WOODCREEPER; and ¶*uniformis*, UNIFORM WOODCREEPER

412 —Delete *Xiphocolaptes franciscanus* entry

412 —*Xiphocolaptes falcirostris*, add groups ¶*falcirostris*, MOUSTACHED WOODCREEPER; and ¶*franciscanus*, SNETHLAGE'S WOODCREEPER

413 —*Dendrocolaptes certhia*, change groups to ¶*sanctithomae*, NORTHERN BARRED-WOODCREEPER; and ¶*certhia*, AMAZONIAN BARRED-WOODCREEPER

413 —*Dendrocolaptes hoffmannsi*, HOFFMANNS'S WOODCREEPER (not HOFFMANNS')

416 —*Chamaeza [campanisoma] campanisoma* and *Chamaeza [campanisoma] nobilis* (add superspecies)

416 —After *Chamaeza nobilis* add **Chamaeza [meruloides] turdina**, SCHWARTZ'S ANTTHRUSH, and **Chamaeza [meruloides] meruloides**, SUCH'S ANTTHRUSH

416 —*Grallaria gigantea*, add groups ¶*gigantea*, GIANT ANTPITTA; and ¶*hylodroma*, PICHINCHA ANTPITTA

417 —After *Grallaria [dignissima] eludens*, add **Grallaria kaestneri**, CUNDINAMARCA ANTPITTA

418 —Split *Hylopezus [fulviventris] fulviventris* into **Hylopezus [fulviventris] dives**, FULVOUS-BELLIED ANTPITTA (with groups ¶*dives* and ¶*flammulatus*); and **Hylopezus [fulviventris] fulviventris**, WHITE-LORED ANTPITTA

421 —Split *Scytalopus indigoticus* into **Scytalopus [indigoticus] psychopompus**, CHESTNUT-SIDED TAPACULO, and **Scytalopus [indigoticus] indigoticus**, WHITE-BREASTED TAPACULO

423 —*Amblyornis macgregoriae*, MACGREGOR'S BOWERBIRD (not MACGREGOR'S)

434 —*Philemon [buceroides] buceroides*, ¶*gordoni*, MELVILLE ISLAND FRIARBIRD (not MELVILLE FRIARBIRD)

435 —*Melipotes ater*, remove superspecies

438 —*Epthianura* (not *Ephthianura*), change in all four species

438 —*Pardalotus (punctatus) xanthopygus* (not *xanthopygos*)

441 —*Acanthiza [pusilla] pusilla*, add [BROWN THORNBILL] for superspecies
444 —*Gerygone [fusca] insularis*, LORD HOWE ISLAND GERYGONE (not LORD HOWE GERYGONE)
444 —*Gerygone [igata] modesta*, NORFOLK ISLAND GERYGONE (not NORFOLK GERYGONE)
444 —*Gerygone albofrontata*, CHATHAM ISLANDS GERYGONE (not CHATHAM GERYGONE), and remove from
    superspecies
444 —Family **Petroicidae** (not **Eopsaltriidae**)
444 —*Culicicapa ceylonensis* and *C. helianthea* (both CANARY-FLYCATCHER, not CANARY-FLYCATCHER), belong
    in Muscicapidae on p. 531 before *Horizorhinus dohrni*
446 —*Petroica [australis] traversi*, CHATHAM ISLANDS ROBIN (not CHATHAM ROBIN)
449 —*Pomatostomus isidorei*, NEW GUINEA BABBLER (not RUFOUS)
449-450 —*Lanius [cristatus] cristatus*, add groups ¶*cristatus*, BROWN SHRIKE; and ¶*superciliosus*, JAPANESE
    SHRIKE
450-451 —*Lanius excubitor*, after ¶*meridionalis*, add ¶*leucopygos* SAHARAN SHRIKE
452 —*Eurocephalus [anguitimens] rueppelli* (not *rueppellii*)
454 —*Vireo [solitarius] solitarius*, change English name to BLUE-HEADED VIREO
455 —Split *Hylophilus poicilotis* into **Hylophilus amaurocephalus**, GREY-EYED GREENLET, and **Hylophilus
    poicilotis**, RUFOUS-CROWNED GREENLET
460 —*Pachycephala [simplex] griseiceps*, GREY-HEADED WHISTLER (not GREY)
460 —*Pachycephala [caledonica] pectoralis*, ¶*xanthoprocta*, NORFOLK ISLAND WHISTLER (not NORFOLK
    WHISTLER)
461 —*Pachycephala implicata*, HOODED WHISTLER (not MOUNTAIN)
466 —*Urocissa caerulea*, FORMOSAN MAGPIE (not TAIWAN)
466 —Split *Cissa thalassina* into **Cissa hypoleuca**, YELLOW-BREASTED MAGPIE, and **Cissa thalassina**, SHORT-
    TAILED MAGPIE, with groups ¶*jefferyi*, BORNEAN MAGPIE, and ¶*thalassina*, SHORT-TAILED MAGPIE,
    under *thalassina*
467 —*Pica [pica] pica*, add groups ¶*pica*, BLACK-BILLED MAGPIE; and ¶*mauritanica*, NORTH AFRICAN MAGPIE
469 —*Corvus [woodfordi] meeki* before *C. [woodfordi] woodfordi* (ranges only are reversed in accounts)
469 —*Corvus [woodfordi] woodfordi*, change English name of superspecies to [SOLOMON ISLANDS CROW]
470 —*Corvus ossifragus* superspecies: *C. [ossifragus] ossifragus*, *C. [ossifragus] imparatus* and *C. [ossifragus]
    sinaloae*, in that sequence; delete superspecies name
*472 —*Loboparadisea* (not *Loboparadisaea*)
472 —*Macgregoria pulchra*, MACGREGOR'S BIRD-OF-PARADISE (not MACGREGOR'S)
474 —Split *Ptiloris magnificus* into **Ptiloris [magnificus] magnificus**, MAGNIFICENT RIFLEBIRD, and **Ptiloris
    [magnificus] intercedens**, EASTERN RIFLEBIRD; use [MAGNIFICENT RIFLEBIRD] for superspecies
474 —*Ptiloris [paradiseus]* superspecies: *P. [paradiseus] victoriae* and *P. [paradiseus] paradiseus*; use
    [PARADISE RIFLEBIRD] for superspecies
476-477 Change "WOOD-SWALLOW" to "WOODSWALLOW" in all cases
479-485 Change "CUCKOO-SHRIKE" to "CUCKOOSHRIKE" in all cases
479 —*Coracina [caledonica] javensis*, JAVAN CUCKOOSHRIKE (not MALAYSIAN)
481 —*Coracina cinerea*, ASHY CUCKOOSHRIKE (not MADAGASCAR)
482 —*Coracina holopolia*, SOLOMON ISLANDS CUCKOOSHRIKE (not SOLOMON CUCKOOSHRIKE)
483 —*Lalage [aurea] leucomela*, add groups ¶*leucomela*, VARIED TRILLER; and ¶*conjuncta*, MUSSAU TRILLER
491 —*Terpsiphone rufiventer*, add groups ¶*rufiventer*, BLACK-HEADED PARADISE-FLYCATCHER; and ¶*smithii*,
    ANNOBON PARADISE-FLYCATCHER
493 —*Mayrornis versicolor*, OGEA MONARCH (not VERSICOLORED)
495 —*Myiagra [oceanica] erythrops*, MANGROVE FLYCATCHER (not PALAU)
496 —*Myiagra [rubecula] caledonica*, MELANESIAN FLYCATCHER (not NEW CALEDONIAN)
499 —After *Laniarius [luehderi] amboimensis*, add **Laniarius liberatus**, BULO BURTI BUSHSHRIKE
499 —*Laniarius [ferrugineus] bicolor*, GABON BOUBOU (not GABOON)
501 —*Prionops [caniceps] rufiventris*, GABON HELMETSHRIKE (not GABOON)
504 —*Calicalicus*, not *Calicalius*
505 —*Leptopterus chabert*, CHABERT'S VANGA (not CHABERT)
505 —*Euryceros prevostii*, HELMET VANGA (not the HELMETBIRD)
505 —*Tylas edouardi*, TYLAS VANGA (not the KINKIMAVO)

505 —*Hypositta corallirostris*, NUTHATCH VANGA (not CORAL-BILLED NUTHATCH)

505 —*Philesturnus carunculatus* (not *Creadion*)

*505 —*Heteralocha* (not *Heterolocha*)

507 —*Pseudocossyphus [imerinus] sharpei*, FOREST ROCK-THRUSH (not EASTERN ROBINCHAT)

507 —*Pseudocossyphus [imerinus] bensoni*, BENSON'S ROCK-THRUSH (not FARKAS'S ROBINCHAT)

507 —*Pseudocossyphus [imerinus] imerinus*, LITTORAL ROCK-THRUSH (not MADAGASCAR ROBINCHAT)

509 —*Myiophonus [caeruleus] insularis*, FORMOSAN WHISTLING-THRUSH (not TAIWAN)

511 —*Zoothera guttata*, delete groups

516 —*Turdus unicolor*, TICKELL'S THRUSH (not INDIAN GREY THRUSH)

523 —*Melaenornis annamarulae*, WEST AFRICAN BLACK-FLYCATCHER (not LIBERIAN)

525 —*Muscicapa ussheri* and *M. infuscata*, remove superspecies

526 —*Muscicapa tessmanni*, TESSMANN'S FLYCATCHER (not TESSMAN'S)

527 —*Ficedula [parva] parva*, add groups ¶*parva*, RED-BREASTED FLYCATCHER; and ¶*albicilla*, RED-THROATED FLYCATCHER

530 —*Cyornis concretus*, WHITE-TAILED FLYCATCHER (not WHITE-TAILED BLUE-FLYCATCHER)

539 —*Enicurus scouleri*, ¶*fortis*, FORMOSAN FORKTAIL (not TAIWAN)

540 —*Saxicola dacotiae*, CANARY ISLANDS CHAT (not CANARY CHAT)

540 —*Saxicola [torquata] torquata*, add *maura* as group: ¶*torquata*, COMMON STONECHAT; ¶*maura*, SIBERIAN STONECHAT; and ¶*albofasciata*, ETHIOPIAN STONECHAT; change superspecies name to [COMMON STONECHAT] (not STONECHAT)

540 —Delete *Saxicola maura* entry

542 —*Oenanthe [hispanica]* superspecies: *O. [hispanica] hispanica*, *O. [hispanica] pleschanka* and *O. [hispanica] cypriaca*, in that sequence

545 —*Aplonis striata*, ¶*atronitens*, LOYALTY ISLANDS STARLING (not LOYALTY STARLING)

550 —*Acridotheres [cinereus] grandis* (change superspecies)

550 —*Acridotheres [cinereus] cinereus* (not *[javanicus] javanicus*); change English name to PALE-BELLIED MYNA (not JAVAN)

558 —*Campylopterus [zonatus] megalopterus* (add to superspecies)

559 —*Hylorchilus sumichrasti* (not *Catherpes*); add groups ¶*sumichrasti*, SUMICHRAST'S WREN; ¶*navai*, NAVA'S WREN

567 —*Parus lugubris*, add groups ¶*lugubris*, SOMBRE TIT; and ¶*hyrcanus*, HYRCANIAN TIT

569 —*Parus [niger] guineensis*, WHITE-SHOULDERED TIT (not BLACK-TIT)

569 —*Parus [niger] leucomelas*, WHITE-WINGED TIT (not BLACK-TIT); add groups ¶*leucomelas*, WHITE-WINGED TIT; ¶*carpi*, CARP'S TIT (moved from under *P. niger*)

569 —*Parus [niger] niger*, BLACK TIT (not SOUTHERN BLACK-TIT); delete groups

569 —*Parus leuconotus*, WHITE-BACKED TIT (not BLACK-TIT)

570 —*Parus nuchalis*, WHITE-NAPED TIT (not WHITE-WINGED)

572 —*Aegithalos [iouschistos] iouschistos*, add groups ¶*iouschistos*, BLACK-BROWED TIT; and ¶*bonvaloti*, BLACK-HEADED TIT

575 —*Riparia [riparia] riparia*, add groups ¶*riparia*, COMMON SAND-MARTIN; and ¶*diluta*, EASTERN SAND-MARTIN

577 —*Hirundo [rustica] rustica*, group ¶*rustica*, EURASIAN SWALLOW (not EUROPEAN SWALLOW)

577 —*Hirundo [rustica] domicola* (not *dumicola*)

581 —*Regulus regulus*, remove superspecies and change English name to GOLDCREST (not COMMON GOLDCREST)

581 —*Regulus teneriffae*, remove superspecies and change English name to CANARY ISLANDS KINGLET (not TENERIFE GOLDCREST)

585 —*Andropadus [montanus] montanus*, change English name of superspecies to [MONTANE GREENBUL]

586 —Split *Andropadus tephrolaemus* into **Andropadus tephrolaemus**, GREY-THROATED GREENBUL, and **Andropadus nigriceps**, MOUNTAIN GREENBUL; remove superspecies

586 —*Andropadus chlorigula*, remove superspecies

587 —Sequence *Phyllastrephus [baumanni] poensis* before *Phyllastrephus [baumanni] hypochloris*

588 —*Phyllastrephus madagascariensis*, LONG-BILLED GREENBUL (not COMMON TETRAKA)

588 —*Phyllastrephus zosterops*, SPECTACLED GREENBUL (not SHORT-BILLED TETRAKA)

588 —*Phyllastrephus apperti*, APPERT'S GREENBUL (not TETRAKA)

588 —*Phyllastrephus tenebrosus*, DUSKY GREENBUL (not TETRAKA)

588 —*Phyllastrephus cinereiceps*, GREY-CROWNED GREENBUL (not TETRAKA)

593 —After *Cisticola [ruficeps] mongalla* add **Cisticola dorsti**, DORST'S CISTICOLA

594 —*Cisticola melanurus*, BLACK-TAILED CISTICOLA (not SLENDER-TAILED)

597 —Change *Prinia substriata* and *P. robertsi* to *Phragmacia substriata*, NAMAQUA WARBLER, and *Oreophilais robertsi*, BRIAR WARBLER; sequence after *Prinia melanops*

598 —Change *Prinia erythroptera* to *Heliolais erythroptera*, RED-WINGED WARBLER

601 —Delete *Zosterops kirki* entry

602 —*Zosterops maderaspatanus*, MALAGASY WHITE-EYE (not MADAGASCAR); add groups ¶*kirki*, KIRK'S WHITE-EYE; and ¶*maderaspatanus*, MALAGASY WHITE-EYE

603 —*Zosterops [conspicillatus] conspicillatus*, add groups ¶*saypani*, SAIPAN WHITE-EYE; ¶*rotensis*, ROTA WHITE-EYE; and ¶*conspicillatus*, BRIDLED WHITE-EYE

603 —*Zosterops semperi*, CAROLINE ISLANDS WHITE-EYE (not CAROLINE WHITE-EYE); remove from superspecies and sequence after *Z. hypolais*

603 —*Zosterops nigrorum*, GOLDEN-GREEN WHITE-EYE (not YELLOWISH)

603 —*Zosterops natalis*, CHRISTMAS ISLAND WHITE-EYE (not CHRISTMAS WHITE-EYE)

605 —*Zosterops [griseotinctus] kulambangrae*, SOLOMON ISLANDS WHITE-EYE (not SOLOMON WHITE-EYE)

606 —*Zosterops lateralis*, change SILVER-EYE to SILVEREYE (including groups and superspecies)

606 —*Zosterops tephropleurus*, LORD HOWE ISLAND WHITE-EYE (not LORD HOWE WHITE-EYE)

607 —*Zosterops [cinereus] cinereus*, GREY-BROWN WHITE-EYE (not GREY); ¶*ponapensis*, GREY-BROWN WHITE-EYE (not POHNPEI)

607 —*Rukia ruki*, sequence after *R. longirostra*

607 —*Heleia [muelleri] muelleri*, SPOT-BREASTED WHITE-EYE (not SPOT-BREATED)

609 —*Cettia [fortipes]* superspecies: *C. [fortipes] fortipes*, *C. [fortipes] vulcania* and *C. [fortipes] carolinae*, in that sequence

609 —*Cettia acanthizoides* (not *C. robustipes*), groups ¶*acanthizoides* and ¶*concolor* (not ¶*robustipes*), FORMOSAN BUSH-WARBLER (not TAIWAN)

610 —*Bradypterus [barratti] lopezi* (not *lopesi*), including groups

611 —*Nesillas [typica] aldabrana*, ALDABRA BRUSH-WARBLER (not TSIKIRITY)

611 —After *Nesillas [typica] aldabrana*, add **Nesillas [typica] longicauda**, ANJOUAN BRUSH-WARBLER

611 —*Nesillas [typica] typica*, MALAGASY BRUSH-WARBLER (not COMMON TSIKIRITY)

611 —After *Nesillas [typica] typica*, add **Nesillas brevicaudata**, GRAND COMORO BRUSH-WARBLER

612 —*Nesillas mariae*, MOHELI BRUSH-WARBLER (not TSIKIRITY)

612 —*Thamnornis chloropetoides*, THAMNORNIS WARBLER (not the THAMNORNIS)

612 —*Locustella naevia*, COMMON GRASSHOPPER-WARBLER (not GRASSHOPPER WARBLER)

612 —*Locustella certhiola*, PALLAS'S GRASSHOPPER-WARBLER (not PALLAS'S WARBLER)

612 —*Locustella ochotensis*, MIDDENDORFF'S GRASSHOPPER-WARBLER (not MIDDENDORFF'S WARBLER)

612 —*Locustella pleskei*, PLESKE'S GRASSHOPPER-WARBLER (not PLESKE'S WARBLER)

613 —Delete *Locustella amnicola* entry

613 —Merge *Locustella fasciolata* and *L. amnicola* as groups under *Locustella fasciolata* (GRAY'S GRASSHOPPER-WARBLER): ¶*fasciolata*, GRAY'S GRASSHOPPER-WARBLER; and ¶*amnicola*, SAKHALIN GRASSHOPPER-WARBLER; delete superspecies

613 —Delete *Acrocephalus tangorum* entry

613 —Merge *Acrocephalus agricola* and *A. tangorum* as species, insert as group under *A. [agricola] agricola* (PADDYFIELD WARBLER): ¶*agricola*, PADDYFIELD WARBLER, and ¶*tangorum*, MANCHURIAN REED-WARBLER

614 —Merge *Acrocephalus arundinaceus* and *A. orientalis* as groups under *Acrocephalus [arundinaceus] arundinaceus* (GREAT REED-WARBLER): ¶*arundinaceus*, GREAT REED-WARBLER; and ¶*oriertalis*, ORIENTAL REED-WARBLER

613 —Delete *Acrocephalus orientalis* entry

615 —*Acrocephalus [luscinia] syrinx*, CAROLINE ISLANDS REED-WARBLER (not CAROLINE REED-WARBLER)

615 —*Acrocephalus [caffer]* superspecies (not *[cafer]*)

615 —Split *Acrocephalus [vaughani] vaughani* into **Acrocephalus [vaughani] rimatarae**, RIMATARA REED-WARBLER, **Acrocephalus [vaughani] vaughani**, PITCAIRN REED-WARBLER, and **Acrocephalus [vaughani] taiti**, HENDERSON ISLAND REED-WARBLER; change English name of superspecies to [POLYNESIAN REED-WARBLER]

615 —Split *Hippolais caligata* into **Hippolais [caligata] caligata**, BOOTED WARBLER, and **Hippolais [caligata] rama**, SYKES'S WARBLER; retain [BOOTED WARBLER] for superspecies

617 —*Orthotomus [nigriceps]* superspecies: *O. [nigriceps] samarensis* and *O. [nigriceps] nigriceps*

617 —*Poliolais lopezi* (not *lopesi*)

618 —*Randia pseudozosterops*, RAND'S WARBLER (not MAROANTSETRA)

618 —*Newtonia amphichroa*, DARK NEWTONIA (not TULEAR)

618 —*Newtonia archboldi*, ARCHBOLD'S NEWTONIA (not TABITY)

619 —*Newtonia fanovanae*, RED-TAILED NEWTONIA (not FANOVANA)

620 —*Phylloscopus [ruficapillus] laetus*, *P. [ruficapillus] laurae* and *P. [ruficapillus] ruficapillus* [genus masculine, *ruficapillus* adjectival]

620 —*Phylloscopus [collybita] collybita*, COMMON CHIFFCHAFF (not EURASIAN); add groups ¶*collybita*, EURASIAN CHIFFCHAFF; ¶*tristis*, SIBERIAN CHIFFCHAFF; and ¶*sindianus*, MOUNTAIN CHIFFCHAFF

620 —Change *Phylloscopus [collybita] sindianus* to *Phylloscopus [collybita] lorenzii*, CAUCASIAN CHIFFCHAFF

621 —*Phylloscopus bonelli*, add groups ¶*bonelli*, WESTERN BONELLI'S-WARBLER; and ¶*orientalis*, EASTERN BONELLI'S-WARBLER

621 —Split *Phylloscopus proregulus* into **Phylloscopus [proregulus] proregulus**, LEMON-RUMPED WARBLER, and **Phylloscopus [proregulus] chloronotus**, PALE-RUMPED WARBLER; retain [PALLAS'S WARBLER] for superspecies

622 —*Phylloscopus inornatus*, add groups ¶*inornatus*, YELLOW-BROWED WARBLER; and ¶*humei*, BUFF-BROWED WARBLER

622 —Merge *Phylloscopus trochiloides*, *P. plumbeitarsus* and *P. nitidus* as groups under *Phylloscopus trochiloides* (GREENISH WARBLER): ¶*trochiloides*, GREENISH WARBLER; ¶*plumbeitarsus*, TWO-BARRED WARBLER; and ¶*nitidus*, BRIGHT-GREEN WARBLER

622 —Delete *Phylloscopus plumbeitarsus* and *P. nitidus* entries

622 —Split *Phylloscopus tenellipes* into **Phylloscopus [tenellipes] tenellipes**, PALE-LEGGED LEAF-WARBLER, and **Phylloscopus [tenellipes] borealoides**, SAKHALIN LEAF-WARBLER; retain [PALE-LEGGED LEAF-WARBLER] for superspecies

624 —*Seicercus xanthoschistos* (not *xanthoschistus*)

625 —*Amphilais seebohmi*, GREY EMU-TAIL (not SEEBOHM'S)

625 —Split *Megalurus punctatus* into **Megalurus [punctatus] punctatus**, NEW ZEALAND FERNBIRD, and **Megalurus [punctatus] rufescens**, CHATHAM ISLANDS FERNBIRD; retain [FERNBIRD] for superspecies

631 —*Malacocincla [malaccensis] malaccensis*, add groups ¶*malaccensis*, SHORT-TAILED BABBLER; and ¶*feriatum*, OCHRACEOUS-THROATED BABBLER

634 —After *Pnoepyga albiventer* add **Pnoepyga immaculata**, NEPAL WREN-BABBLER

635 —*Neomixis tenella*, COMMON JERY (not NORTHERN)

636 —After *Stachyris [striata] striata* add **Stachyris [striata] latistriata**, PANAY STRIPED-BABBLER

639 —*Turdoides [plebejus] plebejus* before *T. [plebejus] leucocephalus*

641 —*Actinodura [egertoni]* superspecies: *A. [egertoni] egertoni* and *A. [egertoni] ramsayi*

641 —*Actinodura morrisoniana*, FORMOSAN BARWING (not TAIWAN)

642 —Split *Alcippe cinereiceps* into **Alcippe [cinereiceps] cinereiceps**, STREAK-THROATED FULVETTA, and **Alcippe [cinereiceps] ludlowi**, LUDLOW'S FULVETTA; retain [STREAK-THROATED FULVETTA] for superspecies

644 —*Yuhina brunneiceps*, FORMOSAN YUHINA (not TAIWAN)

646 —*Rhabdornis mystacalis* (not *mysticalis*)

647 —Split *Sylvia curruca* into **Sylvia [curruca] curruca**, LESSER WHITETHROAT; **Sylvia [curruca] minula**, SMALL WHITETHROAT; and **Sylvia [curruca] althaea**, HUME'S WHITETHROAT; retain [LESSER WHITETHROAT] for superspecies

649 —*Mirafra hova*, MADAGASCAR LARK (not HOVA)

657 —*Dicaeum anthonyi*, YELLOW-CROWNED FLOWERPECKER (not YELLOW-CROWED); add groups ¶*anthonyi*, YELLOW-CROWNED FLOWERPECKER; and ¶*kampalili*, RED-CROWNED FLOWERPECKER

665 —After *Nectarinia loveridgei* add **Nectarinia moreaui**, MOREAU'S SUNBIRD

667 —*Nectarinia [notata] notata*, LONG-BILLED GREEN SUNBIRD (not MADAGASCAR)

667 —*Nectarinia coccinigastra* (not *coccinogastra*)

668 —*Aethopyga mystacalis*, add groups ¶*tenuirostris*, SCARLET SUNBIRD; and ¶*mystacalis*, JAVAN SUNBIRD

670 —*Passer castanopterus* and *P. rutilans*, delete superspecies

670 —*Passer [motitensis] iagoensis*, IAGO SPARROW (not CAPE VERDE)

674 —*Motacilla citreola*, CITRINE WAGTAIL (not YELLOW-HOODED)

674 —*Motacilla flava*, change English names of following groups: ¶*lutea*, YELLOW-HEADED WAGTAIL (not YELLOW-BROWED); ¶*taivana*, GREEN-HEADED WAGTAIL (not GREEN-CROWNED)

677 —*Anthus similis*, groups ¶*similas* and ¶*moco*, in that sequence

679 —*Prunella ocularis*, RADDE'S ACCENTOR (not SPOT-THROATED)

681 —*Philetairus socius* (not *Philetarius*)

683 —After *Ploceus castanops* add **Ploceus burnieri**, KILOMBERO WEAVER

686 —*Malimbus [racheliae] ballmanni*, BALLMANN'S MALIMBE (not BALLMAN'S)

687 —*Foudia madagascariensis*, MADAGASCAR RED FODY (not RED)

687 —*Foudia [rubra] omissa*, FOREST FODY (not ROTHSCHILD'S)

690 —*Pytilia [phoenicoptera]* superspecies: *Pytilia [phoenicoptera] phoenicoptera* and *Pytilia [phoenicoptera] lineata*; remove superspecies from *P. afra*, *P. melba* and *P. hypogrammica*

698 —*Lonchura [malacca] ferruginosa*, change English name to WHITE-CAPPED MUNIA (not CHESTNUT)

700 —Split *Vidua funerea* into **Vidua funerea**, VARIABLE INDIGOBIRD, and **Vidua codringtoni**, TWINSPOT INDIGOBIRD; remove superspecies; remove English name for superspecies

700 —*Vidua purpurascens*, remove superspecies

702 —*Serinus citrinella*, add groups ¶*citrinella*, EUROPEAN CITRIL; and ¶*corsicana*, CORSICAN CITRIL

703 —After *Serinus rothschildi* add **Serinus flavigula**, YELLOW-THROATED SEEDEATER

704 —*Serinus [totta] symonsi*, DRAKENSBERG SISKIN (not DRAKENSBURG)

705 —*Carduelis [spinoides]* superspecies: *C. [spinoides] spinoides*, *C. [spinoides] ambigua* and *C. [spinoides] monguilloti*, in that sequence

706 —*Carduelis [spinus] atriceps* (not *[pinus]*)

712 —*Pyrrhula pyrrhula*, after ¶*cineracea* add group ¶*griseiventris*, GREY-BELLIED BULLFINCH

716 —*Emberiza stewarti*, sequence after *E. leucocephalos* on p. 715

717 —*Emberiza yessoensis*, sequence after *E. schoeniclus* on p. 718

718 —*Emberiza rutila*, sequence after *E. aureola* on p. 717

720 —*Zonotrichia leucophrys*, sequence after *Z. albicollis*

721 —Split *Passerculus sandwichensis* into **Passerculus [sandwichensis] sandwichensis**, SAVANNAH SPARROW, with groups ¶*sandwichensis*, SAVANNAH SPARROW, ¶*princeps*, IPSWICH SPARROW and ¶*beldingi*, BELDING'S SPARROW; and **Passerculus [sandwichensis] rostratus**, LARGE-BILLED SPARROW; retain [SAVANNAH SPARROW] for superspecies

723 —*Amphispiza belli*, add groups ¶*nevadensis*, SAGE SPARROW; and ¶*belli*, BELL'S SPARROW

723 —Change *Amphispiza quinquestriata* to *Aimophila quinquestriata*

725 —*Pipilo crissalis* and *P. fuscus* (delete superspecies); sequence *P. aberti* before *P. crissalis*

726 —*Atlapetes [schistaceus] schistaceus*, SLATY BUSH-FINCH (not BUSH-FINCH)

732 —*Dendroica pharetra*, ARROWHEAD WARBLER (not ARROW-HEADED)

739 —*Schistochlamys ruficapillus* and *melanopis* (not *Schistoclamys*)

775 —*Passerina ciris*, add groups ¶*pallidior*, WESTERN PAINTED-BUNTING; and ¶*ciris*, EASTERN PAINTED-BUNTING

778 —*Icterus cucullatus*, sequence after *I. galbula* on p. 779

779 —*Icterus wagleri* (remove from superspecies)

779 —*Icterus graduacauda*, sequence after *I. cayanensis* on p. 777

781 —*Sturnella [militaris] militaris* (add superspecies name)

Part 2 (complete update)

page #

vii-xv   The following counts (or names) need to be revised:
vii   Subclass NEORNITHES (**2063 genera/9702 species:**
        nonpasserine—895/3963; *passerine*—1168/5739)
vii   Infraclass NEOAVES (2049/9645)
vii   Parvclass GALLOANSERAE (122/443)
vii   Superorder GALLOMORPHAE (74/282)
vii   Order **GALLIFORMES** (57/213)
vii   Parvorder PHASIANIDA (48/182)
vii   Superfamily PHASIANOIDEA (44/176)
vii   Family **Phasianidae** (44/176)
vii   Parvorder ODONTOPHORIDA (9/31
vii   Family **Odontophoridae** (9/31)
viii   Subfamily Oxyurinae (3/9)
viii   Subfamily Anatinae (37/131)
viii   Tribe Anatini (23/88)
viii   Parvclass PICAE (51/356)
viii   Order PICIFORMES (51/356)
viii   Infraorder PICIDES (32/233)
viii   Family **Picidae** (28/216)
viii   Parvclass CORACIAE (67/309)
viii   Superorder CORACIIMORPHAE (40/192)
viii   Subfamily Apalodermatinae [not Apaloderminae]
viii   Order **CORACIIFORMES** (34/153)
ix   Suborder ALCEDINI (28/135)
ix   Infraorder ALCEDINIDES (25/109)
ix   Parvorder ALCEDINIDA (3/25)
ix   Family **Alcedinidae** (3/25)
ix   Superfamily HALCYONOIDEA and Family
        Halcyonidae [not DACELONOIDEA and
        Dacelonidae]
ix   Parvclass PASSERAE (1805/8514)
ix   Superorder PSITTACIMORPHAE (80/360)
ix   Order **PSITTACIFORMES** (80/360)
ix   Family **Psittacidae** (80/360)
ix   Superorder APODIMORPHAE (127/425)
ix   Order **TROCHILIFORMES** (108/322)
ix   Family **Trochilidae** (108/322)
ix   Subfamily Trochilinae (104/293)
x   Superorder STRIGIMORPHAE (50/312)
x   Order **STRIGIFORMES** (45/289)
x   Suborder STRIGI (25/173)
x   Parvorder STRIGIDA (23/156)
x   Family **Strigidae** (23/156)
x   Suborder CAPRIMULGI (19/108)
x   Infraorder CAPRIMULGIDES (17/94)
x   Parvorder CAPRIMULGIDA (15/86)
x   Superfamily CAPRIMULGOIDEA (14/79)
x   Family **Caprimulgidae** (14/79)
x   Subfamily Chordeilinae (4/9)
x   Subfamily Caprimulginae (10/70)
x   Superorder PASSERIMORPHAE (1518/7274)
x   Order **COLUMBIFORMES** (42/316)
x   Family **Columbidae** (40/313)
x   Order **GRUIFORMES** (53/197)
x   Family **Aramidae** (1/1) [before Family **Heliornithidae**]
x   Family **Heliornithidae** (3/3) [delete Tribes]
xi   Suborder RALLI (34/143)
xi   Family **Rallidae** (34/143)
xi   Order **CICONIIFORMES** (255/1022)
xi   Suborder CHARADRII (86/365)

xi   Infraorder CHARADRIIDES (84/349)
xi   Parvorder CHARADRIIDA (53/246)
xi   Superfamily CHIONOIDEA (2/3) [not
        CHIONIDOIDEA]
xi   Family **Chionidae** [not **Chionididae**]
xi   Family **Pluvianellidae** (Magellanic Plover, 1/1) [after
        Family **Chionidae** entry]
xi   Superfamily CHARADRIOIDEA (17/97)
xi   Family **Charadriidae** (16/88)
xi   Subfamily Charadriinae (11/66)
xi   Superfamily LAROIDEA (34/146)
xi   Family **Laridae** (28/128)
xi   Subfamily Larinae (16/105)
xi   Tribe Sternini (7/44)
xi   Suborder CICONII (169/657)
xi   Infraorder FALCONIDES (77/302)
xi   Parvorder ACCIPITRIDA (67/239)
xi   Subfamily Accipitrinae (65/237)
xi   Family **Falconidae** (10/64)
xi   Infraorder CICONIIDES (92/355)
xi   Parvorder PODICIPEDIDA (6/22)
xi   Family **Podicipedidae** (6/22)
xi   Family **Phaethontidae**, change "Tropicbird" to
        "Tropicbirds"
xii   Parvorder SULIDA (5/50)
xii   Superfamily PHALACROCORACOIDEA (1/37)
xii   Family **Phalacrocoracidae** (1/37)
xii   Parvorder CICONIIDA (80/280)
xii   Superfamily ARDEOIDEA (21/65)
xii   Family **Ardeidae** (21/65)
xii   Superfamily THRESKIORNITHOIDEA (14/33)
xii   Family **Threskiornithidae** (14/33)
xii   Superfamily PROCELLARIOIDEA (30/141)
xii   Family **Procellariidae** (22/114)
xii   Subfamily Procellariinae (13/79)
xii   Order **PASSERIFORMES** (1168/5739)
xii   Suborder TYRANNI (292/1159)
xii   Infraorder TYRANNIDES (278/1105)
xii   Parvorder TYRANNIDA (147/539)
xii   Family **Tyrannidae** (147/539)
xii   Subfamily Tyranninae (92/341)
xii   Subfamily Piprinae (12/53)
xii   Parvorder THAMNOPHILIDA (45/190)
xii   Family **Thamnophilidae** (45/190)
xiii   Parvorder FURNARIIDA (86/376)
xiii   Superfamily FURNARIOIDEA (66/279)
xiii   Family **Furnariidae** (66/279)
xiii   Subfamily Dendrocolaptinae (13/48)
xiii   Superfamily FORMICARIOIDEA (20/97)
xiii   Family **Formicariidae** (7/60)
xiii   Family **Rhinocryptidae** (12/29)
xiii   Suborder PASSERI (876/4580)
xiii   Parvorder CORVIDA (228/1103)
xiii   Family **Meliphagidae**, change "*Ephthianura*" to
        "*Epthianura*"
xiii   Superfamily CORVOIDEA (154/796)
xiii   Family **Petroicidae** (13/44) [not **Eopsaltriidae**]
xiii   Family **Vireonidae** (4/52)
xiii   Family **Corvidae** (127/650)
xiii   Subfamily Corvinae (56/299)
xiii   Tribe Corvini (25/118)
xiii   Tribe Paradisaeini (17/46)
xiv   Subfamily Malaconotinae (27/107)

xiv Tribe Malaconotini (8/49)
xiv Parvorder PASSERIDA (646/3473)
xiv Superfamily MUSCICAPOIDEA (1131/613)
xiv Family **Muscicapidae** (69/452)
xiv Subfamily Turdinae (21/179)
xiv Subfamily Muscicapinae (48/273)
xiv Tribe Muscicapini (18/117)
xiv Tribe Saxicolini (30/156)
xiv Superfamily SYLVIOIDEA (203/1204)
xiv Family **Certhiidae** (23/97)
xiv Subfamily Troglodytinae (17/75)
xiv Family **Pycnonotidae** (21/138)
xiv Family **Cisticolidae** (17/120)
xiv Family **Zosteropidae** (13/95)
xiv Family **Sylviidae** (101/560)
xiv Subfamily Acrocephalinae (36/223)
xiv Subfamily Megalurinae (10/22)
xiv Subfamily Sylviinae (53/261)
xiv Tribe Timaliini (51/236)
xiv Tribe Sylviini (1/24)
xiv Superfamily PASSEROIDEA (330/1656)
xiv Family **Alaudidae** (19/91)
xiv Family **Nectariniidae** (8/170)
xiv Subfamily Nectariniinae (7/168)
xv Tribe Nectariniini (5/124)
xv Family **Passeridae** (57/388)
xv Subfamily Ploceinae (17/118)
xv Subfamily Estrildinae (30/156)
xv Tribe Viduini (1/16)
xv Family **Fringillidae** (241/995)
xv Subfamily Fringillinae (39/170)
xv Tribe Carduelini (20/137)
xv Tribe Drepanidini, change "701" to "713"
xv Subfamily Emberizinae (201/824)
xv Tribe Emberizini (32/157)
xv Tribe Thraupini (105/413)

xvii Change "John Ahlquist" to "Jon Ahlquist"
xx Section B.2.f omitted: "f. Superspecies [in square brackets] in LARGE AND SMALL CAPS;" re-letter old section "f" to "g"
xxi Change third paragraph to "We recognize 9699 species (in 2063 genera): 3961 nonpasserine species (...) and 5738 species in the Passeriformes (in 895 and 1168 genera, respectively)..."
xxii change end of last paragraph under "**Abbreviations**" to "...introduced; *"int."* for interior."
xxiv in Acknowledgments change "M. K. Lecroy," to "M. K. LeCroy,"
1 *Struthio camelus,* change range to "...Senegal E to n C. African Rep., Sudan and w,ne Ethiopia, and S in e Africa through Uganda and w,c Kenya to s Tanzania, also from sw Angola...se Sudan and e Kenya (S to Tsavo East...)"; change comments to "*Molybdophanes* may be a distinct species, but it was introduced into a *camelus* population and interbred in central Kenya, producing fertile offspring (Brown, Urban and Newman 1982: 33); *molybdophanes* differs from *camelus* in crown patch and skin and leg color, and both occur naturally in ec Kenya in close proximity, possibly without interbreeding."
1 *Casuarius casuarius,* delete ", but incl. Yapen I."
1 *Dromaius novaehollandiae,* in comments after "respective islands" add "(Jouanin 1959)"

2 Family **Tinamidae** (not **Tinamiidae**)
2 *Tinamus major,* after "Chiapas" add ", s Campeche"
2 *Crypturellus berlepschi,* in heading change "Rothschild" to "(Rothschild)"
3 *Crypturellus obsoletus,* change "(Misione)s" to "(Misiones)"
3 *Crypturellus strigulosus,* change range to "...Madre de Dios), n,e Bolivia (Pando, Beni, Santa Cruz) and Amazonian..."
3 *Crypturellus boucardi,* after "n Oaxaca" add "(also Pacific slope in Sierra Madre de Chiapas)"
4 *Crypturellus variegatus,* after "Pando" add ", n La Paz"
4 *Crypturellus tataupa,* after "Pernambuco S)" add ", Paraguay"
5 Order "CRACIFORMES" not "GALLIFORMES"
6 *Ortalis wagleri,* change English name to RUFOUS-BELLIED CHACHALACA (not WAGLER'S); change end of comments to "...*poliocephala* (Banks 1990b). (WAGLER'S CHACHALACA)."
6 *Ortalis guttata,* change "e Colombia" to "wc S. America in e Colombia"
7 *Penelope montagnii,* insert space between "Santa Cruz)" and "and"
8 *Pipile pipile,* change comments to "...*Aburria* and *Penelope.* [<*Aburria*/...[COMMON PIPING-GUAN]. See *P. cumanensis.*"
8 *Pipile cumanensis,* change comments to 'The Brazilian *P. cujubi* is usually treated as a distinct species because there is sympatry between *cumanensis* and *cujubi* in southern Mato Grosso; *P. cumanensis* seems to be an allospecies, although these two and *P. pipile* may be conspecific. *Grayi* is...PIPING-GUAN). See *P. cujubi.*"
8 *Pipile cujubi,* change end of comments to "See *P. cumanensis.*"
8 *Penelopina nigra,* delete "(at least formerly)"
10 *Megapodius layardi,* change English name to VANUATU SCRUBFOWL (not NEW HEBRIDES); change range to "Lowlands of **Vanuatu** (incl. Banks Is.)."; in comments change "VANUATU" to "NEW HEBRIDES"
10 *Megapodius pritchardii,* change English name to NIAUFOOU SCRUBFOWL (not POLYNESIAN); change comments to "(POLYNESIAN/TONGAN/PRITCHARD'S SCRUBFOWL/THE MALAU)."
11 Under Family **Phasianidae**, change comments to "Sequence of species in the genus *Francolinus* follows Crowe et al. (1992), except where our policy for geographical sequence within superspecies takes precedence, but we have not at this time adopted the proposed generic split of *Francolinus* into four genera. Limits of genera..."
11 *Ammoperdix heyi,* change range to "Cs **Palearctic** in Egypt...ne Sudan, Near East and Arabia."
11 *Alectoris graeca,* change "Italy" to "Switzerland, s Germany,"; change end of comments to "...because of hybridization, but interbreeding is restricted and selective in mostly disturbed areas, and biochemical analysis revealed differences normal for separate species (Randi et al. 1992). [ROCK PARTRIDGE]."
11-12 *Alectoris chukar,* in comments after "supplant *chukar*" add "(Stepanyan 1990a)"
12 *Alectoris barbara,* in heading change "(Reichenow) 1896" to "(Bonnaterre) 1790"; change range to "S **Palearctic** in Canary Is., s Spain (Gibraltar), Sardinia, and from Morocco..."

12-15 Sequence species of *Francolinus* as follows: *francolinus, pictus, pintadeanus, pondicerianus, gularis, coqui, albogularis, schlegelii, lathami, sephaena, streptophorus, finschi, africanus, levaillantii, psilolaemus, shelleyi, levaillantoides, nahani, hartlaubi, bicalcaratus, clappertoni, icterorhynchus, harwoodi, adspersus, capensis, hildebrandti, natalensis, ahantensis, squamatus, griseostriatus, leucoscepus, rufopictus, afer, swainsonii, erckelii, ochropectus, castaneicollis, nobilis, jacksoni, camerunensis* and *swierstrai*

12 *Francolinus lathami*, change "Gambia" to "Sierra Leone"; change end of range to "...Cabinda, sc,ce Zaire and extreme nw Tanzania."; change comments to "(LATHAM'S FOREST FRANCOLIN)."

12 *Francolinus coqui*, at beginning of comments add "[>*Peliperdix* (≈*F. sephaena*)]."

12 *Francolinus albogularis*, change range to "**W Africa** from Senegambia, sw Mali and Guinea E (incl...Volta) to n Cameroon;..."

13 *Francolinus streptophorus*, after "sw Cameroon," add "n C. African Rep.,"; in comments change "*F. shelleyi*" to "*F. levaillantoides*"

13 *Francolinus shelleyi*, in heading change "1891" to "1890"

13 *Francolinus ahantensis*, add comments "[>*Squamatocolinus* (≈*F. griseostriatus*)]."

13 *Francolinus nahani*, change beginning of comments to "[>*Pternistis* (≈*F. jacksoni*); >*Acentrortyx*]..."

13 *Francolinus hartlaubi*, before "Bocage" add "Barboza du"; change comments to "[>*Chaetopus* (≈*F. harwoodi*); >*Chapinortyx*]."

14 *Francolinus bicalcaratus*, change range to "...s Mali, Burkina Faso, s Niger and sw Chad S to Gulf..."

14 *Francolinus clappertoni*, after "s Chad," add "n C. African Rep.,"

14 *Francolinus adspersus*, at end of range add "."; add comments "[>*Notocolinus* (≈*F. natalensis*)]."

14 *Francolinus erckelii*, at beginning of comments add "[>*Oreocolinus* (≈*F. swierstrai*)]."

14 *Francolinus ochropectus*, in heading change "1952" to "(1952)"; change "**n Somalia**" to "**Djibouti**"

14 *Francolinus nobilis*, change end of range to "...w Uganda, Rwanda and Burundi."

14 *Francolinus jacksoni*, change "w,c Kenya" to "**ec Africa** in e Uganda and w,c Kenya"

14 *Francolinus leucoscepus*, change beginning of comments to "AG (~SPURFOWL):..."

14 *Francolinus rufopictus*, in heading change "1867" to "1887"

14 *Francolinus afer*, change range to "...Uganda and w Kenya S to ne Angola, n Zambia, n Malawi and w,s Tanzania ¶*cranchii*...s Malawi, coastal Kenya, e Tanzania, n,e Zimbabwe..."

15 Change spelling of ***Perdix dauuricae*** to ***Perdix dauurica***; at beginning of comments add: "The correct spelling of the specific name is *Perdix dauurica* (Stepanyan 1990a)."

15 *Margaroperdix madagascariensis*, change range to "Lowlands to 2700 m of **Madagascar**. Intro. Réunion."

15 ***Coturnix [coromandelica] coromandelica*** and ***C. [coromandelica] delegorguei*** [*coromandelica* has priority over *delegorguei*]

15 *Coturnix coromandelica*, in heading change "[3059.]" to "[3060.]"

15 *Coturnix delegorguei*, after "Senegal," add "Mali,"

16 *Coturnix chinensis*, change range to "...Taiwan) S through Andaman and Nicobar is., se Asia, Indonesia and Philippines to New Guinea, Bismarck Arch., and coastal n,e,se Australia W to N. Terr. and s S. Australia (Yorke pen.). Intro..."

16 *Perdicula argoondah*, in heading after "BUSH-QUAIL" add "."

16 *Arborophila crudigularis*, change English name to FORMOSAN PARTRIDGE (not TAIWAN); in comments change "FORMOSAN" to "TAIWAN"

17 *Arborophila davidi*, change range to "Lowlands of **s Vietnam**."

17 Move *Arborophila hyperythra* account to follow *A. javanica* and change to "***Arborophila [javanica] hyperythra*** ...Forest. Mts. of **nc Borneo** ¶*hyperythra*, RED-BREASTED PARTRIDGE [3075]; mts. of **ne Borneo** (Mt. Kinabalu) ¶*erythrophrys* (Sharpe) 1890, KINABALU PARTRIDGE [3075.1]."

*17 ***Rollulus rouloul*** (not ***roulroul***); at beginning of comments, add: "For correct spelling of *rouloul*, see Farrand and Olson (1973)."

17 *Bambusicola fytchii*, in heading change "[2081.]" to "[3081.]"; change "Assam" to "Arunachal Pradesh"

18 *Ithaginis cruentus*, change "Nepal" to "n India (from Nepal E to Arunachal Pradesh)"

18 *Tragopan blythii*, in heading change "(Jerson)" to "(Jerdon)"

18-19 *Gallus gallus*, change range to "...Sumatra, Java, Bali, and (possibly intro.) Sulawesi and Philippines..."

19 *Lophura leucomelanos*, after "(Indus r.)" add ", sw Tibet"; after "s Tibet" add "(E of *leucomelanos*)"

19 *Lophura edwardsi*, after "(c Annam)" add "; possibly extinct (last collected 1928, but reported seen in 1985)"

19 ***Lophura hoogerwerfi*** (not ***hoogerswerfi***); change comments to "...regarded *hoogerwerfi* as a distinct species. [>*Houppifer* (≈*L. erythrophthalma*)]. (HOOGERWERF'S PHEASANT)..."

19 *Lophura inornata*, change comments to "See *L. hoogerwerfi*."

*19 ***Lophura erythrophthalma*** (not ***erythropthalma***)

19 Change heading of ***Lophura haitensis*** to "***Lophura hatinhensis*** Vo Quy and Do Ngoc Quang 1965. VIETNAMESE PHEASANT. [3092.1.]" and sequence species after *L. edwardsi*; change range to "Lowlands of **nc Vietnam** (n Annam); males known only from the type specimen (collected 1964), a second specimen not entirely preserved, and identifiable feathers brought in from at least two others."; change comments to "(VO QUY'S PHEASANT)."

20 *Phasianus colchicus*, after "nw Turkey" add "(probably intro.)"

21 *Chrysolophus amherstiae*, add end of range add "Intro. locally British Isles."

21 *Argusianus argus*, remove superspecies; change comments to "*A. bipunctatus* (Wood) 1871, DOUBLE-BANDED ARGUS [3109.1], based on a primary feather alleged to have come from Tioman Island off eastern Malaya (Davison 1983), is insufficiently documented to be recognized as a distinct (and extinct) species (Parkes 1992: 231). (ARGUS PHEASANT)."

21 Delete *Argusianus bipunctatus* entry

23 *Tympanuchus cupido*, in heading change "PRAIRIE-CHICKEN" to "PRAIRIE-chicken"; in comments change "[PRAIRIE-CHICKEN]" to "[PRAIRIE-chicken]"

23 *Tympanuchus pallidicinctus,* in heading change "PRAIRIE-CHICKEN" to "PRAIRIE-chicken"

23 *Agleastes meleagrides,* change range to "Lowlands of **w Africa** in Sierra Leone, Liberia, Ivory Coast and Ghana."

23 *Numida meleagris,* numbers reversed, ¶*galeata* should be [296.1], ¶*meleagris* [7043.1]; after "Ethiopia" add "and nw,s Somalia"; at end of range, add "Intro. (¶*galeata*) W. Indies, various is. (worldwide)."

24 *Callipepla californica,* after "c Chile," add "c Argentina,"

24 *Colinus virginianus,* change "from c Guerrero to s Chiapas" to "in Oaxaca and Chiapas"

25 *Odontophorus dialeucos,* in heading change "1963" to "(1963)"

26 *Odontophorus guttatus,* change "n Oaxaca" to "Oaxaca"

26 *Rhynchortyx cinctus,* change "**C. and nw**" to "**C. and nw**"

26 Under Family **Anseranatidae,** add comments "DNA-DNA hybridization data indicate *Anseranas* is distinct at the family level, supported by morphological studies of Livesey (1986)."

27 *Dendrocygna bicolor,* change range to "Locally in **African region** from...e Africa) to s S. Africa; Madagascar; **s Asia**..."

27 *Dendrocygna arborea,* change range to "...Hispaniola), s Bahama Is. (Great Inagua) and n Lesser..."

28 *Oxyura dominica,* after "Lesser Antilles" delete "("

28 *Oxyura jamaicensis,* change "**El Salvador**" to "**n C. America** in Guatemala and El Salvador"; in comments change "he considered" to "Fjeldså considered"

28 *Oxyura leucocephala,* change range to "...**s Palearctic** from s Europe (rarely s Spain, Sardinia and Romania, formerly more widespread) and nw Africa..."

28 After *Biziura lobata,* insert *Heteronetta atricapilla* from p. 42.

28 Under Subfamily Stictonettinae, at end of comments add "...(1988), supported by Livesey (1986)."

28 *Cygnus olor,* change range to "**N,c Eurasia** from Faroe Is., British Isles, s Scandinavia and w,s Russia S locally through c Europe to s France, n Italy, Greece and Turkey, and E across s S.S.R..."

29 *Cygnus cygnus,* change range to "...(w,n Sinkiang, Tsinghai..."

29 *Cygnus columbianus,* before "**n N. America**" add "**e Siberia** (Chukotski pen.), and"; in comments after "situations" add "(e.g., Stepanyan 1990c)."

29 *Anser brachyrhynchus,* in comments after "*fabalis*" add "; so treated by Stepanyan (1990c)"

29 *Anser fabalis,* change habitat to "Tundra (¶*serrirostris*) and taiga (¶*fabalis*) lakes, ponds,...."; change range to "...Scandinavia E through nw,c Russia and c,se Siberia (S of tundra) to Anadyrland and Kamchatka, and S to Altai, Transbaicalia, Mongolia and Amurland ¶*fabalis,* FOREST BEAN-GOOSE [171.1]; **cn,ne Eurasia** from n Russia (incl. Novaya Zemlya) E through n Siberia to Chukotski pen. ¶*serrirostris* Swinhoe 1871, TUNDRA BEAN-GOOSE [2059.1]. Winters (both groups) in w,c Europe..."

30 *Anser rossii,* before "n Mackenzie" add "n Alaska,"

30 *Branta sandvicensis,* change comments to read "Data from mtDNA studies of Quinn, Shields and Wilson (1991) support *B. sandvicensis* and *B. canadensis* as sister taxa within the genus *Branta,* despite the suggestion for retention of *Nesochen* as distinct from *Branta.* [>*Nesochen*]. (HAWAIIAN GOOSE)."

30 *Branta canadensis,* after "s Kansas," add "n Texas, w Oklahoma,"; change end of comments to "...consists of at least two species, a large one, *B. canadensis* (CANADA GOOSE), and a small one, *B. hutchinsii* (CACKLING GOOSE), that includes the other three groups (see mtDNA data in Quinn, Shields and Wilson 1991). [>*Leucoblepharon*]."

30-31 *Branta bernicla,* change end of range to "...se Alaska S to c Baja Calif."

31 *Alopochen aegyptiacus,* after "Nile v.)" add "; formerly Near East (Palestine)"

32 *Tadorna tadorna,* before "s France," add "Spain,"

32 *Tachyeres pteneres,* at end of comments add "See *T. patachonicus.*"

32 *Tachyeres patachonicus,* in heading change "1828" to "1831"; add comments "*Oidemia Patachonica* King 1828, which pertains to *Tachyeres tachyeres,* has been suppressed, and *Micropterus patachonicus* King 1831 and *Anas pteneres* Forster 1844 have been conserved for their respective species (I.C.Z.N. 1991)."

32 *Pteronetta hartlaubii,* change range to "...s Sudan, n,ne Zaire and w Uganda, and S to ..."

32-33 *Sarkidiornis melanotos,* change "Ihering and Ihering 1819" to "Ihering and Ihering 1907"

33 Under Tribe Anatini, add comments "Livezey (1991) cladistically analyzed the 'dabbling ducks' of the Anatini using characters of plumage, soft parts, tracheae, and nontracheal skeletons. Generic recognition of *Mareca* is not supported by DNA distance data, and species limits do not conform to the 'biological species' definition, thus these proposed generic and species changes are not followed herein. Species splits recommended by Livezey are given as groups; however, species relationships to one another and their sequence, particularly in *Anas,* are adopted, except for our policy of listing members of a superspecies geographically.

33 *Aix sponsa,* after "sw U.S." add ", c Mexico"

34-38 Sequence species of *Anas* as follows: *specularioides, specularis, capensis, strepera, falcata, penelope, americana, sibilatrix, sparsa, rubripes, fulvigula, platyrhynchos, wyvilliana, laysanensis, poecilorhyncha, luzonica, superciliosa, undulata, melleri, discors, cyanoptera, smithii, platalea, rhynchotis, clypeata, bernieri, gibberifrons, gracilis, castanea, chlorotis, aucklandica, bahamensis, erythrorhyncha, flavirostris, acuta, eatoni, georgica, querquedula, formosa, crecca, puna, versicolor* and *hottentota*

34 *Anas falcata,* change "Kurile" to "Kuril"

34 *Anas strepera,* change "n Texas" to "sc Texas"

34 *Anas formosa,* in comments change "(≈*A. flavirostris*)" to "(+N)"

34 *Anas crecca* (remove superspecies); change comments to "Stepanyan (1990c) and Livezey (1991) recognized *A. carolinensis* as a species. (GREEN-WINGED TEAL)."

34 *Anas flavirostris* (remove superspecies); near end of range after "YELLOW-BILLED TEAL" add "(CHILEAN TEAL)"; in comments after "populations." add "Livezey (1991) recognized *A. andium* as a species."

35 *Anas bernieri,* change English name to BERNIER'S TEAL (not MADAGASCAR); change end of comments to "...superspecies. [>*Nesonetta* (≈*A. aucklandica*); >*Nettion*]. (MADAGASCAR TEAL)."

35 *Anas gibberifrons*, at beginning of comments add "Livezey (1991) recognized *A. albogularis* as a species. [>*Virago* (≈*A. aucklandica*)]."

35 *Anas gracilis*, after "**Australasian region** in" add "s Moluccas (Ambon),"

35 *Anas castanea*, delete comments "[>*Virago*]."

35 *Anas aucklandica*, in range before "Auckland," add "**subantarctic is.** in"; in comments delete "[>*Nesonetta*]."

35 *Anas platyrhynchos*, change comments to "...*platyrhynchos*. Livezey (1991) recognized *A. diazi* as a species. [MALLARD]. See *A. rubripes*, *A. fulvigula*, *A. wyvilliana* and *A. superciliosa*."

35 *Anas laysanensis* (remove from superspecies); in comments delete "May be conspecific with *A. platyrhynchos*."

35 *Anas fulvigula* (remove from superspecies)

36 *Anas undulata*, change comments to "[>*Afranas* (+N)]."

36 *Anas poecilorhyncha*, change range to "**E Asia** from s Siberia (...Kuril Is.) S to n,c,e China (...Heilungkiang S to Kwangsi and Kwangtung), Korea and Japan ¶*zonorhyncha* Swinhoe 1866, EASTERN SPOT-BILLED DUCK (CHINESE SPOT-BILLED DUCK) [134.1]; **s Asia** in India (W to...Ceylon), Tibet, sw China (Yunnan), c,s,e Burma,...Annam) ¶*poecilorhyncha*, INDIAN SPOT-BILLED DUCK [3022.2]. Winters (¶*zonorhyncha*) S to s Indochina and Taiwan."; in comments after "140)." add "; Livezey (1991) recognized *A. zonorhyncha* as a species."

36 *Anas superciliosa*, in comments after "GREY/BLACK" add "/AUSTRALIAN BLACK"

*36 **Anas specularioides** (not *specularoides*)

36 *Anas acuta*, in comments delete "[>*Dafila* (≈*A. erythrorhyncha*)]."

37 *Anas bahamensis*, change beginning of comments to "[>*Dafila* (≈*A. georgica*); >*Paecilonetta* (+N)]..."

37 *Anas hottentota*, change "**c,e,se Africa**" to "**c,e,se African region**"; after "...Cape prov.)" add "; Madagascar"; in comments after "(1977)." add "[>*Micronetta*]."

37 *Anas querquedula*, in comments delete "(≈*A. cyanoptera*)"

37 *Anas discors*, in comments after "...clypeata*)" add "; >*Pterocyanea/Querquedula* (+N)]"

37 *Anas cyanoptera*, change "e Montana" to "s Saskatchewan"; in comments delete "[>*Pterocyanea*]."

38 *Anas clypeata*, after "New Brunswick" add "and s Newfoundland"; after "Kansas E to" add "ne Maryland and"

38 *Marmoretta angustirostris*, change range to "...Tunisia) and s Spain (formerly N to France, Italy, Yugoslavia and Greece); from sc Turkey,..."

38 *Netta rufina*, change range to "...Italy, Czechoslovakia, Austria and Romania)..."

*38 **Netta peposaca** (not *peposeaca*)

39 *Aythya innotata*, add "†" in front of name; change range to "Lowlands of **e Madagascar** (L. Alaotra, formerly widespread to 1200 m); probably extinct."

39 *Aythya australis*, change range to "...Banks Is., New Zealand, and (probably)...to Tasmania."

39 *Aythya marila*, change "Baja Calif." to "n Baja Calif."

40 *Somateria mollissima*, change range to "...E to Denmark, Switzerland, Estonia and n Russia); **Arctic**..."

40 *Somateria fischeri*, add comments "[>*Lampronetta*]."

40 *Melanitta nigra*, after "Newfoundland" add "; **N. Carolina** (Pamlico Sound)"; at beginning of comments add "Stepanyan (1990c) recognized *M. americana* as a separate species."

41 *Melanitta fusca*, change range to "...VELVET SCOTER (EUROPEAN WHITE-WINGED SCOTER) [164];...(Ridgway) 1887, ASIATIC SCOTER (ASIATIC WHITE-WINGED SCOTER) [2071.2]; **n N. America**...s Manitoba, n Ontario and w Quebec ¶*deglandi* (Bonapartae) 1850, WHITE-WINGED SCOTER (AMERICAN/DEGLAND'S WHITE-WINGED SCOTER)..."; in comments after "WHITE-WINGED SCOTER" add ", as recognized by Stepanyan (1990c)"

41 *Bucephala albeola*, change range to "**W Palearctic** (Iceland); **n,wc N. America**...n Montana, c Colorado and s Canada..."

41 *Lophodytes cucullatus*, change "c Mexico" to "n Mexico"

42 *Mergus merganser*, change "c Mexico" to "n Mexico"

42 *Mergus australis*, change English name to AUCKLAND ISLANDS MERGANSER (not AUCKLAND MERGANSER); in comments delete "ISLANDS"

42 *Heteronetta atricapilla*, add comments "*Heteronetta* is oxyurine based on behavior (Johnsgard 1978: 365-367) and morphology (Lizesey 1986)."; move to p. 28 and sequence after *Biziura lobata*

42 *Turnix sylvatica*, change "Iberia" to "Iberian"

42 *Turnix maculosa*, change comments to "...Mindanao (Sutter 1955), although the purported overlap has been questioned (Dickinson, Kennedy and Parkes 1991: 138-139), thus the status there is uncertain. *T. maculosa* may be more closely related to..."

42 *Turnix nana*, change "Congo Rep.," to "sw C. African Rep.,"

43 *Turnix suscitator*, change range to "...Sulawesi and n,c Philippines (S to Negros and Cebu) ¶*suscitator*..."

43 *Turnix nigricollis*, at end of range add "Intro. Réunion."

43 *Ortyxelos meiffrenii*, after "S Chad" add ", n C. African Rep."

44 *Indicator minor*, after "s Mali," add "Ivory Coast,"

44 *Indicator conirostris*, change range to "**W,c Africa** from coastal Liberia E through Cameroon..."

44 *Indicator willcocksi*, change range to "Locally in **w,c Africa** from Guinea-Bissau, Liberia and Ivory Coast E to Cameroon, s Chad, C. African Rep., n,c,e Zaire and Uganda."

44 *Indicator exilis*, change range to "...**w,c, Africa** from Senegal, se Guinea and Sierra Leone E to s Cameroon...Uganda, w Kenya and nw Tanzania, and S to c Angola..."

44 *Indicator pumilio*, in heading change "1958" to "(1958)"; change end of range to "...w Uganda, Rwanda and Burundi."

44 *Melichneustes robustus*, change range to "...**w,c, Africa** from Guinea, Liberia, w Ivory Coast and s Nigeria E to s C. African Rep., ne Zaire and sw Uganda, and S to extreme n Angola and sw,c Zaire."

44 *Melignomon eisentrauti*, change range to "Locally in **w Africa** in Liberia, Sierra Leone and sw Cameroon."

44 *Melignomon zenkeri*, change range to "...n Gabon, se C. African Rep., n,ce Zaire and w Uganda."

44 *Prodotiscus insignis*, change range to "**W,c Africa** from Sierra Leone, Liberia,...s Cameroon, C. African Rep., n,ne,ce Zaire,..."

45 *Prodotiscus zambesiae*, change range to "...Malawi to extreme ne Namibia (Caprivi), ne Botswana, Mozambique..."

45 *Prodotiscus regulus*, change "w Ivory Coast" to "Guinea"; at beginning of comments add "Includes *P. whitei* Horniman (1956)."

45 *Jynx torquilla*, before "Sicily" add "Corsica, Sardinia and"

45 *Picumnus aurifrons*, at end of comments add "See *P. fuscus.*"

45 *Picumnus exilis*, at end of comments add "See *P. fuscus.*"

46 *Picumnus cirratus*, change end of comments to "...See *P. varzeae*, *P. dorbygnianus*, and *P. albosquamatus.*"

46 **Picumnus dorbygnianus** (not *dorbygianus*)

46 *Picumnus fuscus*, change range to "...**sc S. America** in r. Guaporé drainage of n Bolivia..."; change comments to "Probably closely related to *P. aurifrons* or *P. exilis* (Parker and Rocha 1991). (NATTERER'S PICULET)."; move to p. 45 and sequence after *P. exilis*

46 *Picumnus rufiventris*, delete comments

46 *Picumnus fulvescens*, in heading change "(1961)" to "(1962)"

47 *Sasia africana*, change range to "...1000 m of **w,c Africa** from Liberia E locally to Ghana and (possibly) Nigeria, and from s Cameroon, s C. African Rep., n,ne Zaire..."

48 *Melanerpes formicivorus*, change range to read "**W N. and Middle America** from cs Washington and nw Oregon S (W of Cascades and Sierra Nevada) to s Baja ... w Panama (Chiriquí, Veraguas); lowland...ne Nicaragua; Andes, 1400-3300 m, of **Colombia** (except Nariño)."

48 *Melanerpes hypopolius*, delete ", Tlaxcala"

49 *Sphyrapicus ruber*, change range to "...Cascades, to cw Calif., and Sierra Nevada to ec Calif. and w Nevada; locally mts. of s Calif. and s Nevada."

50 *Campethera abingoni*, change range to "...**Africa** in Senegambia, Guinea-Bissau, n Ghana, nc Cameroon,..."

50 *Campethera maculosa*, change English name to LITTLE GREEN WOODPECKER (not LITLE)

50 *Campethera caroli*, after "Liberia," add "Ghana, Ivory Coast,"

50 *Dendropicos elachus*, before "Senegal" add "sw Mauritania and"

51 *Dendropicos poecilolaemus*, before "c,s Cameroon" add "extreme se Nigeria,"

51 *Dendropicos fuscescens*, change "Senegal" to "Senegambia"

51 *Dendropicos lugubris*, change "s Nigeria" to "sw Cameroon"

51 *Dendropicos gabonensis*, change English name to GABON WOODPECKER (not GABOON); after "s Cameroon," add "sw C. African Rep.,"; at beginning of comments add "(GABOON WOODPECKER)."

51 *Dendropicos stierlingi*, change range to "...**e Africa** in s Tanzania..."

51 *Dendropicos pyrrhogaster*, before "s Cameroon" add "(questionably)"

51 *Dendropicos elliotii*, after "Gabon," add "sw C. African Rep.,"

51 *Dendropicos griseocephalus*, change range to "...s,ne Tanzania S to nc,ne Namibia, Zambia and nw Malawi; locally in extreme s Mozambique and S. Africa (...)"

52 *Dendrocopos maculatus*, change range to "Lowlands to 2500 m of **Philippines** (except Sulu Arch.) ¶*maculatus*..."

52 *Dendrocopos minor*, change "**Eurasia**" to "**Palearctic**"

53 *Dendrocopos medius*, before "cont. Europe" add "s Sweden and"

53 *Dendrocopos leucotos*, change range to "...s Scandinavia and e Europe (S to Germany, Austria, ne Italy, Hungary, e Yugoslavia and Romania) E across nw,c Russia...Taiwan ¶*leucotos*, WHITE-BACKED WOODPECKER [2377]; locally in **s Europe** in Pyrenees, c Italy, and from Yugoslavia E through Albania, Bulgaria, Greece and w,n Turkey to sw

Russia (Caucasus, Transcaucasus) and w,n Iran ¶*lilfordi* (Sharpe and Dresser) 1871, LILFORD'S WOODPECKER [2377.1]."; change comments to "The two groups are parapatric in eastern Yugoslavia but altitudinally separated and ecologically different, with few hybrids known (Haffer 1989). [>*Dendrodromas*]."

53 *Dendrocopos major*, change "**Eurasia**" to "**Palearctic**"

54 *Picoides scalaris*, change range to "...Belize; int. of c Guatemala and Honduras (also Pacific coast); pine..."

55 *Veniliornis fumigatus*, change range to "...Jalisco, Hidalgo, San Luis Potosí...Darién) and Colombia..."

55 *Veniliornis sanguineus*, in heading change "1783" to "1793"

55 *Veniliornis chocoensis*, in heading change "(Swainson) 1821" to "Todd 1919"

55 *Veniliornis affinis*, change range to "...n,e Bolivia and Brazil (from Amazon..."

56 *Piculus flavigula*, change range to "...e Peru, n Bolivia (Beni, ne Santa Cruz)..."

56 *Piculus rubiginosus*, after "e San Luis Potosí" add "and Hidalgo"

57 *Colaptes auratus*, change "n Baja Calif." to "nw Baja Calif."

57 *Colaptes chrysoides*, change "ne Baja Calif." to "Baja Calif. (except nw)"

58 *Dryocopus galeatus*, change end of range to "...(Misiones); possibly extinct, last reported 1958."

58 *Dryocopus javensis*, change range to "...N. Natuna Is.), Java and Bali; Philippines..."

60 *Picus viridanus*, change range to "Lowlands to 1700 m in **se Asia** from Burma (...) S to pen. Thailand and (mostly in highlands) Malaya."

60 *Picus vittatus*, change range to "Lowlands to 1700 m...(except pen.), Malaya (lowlands only, incl. Langkawi I.), Sumatra..."

60 Split *Picus viridis* into the following two species:

Picus [viridis] viridis Linnaeus 1758. EURASIAN GREEN WOODPECKER. [2387.]

Deciduous and mixed forest edge, second growth, woodland, towns. Lowlands and mts. to 2750 m of **w Eurasia** from British Isles and s Scandinavia S through most of Europe to n Mediterranean region (except Pyrenees and Iberian pen.), and E to w Russia (Volga r., Caucasus, Transcaucasus), Turkey and w,n Iran ¶*viridis*, EURASIAN GREEN WOODPECKER [2387]; **sw Europe** in Iberian pen. and Pyrenees (incl. extreme sw France) ¶*sharpei* (Saunders) 1872, IBERIAN WOODPECKER [2387.1].

Sharpei differs in head coloration, juvenal plumage, and size, and may warrant specific status (L. Larson, pers. comm.). (GREEN/EUROPEAN GREEN WOODPECKER). [EURASIAN GREEN WOODPECKER]. See *P. vaillantii*.

Picus [viridis] vaillantii (Malherbe) 1847. LEVAILLANT'S WOODPECKER. [2388.]

Deciduous forest, second growth, woodland. Mts. (mostly) to 2100 m of **nw Africa** in Morocco, Algeria and Tunisia.

P. vaillantii is generally treated as a species (e.g., Harrison 1982: 191) distinct from *P. viridis* on the basis of morphological differences, especially head pattern (including black instead of red moustache) and sexually dimorphic characters. (NORTH AFRICAN GREEN/ALGERIAN WOODPECKER).

61 *Dinopium shorii*, change end of range to "...(from Garhwal E to n Assam) and w,ne,c,s Burma."

61 *Dinopium javanense*, change "s Asia" to "**s Asia and Malay Arch.**"; after "Java" add ", Bali"

61 *Chrysocolaptes lucidus*, in heading change "1796" to "1786"; in range change "s Asia" to "**s Asia and Malay Arch.**"

62 *Mulleripicus pulverulentus*, change "s Asia" to "**s Asia and Malay Arch.**"

63 *Megalaima corvina*, change English name to BROWN-THROATED BARBET (not BROWN-THRAOTED)

63 *Megalaima flavifrons*, in heading change "1817" to "1816"

63 *Megalaima armillaris*, change English name to FLAME-FRONTED BARBET (not ORANGE-FRONTED); in comments, change "FLAME-FRONTED" to "ORANGE-FRONTED"

64 *Calorhamphus fuliginosus*, at end of range add ", Sumatra and Borneo."

64 *Gymnobucco peli*, after "Gabon" add "and Cabinda"

64 *Gymnobucco sladeni*, change end of range to "...Congo Rep. and Zaire (except se)."

64 *Gymnobucco bonapartei*, after "sw,cs,se Zaire," add "extreme n Angola,"

64 *Stactolaema olivacea*, change range to "...[7189]; **se Africa** disjunctly in se Tanzania and e S. Africa (Natal)..."

64 *Pogoniulus coryphaeus*, change English name to WESTERN TINKERBIRD (not WESTERN GREEN-TINKERBIRD); in range before "Cameroon" add "se Nigeria and"; change end of comments to "...AG (+N): GREEN-TINKERBIRD."

65 *Pogoniulus leucomystax*, change English name to MOUSTACHED TINKERBIRD (not MOUTACHED GREEN-TINKERBIRD); change comments to "(WHISKERED TINKERBIRD)."

65 *Pogoniulus simplex*, change English name to GREEN TINKERBIRD (not AFRICAN GREEN-TINKERBIRD); change comments to "(AFRICAN GREEN-TINKERBIRD)."

65 *Pogoniulus atroflavus*, change range to "...s Cameroon, se African Rep., n,ne Zaire and w Uganda, and S to..."

65 *Pogoniulus subsulphureus*, after "Cameroon" add "(incl. Bioko)"

65 *Pogoniulus bilineatus*, after "Cameroon" add "(incl. Bioko)"; after "Burundi, Tanzania" add "(incl. Zanzibar and Mafia is.)"

65 *Pogoniulus pusillus*, change "e S. Africa" to "**se Africa** in extreme s Mozambique and e S. Africa"

65 *Buccanodon duchaillui*, before "Liberia" add "Sierra Leone,"; change end of range to "...Congo Rep., sw,sc,ce Zaire and Rwanda."

65 *Tricholaema hirsuta*, change range to "**W,c Africa** from Sierra Leone, Liberia, se Guinea and Ivory Coast E to c,e Cameroon,...w Kenya S (E of *flavipunctata*) to n Angola, cs,ce Zaire and extreme nw Tanzania ¶*hirsuta*...**wc Africa** from s Nigeria and w,s Cameroon..."

65 *Tricholaema diademata*, after "c,sw Ethiopia" add "nw Somalia,"

65 *Tricholaema frontata*, after "se Zaire" add ", sw Tanzania"

66 *Tricholaema melanocephala*, before "Ethiopia" add "extreme se Sudan,"

66 *Lybius leucocephalus*, in heading change "Defilippi" to "de Filippi"; at end of range add "[7209.1]; **cw Angola** ¶*leucogaster* (Barboza du Bocage) 1877, WHITE-BELLIED BARBET [7209.3]."; change comments to "...two of the three northern groups in areas of contact (*leucogaster* is an isolate), but pure..."

66 *Lybius guifsobalito*, before "Uganda," add "extreme ne Zaire,"

66 *Lybius torquatus*, after "se Zaire," add "se Rwanda,"

66 *Lybius minor*, in heading change "1817" to "1816"; change range to "...s Burundi, sw Tanzania, Zambia and nw Malawi ¶*macclounii*..."

66 *Lybius dubius*, change end of range to "...Nigeria, Cameroon and sw Chad to w,n C. African Rep."

66 *Lybius rolleti*, in heading change "(Defilippi)" to "(de Filippi)"; after "s Sudan" add ", extreme ne Zaire"

66 *Trachyphonus purpuratus*, after "Sierra Leone" add ", s Guinea"; change end of range to "...nw Angola, sw,cs,ce Zaire, Rwanda and Burundi."; in comments change "(1988)" to "(1988a)"

66 *Trachyphonus vaillantii*, after "se Zaire" add ", Rwanda, Burundi"

67 *Trachyphonus margaritatus*, change "s Mali" to "c Mali"

67 *Trachyphonus erythrocephalus*, after "Somalia," add "e Uganda,"

67 *Capito dayi*, change range to "Locally in lowlands of **wc S. America** in w Amazonian Brazil (e Amazonas, Rondônia, nc Mato Grosso) and ne Bolivia (ne Santa Cruz)."

68 *Eubucco tucinkae*, change range to "Andean slopes of **sw S. America** in e Peru (...) and n Bolivia (n La Paz)."

68 *Semnornis frantzii*, in comments change "(1988)" to "(1988a)"

68 *Aulacorhynchus prasinus*, change beginning of range to "Highlands of **Middle and w S. America** from se San Luis Potosí, Hidalgo, Puebla, Veracruz, Guerrero, Oaxaca,..."

68 *Pteroglossus viridis*, in heading after "ARACARI" delete "]"

68 *Pteroglossus bitorquatus*, before "Santa Cruz" add "Beni,"

69 *Pteroglossus mariae*, change end of range to "...E to r. Purús)."

70 *Selenidera reinwardtii*, after "Pando" add ", n La Paz"

70 *Selenidera maculirostris*, change end of range to "...Sul), n Bolivia (Beni, ne Santa Cruz) and ne Argentina (Misiones)."

70 *Ramphastos vitellinus*, change range to "**N S America** ...Guianas, Trinidad and nw Amazonian Brazil..."

71 *Ramphastos tucanus*, change range to "...1100 m of **c S America**..."

71 *Ramphastos toco*, change range to "Lowlands of **c,se S America**..."

71 Order **GALBULIFORMES** (not **GABULIFORMES**)

72 *Brachygalba lugubris*, habitat and range in one paragraph

72 *Galbula ruficauda*, change range to "...(except Yucatán and Quintana Roo) S to Nicaragua,...w Bocas del Toro), also in w Colombia (Pacific...[1365]; **s C. and n S. America** in e Panama (e Panamá prov., e Darién), n,e Colombia..."

72 *Galbula pastazae*, change end of range to "...(se Nariño) and e Ecuador."

73 *Jacamerops aureus* (not *aurea*)

73 *Notharchus ordii*, change range to "...Amazonas), n,wc Amazonian Brazil (e Amazonas W to Tefé and upper r. Urucu, and in wc Pará)..."

73 *Notharchus tectus*, change range to "...Guianas S, W of Andes to w Ecuador and E of Andes to e Ecuador, e Peru..."

73 *Bucco tamatia,* change range to "...Guianas S to e Ecuador, e Peru, Amazonian Brazil (...) and ne Bolivia (ne Santa Cruz)."

74 *Malacoptila rufa,* change end of range to "...Ucayali), Amazonian Brazil (...) and ne Bolivia (ne Santa Cruz)."

74 *Micromonacha lanceolata,* change end of range to "...(upper r. Juruá, upper r. Urucu."

75 *Nonnula ruficapilla,* change end of range to "...Amazonian Brazil (from r. Juruá E to r. Tocantins, and S to r. Guaporé and r. Paraguai)."

75 *Monasa nigrifrons,* before "e Peru," add "e Ecuador,"

75 *Monasa morphoeus,* change range to "...[1363]; **s C. and nw S. America** in c,e Panama (...) and nw,nc Colombia (Pacific..."

75 *Chelidoptera tenebrosa,* before "e Peru," add "e Ecuador,"

75 Family Bucerotidae, in comments change *"Anthracocerus"* to *"Anthracoceros"*

75 *Tockus albocristatus,* change range to "...Sierra Leone, s Guinea and Liberia E to s Cameroon, cs C. African Rep., n Zaire and w Uganda, and S to Congo Rep., Cabinda and w,sc,ec Zaire."

75 *Tockus hartlaubi,* change range to "...Sierra Leone, s Guinea and Liberia E to s Cameroon, s C. African Rep., n Zaire and w Uganda, and S to Congo Rep., Cabinda and w,sc,ec Zaire."

75 *Tockus camurus,* change range to "...Sierra Leone, s Guinea and Liberia E to Cameroon, s C. African Rep., extreme s Sudan, n,ne Zaire and w Uganda, and S to Congo Rep., Cabinda and w,c,ec Zaire."

76 *Tockus erythrorhynchus,* change range to "**Africa** (except forested w,c) from Senegambia and Guinea-Bissau E in a narrow belt through s Mali, Burkina Faso, n Ghana, s Niger, Benin, n Nigeria, ne Cameroon, s Chad, C. African Rep. and s Sudan..."

76 *Tockus flavirostris,* change end of range to "...Somalia, n Uganda, nc,ec Kenya and ne Tanzania."

76 *Tockus jacksoni,* change range to "**Ne Africa** in se Sudan, ne Uganda and nw Kenya."

76 *Tockus deckeni,* change range to "**E Africa** from c,s Ethiopia and n,s Somalia S through e,s Kenya to sc,ne Tanzania."

76 *Tockus alboterminatus,* change end of range to "...n,e Zimbabwe and e,s S. Africa (e Transvaal, Swaziland, Natal, s Cape prov.)."; change comments to "[>*Rhynchaceros/Protokus* (≈*T. hemprichii*)]."

76 *Tockus fasciatus,* change range to "...n Zaire, s Sudan and Uganda S to..."

76 *Tockus nasutus,* change range to "**African region** from s Mauritania and Senegambia E across...e Natal)."

76 *Tockus pallidirostris,* change account to one paragraph

77 *Anthracotheros montani,* change range to "**Sw Philippines** (Sulu Arch.)."

77 *Anorrhinus tickelli,* change "(Jerdon)" to "Jerdon 1872"

77 **Penelopides manillae** (not *manilloe*); also change spelling in comments of this and following four species; at end of comments add "The correct original spelling is *manillae* (Browning 1992: 25)."

77 *Penelopides samarensis,* after "Samar," add "Calicoan,"

78 *Aceros narcondami,* change English name to NARCONDAM HORNBILL (not NARCODAM); change "Narcodam I." to "Narcondam I."

78 *Aceros subruficollis,* change comments to "...specific status, and the mallophagan..."

78 *Ceratogymna fistulator,* after "Senegal" add ", Guinea-Bissau, Guinea"

79 *Ceratogymna subcylindricus,* change end of range to "...Rwanda, Burundi and nw Tanzania; ne Angola."

79 *Ceratogymna cylindricus,* in heading change "1824" to "1831"; change "s Benin" to "Ghana"

79 *Ceratogymna albotibialis,* change range to "**C Africa** from s Benin, s Nigeria, s Cameroon, sw C. African Rep., n Zaire,...Congo Rep., extreme n Angola and w,sc,ec Zaire."

79 *Ceratogymna atrata,* change range to "...Liberia, Guinea and Ivory Coast...n,ne Zaire, extreme s Sudan and w Uganda, and S to..."

79 *Bucorvus abyssinicus,* after "Ethiopia," add "s Somalia,"; changes comments to "See *B. leadbeateri.*"

79 Change "*Bucorvus cafer* (Schlegel) 1862" to "*Bucorvus leadbeateri* (Vigors) 1825"; change comments to "Browning (1992: 22-24) demonstrated that *Buceros leadbeateri* Vigors 1825 cannot apply to *B. abyssinicus.* [= *B. cafer* (Schlegel) 1862]. (GROUND..."

79 *Upupa epops,* change range to "...except Balearic Is. and...c Malaya; **wc,nc Africa** from sw Mauritania and Senegambia E through s Mali, s Niger, s Chad and s Sudan to Ethiopia and Somalia, and S to Cameroon, C. African Rep., n Uganda and n Kenya. Winters..."

79 *Upupa africana,* change range to "**Sc,s Africa** from Congo Rep., c Zaire, s Uganda and s Kenya S to s S. Africa ¶*africana,* AFRICAN HOOPOE [6282.1]; **Madagascar** ¶*marginata* Cabanis and Heine 1860, MADAGASCAR HOOPOE [6282.2]. Winters (¶*africana*) N to w,ne Africa."; at end of comments add "The two groups may also represent distinct species, differing morphologically and vocally (I. Lewis, pers. comm.)."

79 *Phoeniculus purpureus,* change "nw Somalia" to "extreme s Somalia"

80 *Phoeniculus bollei,* change range to "...**w,c,ec Africa** from Liberia and Ivory Coast...Uganda, w,c Kenya and n Tanzania."

80 *Phoeniculus castaneiceps,* change range to "...se Guinea, Liberia and Ivory Coast...s Cameroon, sw C. African Rep. and n,ne Zaire to Uganda and w Kenya, and S to Gabon and Congo Rep."

80 Subfamily Apalodermatinae (not Apaloderminae)

80 *Apaloderma aequatoriale,* after "Gabon," add "sw C. African Rep.,"

80 *Apaloderma vittatum,* change range to "...1500 m of **c,ec Africa** in se Nigeria and s Cameroon..."

81 *Trogon viridis,* change range to "...**s C. and S. America**..."

81 Sequence *Trogon bairdii* before *T. viridis*

82 *Trogon elegans,* after "Tamaulipas S" add "(incl. Tres Marias Is.)"

82 *Trogon collaris,* change range to "...San Luis Potosí, Hidalgo, Veracruz...Costa Rica and w,e Panama (w Chiriquí, sw Bocas del Toro, e Darién) ¶*puella*...2700 m of **s C. and S. America** from extreme e Panama (Cerro Pirre in e Darién), Colombia (Serranía...)"; at end of comments add "See *T. aurantiiventris.*"

82 *Trogon aurantiiventris,* add comments "This form and *T. collaris,* with which it is partly sympatric, may represent color morphs rather than species (Wetmore 1968: 412; Ridgely 1981: 172; Stiles and Skutch 1989: 236)."

82 *Trogon curucui*, after "s Jujuy" add ", Formosa"

83 *Coracias abyssinica*, change range to "...C. African Rep., s Egypt, Sudan..."

84 *Coracias cyanogaster*, in heading change "1817" to "1816"

84 *Eurystomus glaucurus*, after "forested w,c" add ", but incl. Bioko"

84 *Brachypteracias leptosomus*, change "**ne,ec Madagascar**" to "**ne,e Madagascar**"

84 *Brachypteracias squamigera*, change English name to SCALY GROUND-ROLLER (not SCALED); add at end of comments "(SCALED GROUND-ROLLER)."

84 *Atelornis pittoides*, change "**e Madagascar**" to "**nw,e Madagascar**"

84 *Atelornis crossleyi*, change English name to RUFOUS-HEADED GROUND-ROLLER (not CROSSLEY'S); change "**ne,ec Madagascar**" to "**e Madagascar**"; at end of comments add "(CROSSLEY'S GROUND-ROLLER)."

85 *Leptosomus discolor*, change English name to CUCKOO ROLLER (not COUROL); change comments to "(THE COUROL/THE CUCKOO-ROLLER)."

85 *Eumomota superciliosa*, delete "Oaxaca and"

86 *Alcedo semitorquata*, ranges (only, other parts of account okay) of *A. semitorquata* and *A. quadribrachys* reversed; after reversing, change range of *A. semitorquata* to "w,c Ethiopia and se Kenya; from s Angola...ne Botswana and nw,e,s Tanzania S through..."

86 *Alcedo quadribrachys*, change English name to SHINING-BLUE KINGFISHER (not SHINING BLUE); after reversing ranges (see preceding), change range to "...Uganda, w Kenya and nw Tanzania, and S to..."

86 *Alcedo meninting*, after "Kerala;" add "E. Ghats in Andhra Pradesh;"

87 *Alcedo websteri*, change range to "**Bismarck Arch.** (Umboi, New Britain, New Ireland, New Hanover, Lihir Is.)."

87 *Alcedo cyanopecta*, change heading from "...Lafresnaye 1840. DWARF RIVER KINGFISHER..." to "...(Lafresnaye) 1840. INDIGO-BANDED KINGFISHER..."; in comments after "RIVER" add "/DWARF RIVER"

87 *Alcedo argentata*, change comments to "Dickinson, Kennedy and Parkes (1991: 247) indicated that *argentata* is an allospecies..."

87 Split *Alcedo cristata* into the following two species:

Alcedo [cristata] cristata Pallas 1764. MALACHITE KINGFISH-ER. [6294.]
    Streams, lakes, ponds, marshes. **Africa** from Senegambia E through s Mali, s Niger, s Chad and s Sudan to Ethiopia and s Somalia, and S to s S. Africa.
    A. cristata and *A. leucogaster* are regarded by some as constituting a superspecies, but they are widely sympatric in western and central Africa. [>*Corythornis* (≈*A. leucogaster*)]. (AFRICAN MALACHITE-KINGFISHER). [MALACHITE KINGFISHER]. See *A. vintsioides*, *A. thomensis* and *A. nais*.

Alcedo [cristata] vintsioides Eydoux and Gervais 1836. MALAGASY KINGFISHER. [6294.3.]
    Streams, lakes, ponds, marshes, mangroves.
Madagascar and Comoro Is.
    A. vintsioides is recognized as a species distinct from *A. cristata* by Langrand (1990: 236-237). (MADAGASCAR MALACHITE-KINGFISHER/DIADEMED KINGFISHER).

87 *Alcedo leucogaster*, change habitat to "Forested streams, mangroves."; in range after "s Cameroon" add "(incl. Bioko), C. African Rep."

87 *Alcedo pusilla*, change range to "...Bismarck Arch. (Umboi, New Britain, New Ireland, New Hanover, Tabar Is.), Solomon Is..."

87 *Ceyx lepidus*, in range before "Philippines" add "c,s"; change end of comments to "...FOREST-KINGFISHER/DWARF-KINGFISHER"

87 *Ceyx erithacus*, sequence "Mindoro," before "Camiguin Sur,"

88 *Ceyx rufidorsa*, change end of range to "...Balabac, Sulu Arch.)."

88 *Ceyx melanurus*, before "Samar," add "Catanduanes,"

88 *Ispidina lecontei*, change range to "...**w,c Africa** from Sierra Leone, Liberia and Ivory Coast E to s Cameroon, C. African Rep., n,e Zaire,..."

88 HALCYONOIDEA and **Halcyonidae**, *not* DACELONOIDEA and **Dacelonidae**; under "Family **Halcyonidae**" add "Halcyonidae Vigors 1825 has priority over Dacelonidae Bonaparte 1837."

88 *Dacelo gaudichaud*, change range to "Lowlands to 1300 m of **New Guinea region** in Aru and w Papuan is., and New Guinea (...)."

88 *Cittura cyanotis*, change end of comments to ".../TEMMINCK'S/MASKED KINGFISHER)."

89 *Halcyon badia*, change range to "...s Cameroon, sw C. African Rep., n,ne Zaire,...S to Cabinda, nw Angola and cw,sc,ce Zaire."

89 *Halcyon smyrnensis*, before "Near East" add "ne Egypt,"

89 *Halcyon malimbica*, change range to "...Senegal, sw Mali and Sierra Leone E to Cameroon, s Chad, C. African Rep., s Sudan, Uganda and sw Ethiopia, and S to..."

90 *Todirhamphus macleayii*, change range to "...**Australasian region** in e New Guinea..."

90 *Todirhamphus albonotatus*, at beginning of comments add "(WHITE-MANTLED KINGFISHER)."

90 *Todirhamphus pyrrhopygia*, change comments to "In the early 19th century, most authors, including Gould, considered *Halcyon* as masculine (e.g., Gould's 1838 description of *Halcyon inscriptus*, now a synonym of *Todirhamphus macleayii*). Gould's use of *Halcyon pyrrhopygia* in the original description indicates *pyrrhopygia* is a noun in apposition. [<*Cyanalcyon*]"

90 *Todirhamphus cinnamominus*, change range to "...[2367]; **s Mariana Is.** (Guam) ¶*cinnamominus*, GUAM KINGFISHER [9334]; **Caroline Is.** (Palau, Pohnpei) ¶*reichenbachii* (Hartlaub) 1852, CAROLINE ISLANDS KINGFISHER [9334.1]."

91 *Todirhamphus australasia*, change English name to CINNAMON-BANDED KINGFISHER (not CINNAMON-BACKED); in comments change "CINNAMON-BANDED" to "CINNAMON-BACKED"

91 *Todirhamphus tuta*, in comments after "RESPECTED" add "/POLYNESIAN"

91 *Actenoides lindsayi*, after "Luzon," add "Catanduanes, Marinduque,"

92 *Actenoides monachus*, in comments after "CELEBES LOWLAND/" add "COWLED/"

92 *Actenoides princeps*, in comments after "CELEBES MOUNTAIN/" add "REGENT/"

92 *Tanysiptera hydrocharis*, in comments before "ARU/" add "LESSER/"

92 *Tanysiptera ellioti*, in heading change "1970" to "1870"

92 *Tanysiptera sylvia*, change range to "...Port Moresby area), and coastal ne Australia...Townsville ¶*sylvia*, BUFF-BREASTED PARADISE-KINGFISHER [8240]; **Bismarck Arch.** (Umboi, New Britain, Watom, Duke of York Is.) ¶*nigriceps* Sclater 1877 BLACK-HEADED PARADISE-KINGFISHER [9353.1]. Australian populations (¶*sylvia*) winter in New Guinea."; at beginning of comments add "Coates (1985: 434-436) treated *T. nigriceps* as a distinct species."

93 *Chloroceryle amazona*, delete ", Tobago"

93 *Chloroceryle americana*, before "Sonora," add "s Arizona,"

93 *Chloroceryle aenea*, after "Santa Cruz)" add ", n Paraguay"

94 *Merops muelleri*, change range to "**W,c Africa** from sw Mali, Sierra Leone,...s C. African Rep. and n,ne Zaire, and S to Congo Rep. and cw,sc,ce Zaire; w Kenya."

94 *Merops bulocki*, before "c Ghana," add "Ivory Coast,"; at beginning of comments add "The original name is *Merops Bulocki* and the French name "Le Guêpier Bulock," indicating that the spelling 'Bulock' is not a *lapsus calami*."

94 *Merops bullockoides*, change "sw Uganda" to "sw Rwanda"

94 *Merops variegatus*, change range to "¶*lafresnayii* Guérin-Méneville 1843,...**c Africa** from se Nigeria, c Cameroon,..."

94 *Merops oreobates*, change range to "...**e Africa** from C. African Rep., e Zaire, Uganda, se Sudan and sc Ethiopia S to Rwanda, Burundi, c Tanzania and w,c,se Kenya."

94 ***Merops hirundineus*** (not ***hirundinaceus***); change range to "**Africa** from Senegambia E through s Mali and sw Niger, s Chad and s Sudan to w Ethiopia, Uganda and extreme se Kenya, and S (except...)"

94 *Merops breweri*, change range to "**W,c Africa** in Ghana, Nigeria, Gabon, C. African Rep., Congo Rep. and sw,c,n,ne Zaire."

94 *Merops albicollis*, change range to "...Congo Rep., Cabinda, cw,n,e Zaire, Uganda, Burundi and n Tanzania. Highly migratory; breeding known only from n Senegal E locally to Ethiopia and Kenya."

94 *Merops orientalis*, after "s Chad" add ", n C. African Rep.'

94 *Merops boehmi*, before "Zambia" add "se Zaire,"

95 *Merops persicus*, change range to "...ne Egypt, Near East and n Arabia E through..."

95 *Merops philippinus*, change "**Australasian**" to "**New Guinea**"; change "Astrolabe Bay" to "Collingwood Bay"

95 *Merops ornatus*, change range to "...**Australasian region** in mainland Australia (except extreme se,sw), and locally in Lesser Sunda Is. (Moa) and New Guinea (Sepik-Ramu r. and Port Moresby areas). Winters..."

95 *Merops apiaster*, change "Italy," to "Switzerland,"

95 *Merops malimbicus*, change range to "Lowlands of **w,c Africa** from Ivory Coast E to sw Cameroon and sw C. African Rep., and S to Cabinda and sw,c,nw,nc Zaire."

96 *Colius striatus*, before "Nigeria" add "Ghana and"

96 *Colius castanotus*, before "Cabinda" add "sw Gabon (formerly),"

96 *Colius colius*, habitat and range in one paragraph

96 *Urocolius macrourus*, change range to "...Niger, n Nigeria, Chad, C. African Rep. and Sudan to Ethiopia and Somalia, and S to extreme ne,ce Zaire, Uganda, Rwanda, Kenya and sw,sc Tanzania."

96 *Oxylophus jacobinus*, change "Senegal," to "Senegambia,"

96 *Oxylophus levaillantii*, at end of range add "Primarily a migrant in forested w,c Africa."

96 *Clamator glandarius*, change "Corsica" to "Sardinia"; after "Turkey" add "and Cyprus"

97 *Pachycoccyx audeberti*, change range to "...Sierra Leone E to Nigeria, s Cameroon, cw,cn,ne Zaire, s Sudan, Rwanda, Burundi, Tanzania and se Kenya...Madagascar (at least formerly)."; add comments "[<*Cuculus*]."

97 *Cuculus fugax*, change range to "Lowlands and foothills to 1800 m of **e Asia** in ne China (Heilungkiang, e Liaoning, Hopeh), se Siberia (Amurland, Ussuriland) and Japan (c Honshu, probably Hokkaido) ¶*hyperythrus* Gould 1856, NORTHERN HAWK-CUCKOO [2304.1]; **s Asia** from n,e India (from Nepal E to Arunachal Pradesh, and S to Bangladesh, Manipur and Nagaland) and s,se China (from s Szechwan and Yunnan E to Kiangsi, Fukien and Kwangtung) S to s,e Burma, Malay pen. (incl. Tenasserim), Thailand, n,s Vietnam (Tonkin, s Annam, incl. Con Son Is.), Sumatra, Java and Borneo ¶*fugax*, HODGSON'S HAWK-CUCKOO [2304]; and **Philippines** ¶*pectoralis* (Cabanis and Heine) 1863, PHILIPPINE HAWK-CUCKOO [3209.1]. Winters (¶*hyperythrus*, ¶*fugax*) in s Asia and Greater Sunda Is."

97 *Cuculus micropterus*, change range to "...Ussuriland) S to Andaman and Nicobar is., se Asia,...(where possibly resident), Greater Sunda Is. and Philippines."

97 *Cuculus canorus*, change range to "...Hainan), n Vietnam (Tonkin), Japan...se Asia, and (rarely)..."

98 *Cuculus saturatus*, in comments after "SATURATED" add "/BLYTH'S"

98 *Cuculus poliocephalus*, change range to "...Winters in se Africa, India and..."

98 *Cuculus rochii*, in heading change "Latham 1790" to "Hartlaub 1862"; change end of range to "...Winters in se Africa."

98 *Cercococcyx olivinus*, before "Ivory Coast" add "Liberia,"

98 *Cacomantis sonneratii*, change end of range to "...sw Philippines (Palawan)."

98 *Cacomantis merulinus*, change range to "...and Philippines. Winters S to ec India."

99 *Cacomantis variolosus*, change "Kai Is.," to "Aru and Kai is.,"

99 *Chrysococcyx russatus*, change range to "...Basilan, Sulu Arch.), Lesser Sunda Is..."

100 *Chrysococcyx xanthorhynchus*, after "s Asia" add "**and Malay Arch.**"

100 *Chrysococcyx flavigularis*, change range to "...Sierra Leone, Liberia, Ivory Coast,...n,ne Zaire, sw Sudan and w Uganda..."

100 *Chrysococcyx klaas*, after "s Niger," add "Cameroon (incl. Bioko)"

100 *Chrysococcyx cupreus*, after "Cameroon" add "(incl. Bioko, Príncipe and São Tomé)"

100 *Chrysococcyx caprius*, after "...s Niger," add "Cameroon (incl. Bioko),"

101 *Eudynamys cyanocephala*, after "Moresby)," add "Bismarck Arch., Solomon Is.,"

101 *Ceuthmochares aereus*, change range to "**Africa** from Gambia, Guinea-Bissau,...Cameroon (incl. Bioko), C. African Rep.,...Malawi, se Zimbabwe and Mozambique..."

101 *Phaenicophaeus tristis,* change range to "...n,e India (Himalayan foothills from Garhwal E through Nepal, Sikkim and Bhutan to Arunachal Pradesh and Assam, also SW to e Madhya Pradesh and ne Andrha Pradesh) E to s China..."

101 *Phaenicophaeus viridirostris,* habitat and range in one paragraph

102 *Phaenicophaeus pyrrhocephalus,* change range to "...1700 m of **Ceylon**; records from Kerala are unsubstantiated."

102 *Phaenicophaeus cumingi,* after "Luzon," add "Catanduanes,"

102 *Coua delalandei,* change English name to SNAIL-EATING COUA (not DELALANDE'S); in range after "extinct" add "(ca. 1834)"; at end of comments add "(DELALANDE'S COUA)."

102 *Coua reynaudii,* change English name to RED-FRONTED COUA (not REYNAUD'S); change comments to "(REYNAUD'S COUA)."

102 *Coua ruficeps,* change English name to RED-CAPPED COUA (not OLIVE-CAPPED); add comments "(OLIVE-CAPPED COUA)."

103 *Centropus menbeki,* change comments to "JUNGLE/MENBEK'S/MENBEKI/GREATER COUCAL"

103 *Centropus ateralbus,* change habitat and range to "Forest, edge, second growth. Lowlands to 1200 m of **Bismarck Arch.** (Umboi, New Britain, New Ireland)."

103 *Centropus sinensis,* before "Cagayan Sulu," add "Balabac,"

103 *Centropus nigrorufus,* in heading change "1817" to "1816"; change range to "Lowlands of **w Indonesia** in Java; a Sumatran record is probably erroneous."

104 *Centropus grillii,* change range to "...Liberia E through s Mali and s Niger to Cameroon, s Chad, n,ne Zaire..."

104 *Centropus leucogaster,* delete "(possibly)"

104 *Centropus anselli,* change English name to GABON COUCAL (not GABOON); in comments change "GABON" to "GABOON"

104 *Centropus monachus,* change end of range to "...Rwanda, Uganda and nw Tanzania."

105 *Coccyzus americanus,* change "n Colorado" to "Wyoming"

105 *Coccyzus [americanus] euleri* Cabanis 1873 (not *Coccyzus [americanus] julieni* Lawrence 1864); change comments to "...; although *C. julieni* has priority, there is a petition pending before the I.C.Z.N. to conserve *C. euleri.*"

106 Headings for *H. pluvialis* and *H. rufigularis* are reversed; after switching headings only, *H. pluvialis* will precede *H. rufigularis;* also change English name of *H. rufigularis* to BAY-BREASTED CUCKOO (not RUFOUS-BREASTED)

106 *Piaya melanogaster,* after "Pando" add ", La Paz, ne Santa Cruz"

106 *Piaya minuta,* change range to "...s C. and S. America..."

106 *Saurothera merlini,* change English name to GREAT LIZARD-CUCKOO (not CUBAN); at end of comments add "(CUBAN LIZARD-CUCKOO)"

106 *Opisthocomus hoazin,* change comments to "...discussed the relationships..."

107 *Crotophaga sulcirostris,* after "Baja Calif." add "(formerly)"; delete ", Trinidad"

107 *Tapera naevia,* delete "s" before "Quintana Roo"

108 *Chalcopsitta cardinalis,* before "Feni," add "New Hanover,"

110 *Lorius albidinuchus,* change habitat and range to "Forest. Mts., 500-2000 m, of **ec Bismarck Arch.** (s New Ireland)."

110 *Vini australis,* change "SC Polynesia" to "**Sc Polynesia**"

110 *Vini stepheni,* change English name to STEPHEN'S LORIKEET (not STEPHENS'S; change habitat to "Forest, edge."

110 *Vini peruviana,* change English name to BLUE LORIKEET (not TAHITIAN); change end of comments to "...(+N)]. (TAHITI/TAHITIAN LORIKEET)."

110 *Charmosyna palmarum,* change range to "**E Melanesia** in Vanuatu (incl. Banks Is.) and Santa Cruz Is. (incl. Duff Is.)."

110 *Charmosyna rubrigularis,* change range to "...Bismarck Arch. (New Britain, New Ireland, New Hanover), occurring..."

110 *Charmosyna rubronotata,* change "Sepik r." to "Ramu r."

110 *Charmosyna placentis,* before "Bougainville," add "Buka,"

111 *Charmosyna margarethae,* change range to "Lowlands to 1350 m of **Solomon Is.**"

111 *Charmosyna josefinae,* change habitat and range to "Forest, edge. Mts., 750-2200 m, of **w,c New Guinea**..." and merge into one paragraph

112 *Cacatua leadbeateri,* in comments before "MAJOR MITCHELL'S" add "MITCHELL'S/"

112 *Cacatua ophthalmica,* change end of range to "...(New Britain)."

112 *Cacatua ducorpsii,* in comments after "WHITE" add "/SOLOMON"

113 *Nymphicus hollandicus,* change comments to "...to *Cacatua* are discussed..."

113 *Nestor productus,* change English name to NORFOLK ISLAND KAKA (not NORFOLK KAKA); change comments to "(NORFOLK KAKA)."

113 *Nestor meridionalis,* change English name to NEW ZEALAND KAKA (not COMMON)

113 *Micropsitta meeki,* in heading change "1924" to "1914"; change range to "**Bismarck Arch.** (Admiralty and St. Matthias is., except Tench)."

113 *Micropsitta finschii,* change range to "Lowlands to 750 m of **e New Guinea region** in Bismarck Arch. (New Hanover, New Ireland, Tabar and Lihir is.) and Solomon Is. (from Bougainville to San Cristobal)."; add comments "(GREEN PYGMY-PARROT)."

114 *Geoffroyus geoffroyi,* after "Fergusson" add ", Normanby"

114 *Geoffroyus heteroclitus,* change range to "...Bismarck Arch. (Umboi, New Britain, New Ireland, New Hanover, Lihir Is.) and Solomon Is."

114 *Prioniturus montanus,* change English name to MONTANE RACQUET-TAIL (not LUZON); in comments after "RED-CROWNED/" add "LUZON/"

114 *Prioniturus verticalis,* change range to "**Sw Philippines** (Sulu Arch.)."

115 *Prosopeia splendens,* at end of comments add "AG (~*Prosopeia*): MUSK-PARROT."

117 *Cyanoramphus cookii,* change English name to NORFOLK ISLAND PARAKEET (not NORFOLK PARAKEET); in comments before "See" add "(NORFOLK PARAKEET)."

117 *Cyanoramphus novaezelandiae*, change range to "...1891, LORD HOWE ISLAND PARAKEET (LORD HOWE PARAKEET) [8195.3];..."

117 *Cyanoramphus ulietanus*, change English name to RAIATEA PARAKEET (not SOCIETY); change comments to "(SOCIETY PARAKEET)."

118 *Neophema elegans*, change range to "Disjunctly in **sw,sc Australia** in sw W. Australia (N to Merredin and E to Esperance) and se S. Australia (W to Kangaroo I..."

118 *Geopsittacus occidentalis* (not *Pezoporus*); change comments to "[*<Pezoporus*]."

118 *Strigops habroptilus* (not *hapbroptilus*)

118 *Coracopsis vasa*, add comments "(GREATER VASA-PARROT)."

118 *Coracopsis nigra*, add comments "(LESSER VASA-PARROT)."

119 *Psittacus erithacus*, after "Guinea-Bissau" add ", s Mali"

119 *Poicephalus robustus*, change range to "...n Ghana, Togo and c Nigeria; from sw Congo...Rwanda, Burundi and c Tanzania..."

119 *Poicephalus senegalus*, change range to "...s Mali and s Niger to Nigeria, Cameroon and sw Chad, and S to Gulf of Guinea (except Liberia)."

119 *Poicephalus crassus*, change range to "**C Africa** from sw Chad E through C. African Rep. to extreme n Zaire and sw Sudan."

119 *Agapornis canus*, delete "Zanzibar, Mafia,"

119 *Agapornis pullarius*, after "Sierra Leone" add "and sw Mali"

119 *Agapornis swindernianus*, after "Liberia," add "Ivory Coast,"

119 *Agapornis roseicollis*, change end of range to "...(except ne) and nw S. Africa (n Cape prov.)."

120 *Agapornis fischeri*, before "nw,cn Tanzania" add "Rwanda, Burundi and"

120 *Loriculus vernalis*, before "Burma" add "Andaman and Nicobar is.,"

120 Change range of *Loriculus philippensis* to read "Lowlands and mts. to 2500 m of **Philippines** (except Sulu Arch.) ¶*philippensis*, COLASISI [3198]; **Sulu Arch.** ¶*bonapartei* Souancé 1856, BLACK-BILLED HANGING-PARROT [3198.1]."

120 *Loriculus tener*, at end of comments add "(BISMARCK HANGING-PARROT)."

121 *Psittacula krameri*, change "Senegal," to "Senegambia, Guinea-Bissau,"

121 *Psittacula intermedia*, change comments to "...but is a good species sympatric with *himalayana* (Walters 1985; Sane et al. 1986). (ROTHSCHILD'S PARAKEET)."

121 *Psittacula roseata*, in heading change "1951" to "(1951a)"

122 *Psittacula longicauda*, at end of comments add "(RED-CHEEKED PARAKEET)."

122 *Anodorhynchus hyacinthinus*, change range to "...(e Santa Cruz), int. Brazil (...) and n Paraguay."

122 *Cyanopsitta spixii*, change range to "Effectively extinct in wild (one living bird in 1990, but still exists in captivity); formerly lowlands of **e Brazil** (s Piauí, nw Bahia)."

122 *Ara militaris*, after "Chiapas" add "(extirpated in most n portions of range)"

122 *Ara macao*, change "**Meotropical**" to "**Neotropical**"

123 *Ara rubrogenys*, change range to "Andean valleys, 1300-2400 m, of **c Bolivia** (se Cochabamba, w Santa Cruz, ne Potosí, nw Chuquisaca)."; add comments "Lanning

(1991) discussed distribution and breeding biology of *A. rubrogenys*."

123 *Ara couloni*, after "Pando" add ", n La Paz"

123 *Aratinga holochlora*, change range to "...ne, Sinaloa, s Sonora, and from s Nuevo León...[1123]; **Revillagigedo Is.** (Socorro) ¶*brevipes* (Lawrence) 1871, SOCORRO PARAKEET [1123.2]; mts., 900-2600 m,..."

124 *Aratinga leucophthalmus*, after "Entre Ríos" add ")"

125 *Nandayus nenday*, change "(probably)" to "(se Santa Cruz)"

125 *Rhynchopsitta pachyrhyncha*, in comments after "PARROT]." add "AG (+N): MACAWLET."

125 *Rhynchopsitta terrisi*, change "1800,3100" to "1800-3100"

126 *Pyrrhura rhodogaster*, change end of range to "...Grosso) and n,e Bolivia (Beni, Santa Cruz)."

128 *Brotogeris versicolurus*, change range to "...e Peru, Amazonian Brazil (...) and e Paraguay. Intro..."

128 *Brotogeris chiriri*, after "w São Paulo)" add "and n Paraguay."

128 *Nannopsittaca panychlora*, change scientific name to "*Nannopsittaca [panychlora] panychlora*"; add comments "See *N. dachilleae*."; after account, insert new species:

Nannopsittaca [panychlora] dachilleae O'Neill, Munn and Franke (1991). AMAZONIAN PARROTLET. [4120.1.]
Humid forest. Lowlands of **sw S. America** in southeastern Peru (Ucayali, Madre de Dios) and northwestern Bolivia (La Paz).
A distinct species that appears to be an allospecies of *N. panychlora* (O'Neill, Munn and Franke 1991).

129 *Touit huetii*, after "Pando" add ", n La Paz"

129 *Pionopsitta barrabandi*, after "Beni" add ", n La Paz"

130 *Pionopsitta caica*, change "**nc N. America**" to "**nc S. America**"

131 *Amazona viridigenalis*, after "s Calif.," add "s Texas (perhaps from wild vagrants),"

131 *Amazona autumnalis*, change "Yucatán pen." to "Yucatán and Quintana Roo"

131 *Amazona dufresniana*, change "morpholgocial" to "morphological"

132 *Amazona aestiva*, change range to "...ne Argentina (S to..."

132 *Amazona farinosa*, change "Yucatán pen." to "Yucatán and Quintana Roo"; at end of comments add "See *A. kawalli*."

132 After *Amazona farinosa*, add new species:

Amazona kawalli Grantsau and Camargo (1989). KAWALL'S PARROT. [5215.1.]
Humid forest. **C Amazonian Brazil** (r. Juruá, Amazonas; r. Tapajós, Pará).
Related to *A. farinosa* and occurring within the range of that species, perhaps sympatrically (Grantsau and Camargo 1989).

133 *Cypseloides rutilus*, change "Puebla" to "Hidalgo"

133 *Cypseloides phelpsi*, in heading change "1972" to "(1972)"

133 *Cypseloides niger*, change range to "...c Utah, se Arizona, nc New Mexico;...Nayarit, Hidalgo and Veracruz..."

133 *Cypseloides lemosi*, in heading change "1962" to "(1963)"

133 After *Cypseloides cherriei*, add the following species:

Cypseloides [cryptus] storeri Navarro et al. (1992). WHITE-
     FRONTED SWIFT. [1220.1.]
     Presumably forest and open country. Locally in mts.,
1500-2500 m, of **wc Mexico** in Michoacán and Guerrero.
     This recently described form, known from four speci-
mens, is morphologically similar to *C. cryptus* and may be a
race of that species (S. Howell, pers. comm.).

133-134 *Cypseloides [cryptus] cryptus*, add superspecies;
         change comments to "(ZIMMER'S SWIFT). [WHITE-
         CHINNED SWIFT]. See *C. storeri*."
134 *Streptoprocne zonaris*, in comments change
     "ALTILLEAN" to "ANTILLEAN"
134 *Streptoprocne semicollaris*, in heading change
     "(DeSaussure)" to "(Saussure)"
134 *Collocalia esculenta* (remove superspecies); change
     range to "...¶*affinis* Beavan 1867, WHITE-BELLIED...
     [3292.1]; **Philippines** ¶*marginata* Salvadori 1882,
     GREY-RUMPED SWIFTLET (PHILIPPINE SWIFTLET) [3292];
     e Indonesia..."; change comments to "Dickinson
     (1989b: 23-30) discussed conspecificity of *marginata*
     and *esculenta*. (WHITE-BELLIED SWIFTLET)."
134 Delete *Collocalia marginata* entry
135 Before *Collocalia infuscata*, insert *C. mearnsi* from p.
     136
135 *Collocalia hirundinacea*, change "Japen" to "Yapen";
     change comments to "See *C. mearnsi* and *C.
     spodiopygius*."
135 *Collocalia spodiopygius*, change range to "...Bismarck
     Arch., Solomon Is. (S to Guadalcanal), Vanuatu..."
135 *Collocalia rogersi*, in heading change "1955" to "(1955)"
135 *Collocalia whiteheadi*, change comments to "...*C. amelis*
     (Dickinson 1989a: 22-27). See *C*..."
135 *Collocalia nuditarsus*, change end of range to "...**c,e New
     Guinea** (from Snow Mts. and Mimika r. E to se ranges)."
135 *Collocalia salangana*, change end of range to "...Java,
     c,s,se Sulawesi (...) and s Philippines (Balabac)."
135 *Collocalia palawanensis*, change end of comments to
     "...*C. amelis*. *C. amelis* has most frequently been
     associated with the *C. [fuciphaga]* superspecies, but both
     palawanensis and *amelis* are part of the *C. vanikorensis*
     complex and may be races of the latter, as treated by
     Dickinson (1989a: 27-36). See *C. vanikorensis*."
135 After *C. palawanensis*, insert *C. amelis* from p. 136
136 *Collocalia vanikorensis*, change range to "...(Waigeo,
     Misool), New Guinea...D'Entrecasteaux Arch.
     (Goodenough, Fergusson), Louisiade..."; at end of
     comments add "See *C. amelis*."
136 *Collocalia [spodiopygius] mearnsi* (not *[vanikorensis]*),
     move to p. 135, and sequence before *C. infuscata*; after
     "Bohol," add "Camiguin Sur,"; at beginning of
     comments add "Dickinson (1989a: 37-45) discussed
     relationships of *mearnsi* and its association in the same
     superspecies as *C. hirundinacea*."
136 *Collocalia pelewensis*, change comments to "...*C.
     bartschi* is comparable to that among other allospecies in
     the *C. [vanikorensis]* superspecies, thus it is better
     retained in that status (M. R. Browning, pers. comm.). H.
     D. Pratt (pers. comm.) indicates that *pelewensis* differs
     from *inquieta* in vocalizations, flight behavior and
     morphology; on this basis, *pelewensis* seems better
     retained as an allospecies."
136 Delete *Collocalia bartschi* account

136 *Collocalia inquieta*, change English name to
     MICRONESIAN SWIFTLET (not CAROLINE); change range
     to "Lowlands of **s Mariana Is.** (Guam) ¶*bartschi*
     (Mearns) 1909, MARIANA SWIFTLET (GUAM CAVE/GUAM
     SWIFTLET) [9308.1]; **Caroline Is.** (from Yap E to
     Kosrae ¶*inquieta*, CAROLINE SWIFTLET
     (CAROLINES/CAROLINE ISLANDS SWIFTLET) [9308]).
     Intro. (¶*bartschi*) Hawaiian Is. (Oahu)."; change
     comments to "H. D. Pratt (pers. comm.) suggests there is
     no evidence that *bartschi* and *inquieta* are specifically
     distinct. (VANIKORO SWIFTLET). See *C. vanikorensis*
     and *C. pelewensis*."
136 *Collocalia sawtelli*, change English name to ATIU
     SWIFTLET (not SAWTELL'S); change "(Atiu.)" to
     "(Atiu)."; change end of comments to "...1978).
     (SAWTELL'S/COOK ISLANDS SWIFTLET)."
136 *Collocalia leucophaeus*, change English name to TAHITI
     SWIFTLET (not POLYNESIAN); change range to "**E Society
     Is.** (Moorea, Tahiti)."; change comments to "The name
     leucophaeus...retained. [POLYNESIAN SWIFTLET]. See *C.
     sawtelli* and *C. ocista*."
136 After *Collocalia leucophaeus* add the following account:

Collocalia [leucophaeus] ocista (Oberholser) 1906. MAR-
     QUESAN SWIFTLET. [9310.1.]
     Forest, open country. **Marquesas** (except Hiva Oa).
     H. D. Pratt informs us (pers. comm.) that *C. sawtelli*, *C.
leucophaeus* and *C. ocista* differ about equally and should be
treated either as allospecies following Holyoak and Thibault
(1978) or conspecific following Mayr and Vuilleumier (1983:
217-218). Because of reasons given under *C. sawtelli*,
allospecies treatment seems more appropriate. (MARQUESAS
SWIFTLET). See *C. sawtelli*.

136 *Collocalia fuciphaga*, in heading change "(Gmelin)
     1789" to (Thunberg) 1812"; change end of comments to
     "...See *C. francica* and *C. palawanensis*."
136 *Collocalia germani*, change "Cayo Is.," to "Cuyo Is.,"
136 *Collocalia [vanikorensis] amelis* (not *[fuciphaga]*), move
     to p. 135, and sequence after *C. palawanensis*; change
     end of range to "...and Philippines."; change comments
     to "See *C. whiteheadi* and *C. palawanensis*."
137 *Schoutedenapus myoptilus*, change range to "...extreme s
     Sudan, s Ethiopia, Uganda, Rwanda, Burundi, w,c
     Kenya..."
137 *Schoutedenapus schoutedeni*, in heading change
     "(Prigogine) 1960" to "(Prigogine 1960)"
137 *Zoonavena grandidieri*, MALAGASY SPINETAIL (not
     MADAGASCAR); at beginning of comments add
     "(MADAGASCAR SPINETAIL)."
137 *Zoonavena thomensis*, change "São Tomé" to "**Príncipe
     and São Tomé**"
137 *Telacanthura ussheri* (not *Telecanthura*); change range
     to "**Africa** from Senegambia and s Mali E to Nigeria, sw
     Cameroon, sw C. African Rep., n,ne Zaire,..."
137 *Telacanthura melanopygia* (not *Telecanthura*); change
     range to "...Ghana, Nigeria, sw Cameroon, Gabon, sw C.
     African Rep. and ne Zaire."
137 *Rhapidura sabini*, change range to "Locally in **w,c
     Africa** from Sierra Leone E to s Cameroon (incl. Bioko),
     Rio Muni, Gabon, sw Congo Rep., s C. African Rep.,
     w,n,ne,ce Zaire,..."

137 *Neafrapus cassini*, change range to "Lowlands in **w,c Africa** in Liberia, Ivory Coast, Ghana, s Nigeria, sw Cameroon (incl. Bioko), Gabon, Congo Rep., Cabinda, sw C. African Rep., n,nc,ce Zaire and w Uganda."

137 *Neafrapus boehmi*, delete "e Uganda,"

137 *Hirundapus caudacutus*, change range to "...Kuril Is.), ne China..."

138 *Hirundapus cochinchinensis*, in range change "1951" to "(1951b)"; in comments change "(1951)" to "(1951b)"

138 *Hirundapus celebensis*, change range to "...Philippines (Calayan, Luzon, Mindoro, Catanduanes, Marinduque,..."

138 *Chaetura cinereiventris*, change range to "...Trinidad, Tobago and Guianas...e Peru to n,e Bolivia (Pando, Beni, La Paz, Santa Cruz) and w Amazonian...GREY-RUMPED SWIFT [5237.2]."

138 *Chaetura vauxi*, change range to "...sw Tamaulipas, se San Luis Potosí and Hidalgo ¶*vauxi*..."

139 *Chaetura brachyura*, after "Trinidad" add ", Tobago"

139 *Panyptila sanctihieronymi*, change range to "...s Mexico (Nayarit, Jalisco, Colima, México, Michoacán,..."

139 *Panyptila cayennensis*, change range to "...Belize, Guatemala, Honduras...Trinidad and Guianas,...Bolivia (Pando, Beni, n La Paz), locally..."

139 *Cypsiurus parvus*, in heading change "Lichtenstein" to "(Lichtenstein)"; change beginning of range to "**African region** from s Mauritania, Senegambia, s Mali,..."

140 *Tachymarptis melba*, change range to "...Ceylon; largely in highlands of **African region** in s Mali, from w,c Ethiopia...n Tanzania, and in sw Angola...1300 m of Madagascar. N populations..."

140 *Tachymarptis aequatorialis*, change range to read "Locally in highlands (mostly) of **Africa** in Sierra Leone, s Ghana, Nigeria, Cameroon, w,c Angola, and from w Sudan and Ethiopia S...Mozambique. Recorded in nonbreeding season from trop. Africa S to s S. Africa."

140 *Apus alexandri*, change "*A. barbatus* complex" to "*A. [pallidus]* superspecies."

140 *Apus pallidus*, change "1855" to "1870"; before "Yugoslavia" add "Switzerland,"; at end of comments add "See *A. alexandri.*"

140 *Apus barbatus*, change range to "Locally in **wc Africa** in s Nigeria, s Cameroon (incl. Bioko) and wc Angola (Mt. Moco) ¶*sladeniae*..."; in comments delete "*A. alexandri,*"

140 *Apus berliozi*, change range to "Lowlands of **Somalia** (incl. Socotra I.). Ranges to coastal Kenya."

141 *Apus nipalensis*, change range to "...Hainan), Taiwan and s Japan (N to c Honshu), and S through..."

141 *Apus horus*, change range to "**C,s,ne Africa** from n Cameroon, s Chad, nw,cn,ne,ce Zaire, e Sudan and Ethiopia..."

141 *Apus caffer*, change range to "...**Africa** from Senegambia and Mali E to Nigeria, s Chad,...Somalia, and S (except most of forested w,c and desert sw) to s S. Africa."

141 *Apus batesi*, change range to "Locally in **w,c Africa** in Ghana, s Cameroon, n Gabon, C. African Rep. and ne Zaire."

142 *Hemiprocne mystacea*, change range to "...Bismarck Arch. and Solomon Is...."

142 *Glaucis hirsuta*, in heading change "1758" to "1788"

142 ***Threnetes [leucurus] ruckeri*** and ***Threnetes [leucurus] leucurus***, add superspecies and reverse sequence

143 *Phaethornis superciliosus*, change range to read "Lowlands to 1800 m of **nw Mexico** on Pacific slope from wc Nayarit S to Jalisco and Colima ¶*griseoventer* Phillips 1962, JALISCO HERMIT [1237.1]; **wc Mexico** in Guerrero and w Oaxaca ¶*mexicanus* Hartert 1897, HARTERT'S HERMIT [1237.2]; **Middle and nw S. America** on Gulf-Caribbean slope from Veracruz S to Nicaragua, both slopes of Costa Rica and Panama, and in n Colombia (from Chocó E to Sierra de Perijá and middle Magdalena v.) and nw Venezuela (Sierra de Perijá) ¶*longirostris* DeLattre 1843, LONG-TAILED HERMIT [1237]; and **S. America** W of Andes in w Ecuador and nw Peru, and E of Andes from se Colombia (N to Meta, Vichada and Guainía) and s Venezuela (Amazonas, nw,e Bolívar) S through e Ecuador and e Peru to n,e Bolivia and Amazonian Brazil (E to Amapá, e Pará, Bahia and Alagoas) ¶*superciliosus*, RUSTY-BREASTED HERMIT [4172.1]."

143 *Phaethornis eurynome*, in comments change "1622-163" to "162-163"

143 *Phaethornis augusti*, change "fraom" to "from"

144 *Phaethornis longuemareus*, change account to read "Lowlands to 1300 m of **Middle and nw S. America** on Gulf-Caribbean slope from Veracruz...Panama, and on Pacific slope of Colombia and w Ecuador ¶*adolphi* Gould 1857, BOUCARD'S HERMIT [1239]; lowlands to 1300 m of **n,c Colombia** (from Santa Marta Mts. S to Tolima) ¶*striigularis* Gould 1854, STRIPE-THROATED HERMIT [4178.3]; and in **S. America** E of the Andes from e Colombia (N to Meta), Venezuela (locally) and Guianas...sr. Tapajós) ¶*longuemareus*, LITTLE HERMIT [4178.2]."; at beginning of comments add "[>*Pygmornis* (+N)]."

*145 ***Doryfera ludovicae*** (not *ludoviciae*)

145 *Campylopterus hyperythrus*, change "nc S. American" to "**nc S. America**"

148 Split *Lophornis delattrei* into the following two species:

Lophornis [delattrei] brachylopha Moore 1949. SHORT-CRESTED COQUETTE. [1260.1.]
Evergreen subtropical forest. Lowlands and foothills of **sw Guerrero.**
Banks (1990a) recognized *L. brachylopha* as a species distinct from *L. delattrei.*

Lophornis [delattrei] delattrei (Lesson) 1839. RUFOUS-CRESTED COQUETTE. [1260.]
Humid forest edge, open woodland. Locally in lowlands and foothills to 2000 m of **s C. and nw,nc S. America** in c Costa Rica (San José region), Panama, sc,e Colombia (Madgalena v. in Huila and Tolima; E of Andes from Norte de Santander S to Meta), e Peru and n,e Bolivia (Beni, La Paz, Cochabamba, w Santa Cruz).
[RUFOUS-CRESTED COQUETTE]. See *L. brachylopha.*

148 *Popelairia letitiae*, in heading change "1846" to "1852"

149 *Chlorostilbon canivetii*, change range to "Lowlands to 1800 m on the Pacific slope of **w Mexico** from Sinaloa S to Oaxaca, and inland to s Morelos ¶*auriceps* (Gould) 1852, GOLDEN-CROWNED EMERALD [1264.1]; **Cozumel I.** ¶*forficatus* Ridgway 1885, COZUMEL EMERALD [1264.2]; Gulf-Caribbean slope of **n Middle America** from s Tamaulipas S (incl. Yucatán pen. and I. Holbox)

to n Guatemala and Belize, also Bay Is. off n Honduras ¶*canivetii*, CANIVET'S EMERALD [1264]; both slopes of **Middle America** from se Chiapas, w,e Guatemala and Honduras S to Nicaragua and nw Costa Rica ¶*salvini* Cabanis and Heine 1860, SALVIN'S EMERALD [1264.3]."; change comments to "Morphological differences as well as lack of evidence for interbreeding suggest that the groups may represent distinct species (S. Howell, pers. comm.). See *C. mellisugus*."

149 *Chlorostilbon mellisugus*, in comments after "*C. mellisugus*." add "Includes *C. vitticeps* (Simon) 1910 [SIMON'S EMERALD]."

149 *Chlorostilbon ricordii*, in heading change "1935" to "1835"

149 *Chlorostilbon alice*, at beginning of comments add "Includes *Panychlora micans* Salvin 1891, based on a unique specimen of unknown origin that is usually regarded as a variant of *C. alice* despite its striking appearance."

150 Split *Thalurania colombica* into the following three species:

Thalurania [furcata] ridgwayi Nelson 1900. MEXICAN WOODNYMPH. [1271.]
  Humid forest, edge, second growth, open woodland. Lowlands of **w Mexico** in Nayarit, w Jalisco and Colima.
  Escalante-Pliego and Peterson (1992) recognized *T. ridgwayi* and *T. fannyi* as species distinct from *T. colombica.*

Thalurania [furcata] colombica (Bourcier) 1843. BLUE-CROWNED WOODNYMPH. [1271.1.]
  Humid forest, edge, second growth, open woodland. Lowlands of Caribbean slope of **C. America** from Guatemala and Belize S to Costa Rica and w,c Panama (E to Canal Zone and e Panamá prov.) ¶*townsendi* Ridgway 1888, BLUE-CROWNED WOODNYMPH [1271.1]; lowlands to 1900 m of **n S. America** in ne Colombia (upper Magdalena v., Santa Marta region, "Bogotá" region of E. Andes) and w Venezuela (from Zulia S to Táchira and w Barinas, and E to ne Lara) ¶*colombica*, COLOMBIAN WOODNYMPH [4202.2].
  T. colombica may be conspecific with *T. furcata*. *T. lerchi* Mulsant and Verreaux 1872, LERCH'S WOODNYMPH, known only from "Bogotá" skins, is probably a hybrid *T. furcata* x *Chrysuronia oenone*. (COLOMBIAN/CROWNED WOODNYMPH). See *Thalurania ridgwayi* and *Aglaiocercus kingi.*

Thalurania [furcata] fannyi (DeLattre and Bourcier) 1846. GREEN-CROWNED WOODNYMPH. [1271.2.]
  Humid forest, edge, second growth, open woodland. Lowlands of **s C. and nw S. America** in e Panama (e Colón, Darién, e San Blas) and nw Colombia ¶*fannyi*, GREEN-CROWNED WOODNYMPH [1271.2]; lowlands of **nw S. America** on Pacific slope of sw Colombia (w slope of W. Andes in Nariño) and w Ecuador (S to El Oro) ¶*hypochlora* Gould 1871, EMERALD-BELLIED WOODNYMPH [4202.3].
  See *Thalurania ridgwayi.*

150 *Thalurania furcata*, at end of comments add "See *Aglaiocercus kingi*."
151 *Hylocharis eliciae*, delete "(not recorded Belize)"
151 *Hylocharis grayi*, in heading before "DeLattre" add "("
152 *Goethalsia bella*, change "600-1650m" to "600-1650 m"

152 *Trochilus polytmus*, change range to "...¶*polytmus*, RED-BILLED STREAMERTAIL (WESTERN STREAMERTAIL)...1901, BLACK-BILLED STREAMERTAIL (EASTERN STREAMERTAIL) [1279.1]."; at end of comments add "(THE DOCTORBIRD)."

152 *Polytmus milleri*, in heading change "Chapman" to "(Chapman)"

153 *Amazilia distans*, in heading change "1956" to "(1956)"

154 *Amazilia cyanocephala*, change comments to "...Honduras, is a young *A. cyanocephala* (S. Howell, pers. comm.). See *A. violiceps*."

154 *Amazilia beryllina*, change "Hybridizes" to "May hybridize"

154 *Amazilia yucatanensis*, delete "(lower Rio Grande v.)"

155 *Amazilia tzacatl*, in heading change "(De La Llave)" to "(de la Llave)"; change "1963" to "(1963)"

155 *Amazilia viridifrons*, change range to "...c Guerrero S to w Oaxaca, and in e Oaxaca and w Chiapas ¶*viridifrons*, GREEN-FRONTED HUMMINGBIRD [1291]; **s Oaxaca** ¶*wagneri* Phillips (1965), CINNAMON-SIDED HUMMINGBIRD [1291.1]."; at end of comments add "The form *wagneri* is probably a good species (S. Howell, pers. comm.)."

155 *Elvira cupreiceps*, in heading change "1866" to "1867"

156 **Aphantochroa** (not **Aphanotochroa**)

156 *Lampornis clemenciae*, change end of range to "...Oaxaca and Chiapas."

156 *Lampornis hemileucus*, change "Chiriqú" to "Chiriquí"

156 *Lampornis castaneoventris*, change "Highlands" to "Locally in highlands"

157 *Topaza pyra*, change end of range to "...Loreto) and wc Amazonian Brazil (r. Negro region, upper r. Urucu)."; in comments change "*T. pella*" to "*T. pella*"

158 *Oreotrochilus chimborazo*, change "*Polyonomus*" to "*Polyonymus*"

158-162 Change "Boissoneau" to "Boissonneau" in the following accounts: 158, *Lafresnaya lafresnayi*; 159, *Coeligena torquata, C. bonapartei* and *Ensifera ensifera*; 161, *Ramphomicron microrhynchum*; 162, *Chalcostigma heteropogon* and *Oxypogon guerinii*

158 *Coeligena coeligena*, change "w.n" to "w,n"

159 *Coeligena torquata*, change range to "...wc Bolivia (La Paz,..."

160 *Heliangelus amethysticollis*, add comments "*H. squamigularis* Gould 1871, OLIVE-THROATED SUNANGEL, *H. rothschildi* Boucard 1892, ROTHSCHILD'S SUNANGEL, *Iolaema luminosa* Elliot 1878, GLISTENING SUNANGEL, *Heliotrypha speciosa* Salvin 1891, GREEN-THROATED SUNANGEL, and *H. barralli* Mulsant and Verreaux 1872 are all regarded as hybrids, mostly *Heliangelus amethysticollis* x *Eriocnemis cupreoventris* (Meyer de Schauensee 1966: 184; Graves 1990)."

160 *Heliangelus viola*, delete comments

160 *Eriocnemis luciani*, delete "in **S. America**"

160 *Eriocnemis cupreoventris*, add comments "See *Heliangelus amethysticollis*."

161 **Polyonymus** (not **Polyonomus**)

162-163 *Aglaiocercus kingi*, change end of comments to "...NEHRKORN'S SYLPH, known from several specimens from Colombia, is probably a hybrid *A. kingi* x *Thalurania furcata* or *T. colombica* (Hinkelmann, Nicolai and Dickerman 1991). [>*Cyanolesbia* (+N)]. See *A. coelestis*."

164 *Archilochus alexandri*, delete ", w Wyoming"; in comments change "Obserholser" to "Oberholser"

166 *Tauraco persa*, change comments to "...areas where two or more..."

166 *Tauraco schuettii,* before "s Sudan" add "s C. African Rep.,"

166 *Tauraco schalowi,* change range to "**Sc Africa** from w,c,s Angola, Zambia, Malawi, sw,nc Tanzania and sw Kenya S to extreme ne Namibia (Caprivi) and ne Zimbabwe."

167 *Tauraco livingstonii,* change comments to "...TURACO, now recognized as the southern subspecies of *T. livingstonii* (Clancey 1992). See..."

167 *Tauraco macrorhynchus,* after "sw Congo Rep." add ", Cabinda"

167 *Musophaga violacea,* change range to "**W Africa** from Senegambia and sw Mali E to c,n Cameroon (absent Sierra Leone and Liberia); isolated..."

167 *Musophaga rossae,* change "C. Africa Rep.," to "C. African Rep.,"

167 *Corythaixoides [personatus] concolor* and *Corythaixoides [personatus] personatus* (genus is masculine)

167 *Corythaixoides personatus,* before "w Kenya," add "w Uganda,"

168 *Crinifer piscator,* before "Senegal" add "s Mauritania,"

168 *Corythaeola cristata,* after "s Cameroon" add "(incl. Bioko)"

168 *Tyto multipunctata,* change range to "Lowlands of **ne Australia** in ne Queensland (from Cooktown to Townsville)."; sequence after *T. tenebricosa*

168 *Tyto tenebricosa,* change range to "Lowlands and mts. to 3650 m of **Australian region** in New Guinea (incl. Yapen I.), and e,se Australia from extreme..."

168 *Tyto soumagnei,* change English name to MADAGASCAR RED OWL (not SOUMAGNE'S); change comments to "[>*Heliodilus*]. (SOUMAGNE'S OWL)..."

168-169 *Tyto alba,* change range to "...Bismarck Arch. (Long I., New Ireland, and Boang in Tanga Is.), Solomon Is. (Green Is., Buka, Vella Lavella,..."

169 *Tyto longimembris,* change range to "...and Philippines; lowlands and mts. to 2500 m of **c,e New Guinea**...Huon pen., and S to Merauke region); **New Caledonia**..."

169 *Phodilus badius,* change range to "...Laos, Vietnam (Tonkin, n Annam, Cochinchina),...Natuna Is.), Java and Bali; one record..."

169 Under Family **Strigidae,** change "is based" to "are based"; change "follows" to "follow"

169-174 Sequence species of *Otus* as follows: *sagittatus, rufescens, icterorhynchus, ireneae, balli, spilocephalus, umbra, angelinae, manadensis, longicornis, mindorensis, mirus, hartlaubi, brucei, flammeolus, scops, elegans, mantananensis, magicus, rutilus, pauliani, brookii, bakkamoena, mentawi, fuliginosus, megalotis, silvicola, leucotis, kennicottii, asio, trichopsis, choliba, koepckeae, roboratus, clarkii, barbarus, ingens, marshalli, watsonii, atricapillus, vermiculatus, sanctaecatarinae, lawrencii, nudipes, podarginus, albogularis*

170 *Otus rufescens,* change comments to "[>*Athenoptera* (≈*O. spilocephalus*)]."

170 *Otus icterorhynchus,* change end of range to "...(Mt. Nimba), Ivory Coast, s Ghana, s Cameroon and c,ne,ce Zaire."

170 *Otus spilocephalus,* remove superspecies; change range to "...Nagaland) and se China (...) S to se Asia...[3244]; mts. of **Taiwan** ¶*hambroecki* (Swinhoe) 1870, FORMOSAN SCOPS-OWL [3244.4]; mts. of **Sumatra** ¶*vandewateri* (Robinson and Kloss) 1916, VANDEWATER'S SCOPS-OWL [3244.1]; mts. of **Borneo** ¶*luciae* (Sharpe) 1888,

BORNEAN SCOPS-OWL [3244.5]."; change comments to "The form *vandewateri* of Sumatra may be identical with *luciae* of Borneo (Marshall 1978); if so, the merged taxon on Sumatra and Borneo will be *O. (spilocephalus) luciae,* SUNDA SCOPS-OWL [3244.1]. *O. stresemanni*...color morph of *luciae* by J. T. Marshall and B. King (pers. comm.). (SPOTTED SCOPS-OWL)."

170 *Otus mirus,* change superspecies to [*manadensis*]; change comments to "Vocal differences suggest species status and close relationships with *O. manadensis* (J. T. Marshall and B. King, pers. comm.). [>*Athenoptera*]."

170 *Otus brucei,* change comments to "Sympatric with *O. scops* in Pakistan (Roberts and King 1986: 300-301). [>*Zorca* (≈*O. rutilus*)]. (STRIATED/..."

170 *Otus flammeolus,* change end of range to "c,s Mexico and Guatemala."; change comments to "Formerly considered conspecific with *O. scops,* but probably related to *O. brucei* (J. T. Marshall and B. King, pers. comm.). AG: SCREECH-OWL."

170 *Otus scops,* change English name to COMMON SCOPS-OWL (not EURASIAN); remove superspecies; change world no. to [374.1.] (not [2316.])"; change range to "Lowlands to 2500 m of **Palearctic** from...(Baluchistan) ¶*scops,* EURASIAN SCOPS-OWL (SCOPS OWL/EUROPEAN/COMMON SCOPS-OWL) [2316]; **e Asia and Malay Arch.** from Mongolia, extreme se Siberia (Amurland, Ussuriland, Sakhalin), c,s China (from e Kansu, s Shensi and c Heilungkiang S to w Yunnan, Kwangsi and Kwangtung), Korea and Japan S to e Pakistan, India, Ceylon, Andaman and Nicobar is., se Asia (throughout, incl. Malay pen.), sw Borneo, s Philippines (Romblon, Cuyo Is., Mindanao, Tawitawi), Taiwan, and Daito (Minami) and Izu is. ¶*sunia* (Hodgson) 1836, ORIENTAL SCOPS-OWL (ASIAN SCOPS-OWL) [374.1.]; **African region** from Senegambia, sw Mali and Ivory Coast E to Nigeria, Cameroon (incl. Pagalu), s Chad, s Sudan, Ethiopia, Somalia and s Arabia, and S (except forested c and sw deserts) to s S. Africa ¶*senegalensis* (Swainson) 1834, AFRICAN SCOPS-OWL [6232]. Winters (¶*scops*) from Mediterranean region E to c India, and S to c Africa; (¶*sunia*) from s Asia, se China and Japan S to Sumatra."; change comments to "Although the groups are sometimes treated as distinct species (e.g., Dowsett and Dowsett-Lemaire 1980: 162; Hekstra, in Burton et al. 1973: 104-108), J. T. Marshall and B. King (pers. comm.) indicate that they are conspecific. See *O. brucei, O. flammeolus* and *O. mantananensis.*"

170 Delete *Otus senegalensis* and *O. sunia* entries

171 *Otus manadensis,* add superspecies [*manadensis*]; at beginning of comments add "[>*Zorca* (≈*O. rutilus*)]."

171 *Otus longicornis,* add superspecies [*manadensis*]

171 *Otus mindorensis,* add superspecies [*manadensis*]; change range to "Mts. of **c Philippines** (Mindoro)."

171 Delete *O. alfredi* entry

171 *Otus angelinae,* add superspecies [*manadensis*]; change comments to "Vocalizations are unknown. [>*Athenoptera*]. (ANGELINA'S SCOPS-OWL)."

171 *Otus umbra,* add superspecies [*manadensis*]; in comments delete "(≈*O. rutilus*)"

171 *Otus hartlaubi,* change comments to "de Naurois (1975) and Snow (1978: 254) gave it species status because of vocalizations and its robust build; J. T. Marshall and B. King (pers. comm.) suggest it is part of the *O. [manadensis]* superspecies."

171 *Otus elegans*, change comments to "A member of the *O. [magicus]* superspecies (J. T. Marshall and B. King, pers. comm.). (RYUKYU SCOPS-OWL)."

171 *Otus mantananensis*, change "(Mantanani I) to "(Mantanani I.)"; change comments to "Sometimes considered conspecific with *O. scops* or *O. manadensis* but appears to be part of the *O. [magicus]* superspecies."

171 *Otus magicus*, change range to "...(BARE-LEGGED SCOPS-OWL) [6234]; **Enggano** (off w Sumatra) ¶*enganensis* Riley 1927, ENGGANO SCOPS-OWL (ENGANO SCOPS-OWL) [3246.1]; **Wallacea**...[3248.1]; **Flores** ¶*albiventris* (Sharpe) 1875 [=*alfredi* (Hartert) 1897], FLORES SCOPS-OWL [9282]; **nw New Guinea**..."; change comments to "*O. alfredi* is the red phase of *O. (magicus) albiventris* (J. T. Marshall and B. King, pers. comm.). Relationships of *O. magicus* are with the other species now included in the *O. [magicus]* superspecies; recent data also suggest *enganensis* is a race of *magicus* (J. T. Marshall and B. King, pers. comm.). (MYSTERIOUS SCOPS-OWL). [INSULAR SCOPS-OWL]. See *O. elegans* and *O. mantananensis*."

171 Delete *Otus enganensis* entry

171 *Otus rutilus*, add superspecies *[rutilus]*; change English name to MALAGASY SCOPS-OWL (not MADAGASCAR); change range to "...[6233.1]; **Comoro Is.** (Anjouan) ¶*capnodes* (Gurney) 1889, ANJOUAN SCOPS-OWL [6233.3]; **lowlands**..."; change comments to "(MADAGASCAR SCOPS-OWL). [MALAGASY SCOPS-OWL]. See *O. magicus*."

171 After *Otus rutilus* insert:

Otus [rutilus] pauliani Benson (1960). COMORO SCOPS-OWL. [6233.2.]
Forest. Mts., 1000-1900 m, in **Comoro Is.** (Grand Comoro).
Affinities uncertain. A distinctive form differing in morphology and vocalizations (Herremans, Louette and Stevens 1991); J. T. Marshall and B. King (pers. comm.) suggest that *pauliani* is a race of *O. rutilus*. (GRAND COMORO SCOPS-OWL).

171 *Otus brookii*, change end of range to "...Sumatra, Java and Borneo."

171 *Otus bakkamoena*, change range to "...Ceylon) ¶*bakkamoena*, INDIAN SCOPS-OWL [2314]; lowlands and mts. to 2400 m of **e,se Asia** from ne,e India (Himalayas from c Nepal E to Arunachal Pradesh, and S to Bangladesh, Mizoram, Manipur and Nagaland), China (incl. Taiwan) and se Siberia (s Ussuriland, Sakhalin) S through se Asia to Sumatra (incl. Bangka and Belitung), Borneo (incl. N. Natuna Is.), Java and Bali (incl. Kangean Is.) ¶*lempiji* (Horsfield) 1821, COLLARED SCOPS-OWL [2314.2]; **e Asia** in Kuril Is., Japan and Izu Is. ¶*semitorques* Temminck and Schlegel 1850, JAPANESE SCOPS-OWL [2314.3]."; change comments to "Roberts and King (1986: 303-305) recognized *lempiji* as a species, but J. T. Marshall and B. King (pers. comm.) now consider it a race of *O. bakkamoena*. *Semitorques* possibly represents a distinct species, differing in vocalizations and eye color (J. T. Marshall and B. King, in Amadon and Bull 1988: 334), but they now consider it better treated as a race of *O. bakkamoena*."

171 Delete *Otus lempiji* entry

172 *Otus mentawi*, delete comments

172 *Otus megalotis*, change range to "Lowlands to 1600 m of **n Philippines** (Luzon, Catanduanes, Marinduque) ¶*megalotis*, PHILIPPINE SCREECH-OWL [3249]; **sc Philippines** (Negros) ¶*nigrorum* Rand 1950, NEGROS SCREECH-OWL [3249.2]; **ce,s Philippines** (Samar, Leyte, Bohol, Dinagat, Mindanao, Basilan) ¶*everetti* (Tweeddale) 1879, EVERETT'S SCREECH-OWL [3249.3]."; change comments to "[=*O. whiteheadi* Ogilvie-Grant 1895]. See *O. fuliginosus*."

172 *Otus kennicottii*, change range to "...Federal) and w,sc Texas...[1182.1]; **cw Mexico** in Colima, and r. Balsas drainage of Michoacán and w Guerrero ¶*seductus* Moore 1941, BALSAS SCREECH-OWL [1183]; **w,c Oaxaca** ¶*lambi* Moore and Marshall (1959), OAXACA SCREECH-OWL [1183.1]; Pacific slope of **c Middle America** from e Oaxaca and Chiapas S through C. America to nw Costa Rica (Guanacaste) ¶*cooperi* (Ridgway) 1878, PACIFIC SCREECH-OWL [1184]."; change comments to "J. T. Marshall and B. King (pers. comm.) consider *seductus*, *lambi* and *cooperi* as races of *O. kennicottii*. [>*Megascops* (≈*O. vermiculatus*)]. (KENNICOTT'S SCREECH-OWL)."

172 *Otus asio*, change comments to "[COMMON SCREECH-OWL]."

172 Delete *Otus seductus* and *O. cooperi* entries

173 *Otus roboratus*, change range to read "Lowlands of **nw Peru** (Tumbes, Piura) ¶*pacificus* Hekstra (1982), COASTAL SCREECH-OWL [5222.3]; mts. to 3200 m of **nw Peru** (w Andes and upper Marañón v. from Cajamarca S to Lima) ¶*roboratus*, WEST PERUVIAN SCREECH-OWL [5222]."; change comments to read "*Pacificus* is morphologically and vocally similar to *roboratus* except in its much smaller size (Johnson and Jones 1990)."

173 *Otus barbarus*, change English name to SANTA BARBARA SCREECH-OWL (not BRIDLED); change comments to "(BRIDLED/BEARDED SCREECH-OWL)."

173 *Otus vermiculatus*, add superspecies *[atricapillus]*; change comments to "A vocally distinct form supplanting *O. (atricapillus) guatemalae* in southern Central America (Marshall, Behrstock and König 1991). See *O. atricapillus*."

173 After *Otus vermiculatus* insert:

Otus [atricapillus] sanctaecatarinae (Salvin) 1897. LONG-TUFTED SCREECH-OWL. [5222.1.]
Humid forest, open woodland. Foothills of **se S. America** in s Brazil (Santa Catarina, Rio Grande do Sul) and extreme ne Argentina (Misiones).
A distinct species differing from *O. atricapillus* in calls and morphology (Marshall, Behrstock and König 1991: 313).

173 *Otus atricapillus*, add superspecies *[atricapillus]*; change range to "...Honduras, nc Nicaragua and ne Costa Rica, also in n Venezuela...¶*atricapillus*, BLACK-CAPPED SCREECH-OWL [5223]."; change comments to "All populations formerly included in *O. atricapillus*, *O. guatemalae*, and the recently described *O. hoyi* (except for *O. vermiculatus* and *O. sanctaecatarinae*) are vocally identical and apparently constitute a single species with considerable variation in size (Marshall, Behrstock and König 1991). [>*Megascops* (≈*O. nudipes*)]. [VARIABLE SCREECH-OWL]. See *O. vermiculatus*."

173 *Otus watsonii*, remove superspecies; change range to "...(r. Negro region) ¶*watsonii*, TAWNY-BELLIED SCREECH-OWL [4146]; **sc S. America** in Amazonian Brazil (S of Amazon, from r. Juruá E to r. Tapajós and S to n Mato Grosso), e Peru (Ucayali, Madre de Dios) and extreme n Bolivia (Pando), although a record from n Argentina (Tucumán) is erroneous ¶*usta* (Sclater) 1859, AUSTRAL SCREECH-OWL (SOUTHERN SCREECH-OWL) [4146.1]."; "Differences in calls between *watsonii* and *usta*, which are identical morphologically, are bridged by intermediate ones, indicating conspecificity of the groups (Marshall, Behrstock and König 1991: 313)."

173 Delete *Otus usta* and *O. petersoni* entries

173 *Otus marshalli*, remove superspecies; change range to "Andes, 1500-2700 m, of **cw S. America** in s Ecuador and n Peru (Piura, Cajamarca, Amazonas) ¶*petersoni* Fitzpatrick and O'Neill (1986), CINNAMON SCREECH-OWL [5223.2]; Andes, 1900-2250 m, of **e Peru** (Pasco, Cuzco) ¶*marshalli*, CLOUD-FOREST SCREECH-OWL [5223.1]."; change comments to "*Petersoni* is a morphologically distinct subspecies of *O. marshalli* (J. T. Marshall and B. King, pers. comm.)."

173 *Otus ingens*, change "1952" to "(1952)"; change end of comments to "...identical. [>*Macabra*]."

173 *Otus clarkii*, change end of comments to "...[=*O. nudipes*]. [>*Macabra*]."

174 *Otus nudipes*, add superspecies *[nudipes]*; delete comments

174 *Otus lawrencii*, add superspecies *[nudipes]*; change beginning of comments to "...[>*Gymnasio* (+N); >*Gymnoglaux*]..."

174 *Otus podarginus*, change English name to PALAU OWL (not PALAU SCOPS-OWL); in comments, change "OWL" to "SCOPS-OWL"

174 *Mimizuku gurneyi*, change English name to LESSER EAGLE-OWL (not GIANT SCOPS-OWL); change end of comments to "...(MINDANAO EAGLE-OWL/GIANT SCOPS-OWL)."

174 *Bubo virginianus*, change end of comments to "...Bull (1988: 336)."

174 *Bubo bubo*, after "/NORTHERN" add "/GREAT"

174 Split *Bubo poensis* into the following two species:

Bubo [poensis] poensis Fraser 1853. FRASER'S EAGLE-OWL. [7120.]
Humid forest. **W,c Africa** from Liberia and Ivory Coast E to s Cameroon (incl. Bioko), s C. African Rep. and n,ne Zaire to extreme sw Uganda, and S to Cabinda and sw,sc,ce Zaire.
[FRASER'S EAGLE-OWL]. See *B. vosseleri*.

Bubo [poensis] vosseleri Reichenow 1908. USAMBARA EAGLE-OWL. [7120.1.]
Humid forest. **Ne Tanzania** (Usambara Mts.).
B. vosseleri is recognized as a separate species by Collar and Stuart (1985) and Turner, Pearson and Zimmerman (1991: 87), based primarily on their widely disjunct ranges and differences in vocalizations, as reported by White (1974). (NDUK EAGLE-OWL).

175 *Bubo sumatranus*, change end of range to "...Borneo, Java and Bali."

175 *Bubo shelleyi*, change range to "...Liberia, Ivory Coast, s Ghana, s Cameroon, Gabon and cn Zaire."

175 *Bubo lacteus*, change range to "**Africa** from Senegambia, c Mali, Guinea,..."

175 *Bubo leucostictus*, change range to "**W,c Africa** from Guinea and Liberia E to s Cameroon, sw C. African Rep. and n,sc,ce Zaire, and S to Rio Muni, Gabon and Cabinda."

175 *Scotopelia peli*, change range to "Locally in **Africa** from Senegambia, sw Mali, Guinea-Bissau and Sierra Leone...s Sudan, w,c Ethiopia and s Somalia, and S to..."

175 *Scotopelia bouvieri*, change range to "...Liberia, s Nigeria, extreme s Cameroon, sw C. African Rep., Rio Muni,..."

176 *Strix seloputo*, in heading change "1878" to "1821"

176 *Strix occidentalis*, change reference in comments to "(Barrowclough and Gutiérrez 1990)."

176 *Strix rufipes*, after "Santa Cruz)" add ", se Bolivia (se Santa Cruz)"

176 *Strix uralensis*, change range to "...locally mts. (mostly) of ec Europe in extreme se W. Germany, Poland, Carpathian Mts., Transylvanian Alps,"

177 *Strix nebulosa*, in heading change "Thunberg 1798" to "Forster 1772"; change range to "...n Manitoba, n Ontario and wc Quebec S locally..."

177 *Strix huhula*, in heading remove parentheses around "Daudin"

177 *Strix woodfordii*, change range to "**Africa** from Senegal, Guinea-Bissau,...s Cameroon (incl. Bioko), C. African Rep..."

177 *Jubula lettii*, change "Equatorial Guinea" to "Rio Muni"

177 *Pulsatrix melanota*, after "Cochabamba" add ", w Santa Cruz"; in comments change "[RUSTY-BARRED OWL]." to "[WHITE-CHINNED OWL]."

178 *Glaucidium californicum*, change range to "...se Alaska, n British Columbia,...s Calif., c Arizona and c New Mexico; mts. of..."

178 *Glaucidium minutissimum*, at end of comments add "See *G. hardyi*."

178 Before *Glaucidium minutissimum* insert:

Glaucidium [passerinum] hardyi Vielliard (1990a). HARDY'S PYGMY-OWL. [5224.2.]
Humid forest. Lowlands of **Amazonian Brazil** (Rondônia, n Pará).
A distinct species, differing from *G. minutissimum* in vocalizations and shorter tail (Vielliard 1990a) but apparently related to *G. jardinii* (König 1991: 46-50). (AMAZONIAN PYGMY-OWL).

179 Split *Glaucidium brasilianum* into the following three species:

Glaucidium [brasilianum] brasilianum (Gmelin) 1788. FERRUGINOUS PYGMY-OWL. [380.]
Open woodland, forest edge, riparian woodland, thornscrub, brush. Lowlands of **Neotropical** from sc Arizona, Sonora, Chihuahua, Coahuila, Nuevo León and extreme s Texas (lower Rio Grande v.) S (incl. I. Cancun off Quintana Roo) to Costa Rica (mostly Pacific slope) and w,c Panama (Pacific slope E to w Panamá prov.), and from n,se Colombia (Caribbean lowlands, and Meta), Venezuela (incl. Margarita I.), Trinidad and Guianas S through e Ecuador, e Peru, Bolivia, Brazil and Paraguay to n Chile (Arica, Tarapacá), c Argentina (to La Rioja, Córdoba and Santa Fe) and Uruguay.
[FERRUGINOUS PYGMY-OWL]. AG: OWL. See *G. jardinii* and *G. nanum*.

Glaucidium [brasilianum] peruanum König 1991. PERUVIAN
PYGMY-OWL. [4147.2.]

Riparian woodland, thickets, mesquite. **Cw S. America**
in w Ecuador (N to Guayas) and Peru (S to Lima and Apuri-
mac).

Glaucidium [brasilianum] nanum (King) 1828. AUSTRAL
PYGMY-OWL. [5225.]

Open woodland, thornscrub. **S S. America** in s Chile (N
to Tarapacá) and s Argentina (N to Neuquén and Río Negro) S
to Tierra del Fuego. Winters N to n Argentina.

Nanum was reported to consist of a greater percentage of
dark morphs of *G. brasilianum* rather than constituting a distinct species by Marin, Kiff and Peña (1989: 69-71), but König
(1991: 62-70) recognized it as a distinct species. Jiménez and
Jaksić (1989) discussed the biology of *nanum*.

179 Split *Glaucidium jardinii* into the following two species
and move to p. 178 following *G. gnoma:*

Glaucidium [passerinum] jardinii (Bonaparte) 1855.
ANDEAN PYGMY-OWL. [1193.]

Humid forest, edge, woodland. Mts. of **s C. America** in
c Costa Rica and w Panama (Chiriquí, Veraguas); locally in
mts. of **w S. America** from Colombia (Andes, Sierra de Perijá)
and w Venezuela (Sierra de Perijá of Zulia, and Andes of
Mérida and Táchira) S through Andes of Ecuador to c Peru (S
to Junín).

Closely related to *G. gnoma*. See *G. hardyi*.

Glaucidium [passerinum] bolivianum König 1991. YUNGAS
PYGMY-OWL. [4147.1.]

Humid forest. Andes, 1400-2000 m, of **wc S. America**
in sw Peru (Cuzco, Puno), wc Bolivia (La Paz, Cochabamba, w
Santa Cruz) and nw Argentina (Jujuy, Salta).

179 *Glaucidium tephronotum*, after "ne Liberia," add "Ivory
Coast,"
179 *Glaucidium sjostedti*, after "Gabon," add "Congo Rep.,"
179 *Glaucidium radiatum*, change range to read "Lowlands to
2000 m of **s Asia** in India (...) and w Burma."; in
comments change *"castanonotus"* to *"castanonotum"*
179 **Glaucidium castanonotum** (not *castanonotus*)
179 *Glaucidium capense*, change range to "**Sc,s Africa** from
se Zaire, Tanzania and se Kenya S to s Mozambique and
e S. Africa (Natal, e Cape prov.)."
179 *Glaucidium castaneum*, change range to "Locally in **w,c
Africa** in ne Liberia, Ivory Coast, ne Zaire and sw
Uganda."
179 *Glaucidium ngamiense*, change range to "...se Zaire, s
Tanzania, w Zambia, n Botswana, n,c Namibia and
extreme ne S. Africa (Transvaal)."
179 *Glaucidium scheffleri*, change range to "Locally in
coastal **ce Africa** in s Somalia, e Kenya and..."
179 *Glaucidium albertinum*, delete ", w Uganda"
179-180 **Athene [noctua] noctua**, add superspecies; change
range to "**Palearctic and n African region** from cont.
Europe...Arabia, n,c Iran, Afghanistan,
Pakistan...Shantung). Intro. s British Isles, New
Zealand."; change comments to "...[>*Heteroglaux*
(+N)]..."
180 **Athene [noctua] brama**, add superspecies; in comments
delete first sentence

180 *Aegolius funereus*, change "c Alberta" to "c Idaho";
before "nw Wyoming" add "Montana,"
180 *Aegolius acadicus*, remove superspecies and change
English name to SAW-WHET OWL; change habitat to
"Forest, tamarack swamps, cedar groves, humid forest
edge, open pine-oak woodland."; change range to
"...New York ¶*acadicus*, NORTHERN SAW-WHET OWL
[372]; highlands, 1350-2500 m., of **c Middle America** in
Chiapas, Guatemala, El Salvador and Costa Rica.
¶*ridgwayi* (Alfaro) 1905, UNSPOTTED SAW-WHET OWL
[1202]. Winters (¶*acadicus*) S irregularly to s U.S.";
change comments to "Vocalizations of the two groups
are the same (J. T. Marshall, pers. comm.). Supposed
overlap of the groups west of the Isthmus of Tehuantepec
is based on a specimen of questionable origin (Binford
1989: 279). [>*Microscops* (+N)]."
180 *Aegolius harrisii*, delete superspecies; merge habitat and
range into one paragraph
181 **Ninox rudolfi** (not *rudolphi*), change also in comments
181 *Ninox novaeseelandiae*, change range to "...1888, LORD
HOWE ISLAND BOOBOOK (LORD HOWE BOOBOOK)
[9287.1];...1801, NORFOLK ISLAND BOOBOOK (NORFOLK
BOOBOOK) [9287.2]."
181 *Ninox scutulata*, change range to read "Lowlands to ...
Ryukyu Is. S to se Asia,...Sulawesi, Philippines and
Taiwan (incl. Lan Yü I.) ¶*scutulata*, BROWN HAWK-OWL
[2324]; **Andaman and Nicobar is.** ¶*obscura* Hume
1872, HUME'S HAWK-OWL [2324.1]. Winters
(¶*scutulata*) from..."; at beginning of comments, add
"Striking morphological differences suggest *obscura* may
be a distinct species (B. King, pers. comm.)."
181 *Ninox superciliaris*, change English name to WHITE-
BROWED HAWK-OWL (not MADAGASCAR); change range
to "Lowlands of **w,sw,n Madagascar**."; change
comments to "(MADAGASCAR HAWK-OWL). AG: OWL."
181 *Ninox philippensis*, change range to "**N,c Philippines**
(Polillo Is.,...Negros, Siquijor, Bohol and Leyte, except
for range of *spilonota*) ¶*philippensis*,...**s Philippines**
(Dinagat, Siargao, Mindanao,..."
181 *Ninox squamipila*, change range to "...1889, CHRISTMAS
ISLAND HAWK-OWL (CHRISTMAS HAWK-OWL)
[3259.4];..."; add comments "Although morphological
differences between *squamipila* and *natalis* are slight,
they differ vocally and probably represent distinct species
(B. King, P. Snetsinger, pers. comm.)."
181 *Ninox theomacha*, change end of range to
"...D'Entrecasteaux Arch. and Louisiade Arch. (Tagula,
Rossel)."
181 *Ninox meeki*, before "Admiralty Is." add "Manus, in"
182 *Ninox jacquinoti*, change English name to SOLOMON
ISLANDS HAWK-OWL (not SOLOMON HAWK-OWL); in
comments delete "ISLANDS"
182 *Sceloglaux albifacies*, change end of range to "...formerly
New Zealand (North and South is.)."
182 *Asio stygius*, before "Paraguay'" add "ne Bolivia (ne
Santa Cruz),"
182 *Asio otus*, delete "n Nuevo León,"
183 *Asio flammeus*, before "n Virginia" add "w Kentucky,";
change "Philppines" to "Philippines"
183 *Asio capensis*, change range to "...Tunisia, Gambia, s
Mali, Burkina Faso, s Niger, Benin, Nigeria, Cameroon,
and from c,e Angola, s,e Zaire,..."

183 *Aegotheles archboldi*, in heading remove ")" after "ARCHBOLD'S OWLET-NIGHTJAR"

184 *Batrachostomus mixtus*, change range to "Highlands of **n,c Borneo.**"

184 *Batrachostomus affinis*, in comments after "(1967: 25)" add "and Marshall (1978: 28-30)"

184 *Batrachostomus javensis*, in comments change "[JAVAN FROGMOUTH]." to "[HORSFIELD'S FROGMOUTH]."

184 *Batrachostomus cornutus*, change end of range to "...Belitung) and Borneo (incl. Banggi)."

185 *Nyctibius aethereus*, change range to "...e Pará) and ne Bolivia (ne Santa Cruz) ¶*longicaudatus*...S to Paraná), Paraguay and ne Argentina (Misiones) ¶*aethereus*..."

185 *Nyctibius griseus*, after "Trinidad" add ", Tobago"

185 *Eurostopodus argus*, in comments change "Horsfleid" to "Horsfield"

186 Split *Lurocalis semitorquatus* in the following two species:

Lurocalis [semitorquatus] semitorquatus (Gmelin) 1789.
SHORT-TAILED NIGHTHAWK. [1203.]
Forest, edge. Lowlands of **Middle and n,wc S. America** in e Chiapas, e Guatemala, n Honduras, ne Nicaragua, Costa Rica (Caribbean slope, Pacific sw), Panama (incl. I. Cébaco), n,ne Colombia (Santa Marta region, Guainía), nw,c,s Venezuela (se Zulia, Aragua, ne Portuguesa, s Amazonas, se Bolívar), Trinidad, Guianas and extreme nw Brazil (r. Negro region) ¶*semitorquatus*, SHORT-TAILED NIGHTHAWK [1203]; lowlands of **c,se S. America** E of Andes in e Ecuador, e Peru, n,e Bolivia (Pando, Beni, Cochabamba, Santa Cruz), Amazonian,e,s Brazil (S of Amazon E to Pará and Mato Grosso; from Bahia, Alagoas and Rio de Janeiro S to Rio Grande do Sul) and n Argentina (e Formosa, Misiones) ¶*nattereri* (Temminck) 1822, CHESTNUT-BANDED NIGHTHAWK (NATTERER'S NIGHTHAWK) [4151.2]. Winters (¶*nattereri*) N to Venezuela.
(SEMICOLLARED NIGHTHAWK). [SEMICOLLARED NIGHT-HAWK]. See *L. rufiventris*.

Lurocalis [semitorquatus] rufiventris Taczanowski 1884.
RUFOUS-BELLIED NIGHTHAWK. [1203.]
Forest, edge. Mts. of **w S. America** from Colombia (C.,E. Andes, Sierra de Perijá) and w Venezuela (Mérida, Táchira) S through Andes of Ecuador and Peru to c Bolivia.
Differences in vocalizations, morphology and ecology warrant treatment of *L. rufiventris* as a species distinct from *L. semitorquatus* (Parker et al. 1991: 125). (TACZANOWSKI'S NIGHTHAWK).

186 *Chordeiles pusillus*, change range to "... Guyana, n,e,se Brazil (...) and ne Bolivia (ne Santa Cruz)."

187 *Nyctiprogne leucopyga*, change end of range to "...French Guiana, Amazonian Brazil (...) and n,e Bolivia (Beni, Santa Cruz)."

187 *Nyctiphrynus yucatanicus*, at end of comments add "See *Caprimulgus badius*."

187 *Caprimulgus rufus*, at beginning of comments add "Includes *C. saltarius* Olrog (1979), SALTA NIGHTJAR, of Bolivia and northwestern Argentina (Salta), originally described as a race of *C. sericocaudatus* and sometimes treated as a distinct species (e.g., Narosky and Yzurieta 1987: 148) but probably identical to *C. rufus*."

188 *Caprimulgus badius*, change end of comments to "...a subspecies of *C. salvini*. Previous reports of vocalizations differing from those of *C. sericocaudatus* resulted from confusion in the field between calls of *C. badius* and *Nyctiphrynus yucatanicus* (Hardy and Straneck 1989). [>*Annamormis*]. AG: WILL."

188 *Caprimulgus sericocaudatus*, change end of comments to "...See *C. rufus*, *C. salvini* and *C. badius*."

188 *Caprimulgus ridgwayi*, after "Oaxaca" add ", c Veracruz"

188 *Caprimulgus saturatus*, add superspecies *[vociferus]*

188 *Caprimulgus longirostris*, before "Uruguay," add "Paraguay,"

188 *Caprimulgus cayennensis*, before "Venezuela" add "n Ecuador (Imbabura),"

189 *Caprimulgus anthonyi*, change English name to SCRUB NIGHTJAR (not ANTHONY'S); at end of comments add "(ANTHONY'S NIGHTJAR)."

189 *Caprimulgus binotatus*, before "s Ghana," add "Liberia,"

189 *Caprimulgus ruficollis*, change end of range to "...e Atlantic is., w Mediterranean region and w Africa."

189 *Caprimulgus europaeus*, in comments change "19882" to "1988a"

190 *Caprimulgus fraenatus*, after "Uganda," add "Burundi,"

190 *Caprimulgus eximius*, change range to "...**Subsaharan Africa** from s Mauritania and n Senegal E through Mali, s Niger..."

190 *Caprimulgus macrurus*, change "Calamanian Is." to "Calamian Is."

190 Split *Caprimulgus manillensis* into two species:

Caprimulgus [macrurus] manillensis Walden 1875.
PHILIPPINE NIGHTJAR. [3265.2.]
Forest edge, woodland, open country, towns. Lowlands to 2000 m of **Philippines** (except Palawan and Calamian Is.).
Differs from *macrurus* in morphology and egg color (Mees 1985). See *C. macrurus* and *C. celebensis*.

Caprimulgus [macrurus] celebensis Ogilvie-Grant 1894.
SULAWESI NIGHTJAR. [9304.1.]
Forest edge, woodland, open country. Lowlands of **n Sulawesi** (incl. Taliabu).
Formerly considered conspecific with *manillensis* but differs from that species in morphology and vocalizations (Rozendaal 1990).

190 *Caprimulgus nigriscapularis*, change range to "...**w,c Africa** from Senegal, Guinea-Bissau, Guinea and Sierra Leone E to sw Cameroon (...), sw C. African Rep., n,ne,ce Zaire...Uganda, Rwanda and Burundi."; in comments after "...1988a)" add ", although the specific separation is questioned by Louette (1990a: 73-75)"

191 *Caprimulgus pectoralis*, in heading change "1817" to "1816; change range to "¶*fervidus* Sharpe 1875, FIERY-NECKED NIGHTJAR [6245.2]; **S. Africa**..."

191 After *Caprimulgus pectoralis* add:

Caprimulgus prigoginei Louette (1990b). ITOMBWE NIGHTJAR. [6244.1.]
Woodland. **Extreme ce Zaire** (just NW of L. Tanganyika).
Known from a single specimen, representing a new species of unknown relationships (Louette 1990b).

191 *Caprimulgus poliocephalus*, change range to "...[7130.2]; **wc Africa** in cw Angola (Mt. Moco area) and sw Zaire ¶*koesteri*..."

191 *Caprimulgus ruwenzorii*, change end of comments to "... specifically distinct, although the specific separation is questioned by Louette (1990a: 75)."

191 *Caprimulgus natalensis*, change range to "**Africa** from Gambia, cs Mali, Liberia, Ivory Coast and Ghana..."

191 *Caprimulgus inornatus*, after "c Tanzania" add "(mostly a nonbreeder in s half of range)"

191 *Caprimulgus stellatus*, delete ", ne Uganda"

191 *Caprimulgus tristigma*, change range to "...C. African Rep., n Zaire, se Sudan, w,c Ethiopia and c Kenya, thence S locally through e,s Zaire..."

191 *Caprimulgus batesi*, change end of range to "...s Cameroon, sw C. African Rep., Gabon, Zaire (except s) and sw Uganda."

192 *Caprimulgus climacurus*, change range to "...sw Mauritania E through s Mali, s Niger and s Chad to c Sudan,...nw Tanzania, and S to Gulf of Guinea, n,c Zaire and nw Uganda. Winters..."

192 *Caprimulgus clarus*, change range to "**Ne Africa** in c,e Zaire, c,s Uganda, Ethiopia, s Somalia, Kenya and n Tanzania."

192 *Caprimulgus fossii*, change range to "...Congo Rep., s,e Zaire, s Uganda,..."

192 *Macrodipteryx longipennis*, at end of range add "Mostly nonbreeding visitor in n,e portions of range."

192 *Uropsalis lyra*, after "Cochabamba," add "w Santa Cruz,"

193 *Columba livia*, change range to "...native of **Palearctic** in Faroes,...(Senegal, Mali, Niger, Ghana, Chad, Mediterranean region, Egypt, Sudan, Ethiopia), Arabia..."

193 *Columba guinea*, change range to "...**w,nc,e Africa** from s Mauritania, Senegambia and Guinea-Bissau..."

193 *Columba trocaz*, delete "(perhaps near extinction)"

193 *Columba bollii*, replace range with "Highlands of **w,c Canary Is.** (La Palma, Gomera, Tenerife)."

193 *Columba junoniae*, replace range with "**W,c Canary Is.** (La Palma, Gomera, Tenerife)."

194 *Columba unicincta*, change range to "...Cameroon, sw C. African Rep., n,ne Zaire,...cs,ce Zaire, extreme nw Zambia and Burundi."

194 *Columba punicea*, change range to "...e India (W to Bihar, e Madhya Pradesh and n Andhra Pradesh), s Tibet..."

194 *Columba vitiensis*, change range to "...Lombok), is. off e Borneo, Banggai...Philippines E through..."

195 *Columba pallidiceps*, after "New Britain," add "New Ireland,"

195 *Columba corensis*, in heading change "1794" to "1784"

196 *Columba cayennensis*, in comments change "1810" to "1809"

196 *Columba iriditorques*, change range to "...C. African Rep., n,ne Zaire, sw Uganda and Rwanda, and S to..."

196 *Columba delegorguei*, change beginning of comments to "Dowsett and Dowsett-Lemaire (1980:..."

196 *Columba picturata*, after "Mauritius," add "Réunion,"; change beginning of comments to "Fry, Keith and Urban (1985)..."

197 *Columba larvata*, in heading change "1810" to "1809"

197 *Streptopelia turtur*, change range to "...Tsinghai), and S to Canary Is., n Africa (from Morocco E to Egypt, and S to c Niger, n Chad and n Sudan), Turkey,..."

197 *Streptopelia hypopyrrha*, change English name to ADAMAWA TURTLE-DOVE (not ANDAMAWA)

197 *Streptopelia lugens*, after "ce,se Zaire," add "e Zambia, n Malawi,"

197 *Streptopelia orientalis*, change end of range to "...Hainan), Taiwan and Ryukyu Is."

197 *Streptopelia senegalensis*, after "Príncipe" add ", São Tomé"

197 *Streptopelia chinensis*, change range to "... and Philippines. Intro...s Calif."

197 *Streptopelia decipiens*, change range to "**Africa** from s Mauritania and Senegambia E through..."; in comments change "juvenile" to "juvenal"

198 *Streptopelia semitorquata*, change range to "**African region** from s Mauritania and Senegambia E through..."; at end of comments add "."

198 *Streptopelia bitorquata*, in heading change "1810" to "1809"

199 *Macropygia phasianella*, in comments change "amoinensis" to "amboinensis"

199 *Macropygia ruficeps*, before "Burma" add "sw China (s Yunnan),"

199 *Macropygia nigrirostris*, after "Goodenough" add ", Fergusson"

199 *Macropygia mackinlayi*, change "Squally" to "Admiralty"

199 *Reinwartoena reinwardtsi*, change end of range to "...w Papuan is., New Guinea (...) and D'Entrecasteaux Arch. (Goodenough, Fergusson)."

199 *Reinwardtoena browni*, change range to "**Bismarck Arch.** (incl. Lihir Is.)."

199 *Turtur abyssinicus*, change end of range to "...c Cameroon, C. African Rep., nw Uganda and extreme n Kenya."

199 *Turtur chalcospilos*, change beginning of range to "**S,e Africa** from Gabon, sw Congo Rep., w,s,e Angola,..."

199 *Turtur afer*, change beginning of range to "**Africa** from Senegambia E through s Mali, sw Niger, c Nigeria,..."

199 *Turtur tympanistria*, in heading change "1810" to "1809"; change range to "**African region** from s Senegal, Guinea-Bissau and Guinea E through Cameroon (incl. Bioko), C. African Rep. and s Sudan to sw,cs Ethiopia, Kenya and s Somalia, and S to..."

199 *Turtur brehmeri*, in heading change "1875" to "1865"; change range to "**W,c Africa** from sw Mali, Sierra Leone,...s Cameroon, sw C. African Rep., n,ne Zaire,..."

200 *Oena capensis*, change range to "**African region** from Mauritania, s Algeria, Mali, c Niger, c Chad, se Egypt..."

200 *Chalcophaps indica*, change range to "...Hainan), Taiwan (incl. Lan Yü Is.) and s Ryukyu Is. S through se Asia and Philippines to Andaman and Nicobar is., Christmas I...e New Guinea (W to Sepik r..."

200 *Henicophaps foersteri*, before "New Britain" add "Umboi,"

200 *Phaps elegans*, in heading change "1810" to "1809"

201 *Geopelia striata*, change range to "...Borneo, Java and (intro.?) w Lesser Sunda Is. (Java, Bali) and Philippines. Intro. Sulawesi, Moluccas (Ambon), Society..."

201 *Geopelia maugeus*, in heading change "1811" to "1809"; after "Lesser Sunda" add "(W to Sumbawa)"

202 *Columbina inca,* before "c Arizona," add "s Nevada,"

202 *Columbina passerina,* delete "and Tobago"

202 *Columbigallina talpacoti,* in heading change "1810" to "1809"

202 *Columbina cruziana,* in heading change "(Prévost and Knip)" to "(Prévost)"

203 Change scientific names and sequence of *Claravis godefrida* and *C. mondetoura* to *Claravis [godefrida] mondetoura* and *Claravis [godefrida] godefrida*

203 *Claravis godefrida,* at end of comments add "[MAROON-CHESTED GROUND-DOVE]."

203 *Metropelia aymara,* in heading change "(Prévost and Knip)" to "(Prévost)"

203 *Leptotila verreauxi,* in range change "1956" to "1856"

204 *Leptotila rufaxilla,* after "Orinoco)" add ", Trinidad"

204 *Leptotila jamaicensis,* before "Barbareta" add "Roatán and"

204 *Geotrygon albifacies,* before "Veracruz," add "Hidalgo,"

205 *Geotrygon chrysia,* change range to "...sw Puerto Rico (incl. Culebra I., possibly Mona I.); formerly..."

205 *Geotrygon montana,* change range to "...Virgin Is.), s Lesser Antilles (Grenada), and lowlands to 2600 from s Sinaloa, Puebla and Veracruz S along both slopes of Middle America (incl. Yucatán pen.) to Panama (...), and in S. America from Colombia, Venezuela, Trinidad and Guianas S..."

205 *Caloenas nicobarica,* change end of range to "... E. Indies, Philippines, is. off w,n New Guinea, Trobriand Is., and D'Entrecasteaux and Louisiade arch. to Palau,..."

206 *Gallicolumba kubaryi,* change English name to CAROLINE ISLANDS GROUND-DOVE (not CAROLINE GROUND-DOVE); in comments delete "ISLANDS"

206 *Gallicolumba xanthonura,* change range to "**Micronesia** in Mariana (from Saipan S to Guam) and w Caroline is. (Yap)."

206 *Gallicolumba sanctaecrucis,* change "**Sw Polynesia**" to "**E Melanesia**"

206 *Gallicoluma beccarii,* change range to "...(incl. Admiralty, St. Matthias and Green is.) and Solomon Is. (...)."

207 *Microgoura meeki,* in heading add "†" before scientific name; change range to "Extinct (not recorded since 1904); formerly **nw Solomon Is.** (Choiseul)."

207 *Phapitreron amethystina,* change range to "Mts., 1000-2500 m, of **Philippines.**"

207 *Phapitreron cinereiceps,* change "Katanglad" to "Malindang"; change comments to "...Mindanao; treated as a species by Dickinson, Kennedy and Parkes (1991: 184)."

207 *Treron pompadora,* boldface "**Philippines**"

208 *Treron waalia,* after "n Ivory Coast," add "Burkina Faso,"

208 *Treron calva,* change range to "**W,c,ne Africa** from Senegambia, s Mali, Guinea-Bissau,..."; change comments to "This and the following three species may be conspecific, but they are treated as allospecies by Urban, FRY and KEITH (1986: 443-446)."

208 Split *T. australis* into two species:

Treron [australis] pembaensis Pakenham 1940. PEMBA GREEN-PIGEON. [7077.]
Open woodland. Lowlands of **Pemba.**
See *T. calva.*

Treron [australis] australis (Linnaeus) 1771. MADAGASCAR GREEN-PIGEON. [6181.]
Open woodland, savanna (Madagascar), evergreen forest (Mohéli). Lowlands of **Madagascar,** incl. Comoro Is. (Mohéli, probably formerly Grand Comoro and Anjouan). [AFRICAN GREEN-PIGEON]. See *T. calva.*

209 *Ptilinopus cinctus,* in heading change "1810" to "1809"

209 *Ptilinopus marchei,* delete ", Polillo Is."

209 *Ptilinopus merrilli,* change range to "Lowlands to 1000 m of **n Philippines** (Luzon, Polillo Is., Catanduanes)."

209 *Ptilinopus leclancheri,* change range to "**se China** (Lan Yü Is.); **Philippines.**"

209 *Ptilinopus bernsteinii,* in heading change "(Gray) 1861" to "Schlegel 1863"; in comments after "[=*P. superbus*]" add "(White and Bruce 1986: 200)"

210 *Ptilinopus superbus,* in heading change "1810" to "1809"

210 *Ptilinopus porphyraceus,* change range to "...Kosrae, Truk), and sw Marshall...Finsch 1878, PURPLE-CAPPED FRUIT-DOVE (POHNPEI/PONAPE FRUIT-DOVE)..."

210 *Ptilinopus rarotongensis,* change English name to COOK ISLANDS FRUIT-DOVE (not RAROTONGAN); change comments to "(RAROTONGAN FRUIT-DOVE)."

210 *Ptilinopus coralensis,* change "Mahatea" to "Makatea"

211 *Ptilonopus chalcurus,* change English name to MAKATEA FRUIT-DOVE (not MAHATEA); in range change "(Mahatea)" to "(Makatea)"

211 *Ptilinopus [purpuratus] insularis,* change English name to HENDERSON ISLAND FRUIT-DOVE (not HENDERSON FRUIT-DOVE) and add superspecies; in comments delete "ISLAND"

211 *Ptilinopus mercierii,* after "Fatu Hiva)" add "; possibly extinct"

211 *Ptilonopus solomonensis,* change range to "Lowlands to 750 m of **New Guinea region**...Bismarck Arch. (Umboi, Witu, Watom, and from Wuvulu E to Tench and New Hanover, but absent from New Britain and New Ireland) and Solomon Is. (from Green Is. SE)."

211 *Ptilinopus viridis,* change range to "...Trobriand Is., D'Entrecasteaux Arch., Bismarck Arch. (Lihir Is.) and Solomon Is. (S to Guadalcanal and Malaita) ¶*pectoralis*..."

211 *Ptilinopus eugeniae,* change range to "**Se Solomon Is.** (Ugi, San Cristobal)."

211 *Ptilinopus arcanus,* change "Canloan" to "Canlaon"

211 *Ptilinopus victor,* in heading change "(Layard) 1875" to "(Gould) 1872"

212 *Ptilinopus layardi,* change English name to WHISTLING DOVE (not VELVET); in comments change "WHISTLING" to "VELVET"

212 *Drepanoptila holosericea,* in heading change "1810" to "1809"

212 *Alectroenas madagascariensis,* change range to "Lowlands to 1800 m of **n,e Madagascar.**"

212 *Alectroenas nitidissima,* after "Extinct" add "(ca. 1826)"

212 *Alectroenas pulcherrima,* in English name remove hyphen after "SEYCHELLES"

212 *Ducula poliocephala,* change end of range to "...of **Philippines.**"

213 *Ducula rubricera,* change "(Lihir Is.)" to "(W to New Hanover and Umboi)"

213 *Ducula pistrinaria,* change range to "...Louisiade arch.), Bismarck Arch. (...) and Solomon Is."

213 *Ducula whartoni,* change English name to CHRISTMAS ISLAND IMPERIAL-PIGEON (not CHRISTMAS IMPERIAL-PIGEON); in comments delete "ISLAND"

213 *Ducula pickeringii,* change end of range to "...s Philippines (islets from Balabac to Cagayan Sulu and Cagayan Is., Sulu Arch., and off Basilan)."

213 *Ducula finschii,* in comments after "*D. rufigaster*" add "; recognized as a full species by Coates (1985: 259)."

213 *Ducula pinon,* change "PINYON" to "PINON"

214 *Ducula melanochroa,* before "New Britain," add "Umboi,"

214 *Ducula zoeae,* before "Fergusson" add "Goodenough,"

214 *Ducula bicolor,* change beginning of range to "Widely distibuted in coastal regions of **se Asia,**..."; in comments change "(≈*D. luctuosa*)" to "(≈*D. subflavescens*)"

214 *Ducula spilorrhoa,* change range to "...far w), is. in Torres...n Australia from extreme ne W. Australia Eto n Queensland..."; sequence after *D. luctuosa*

214 After *Ducula spilorrhoa* add the following two species:

Ducula [bicolor] constans Bruce (1989). KIMBERLEY IMPER-IAL-PIGEON. [8145.1.]
Vine forest, mangroves, thickets near water. **Nw Aus-tralasia** in ne W. Australia (Kimberleys).
Recognized as an allospecies by Bruce (1989).

Ducula [bicolor] subflavescens (Finsch) 1886. YELLOW-TINTED IMPERIAL-PIGEON. [8145.2.]
Woodland, mangroves. **Bismarck Arch.** (incl. Admiral-ty Is.)
Recognized as an allospecies by Bruce (1989).

214 *Hemiphaga novaeseelandiae,* change range to "...1801, NORFOLK ISLAND PIGEON (NORFOLK PIGEON) [8147.1];..."

215 *Neotis nuba,* change range to "Locally in **subsaharan Africa** from Mauritania E through Mali, Niger, c Chad and..."

216 *Ardeotis arabs,* change beginning of comments to "[=*Choriotis* (~*Ardeotis*); <*Otis* (~*Ardeotis*)]...."

216 *Chlamydotis undulata,* afater "n Libya" add ", n Sudan"

216 *Eupodotis rueppellii,* in comments change "1972:" to "1972a:"

217 *Eupodotis senegalensis,* change range to "...s Mali, Burkina Faso, s Niger,...Cameroon, n C. African Rep., n Uganda,..."

217 *Eupodotis melanogaster,* after "and S" add "(except forested w,c)"

217 *Balearica pavonina,* change range to "**Subsaharan Africa** from s Mauritania and Senegambia S to Sierra Leone, Ivory Coast and Ghana, and E (...) to C. African Rep., s Sudan..."

218 *Grus rubicunda,* change beginning of range to "**Australian region** in s New Guinea (from Frederik Hendrik I. E to Fly r.), and n,nc,e,se Australia..."

218 *Grus virgo,* change range to "...(locally n Morocco, formerly Algeria and Tunisia)..."

219 Under Tribe Aramini, add comments "The relationships among the cranes, Limpkin *(Aramus),* and Sungrebe *(Heliornis)* are controversial. Our DNA hybridization data indicate that *Aramus* and *Heliornis* are more closely related to one another than *Aramus* is to the cranes. F. H. Sheldon (pers. comm.) obtained DNA hybridization data that place *Aramus* closer to the cranes than to *Heliornis.*

We have re-examined our DNA hybridization experiments and find no reason to change our earlier conclusion; neither do we doubt the validity of Sheldon's evidence. It seems best to leave the question open and to obtain additional evidence before changing the classification."

219 Under Tribe Heliornithini, change comments to "See Tribe Aramini"

219 ***Rhynochetos jubatus*** (not ***Rhynochetus jubata***)

220 *Sarothrura elegans,* after "Liberia," add "Ivory Coast,"

220 *Sarothrura rufa,* change range to "...Gabon, s C. African Rep., sc,ce,ne Zaire,...Zanzibar is.) S (except forested w,c and desert sw) to S. Africa..."

220 *Sarothrura lugens,* in heading after "(Böhm)" add "1884"

220 *Sarothrura affinis,* change range to "...w,c Kenya, extreme n Tanzania, Malawi, extreme ne Zambia, e Zimbabwe..."

220 *Sarothrura insularis,* change "**Madagascar**" to "**e Madagascar**"

220 *Sarothrura watersi,* change English name to SLENDER-BILLED FLUFFTAIL (not WATERS'S); change comments to "[>*Lemurolimnas*]. (WATERS'S FLUFFTAIL)."

220 *Canirallus oculeus,* after "Gabon" add ", C. African Rep."

220 *Canirallus kioloides,* change end of comments to "...WOOD RAIL/MADAGASCAR WOOD-RAIL)."

221 *Micropygia schomburgkii,* change range to "...Heath), n,e Bolivia (Beni, La Paz, Santa Cruz) and c,se Brazil..."

221 *Rallina forbesi,* change "New Guinea" to "**New Guinea**"

221 *Rallina fasciata,* after "Luzon," add "Culion, Palawan,"

221 *Amaurolimnas viridis,* after "e Peru" add ", n Bolivia (Beni)"

222 *Laterallus melanophaius,* delete "e Ecuador,"

222 *Laterallus exilis,* change range to" ...Belize, e Guatemala, se Honduras...e Peru, n,c Bolivia (Pando, La Paz), Paraguay..."

222 *Laterallus jamaicensis,* before "Veracruz" add "Greater Antilles (Cuba, Jamaica, formerly Puerto Rico); "

222 *Laterallus leucopyrrhus,* before "Santa Fe," add "Misiones,"

222 *Nesoclopeus poecilopterus,* before "rediscovered" add "supposedly"; in comments before "FIJI" add "BARREDWING""

223 *Gallirallus sylvestris,* change English name to LORD HOWE ISLAND RAIL (not LORD HOWE RAIL); in comments delete "ISLAND"

223 ***Gallirallus conditicius*** (not ***conditicus***); in range change "**Kiribati**" to "**sw Marshall Is.**"; in comments change "Wolters" to "Walters"

223 *Gallirallus philippensis,* change range to "...Mindoro, Cebu, Mindanao), s Moluccas,...Bismarck Arch. (New Ireland, New Britain and Witu Is.), Palau,...Solomon Is. (Bougainville, Choiseul, Ysabel, Guadalcanal), Fiji..."; change end of comments to "...See *G. rovianae* and *G. pacificus.*"

223 After *Gallirallus philippensis,* insert:

Gallirallus [philippensis] rovianae Diamond (1991). ROVIANA RAIL. [9049.1.]
Woodland. Lowlands of **c Solomon Is.** (Kulambangra, New Georgia, Rendova, and small adjacent islands).
Described as a new species distinct from the widespread *G. philippensis* (Diamond 1991).

223 *Gallirallus wakensis*, change English name to WAKE ISLAND RAIL (not WAKE RAIL); in comments delete "ISLAND"

223 *Gallirallus modestus*, change English name to CHATHAM ISLANDS RAIL (not CHATHAM RAIL); in comments delete "ISLANDS"

223-224 *Rallus longirostris*, delete "Nayarit,"

224 *Rallus limicola*, change end of range to "... Chiapas); **w S. America** in sw Colombia (Nariño) and Peru (S to Lima). N Populations winter from sw Canada and coastal U.S. S to n C. America."

224 *Rallus semiplumbeus*, after "¶*peruvianus*" add "Taczanowski 1886"

224 *Rallus caerulescens*, after "Angola," add "C. African Rep.,"

225 *Lewinia muelleri*, change English name to AUCKLAND ISLANDS RAIL (not AUCKLAND RAIL); in comments delete "ISLANDS"

225 *Dryolimnas cuvieri*, WHITE-THROATED RAIL (not CUVIER'S); change comments to "[<*Canirallus*]. (CUVIER'S RAIL)..."

225 *Crecopsis egregia*, change "s Sudan" to "wc,s Sudan"

225 *Rougetius rougetii*, in heading after "(Guérin-Méneville)" add "1843"

225 *Atlantisia rogersi*, change English name to INACCESSIBLE ISLAND RAIL (not INACCESSIBLE RAIL); in comments delete "ISLAND"

225 *Aramides axillaris*, change range to "...Guerrero, El Salvador, Honduras, w Nicaragua,...Belize and Honduras (Guanaja and Roatán in Bay Is.);..."

225 *Aramides cajanea*, delete ", Hidalgo, Distrito Federal"

226 *Amaurolimnas concolor*, after "...São Paulo" add ")"

226 *Amaurornis isabellinus*, change English name to ISABELLINE WATERHEN (not BUSH-HEN); change comments to "(CELEBES WATERHEN). AG (+N): BUSH-HEN/SWAMPHEN/..."; sequence after *A. olivaceus*

226 *Amaurornis olivaceus*, change English name to BUSH-HEN (not PLAIN BUSH-HEN); sequence before *A. isabellinus*; change comments to "[≠*Gallinula*]. (PLAIN BUSH-HEN). [BUSH-HEN]..."

226 *Amaurornis moluccanus*, change English name to RUFOUS-TAILED WATERHEN (not BUSH-HEN); change end of comments to "...1869]. [≠*Gallinula*]. (EASTERN/RUFOUS-VENTED WATERHEN)."

226 *Amaurornis olivieri*, change English name to SAKALAVA RAIL (not OLIVIER'S CRAKE); at beginning of comments add "(OLIVIER'S CRAKE)."

226 *Porzana parva*, change range to "...Tadzhikistan; formerly in n Africa (Algeria, Egypt). Winters...and n,e Africa E to n India."

226-227 *Porzana pusilla*, change range to "...**e,c African region** from cw Angola,...c Ethiopia, n Somalia and w Kenya...s S. Africa; Madagascar; **w Indonesia** in Belitung (off Sumatra), e Borneo (...) and Sulawesi; lowlands to 2450 m in **Australasian**...s,se Asia, Indonesia and Philippines."

227 *Porzana carolina*, after "c Illinois," add "sw Tennessee,"

227 *Porzana fusca*, change range to "...Negros, Samar, Leyte, Bohol, Mindanao). N populations..."

228 *Porzana atra*, change English name to HENDERSON ISLAND CRAKE (not HENDERSON CRAKE); in comments delete "ISLAND"

228 *Aenigmatolimnas marginalis*, at beginning of range add habitat "Wet grassy areas in savanna."; in range after "n Zaire" add ", Uganda"

228 *Pardirallus maculatus*, after "Belize," add "El Salvador,"

228 *Pardirallus nigricans*, after "Pando" add ", n La Paz"

229 *Porphyrio porphyrio*, change range to "...(Morocco, Algeria, Tunisia)...**African region** in Senegambia, s Mali,...Basilan) and Talaud Is. (where..."

229 *Porphyrio albus*, change English name to LORD HOWE ISLAND SWAMPHEN (not LORD HOWE SWAMPHEN); in comments before "WHITE" add "LORD HOWE/"

229 *Porphyrio mantelli*, change end of range to "...(750-1200 m)."; change comments to "[>*Notornis*]. (THE NOTORNIS). See *P. albus*."

230 *Gallinula chloropus*, after "S locally" add "(incl. e Atlantic is. and São Tomé)"

231 *Fulica atra*, in comments delete "*Gallinula chloropus*,"

231 *Fulica caribaea*, change range to "**W Indies and cn S. America** in s Bahama Is. (N. Caicos), Hispaniola, Puerto Rico, Virgin Is., Lesser Antilles...Curaçao and nw Venezuela (Zulia, Aragua)."

231 *Mesitornis variegata*, change English name to WHITE-BREASTED MESITE (not ROATELO); change range to "Lowlands of **w,n Madagascar**."; change end of comments to "...AG (+N): ROATELO."

232 *Mesitornis unicolor*, change English name to BROWN MESITE (not ROATELO); change range to "Lowlands to 900 m of **e Madagascar**."

232 *Monias benschi*, change English name to SUBDESERT MESITE (not MONIAS); change comments to "(BENSCH'S RAIL/THE MONIAS)."

232 *Syrrhaptes paradoxus*, at end of range add "Breeds irregularly W to British Isles and w Europe."

232 *Pterocles exustus*, change range to "**Nc,n African region** from s Mauritania and Senegambia E across Mali, c,se Niger, L. Chad area, Egypt (Nile v.) and c,e Sudan to Ethiopia, Somalia, Near East and coastal Arabia,..."

232 *Pterocles senegallus*, before "c Ethiopia" add "Mauritania, n Mali, n Niger, n Chad, n Sudan,"

232 *Pterocles coronatus*, before "w Sudan," add "n Chad,"

232 *Pterocles personatus*, change English name to MADAGASCAR SANDGROUSE (not MASKED); change range to "Lowlands of **Madagascar** (except e)."; at end of comments add "(MASKED SANDGROUSE)."

233 *Pterocles lichtensteinii*, change range to "...c Chad, c,ne Sudan and se Egypt to Ethiopia..."

233 *Pterocles burchelli*, change range to "...extreme w Zimbabwe and cn S. Africa (cn Cape prov., nw Orange Free State, w,n Transvaal)."

234 *Scolopax saturata*, change "**W Indonesia**" to "**w Indonesia**"; in comments after "DUSKY" add "/INDONESIAN"

234 *Gallinago solitaria*, at beginning of comments add "*Gallinago* Brisson 1760 has priority over *Capella* Frenzel 1801 (Mayr 1963)."

234 *Gallinago megala*, in comments after "MARSH" add "/FOREST"

235 *Gallinago nigripennis*, change range to "Locally in **e,s Africa** from Angola, Zambia, e Zaire, s Sudan, Ethiopia and Kenya S (except desert sw) to S. Africa."

235 *Gallinago jamesoni*, in comments after "*G. stricklandii*" add "(e.g., Vuilleumier 1969b: 599-600)"

235 *Gallinago imperialis*, in heading change "2869" to "1869"

235 *Coenocorypha pusilla*, change English name to
    CHATHAM ISLANDS SNIPE (not CHATHAM SNIPE); in
    comments delete "ISLANDS"

236 *Limoa fedoa*, after "c Montana," add "ne Colorado,"

236 *Numenius phaeopus*, after "Faroe Is.," add "n British
    Isles,"

236 *Numenius arquata*, before "British Isles" add "Iceland,"

238 *Tringa glareola*, change range to "**N Eurasia** from
    British Isles and Scandinavia...and S to Denmark,
    Germany, c Russia,...w,c Aleutian Is. (Attu,
    Amchitka,..."

238 *Tringa [hypoleucos] hypoleucos*, add superspecies

238 *Tringa [hypoleucos] macularia*, add superspecies

238 *Catoptrophorus semipalmatus*, after "Prince Edward I."
    add ", w Newfoundland"

238 *Prosobonia leucoptera*, in heading change "[9066.1.]" to
    "[9067.]"

239 *Limnodromus griseus*, delete "(Fort Albany)"

239 *Limnodromus semipalmatus*, change end of range to
    "...Winters in s,se Asia (incl. Greater Sunda Is.)."

239 *Calidris alba*, change "**Palaeartic**" to "**Palearctic**";
    before "Prince Patrick," add "Banks,"

239 *Calidris pusilla*, change beginning of range to "**E Siberia**
    (Chukotski pen.); **n N. America**..."

240 *Calidris temminckii*, before "n Scandinavia" add "British
    Isles and"

240 *Calidris minutilla*, before "Newfoundland" add "New
    Brunswick,"

240 *Calidris melanotos*, change comments to "The taxonomic
    and biological status of *Calidris paramelanotos* S. A.
    Parker (1982, type from Price Saltfields, upper Gulf St.
    Vincent, South Australia), COX'S SANDPIPER [8117],
    remains in doubt (A.O.U. 1989). *C. paramelanotos* may
    be a valid species but is more likely a hybrid between *C.
    melanotos* and *C. ferruginea* (Cox 1987, 1989, 1990),
    although one possible parental species was suggested by
    Buckley (1988) to be *C. fuscicollis*, and by Stepanyan
    (1990b) to be *Philomachus pugnax*. Present
    evidence...hybrid origin. (AMERICAN PECTORAL
    SANDPIPER)."

240 *Calidris acuminata*, change end of comments to "See *C.
    ferruginea*."

241 *Calidris ptilocnemis*, change "Kurile" to "Kuril"

241 *Calidris alpina*, change range to "...British Isles and
    Baltic region; **n N. America**...ne Keewatin, and s
    Somerset and Baffin is. S to...n Mexico, rarely C.
    America."

241 *Calidris ferruginea*, change comments to "*Calidris
    cooperi* (Baird) 1858, COOPER'S SANDPIPER, appears to
    be a hybrid between *C. acuminata* and *C. ferruginea*
    (Cox 1989). [>*C. testacea*..."

241 *Philomachus pugnax*, change range to "**Eurasia** from s
    British Isles and n Scandinavia...Anadyrland, and S
    locally to nc Europe and c Russia,..."

241 *Steganopus tricolor*, change range to "...(Vancouver I.);
    from s Yukon, n Alberta, c Saskatchewan and s,ne
    Manitoba E...s Ontario, s Quebec and New Brunswick,
    and S in..."

242 *Rostratula benghalensis*, after "Madagascar" add
    "(except s)"

242 *Microparra capensis*, after "Chad" add ", C. African
    Rep."

242 *Hydrophasianus chirurgus*, change range to "...Ceylon
    and Philippines...breeding range and to Greater Sunda
    Is."

243 CHIONOIDEA and **Chionidae**, not CHIONIDOIDEA and
    Chionididae

243 After *Chionis minor* entry, add "Family **Pluvianellidae**"
    with account of *Pluvianellus socialis* from p. 350

243 *Burhinus senegalensis*, after "L. Chad," add "C. African
    Rep.,"

243 *Burhinus bistriatus*, change "**c C. America**" to "**c
    Middle America**"

244 *Burhinus giganteus*, change range to "...Indonesia, New
    Guinea and Bismarck Arch. to Solomon Is..."; in
    comments change "*Orthorhamphus*" to "*Esacus*"; after
    "[=*B. grallarius*]." add "[>*Esacus*]."

244 *Haematopus meadewaldoi*, change English name to
    CANARY ISLANDS OYSTERCATCHER (not CANARY
    OYSTERCATCHER); in comments delete "ISLANDS"

244 *Haematopus palliatus*, change "W.I." to "W. Indies"

244 *Haematopus unicolor*, change end of range to "...1927,
    CHATHAM ISLANDS OYSTERCATCHER (CHATHAM
    OYSTERCATCHER) [8112]."

245 *Himantopus himantopus*, after "Hungary" add ", and incl.
    Canary and Cape Verde is."

245 *Himantopus mexicanus*, change range to "**Americas**
    locally from cs British Columbia, s Alberta, s
    Saskatchewan,...BLACK-NECKED STILT [226]. Winters..."

246 *Recurvirostra americana*, change range to "**W N.
    America** from s British Columbia...coastal Texas; **ce
    U.S.** in coastal Virginia and N. Carolina. Winters..."

246 *Pluvialis apricaria*, change range to "...British Isles,
    Scandinavia and n Europe E across n Russia..."

246-247 *Charadrius hiaticula*, change range to "...Faroe Is.,
    Spitsbergen, Bear I. and Scandinavia E through n Russia
    (incl. s Novaya Zemlya) and n Siberia to Chukotski pen.,
    Anadyrland and Sea of Okhotsk, and S to British Isles
    and n Europe (W to n France); w Alaska..."

247 *Charadrius semipalmatus*, before "se Yukon," add "w
    Washington, sc Oregon,"

247 *Charadrius dubius*, change "s England" to "British
    Isles"; delete ", Sumatra and Borneo"

247 *Charadrius wilsonia*, delete "Tobago,"

247 *Charadrius thoracicus*, change English name to
    MADAGASCAR PLOVER (not BLACK-BANDED); change
    range to "Coast of sw **Madagascar** (formerly also se).";
    in comments before "AG" add "(BLACK-BANDED
    PLOVER)."

247 *Charadrius forbesi*, change "Guinea-Bissau" to
    "Senegambia"

248 *Charadrius melodus*, after "e Montana," add "e
    Colorado,"

248 *Charadrius alexandrinus*, change range to "...Java and
    Bali ¶*alexandrinus*..."

248 *Charadrius marginatus*, change range to "**African
    region** from Senegambia, s Mali, se Niger (L. Chad
    region), sw C. African Rep., n Zaire, Uganda, Ethiopia
    and Somalia to s S. Africa; Madagascar."

249 *Charadrius rubricollis*, in comments delete "[>*Thinornis*
    (+N)]."

249 Change name to ***Thinornis novaeseelandiae*** (Gmelin)
    1789."; at beginning of comments add "[<*Charadrius*
    (≈*Oreopholus*)]."

249 *Erythrogonys cinctus*, in comments delete "[<*Charadrius* (≈*Oreopholus*)]."

249 *Eudromias morinellus*, change comments to "(THE DOTTEREL/MOUNTAIN DOTTEREL)."

250 *Pluvianellus socialis*, change comments to "This species is peculiar in many aspects of its morphology and behavior, and almost certainly is not charadriine; it appears to be more closely related to *Chionis* than to any charadriine (Jehl 1975; Strauch 1978). Until biochemical or genetic data are available, *Pluvianellus* is tentatively placed in a monotypic family Pluvianellidae in the Superfamily Chionoidea."; sequence under monotypic Family **Pluvianellidae** on p. 243 following Family **Chionidae**

250 *Vanellus crassirostris*, change "e Nigeria," to "L. Chad area,"

250 *Vanellus miles*, after "Victoria" add "and Tasmania"

251 *Vanellus spinosus*, change beginning of range to "**Sc Palearctic** in Greece, Turkey and Near East; **w,c,ne African region** from s Mauritania and Senegal E..."

251 *Vanellus tectus*, change range to "...**Africa** from Mauritania, Senegambia and Guinea-Bissau...ne Cameroon, n C. African Rep., ne Uganda and Kenya."

251 *Vanellus senegallus*, change beginning of range to "**Africa** from sw Mauritania and Senegambia E to..."

251 *Vanellus lugubris*, after "Sierra Leone" add "and s Mali"

251 *Vanellus melanopterus*, at end of range add "Winters N to s Mozambique."

251 *Vanellus superciliosus*, change range to "**W Africa** from e Ghana e to n Zaire (verified breeding known only from Nigeria). Winters..."

252 *Pluvianus aegyptius*, after "Nile r. basin" add ", at least formerly"

252 *Rhinoptilus africanus*, in heading change "Temminck" to "(Temminck)"

253 *Cursorius temminckii*, change range to "**Africa** from s Mauritania and Senegambia E to..."

253 *Glareola pratincola*, change range to "...s France, Italy, Hungary and Romania S to Sicily,..."

253 *Glareola cinerea*, before "sw,sc,nc Zaire" add "n Angola and"

253 *Stiltia isabella*, change beginning of range to "**Australian region** in s New Guinea, and n,c,int. Australia..."

253 *Catharacta skua*, change range to "...Iceland, Spitsbergen, and Faroe, Shetland, Orkney and Bear is. Ranges...n S. America, Mediterranean region and nw Africa."; in comments after "*C. skua*" add "(e.g., Devillers 1978)"

254 *Catharacta antarctica*, change comments to "(FALKLAND/SUBANTARCTIC SKUA). See *C. skua*."

254 *Stercorarius pomarinus*, change range to "...w Greenland; and n Russia (incl. Novaya Zemlya) and n Siberia..."

254 *Stercorarius parasiticus*, after "Iceland," add "Faroe Is.,"

254 *Stercorarius longicaudus*, change beginning of range to "**N Palearctic** from Greenland, Spitsbergen and n Scandinavia E..."

254 *Rynchops niger*, change range to "...coasts) from c Calif., Sonora..."

255 *Larus atlanticus*, in heading change "1958" to "(1958)"

255 *Larus canus*, change range to "**Eurasia** from Iceland, Faroe Is.,...n Europe (to n France, Switzerland, Austria and Poland), c Russia,..."

255 *Larus audouinii*, after "Spain," add "Italy,"; before "Cyclades," add "Balearic Is.,"

255 *Larus delawarensis*, change "nc Calif." to "c Calif."

256 *Larus marinus*, change "n Quebec" to "w,n Quebec"

256 *Larus dominicanus*, change range to "...coasts of **s African region** N to... Natal); sw,s Madagascar; coasts of **sw,se Australia**..."

256 *Larus glaucescens*, change range to "...s,se Alaska S to e Washington and nw Oregon..."

256 *Larus hyperboreus*, before "Prince Patrick," add "Banks,"

256 *Larus glaucoides*, change range to "...Greenland and (formerly) Jan Mayen...Winters (¶*glaucoides*) in Iceland, rarely S to n Europe and (probably) ne Canada; (¶*kumlieni*) to..."

256 *Larus argentatus*, change range to "**N Europe** from Iceland...n Russia to Kanin pen., and in **n,c,e N. America**...to ne S. Carolina, with isolated breeding in s Texas and s Alabama ¶*argentatus*, HERRING GULL [51]; **n Russia and nw Siberia** from Kanin pen. E to w Taimyr pen. ¶*heuglini* Bree 1876, HEUGLIN'S GULL [2253.2]; **n Siberia** from e Taimyr pen. E to Chukotski pen., Anadyrland and Koryakland ¶*vegae* Palmén 1887, VEGA GULL [52]. Winters (¶*argentatus*) S to c Europe, Panama and s Lesser Antilles; (¶*heuglini*) S to Mediterranean region (rarely e,se Africa) and s Asia E to India; and (¶*vegae*) S to s China, Japan, Bonin Is., w Alaska and Aleutian Is."; at beginning of comments add "Status of *heuglini* and *vegae* uncertain. Both groups hybridize or intergrade with each other and with *L. argentatus;* they are sometimes considered a single species *L. heuglini* distinct from *L. argentatus* (e.g., Stepanyan 1990c). The form *heuglini* is also sometimes treated as a group or race of *L. fuscus*."

257 *Larus cachinnans*, remove from superspecies and sequence after *L. schistisagus;* change range to "**E Atlantic Is.** (...), questionably also sw Europe (Iberian pen.) ¶*atlantis* Dwight 1922, ATLANTIC ISLANDS GULL [2254.1]; **s Palearctic** on Atlantic coast of w France, and from Mediterranean...Heilungkiang) ¶*cachinnans*, YELLOW-LEGGED GULL [2254]. Winters (¶*cachinnans*) S to ne Africa and Persian Gulf."; change comments to "...and displays; there is a 250 km overlap in the breeding ranges along the coast of France (Marion et al. 1985), and the two species have been reported to breed sympatrically (Yésou 1991). Relationships of *L. cachinnans* may be with *L. fuscus* rather than *L. argentatus* (Yésou 1991). The group *atlantis* may also represent a distinct species; the Iberian population is of uncertain relationships and is tentatively assigned to *atlantis* (Yésou 1991). [=*L. michahellis*..."

257 *Larus fuscus*, change range to "**Nw Europe** in Iceland, Faroe Is., British Isles and w Europe (from Iberian pen. and France E to w Germany) ¶*graellsi* Brehm 1858, DARK-BACKED GULL [50]; **cn Eurasia** from n Scandinavia, n Russia and nw Siberia E to Taimyr pen., and S to coasts of North and Baltic seas (W to Denmark) ¶*fuscus*, LESSER BLACK-BACKED GULL [2254.2]. Winters (¶*graellsi*) S to w Mediterranean and w Africa, and in e N. America from Great Lakes and Labrador S to Florida; and (¶*fuscus*) from e Mediterranean, Baltic and Caspian seas S to e,s Africa and Persian Gulf."; change end of comments to "...See *L. dominicanus, L. argentatus* and *L. cachinnans*."

257 *Larus cirrocephalus*, before "Gambia" add "sw Mauritania,"

258 *Larus genei*, in heading change "1839" to "1840"; after "Sardinia," add "n Italy,"

258 *Larus melanocephalus*, change "Yugoslavia" to "s France, Italy"

258 *Larus relictus*, change range to "Steppe, 300-1500 m, of c Asia in s S.S.R. (L. Alakol and L. Balkhash in se Kazakhstan), Mongolia (L. Orog, probably elsewhere), cs Siberia (...) and nc China (Inner Mongolia). Recorded in migration and winter from n,ce,se China, Korea, Japan and Vietnam."; change comments to "Formerly treated as a race...Kitson 1980); Duff, Bakewell and Williams (1991) presented an extensive summary of its status, including all known records. (LONNBERG'S GULL)."

258 *Larus atricilla*, change "se U.S." to "s,e U.S."; delete "and Trinidad"

258 *Larus minutus*, change range to "...n Michigan, s Ontario and s Quebec. Winters..."

259 *Rissa tridactyla*, change range to "...British Isles, w,n Europe (S to Portugal), coastal nw Russia...Dixon Harbor); from Banks, e Somerset, Prince Leopold,...n,c Baffin I., Labrador..."

259 *Sterna nilotica*, change range to "...nw Africa (Senegal, Mauritania, Tunisia),...Ceylon); **Australia; sw Nearctic**...Indonesia, Philippines and New Guinea, and in Americas..."

259 *Sterna caspia*, change range to "Locally in **African region** in w,n,s Africa (Mauritania, Senegambia, Guinea-Bissau, Tunisia, Namibia, S. Africa); Madagascar; **Eurasia**..."

259 *Sterna maxima*, change "Maryland" to "New Jersey"; after "Mauritania" add ", Senegambia"

260 *Sterna bernsteini*, delete ", Halmahera"

260 *Sterna sandvicensis*, after "India" add ","

260 *Sterna dougallii*, change range to "...Madeira, Canary Is.); along coasts...s S. Africa; Madagascar; **s Asia**...W. Indies S to Indonesia and n S. America."

260 *Sterna hirundo*, change "Iranf," to "Iran,"; change "N. Carolina" to "S. Carolina"

261 *Sterna paradisaea*, change range to "...Iceland, Faroe Is., British Isles, Jan Mayen, Spitsbergen, Bear I., Franz Josef Land, n Europe (W to France) and s Scandinavia E across n Russia (incl. Novaya Zemlya) and n Siberia..."

261 *Sterna forsteri*, after "s New York" add "and s Massachusetts"

261 *Sterna antillarum*, change "s S. Dakota," to "sc N. Dakota"

261 *Sterna superciliaris*, delete "Tobago and"

262 *Sterna aleutica*, change comments to "The correct specific name is *Sterna aleutica*, not *S. camtschatica* Pallas 1811 (Stepanyan 1990a). [>*Onychoprion*..."

262 *Sterna anaethetus*, change range to "...Taiwan, ec Philippines (Maturin) and Palau...W. Indies, and off Yucatán pen., Belize...w India S to Kenya, w Madagascar, Seychelles..."

262 *Sterna fuscata*, before "Mascarene," add "Madagascar,"

262 *Chlidonias hybridus*, change range to "...**e,s African region** from Kenya...prov.); Madagascar;...s Asia and Philippines S to Ceylon,..."

263 *Chlidonias niger*, change "Iceland" to "s Sweden"

263 *Anous stolidus*, after "Belize," add "I. San Andrés,"

263 *Anous minutus*, after "St. Helena," add "Gulf of Guinea"

263 *Procelsterna cerulea*, delete superspecies; change range to "...San Ambrosia ¶*cerulea*, BLUE NODDY [79.2]; **sw Pacific O.** on Lord Howe, Norfolk and Kermadec is., and Tonga ¶*albivitta* Bonaparte 1856, GREY NODDY [8125.1]. Winters at sea..."; change comments to "...1983b). There does not appear to be any evidence that the two groups are specifically distinct (H. D. Pratt, pers. comm.). [<*Anous*]. AG: TERNLET."

263 Delete *Procelsterna albivitta* entry

263 *Gygis alba*, change range to "**Seychelles**, and is in...Oahu) is. S to Bismarck Arch. (Wuvulu, Ninigo, Tench), Nuguria Is., Norfolk I...Sala-y-Gómez is. ¶*candida*"

263 *Gygis microrhyncha*, change range to "...**Pacific O.** in S. China Sea (Paracel Is.), and in Line,..."

264 *Alle alle*, after "N. Atlantic S" add "(rarely)"

264 *Uria aalge*, after "British Isles," add "Iberian pen.,"

264 *Uria lomvia*, after "Franz Josef Land," add "n Norway,"

264 *Alca torda*, after "British Isles," add "Bear I.,"

264 *Cepphus grylle*, change range to "...Iceland, Faroe Is., British Isles, Scandinavia, Jan Mayen, Spitsbergen, Bear I., Franz Josef Land and Estonia..."

264 *Brachyramphus marmoratus*, one paragraph, not two; after "Barren Is.)" add ", w Washington"

265 *Ptychoramphus aleuticus*, before "Asunción" add "incl."

266 *Fratecula cirrhata*, before "from Diomede" add "**nw N. America**"

266 *Pandion haliaetus*, after "s Iberian pen.," add "Balearic Is., Corsica,"

266 *Aviceda jerdoni*, after "s Asia" add "**and Malay Arch.**"

267 *Henicopernis longicauda*, change end of range to "...(incl. Biak and Yapen is.)."

267 *Henicopernis infuscatus*, change range to "**Cs Bismarck Arch.** (New Britain)."

267 *Pernis apivorus*, habitat and range in one paragraph

267 *Pernis ptilorhyncus*, change range to "...Cebu, Negros, Mindanao, Basilan) ¶*philippensis*..."; change comments to "...Amadon and Bull (1988: 307) and Stepanyan (1990c) retained *P. ptilorhyncus* as an allospecies..."

267 *Pernis celebensis*, change end of range to "...and Philippines."

268 *Macheiramphus alcinus*, before "**New Guinea**" add "**se**"

268 *Gampsonyx swainsonii*, change end of range to "...Paraguay and n Argentina (Jujuy, Salta, Tucumán, Misiones)."

268 *Elanus axillaris*, change comments to "...according to Schodde and Mason (1980: 12). [=*E. notatus*..."

268 *Elanus leucurus*, change range to "...**w N. America** from sw Washington S to nw Baja Calif.;...S. Carolina S to s Florida;...**n S. America** from se Kansas, s Oklahoma,..."

268 *Chelictinia riocourii*, at beginning of comments add "[<*Elanus*]."

268 *Rostrhamus sociabilis*, change "**Cuba**" to "Cuba"

269 *Harpagus bidentatus*, before "Oaxaca" add "Guerrero,"

269 *Ictinia mississippiensis*, delete comments

269 *Ictinia plumbea*, delete comments

269 *Milvus migrans*, change range to "**Old World** (except African and e Asian regions) from cont. Europe... Australia (except s) ¶*migrans*, BLACK KITE [2076]; widely in **African region** in Nile v., Red Sea area, s Arabia, and from s Mauritania...Somalia, and S (incl. São

Tomé) to s S. Africa, also lowlands to 2000 m. of Madagascar (incl. Comoro Is.) ¶*aegyptius* Gmelin 1788, YELLOW-BILLED KITE [6038.1]. Winters (¶*migrans*) from s Eurasia...s Australia; and (¶*aegyptius*) throughout most of the African region."

270 *Haliaeetus sanfordi*, change English name to SANFORD'S FISH-EAGLE (not SOLOMON); change end of comments to "...pers. comm.); treated as a species by Coates (1985: 117). (SOLOMON FISH-EAGLE)."

271 *Gypaetus barbatus*, change range to "...**and s Asia** in sw France, Spain, nw Africa (Atlas Mts.), Corsica, and from e Mediterranean..."

271 *Neophron percnopterus*, after "s Niger," add "n Nigeria,"

271 *Necrosyrtes monachus*, after "Somalia, and S" add "(except forested w,c and desert sw)"

272 *Aegypius monachus*, change range to "...s Yugoslavia, Romania and Greece (formerly...Sicily, and N to Poland) E through..."

272 *Torgos tracheliotus*, change range to "**African region** from Senegambia E through sw Mali, c,s Niger, L. Chad area...(Israel, nearly extirpated)."

272 *Circaetus gallicus*, change range to "...(Nile delta), ne Arabia (Oman), Iran,...**subsaharan Africa** in Senegambia, sw Mali, Guinea-Bissau, Ivory Coast, Nigeria, s Chad,..."

273 *Circaetus pectoralis*, after "s,e Zaire," add "C. African Rep."

273 *Circaetus cinerascens*, before "s Niger," add "sw Mali,"

273 *Spilornis cheela*, change range to "...Hainan) and Taiwan S through se Asia...cw Philippines (Calamian Is., Palawan, Balabac) ¶*cheela*, CRESTED SERPENT-EAGLE [2093]; **sw Ryukyu Is.** (Iriomote, Ishigaki) ¶*perplexus* Swann 1922, RYUKYU SERPENT-EAGLE [2093.3]; **Simeulue**..."

273 *Spilornis rufipectus*, in heading change "Sclater 1919" to "Gould 1858"

273 *Spilornis holospilus*, change range to "**Philippines** (except Calamian Is., Palawan and Balabac)."

273 *Eutriorchis astur*, change end of range to "...**ne Madagascar**; rare and in danger of extinction."; change comments to "For a recent report (1990) of this species, see Raxworthy and Colston (1992). (LONG-TAILED SERPENT-EAGLE)."

274 *Circus aeruginosus*, change comments to "...C. aeruginosus and C. spilonotus interbreed in western Siberia...Baker-Gabb 1979), although they are considered conspecific by Stepanyan (1990c). (SWAMP..."

274 *Circus ranivorus*, after "w,sc Kenya" add ", s Ethiopia"

274 *Circus cyaneus*, after "e Austria," add "Hungary,"

275 *Polyboroides typus*, before "s Niger," add "sw Mali,"

275 *Melierax metabates*, after "Arabia, and S" add (except forested w,c)"

275 *Micronisus gabar* (not *Melierax*); change comments to "We follow the analyses of Smeenk and Smeenk-Enserink (1975), Brown, Urban and Newman (1982: 366-368), and Kemp (1986) in recognizing *Micronisus* as a genus distinct from *Melierax*; for a contrary opinion, see Dowsett and Dowsett-Lemaire (1980: 154-155) and Colebrook-Robjent (1986). [<*Melierax*]."

276 *Accipiter trivirgatus*, change range to "...Ceylon; E. Ghats in Andhra Pradesh), s China...Java and Philippines."

276 *Accipiter tousenelii*, before "Sierra Leone" add "Gambia, sw Mali,"

276 *Accipiter castanilius*, change range to "**W,c Africa** in s Nigeria, s Cameroon, Rio Muni, Gabon,..."

276 *Accipiter badius*, change range to "...**s Asia** in s S.S.R. (N to Aral Sea and Kazakhstan), n Iran..."

276 *Accipiter trinotatus*, at end of comments add "AG: SPARROWHAWK."

277 *Accipiter rufitorques*, in heading change "(Leale)" to "(Peale)"

277 *Accipiter luteoschistaceus*, before "New Britain" add "Umboi,"; in comments after "BLUE-AND-GREY" add "/SLATY-BACKED"

277 *Accipiter poliocephalus*, before "w Papuan" add "Aru and"

277 *Accipiter superciliosus*, in heading change "1758" to "1766"

277 *Accipiter erythropus*, change range to "**W,c Africa** from Senegambia, sw Mali, Guinea-Bissau and Sierra Leone E to s Cameroon, sw C. African Rep. and n,ne Zaire,..."

278 *Accipiter virgatus*, before "se Asia" add "Andaman and Nicobar is. and"

278 *Accipiter nisus*, change end of range to "...n,ne Africa and s Asia."

279 *Accipiter chionogaster*, at end of range add "."

279 *Accipiter gundlachi*, delete "Lowlands of"

279 *Accipiter bicolor*, change "Veracruz," to "s Tamaulipas"

279 *Accipiter melanoleucus*, after "s Cameroon," add "C. African Rep.,"

279 *Accipiter gentilis*, in heading after "(Linnaeus)" add "1758"; in range after "Turkey," add "n Iran,"

280 *Accipiter meyerianus*, before "New Britain," add "Umboi,"

281 *Leucopternis albicollis*, after "Valle;" add space

281 *Buteogallus urubitinga*, after "Santa Fe" add ", Buenos Aires"

282 *Geranoaetus melanoleucus*, after "Santa Cruz," add "Oruro,"

282 *Harpyhaliaetus solitarius*, change range to "...Oaxaca, Chiapas, Guatemala, Belize (unverified), Honduras,...e,c Peru, n,c Bolivia (Beni, La Paz,..."

283 *Buteo leucorrhous*, before "n Argentina" add "Paraguay,"

283 *Buteo swainsoni*, after "c,s Texas" add ", c Arkansas"

283 *Buteo polyosoma*, change ***Buteo polyosoma*** to ***Buteo [albicaudatus] polyosoma***; change comments to "*B. polyosoma* and *B. poecilochrous* are better treated as part of the *B. [albicaudatus]* superspecies, as suggested by D. Amadon, in Peters (1979a: 367, footnote); these two and *B. albicaudatus* are largely separate altitudinally, with at most marginal overlap between *albicaudatus* and *polyosoma* in Colombia and Argentina (C. C. Farquhar, pers. comm.). See *B. poecilochrous*."

284 *Buteo poecilochrous*, change ***Buteo poecilochrous*** to ***Buteo [albicaudatus] poecilochrous***

284 *Buteo solitarius*, add comments "(THE IO)."

284 *Buteo oreophilus*, change range to "...Burundi, Tanzania and Malawi; **s Africa**..."

284 *Buteo rufinus*, after "Greece," add "Bulgaria,"

285 *Buteo hemilasius*, delete "Japan,"

285 *Buteo regalis*, delete "(probably)"

285 *Buteo auguralis*, change range to "**N,wc Africa** from sw Mauritania, Senegambia, sw Mali and Sierra Leone..."

286 *Aquila rapax*, change account to the following:

Aquila rapax (Temminck) 1828. TAWNY EAGLE. [2111.]
Desert, savanna, bushveld. Locally in **African region** in Morocco, n Algeria, and locally from sw Mauritania and Senegambia E through s Mali, c,s Niger, s Chad and c,s Sudan to Ethiopia, Somalia and s Arabia, and S (except forested w,c) to S. Africa ¶*rapax*, AFRICAN TAWNY-EAGLE [2111]; locally **s Asia** in se Iran, Pakistan and India (except Assam, but incl. Ceylon) ¶*vindhiana* Franklin 1831, ASIAN TAWNY-EAGLE [2111.2].
Although A. C. Kemp (pers. comm.) stated that *vindhiana* differed from *rapax* in morphology, habitat and feeding behavior, morphological and habitat differences are slight and largely bridged by individual variation, and behavior of *vindhiana* is insufficiently studied to warrant treatment of the two groups as species (W. S. Clark, pers. comm.). [>*Psammoaetus* (+N)]. See *A. nipalensis*.''

286 Delete *Aquila vindhiana* account
286 *Aquila nipalensis*, delete superspecies; change range to "Locally in **wc Eurasia** from Romania E to sw,sc Russia (from Ukraine E to upper Irtysh r., and S to Caucasus, Caspian-Aral seas and Kirghiz steppes) ¶*orientalis* Cabanis 1854, WESTERN STEPPE-EAGLE [2111.3]; **c Asia** in ce Russia (Altai), Mongolia, w China (Sinkiang) and sw Siberia (sw Transbaicalia) ¶*nipalensis*, EASTERN STEPPE-EAGLE [2111.1]. Winters (¶*orientalis*) SW to Near and Middle East, Arabia and e (rarely s) Africa; and (¶*nipalensis*) from s Russia, Afghanistan, Pakistan and India E to Burma and se China."; change end of comments to "...treated *rapax* and *nipalensis* as distinct species, although Stepanyan (1990c) considered them conspecific. W. S. Clark (pers. comm.), based on extensive study of both living eagles and specimens, believes they are not closely related and therefore not allospecies. [=*A. orientalis* Cabanis 1854]."
286 *Aquila wahlbergi*, sequence after *A. verreauxii*, p. 287; change comments to "There is controversy over the placement of *wahlbergi* in *Aquila* or in *Hieraaetus* (Debus 1986, Amadon 1987, Auburn 1988). [>*Afraetus*; ≠*Hieraaetus*]."
286 *Aquila chrysaetos*, change "Kanchatka" to "Kamchatka"
287 *Aquila verreauxii*, before "se Zaire," add "n C. African Rep.,"
287 *Hieraaetus pennatus*, add comments "See *H. ayresii*."
287 *Hieraaetus spilogaster*, change range to "...Ivory Coast, Burkina Faso, Ghana...Somalia S (except forested w,c) to sc Namibia,..."
287 *Hieraaetus ayresii*, change comments to "*H. dubius* (Smith) 1830 pertains to *H. pennatus*, according to Brooke and Vernon (1981). [>*Anomalaetus*]."
287 *Hieraaetus kienerii*, after "Luzon," add "Mindoro,"
287 *Polemaetus bellicosus*, before "Nigeria," add "sw Mali,"
287 *Spizastur melanoleucus*, change range to "...**Neotropical** from Nayarit, Oaxaca,...(Loreto), n,e Bolivia (...) and Paraguay to n Argentina (...)."
*287 **Lophaetus** (not *Lophoaetus*); also change spelling in comments under *L. occipitalis*
288 *Spizaetus philippensis*, after "Siquijor," add "Mindanao,"
288 *Spizaetus ornatus*, change range to "...from Colima, Hidalgo and Tamaulipas S to Panama..."
288 *Stephanoaetus coronatus*, after "s Cameroon," add "sw C. African Rep.,"; in comments change "*Lophoaetus*" to "*Lophaetus*

288 *Oroaetus isidori*, after "Cochabamba" add ", w Santa Cruz"; in comments change "*Lophoaetus*" to "*Lophaetus*"
288 *Sagittarius serpentarius*, change English name to SECRETARYBIRD (not SECRETARY-BIRD)
289 *Phalcobaenus australis*, change end of range to "...Staten is.), also Falkland Is."
290 *Micrastur ruficollis*, change "Puebla" to "Hidalgo"
290 *Micrastur gilvicollis*, change comments to "...but Schwartz (1972) gave..."
290 *Micrastur semitorquatus*, after "Tarija)" add ", Paraguay"
290 *Spiziapteryx circumcinctus*, at beginning of comments add "*Spiziapteryx* is not related to the other 'falconets' but appears to be closest to the caracaras (Olson 1976; Becker 1987)."
290 *Polihierax semitorquatus*, before "extreme se Sudan," add "n C. African Rep.,"
291 *Microhierax latifrons*, change range to "**N Borneo** (Sarawak, Sabah)."
291 *Microhierax erythrogenys*, change "Calicaon" to "Calicoan"
291 *Falco newtoni*, change English name to MADAGASCAR KESTREL (not NEWTON'S)
292 *Falco dickinsoni*, change "Palms, savanna." to "Palm savanna."
292 *Falco zoniventris*, change English name to BANDED KESTREL (not BARRED); change comments to "(BARRED/MADAGASCAR BANDED KESTREL)."
292 *Falco vespertinus*, change range to "...Poland, Czechoslovakia, Hungary, Romania and Bulgaria E across c,se Russia..."
292 *Falco amurensis*, after "e,s Africa" add "and se Asia"
292 *Falco femoralis*, after "Sinaloa" add "(at least formerly)"
293 *Falco rufigularis*, in comments change "*rufogularis*" to "*rufigularis*"
293 **Falco cuvierii** (not *cuvieri*); add comments "The original spelling is '*cuvierii*.'"
293 *Falco severus*, in heading change "821" to "1821"
293 *Falco longipennis*, change "(possibly breeding)" to "(probably breeding)"
293 **Falco novaeseelandiae** (not *novaezeelandiae*)
293 *Falco biarmicus*, after "incl. is." add ", formerly sw Spain"
293 *Falco cherrug*, in heading change "1844" to "1834"; change end of comments to "...treatment. Includes *F. altaicus* (Menzbier) 1891, ALTAI FALCON [2126], of the Altai of central Asia, which appears to be a color morph of *F. cherrug* as treated by Amadon and Bull (1988: 329) and Stepanyan (1990c). (THE SAKER)."
294 Delete *Falco altaicus* entry
294 *Falco rusticolus*, change "n Quebec" to "c Quebec"
294 *Falco peregrinus*, change range to "...s Russia, s Siberia, Mongolia, China (except extreme w), Pakistan,...s S. America from Ecuador, Peru, s Chile..."
294 *Falco pelegrinoides*, change range to "Locally in **n African region and s Palearctic** from Morocco and Mauritania E across Algeria, Tunisia, s Niger, Sudan, Egypt (incl. Sinai pen.), n Kenya, n Somalia, Arabia, Near East, Iraq, (probably) w Iran, s S.S.R. and Afghanistan to nw Mongolia, w China (w,s Sinkiang) and w Pakistan. Largely resident, but e populations winter S to s Pakistan and n India."

294 *Rollandia rolland,* change range to "...Oruro, Potosí, Tarija),...CHILEAN GREBE [5030.1]; **Falkland Is.** ¶*rolland,* FALKLAND GREBE [5030]."

295 *Tachybaptus ruficollis,* change "(New Ireland, New Britain)" to "(incl. Admiralty Is.)"; change comments to "AG (≈*T. pelzelnii*): DABCHICK. [<*Poliocephalus* (~*Tachybaptus*)]. (COMMON/RED-THROATED/RED-THROATED LITTLE GREBE/THE DABCHICK). [LITTLE GREBE]. See *T. novaehollandiae* and *T. rufolavatus*."

295 After *Tachybaptus novaehollandiae,* insert:

Tachybaptus rufolavatus (Delacour) 1932. ALAOTRA GREBE. [6001.]
    Lakes, marshes. **Ec Madagascar** (L. Alaotra).
    Confined to L. Alaotra on Madagascar, where it hybridizes intensively with *T. ruficollis,* a recent colonizer; although it is questionable that *rufolavatus* remains a separate taxonomic entity, Langrand (1990: 84-85) reported that the population was estimated at about 20 pairs. (RUSTY/ DELACOUR'S LITTLE/ALAOTRA LITTLE GREBE).

295 *Podilymbus podiceps,* add comments "See *P. gigas*."

295 *Podilymbus gigas,* change range to "Probably extinct (not recorded since 1984); formerly confined to **c Guatemala** (L. Atitlán)."; at beginning of comments add "Hunter (1988) commented on the replacement of *P. gigas* on Lake Atitlán by *P. podiceps*."

295 *Poliocephalus rufopectus,* change "South I." to "North I."

295-296 *Podiceps grisegena,* after "n Montana," add "nw Wyoming,"; change comments to "(HOLBOELL'S/GREY-CHEEKED GREBE)."

296 *Podiceps cristatus,* change range to "...Ethiopia S through Rift v. lakes of nw Rwanda, w Uganda and c Kenya to n Tanzania, occurring elsewhere in Gabon, Angola, Namibia, Zambia,s Mozambique..."

296 *Podiceps nigricollis,* change range to "... c Ethiopia, and Rift v. lakes of c Kenya and n Tanzania;..."

296 *Podiceps andinus,* in heading change "(Meyer de Schauensee) 1959" to "(Meyer de Schauensee 1959)"

296 *Podiceps occipitalis,* before "Cochabamba," add "La Paz,"

296-297 *Aechmophorus occidentalis,* change range to "...nw Iowa, w Minnesota and ec Wisconsin; locally..."; in comments change "nothern" to "northern"

297 *Phaethon aethereus,* change range to "Trop. is. of **w Pacific** in Paracel Is. (S. China Sea); **e Pacific**..."

297 *Phaethon rubricauda,* change range to "Trop. is. of **Pacific O...Indian O.** on is. off sw Madagascar, near Mauritius,..."

297 *Morus bassanus,* change "Van Tets" to "Van Tets et al."

298 *Sula dactylatra,* change range to "...Oahu) S to is. in Sulu Sea (Tubbataha reef), off e Australia...coast of Somalia, se Arabia (off s Oman), and Cocos..."

298 *Sula sula,* change range to "...**Pacific O.** in Paracel Is. (S. China Sea); from Bonin...Moku Manu S to Sulu Sea (Tubbataha reef), ne Australia...(Cocos I.), off Ecuador (I. La Plata), and in Galapagos...**region** off Yucatán (Glover's reef) and Belize...Grenadines, off Tobago, off Venezuela..."

298 *Sula leucogaster,* after "S. China Sea," add "Sulu Sea (Tubbataha reef),"; change "Los Hermanos Is." to "Trinidad"

299 *Phalacrocorax africanus,* change range to "...w,s Somalia S (incl. São Tomé) to s S. Africa;...Wanders irregularly to Zanzibar,..."

299 *Phalacrocorax coronatus,* in heading change "1855" to "1857"

299 ***Phalacrocorax [pygmeus] pygmeus*** (not *pygmaeus*); change "Albania" to "Yugoslavia"; at beginning of comments add "The original spelling is *pygmeus,* not *pygmaeus*."

299 *Phalacrocorax niger,* change spelling of "*pygmaeus*" to "*pygmeus*" in heading and comments; change range to "...Kwangtung) S to se Asia (except Malaya); n Java. Wanders irregularly to Afghanistan, Malaya and Greater Sunda Is."

299 *Phalacrocorax melanoleucos,* change "Galbreath" to "Galbraith"

300 *Phalacrocorax auritus,* change range to "...I. of Pines), formerly off Belize..."

300 *Phalacrocorax carbo,* change range to "...British Isles, Norway and extreme nw Russia (Kola pen.) S to n cont. Europe (...), locally **s Palearctic and s Asia** from n Africa (from Mauritania E to Egypt), Sardinia,...n Philippines (Batan Is., Calayan, Luzon, Ticao), **Australasian region** in Australia...Chatham Is., and **ne N. America**...n Maine ¶*carbo,* GREAT CORMORANT [119]; locally in **African region** in Cape Verde Is., sw Mauritania, L. Chad area, and from s Angola, Namibia, Zambia, ne,ce,se Zaire, Sudan, Ethiopia and s Somalia S to s S. Africa ¶*lucidus* (Lichtenstein) 1823, WHITE-BREASTED CORMORANT [6008]. Winters (¶*carbo*) S to Florida, along coasts of Europe and Mediterranean (S to n Africa, possibly resident in Tunisia), and in s Asia, wandering irregularly to New Guinea, and Lord Howe, Norfolk, Macquarie, and Snares and Campbell is.; ranges (¶*lucidus*) widely in Africa S of Sahara."; change comments to "Eastern African populations were thought to represent two species (Williams 1966b), but one polymorphic species appears to exist there (Urban and Jefford 1974). Siegel-Causey (1988)..."

300 Delete *Phalacrocorax lucidus* entry

301 *Phalacrocorax nigrogularis,* change range to "Is. in **n Indian O.** in Persian Gulf, along se coast of Arabia, and on Socotra I..."

301 *Phalacrocorax georgianus,* in heading change "King 1828" to "Lönnberg 1906"

301 *Phalacrocorax campbelli,* change English name to CAMPBELL ISLAND SHAG (not CAMPBELL SHAG); in comments delete "ISLAND"

301 *Phalacrocorax onslowi,* change English name to CHATHAM ISLANDS SHAG (not CHATHAM SHAG); in comments delete "ISLANDS"

301 *Phalacrocorax colensoi,* change English name to AUCKLAND ISLANDS SHAG (not AUCKLAND SHAG); in comments delete "ISLANDS"

301 *Phalacrocorax ranfurlyi,* change English name to BOUNTY ISLANDS SHAG (not BOUNTY SHAG); in comments delete "ISLANDS"

302 *Phalacrocorax urile,* change comments to "Includes *Stictocarbo kenyoni* Siegel-Causey (1991: 5), described from recent and subfossil skeletal material from Amchitka Island, in the Aleutian Islands; further assessment of the validity of this form must await collection of additional material. [>*Urile* (+N)]."

302 *Phalacrocorax punctatus,* after "w South I." add ", Stewart I."

302 *Phalacrocorax featherstoni,* change English name to PITT ISLAND SHAG (not PITT SHAG); in comments delete "ISLAND"

302 *Egretta vinaceigula,* in comments after "Irwin (1975)" remove "."

302 *Egretta ardesiaca,* change range to "Locally in **African region** in Senegambia, Guinea-Bissau, s Mali, s Ghana, s Niger, Nigeria, s Somalia,...Cape prov.); Madagascar. Ranges..."

303 *Egretta novaehollandiae,* after "Tasmania," add "s New Guinea,"

303 *Egretta caerulea,* after "se New Mexico," add "e Colorado,"

303 *Egretta garzetta,* in heading change "1758" to "1766"; change range to "...c France, Italy and Czechoslovakia), nw Africa...c Honshu), and S through Andaman and Nicobar is. and se Asia..."

303 *Egretta gularis,* change "Senegal," to "Senegambia,"

303 *Egretta dimorpha,* change English name to DIMORPHIC EGRET (not MASCARENE REEF-EGRET); change end of comments to "(MADAGASCAR/MASCARENE REEF-EGRET/MADAGASCAR EGRET)."

304 *Ardea cinerea,* change range to "...Taiwan, and **c,e,s African region** in Ghana and s Nigeria (presumably this group), and from Angola,...Ethiopia S to S. Africa, also Aldabra Is. and Madagascar ¶*cinerea,* GREY HERON [195]; **w Africa** in sw Mauritania and Senegal, perhaps elsewhere in w Africa ¶*monicae* Jouanin and Roux 1963, MAURITANIAN HERON [6012.1]. Winters (¶*cinerea*) from w,s Europe..."; at beginning of comments add "Erard, Guillou and Mayaud (1986) recognized *A. monicae* as a species because of lack of interbreeding with *A. cinerea.*"

304 *Ardea humbloti,* change English name to HUMBLOT'S HERON (not MADAGASCAR); change "**e Madagascar**" to "**w,s Madagascar**"; at end of comments add "(MADAGASCAR HERON)."

304 *Ardea goliath,* change range to "Locally in **African region** in Gambia, Guinea-Bissau, Ghana, and from C. African Rep., se Egypt, coastal Ethiopia, nw,s Somalia and sw Arabia..."

305 *Ardea sumatrana,* after "Basilan" add ", Sulu Arch."

305 *Ardea purpurea,* change range to "...cont. Europe (N to France, Netherlands, Germany and Poland) E across s Russia...n Morocco E to Algeria), n Mediterranean... Andaman and Nicobar is., se Asia,...Senegal, Mali and nw Zaire;...Lesser Sunda Is. ¶*purpurea,* PURPLE HERON..."

305 *Ardea picata,* change range to "...Tanimbar Is., and n Australia...Moluccas, E to New Guinea, and S to c Australia."; change comments to "...[≠*Egretta/Hydranassa;* >*Tonophoyx/Notophoyx*]. (LITTLE PIED HERON). AG: EGRET."

305 *Casmerodius albus,* change range to "...Okarito), locally in Africa from s Mauritania, s Mali, se Niger, C. African Rep., n Ethiopia...e,s Africa, and in lowlands to 800 m of Comoro Is. (Mohéli) and Madagascar ¶*albus,* GREAT EGRET [2034.1]; locally in lowlands to 2600 m of **Americas** from s Oregon,...s Ontario, New York and New England...(Santa Cruz) ¶*egretta* (Gmelin) 1789, AMERICAN EGRET [196]. Winters (¶*albus*) from Mediterranean region, se Europe, s Asia and Philippines S through Africa and Australasian region; and (¶*egretta*) from s U.S. S through Americas."; in comments after "Curry-Lindahl (1971: 66)." add "Behavioral data and coloration of bill in breeding season suggest possible species status of the two groups (Hancock and Elliott 1978), supported by DNA-DNA hybridization data (Sheldon 1987: 100)."

305 *Mesophoyx intermedia,* change range to "Locally in **Africa** S of Sahara in Senegambia, s Mali, L. Chad area and C. African Rep., and from nw Ethiopia...s,e Cape prov.) ¶*brachyrhyncha* (Brehm) 1854, YELLOW-BILLED EGRET [6013.1]; lowlands to 1400 m...Shikoku) S through Andaman and Nicobar is. and se Asia to E. Indies (Sumatra, Java, Sulawesi, possibly vagrants only elsewhere) ¶*intermedia,* LESSER EGRET [2034]; **Australasian region** in New Guinea (possibly), and in n,e,se Australia...se S. Australia ¶*plumifera* (Gould) 1848, PLUMED EGRET [8030.1]. Ranges in winter (¶*brachyrhyncha*) throughout Africa S of Sahara; (¶*intermedia*) in w Pacific to Philippines, rarely to w Micronesia; and (¶*plumifera*) rarely to Tasmania."; change comments to "Although subspecies are often unrecognized in recent literature, the three groups are widely allopatric as well as distinct morphologically with respect to color of soft parts, especially about the bill and head (J. Hancock, pers. comm.); such characteristics suggest possible isolating mechanisms, and it seems best to retain the forms as separate groups. [<*Egretta* (+N); <*Casmerodius*]. (PLUMED / LESSER / YELLOW-BILLED/SMALLER EGRET). See *Casmerodius albus.*"

305-306 *Bubulcus ibis,* in heading after "(Linnaeus)" add "1758"; change range to "...Ethiopia and s Somalia, and S to s S. Africa..."; in comments change "*C. albus*" to "*Casmerodius albus*"

306 *Ardeola ralloides,* change range to "...Yugoslavia, Czechoslovakia and Romania S...s Mali, Ghana, Nigeria,..."

306 *Ardeola idae,* delete ", possibly Mafia I. off Tanzania"; change end of comments to "...(POND/MADAGASCAR SQUACCO HERON/MALAGASY POND-HERON)."

307 *Butorides virescens,* change end of comments to "...present knowledge, *B. striatus* and *B. virescens* are better treated as allospecies (Monroe and Browning 1992). (LITTLE GREEN HERON). See *B. striatus.*"

307 *Butorides sundevalli,* at beginning of comments add "(PLUMBEOUS HERON)."

307 *Agamia agami,* before "Veracruz," add "Nuevo León,"

307 *Nycticorax nycticorax,* change range to "...Germany and Poland) E across...Middle East, Andaman and Nicobar is., se Asia,...Senegal, Liberia, Ivory Coast, Ghana, n Nigeria, nw Angola,..."

307-308 *Gorsachius leuconotus,* change beginning of range to "Locally in **w,e,s Africa** in Gambia, Liberia, Ivory Coast, Ghana, Nigeria,..."

308 *Cochlearius cochlearia* (not *Cochlearius cochlearius*); change range to "...NORTHERN BOAT-BILLED HERON [1017.1]; lowlands...Paulo) to e Paraguay and n Argentina...Rios) ¶*cochlearia,* SOUTHERN BOAT-BILLED HERON [1017]."; at end of comments add "The original description was *Cancroma Cochlearia,* indicating a specific name that is a noun in apposition and therefore does not change ending."

308 *Tigrisoma fasciatum,* before "Rio de Janeiro" add "c Goiás and"

308 *Zonerodius heliosylus,* in comments after "BITTERN" add "/NEW GUINEA TIGER-HERON"

309 *Zebrilus undulatus,* before "e Peru," add "e Ecuador,"

309 *Ixobrychus minutus,* change range to "...(Sind), n India (...) and w China (w Sinkiang); locally in..."

309 *Ixobrychus novaezelandiae,* in comments after "/NEW ZEALAND BITTERN" add "/BROWN-BACKED LITTLE-BITTERN"

309 *Ixobrychus exilis*, change range to "...**w N. America** from s Oregon,...Sonora S to Guerrero; **c,e N**...s Quebec, Maine, New Brunswick and Nova Scotia S to Utah..."

310 *Ixobrychus sturmii*, change range to "...**w,e,s Africa** in Senegambia, Liberia, Ivory Coast, Ghana,..."

310 Change *Ixobrychus flavicollis* to *Dupetor flavicollis*; change range to "...Philippines (Batan Is., Luzon, Mindoro, Marinduque,...Cebu, Siargao, Mindanao),..."; in comments change "[>*Dupetor*]." to "[<*Ixobrychus*]."

310 *Botaurus pinnatus*, change range to "lowlands to 2600 m...Tabasco, Yucatán pen.), Belize,..."

310 *Botaurus stellaris*, change "(n Morocco)" to "(from n Morocco E to Tunisia)"

310-311 *Phoenicopterus ruber*, change "**e,s Africa**"to "**w,e,s Africa**"; change "**Madagascar**" to "**w,s Madagascar**"

311 *Phoenicopterus minor*, after "(mostly e,s)" add "and Madagascar."

311-312 *Plegadis falcinellus*, change range to "Locally distributed: **s Palearctic and s Asia** from s Europe (Austria, Italy, Balkan states, Greece, formerly Iberian pen. and se France) and nw Africa (Morocco, Algeria) E across Turkey, Near East, s Russia... Balkhash), nw Mongolia, Pakistan (Sind),...Mindanao); **w,e,s African region** in s Mali,...ne S. Africa; Madagascar; **n,e,s Australia**...Philippines and New Guinea, and S to..."

313 *Bostrychia olivacea*, after "Gabon" add ", sw C. African Rep."

313 *Bostrychia rara*, change range to "...Cameroon, sw C. African Rep., n,ne Zaire and w Uganda, and S to..."

313 *Geronticus eremita*, after "Morocco" add "and n Algeria"; after "bred" delete "n Algeria,"

313 *Threskiornis aethiopicus*, change range to "...s S. Africa, also **se Iraq** ¶*aethiopicus*, SACRED IBIS [2045]; **Madagascar** (incl. Aldabra Is.) ¶*bernieri* (Bonaparte) 1855, MADAGASCAR IBIS [6020.1]."; change comments to "... following two species, but Snow (1978: 37) and Lowe and Richards (1991) treated this complex as a superspecies; Langrand (1990: 115) and Lowe and Richards also considered *bernieri* a race of *T. aethiopicus*. [SACRED IBIS]."

314 *Nipponia nippon*, change range to "Nearly extinct; **c China** (s Shensi). Formerly bred..."

314 *Platalea regia*, change range to "...w S. Australia), s New Zealand (...) and s Solomon Is. (Rennell). Winters..."

314 *Platalea alba*, change range to "Locally in **African region** from Senegambia, Guinea-Bissau, Sierra Leone and s Mali E to Ethiopia and s Somalia, and S (except for forested wc) to S. Africa; w Madagascar."

314 *Ajaia ajaja*, after "La Paz," add "Cochabamba,"

314 *Pelecanus onocrotalus*, change range to "...**s Asia** in Romania (formerly to Yugoslavia, Hungary and Bulgaria), Greece,...Tanzania, Zambia, Namibia, Botswana and S. Africa. Winters..."

314 *Pelecanus rufescens*, change range to "...Uganda, Kenya and s Somalia S through Tanzania,...Madagascar (formerly), Amirante I. (in Seychelles). Winters..."

315 *Pelecanus erythrorhynchos*, after "se Texas" add "; Durango"

315 *Coragyps atratus*, in heading change "1783" to "1793"

315 *Cathartes aura*, change "c New England" to "New England"; before "Cuba," add "n Bahamas,"

315 *Cathartes burrovianus*, after "Belize," add "Guatemala (Petén),"; after "Beni," add "La Paz,"

316 *Vultur gryphus*, change beginning of range to "Mts., 1500-5200 m,...w Venezuela (Perijá Mts., w Mérida) S through Andes of Ecuador, Peru..."

316 *Sarcoramphus papa*, after "Venezuela" add ", Trinidad"

316 *Mycteria americana*, before "Paraguay," add "n Chile (Tarapacá),"

316 *Mycteria ibis*, change range to "**African region** from sw Mauritania...Natal); w Madagascar**."

316 *Anastomus lamelligerus*, change "**Madagascar**" to "**w Madagascar**"

316 *Ciconia nigra*, after "Greece" add ", formerly N to Denmark and Sweden"

317 *Ciconia episcopus*, before "Sierra Leone," add "sw Mali,"

317 *Ciconia stormi*, change "**w Greater Sunda Is.**" to "**se Asia**"

317 *Ciconia ciconia*, change range to "...w Russia and Austria, formerly s Sweden...nw Heilungkiang); sporadically in **e,s Africa** in Kenya, s Zambia...Zimbabwe and S. Africa. Winters..."

317 *Ciconia boyciana*, in comments after "*C. ciconia*" add ", but Stepanyan (1990c) treated it as a full species."

317 *Ephippiorhynchus senegalensis*, change range to "...n Ivory Coast, Ghana, s Chad, C. African Rep., s Sudan..."

318 *Fregata magnificens*, before "Nayarit" add "Revillagigedo Is. (San Benedicto),"

318 *Fregata ariel*, before "New Caledonia," add "Nuguria Is.,"

318 *Fregata andrewsi*, change English name to CHRISTMAS ISLAND FRIGATEBIRD (not CHRISTMAS FRIGATEBIRD); in comments delete "ISLAND"

318 *Aptenodytes patagonicus*, change range to "**S S. America** in s Chile (Horn I.) and s Argentina (Staten I.); is. in **s oceans** in Macquarie,...Heard is. Ranges..."

318 *Pygoscelis papua*, change range to "**S Argentina** (Staten I.); is., in **s oceans** in Prince Edward,...S. Shetland is., and on Antarctic pen..."

318 *Pygoscelis adeliae*, change range to "Enderby Land); is. in **s oceans** in S. Shetland,..."

319 *Eudyptes robustus*, in heading change "1953" to "(1953)"

319 *Eudyptes chrysolophus*, change "I. Buenaventura" to "I. Desolación, I. Diego Ramírez"

319 *Spheniscus demersus*, change comments to "(CAPE/BLACK-FOOTED PENGUIN)."

320 *Spheniscus magellanicus*, in heading change "[5057.]" to "[5058,]"

320 *Gavia stellata*, after "Iceland," add "Faroe Is.,"

320 *Gavia arctica*, before "Transbaicalia," add "w Mongolia,"

320 *Gavia immer*, change range to "...formerly), Nevada, nw Montana, nw Wyoming, N. Dakota,...Black seas, n Mexico and s U.S."

320 Under Subfamily Procellariinae, change comments to "...*Pterodroma*. Bourne's (1987b) criticisms of generic and specific taxonomy have not been generally accepted, but his sequence of taxa is followed herein."

321 *Pagodroma nivea*, change heading to "***Pagodroma nivea*** (Forster) 1777. SNOW PETREL. [5039.1.]"; change range to "Is. of **s oceans** (S. Georgia...Bouvet, Scott) and coast of **Antarctica** inland to 2000 m. ¶*nivea*, LESSER SNOW-PETREL [5039.1]; **Balleny Is.** and coast of **Antarctica** (Adélie Land) ¶*confusa* Mathews 1912,

GREATER SNOW-PETREL [5039.2]. Ranges at sea (both groups) in Antarctic..."; change comments to "D. I. Rogers, in Marchant and Higgins (1991: 409), reported an extensive zone of hybridization in Antarctica and treated the two groups as conspecific."

321 Delete *Pagodroma confusa*

321 *Pterodroma brevirostris* (not *Lugensa*); change comments to "...unidentifiable. [>*Lugensa*)]. (GREY-FACED PETREL)."

321 *Pterodroma aterrima* (not *Pseudobulweria*); at end of comments add "[>*Pseudobulweria* (≈*P. macgillivrayi*)]."

321 *Pterodroma becki* (not *Pseudobulweria*); in heading change "(Murphy)" to "Murphy"

321 *Pterodroma rostrata* (not *Pseudobulweria*)

321 *Pseudobulweria macgillvrayi*, change heading to "***Pterodroma [rostrata] macgillivrayi*** Gray 1860. FIJI PETREL. [9003.]"; at end of comments add "(MACGILLIVRAY'S PETREL)."

321 *Pterodroma axillaris*, change English name to CHATHAM ISLANDS PETREL (not CHATHAM PETREL); in comments delete "ISLANDS"

321 *Pterodroma nigripennis*, change range to "...Bass Rocks), probably..."

322 *Pterodroma alba*, change "Christmas" to "Kiritimati"

322 Delete *Pterodroma heraldica* entry

322 *Pterodroma arminjoniana*, delete superspecies; change English name to HERALD PETREL (not TRINDADE); change range to "**S Pacific O.** in Chesterfield Reef (Coral Sea), Raine I. (off ne Australia), Tonga (Eau), Cook Is. (Rarotonga), Marquesas (Ua Pu, Tahuata), Tuamotu (incl. Gambier Is.), Pitcairn and Easter is. ¶*heraldica* (Salvin) 1888, HERALD PETREL [98.6]; is. of s **Atlantic O.** (Trindade, Martin Vaz) and s **Indian O.** (Round I. off Mauritius) ¶*arminjoniana*, TRINDADE PETREL (SOUTH TRINIDAD/TRINDADE ISLAND PETREL) [98.2]. Ranges (¶*heraldica*) at sea in s Pacific, rarely N to Hawaiian Is.; (¶*arminjoniana*) in s Atlantic, rarely to n Atlantic."; change comments to "The groups are nearly identical in every respect except for feather-lice, which alone are insufficient grounds for specific separation (Bourne 1987b)."

323 Split *Pterodroma phaeopygia* into the following two species:

Pterodroma [phaeopygia] sandwichensis (Ridgway) 1884. HAWAIIAN PETREL. [98.5]
Pelagic, breeding on islands in burrows at high elevations. Highlands of **Hawaiian Is.** (Kauai, Maui, Hawaii, formerly Oahu). Ranges at sea in Pacific S to Polynesia.

In addition to the wide geographical separation of breeding ranges, *P. sandwichensis* differs from *P. phaeopygia* in vocalizations and morphology to a degree suggesting specific status (Tomkins and Milne 1991). [>*Aestrelata* (≈*P. baraui*)].

Pterodroma [phaeopygia] phaeopygia (Salvin) 1876. GALAPAGOS PETREL. [5041.2]
Pelagic, breeding on islands in burrows at high eleva-tions. **Galapagos Is.** (Isabela, San Salvador, Santa Cruz, Floreana, San Cristóbal). Ranges at sea in e Pacific from Mexico to n Peru.

[DARK-RUMPED/HAWAIIAN PETREL]. See *P. sandwichensis.*

323 *Pterodroma ultima*, change end of range to "...breeding region N. to Hawaiian Is. and off coast of Calif."

323 *Pterodroma feae*, change beginning of range to "**E. Atlantic is.** in Desertas Is. (Bugio), Cape Verde Is. (Santo Antão, São Nicolau, Fogo, São Tiago) and (probably) Azores. Presumably..."; at beginning of comments add "A bird caught in the Azores appears to link *P. feae* with *P. cahow*; the two may be conspecific (Bibby and del Nevo 1991)."

323 *Pterodroma cahow*, at end of comments add "See *P. feae.*"

324 *Halobaena caerulea*, add comments "Bretagnolle (1990) discussed affinities of *Halobaena.*"

324 *Pachyptila salvini*, in comments after "specific status" add ", supported by studies of Bretagnolle, Zotier and Jouventin (1990)"

324 *Pachyptila desolata*, after "Harper (1972)" add "and Bretagnolle, Zotier and Jouventin (1990)"

324 *Bulweria fallax*, in comments change "(1987)" to "(1987a)"

325 *Calonectris diomedea*, change range to "...**Mediterranean Sea** (from Balearic Is., Corsica and Sardinia E to Turkey and Near East, incl. many small islets) ¶*diomedea*, CORY'S SHEARWATER [88]; **Cape Verde Is.** ¶*edwardsii* Oustalet (1883), CAPE VERDE SHEARWATER [2010.4]. Ranges at sea (¶*diomedea*) primarily..."

325 *Puffinus griseus*, change "Guamblin, Guafo" to "Chiloë"

326 *Puffinus tenuirostris*, change "**se Australia**" to "**s Australia**"

326 *Puffinus nativitatis*, change English name to CHRISTMAS ISLAND SHEARWATER (not CHRISTMAS SHEARWATER); in comments delete "ISLAND"

326 *Puffinus puffinus*, after "Madeira," add "Canary Is.,"; after "Bermuda" add "."

326 *Puffinus yelkouan*, change heading to "***Puffinus [puffinus] yelkouan*** (Acerbi) 1827. MEDITERRANEAN SHEARWATER. [2010.2.]"; in comments before "See" add "(YELKOUAN SHEARWATER)."

326 *Puffinus auricularis*, in comments after "species" add "(e.g., Pratt, Bruner and Berrett 1987: 56-57)"

326 *Puffinus lherminieri*, after "**Indian O.**" add "off se Arabia (s Oman), and"

326-327 *Puffinus assimilis*, change range to "...Antipodes and Tubuai (Rapa) is., possibly Chiloé I. off s Chile; **s Indian O.** on St. Paul and (formerly) Amsterdam. Ranges..."

327 *Puffinus heinrothi*, change range to "...collected in **c Bismarck Arch.** (off n New Britain) and **nw Solomon Is.** (Bougainville)."

327 *Pelecanoides magellani*, change "Chila" to "Chile"

327 *Diomedea amsterdamensis*, change heading to "***Diomedea [exulans] amsterdamensis*** Roux, Mougin and Bartles (1983). AMSTERDAM ISLAND ALBATROSS. [6002.1.]"; at end of comments add "(AMSTERDAM ALBATROSS)."

328 *Diomedea cauta*, change range to "...[82.3]; **Crozet, Snares**...1930, CHATHAM ISLANDS ALBATROSS (CHATHAM ALBATROSS) [8008.2]...Ranges at sea in s oceans, occurring (mostly ¶*cauta*) W to S. Africa and E to s S. America."

328 Under Subfamily Hydrobatinae, add comments "There has been a recent trend in some parts of the world to use Oceanitidae. Using strict priority, Thalassidromidae Müller 1865 (based on the type-species *pelagica*, now placed in *Hydrobates*) antedates Oceanitidae Forbes 1882. From a usage standpoint, Hydrobatidae Mathews 1912-13 is the most widely used and one that would qualify as a 'conserved name.' Because under either approach Hydrobatidae is the choice, the Standing Committee on Ornithological Nomenclature of the International Ornithological Congress recommended in its list of accepted family-level names (written by Chair Walter Bock) that Hydrobatidae should be retained, thus Oceanitidae should not be used."

328 *Oceanites oceanicus*, change range to "**S S. America** on islets near Cape Horn; is. of **s oceans** in Falkland,..."

329 *Pelagodroma marina*, before "Cape Verde" add "Canary,"

329 *Fregetta grallaria*, change "Austral " to "Tubuai"

329 *Oceanodroma castro*, after "São Tomé" add ", also Is. Farilhões off c Portugal"

329 *Oceanodroma leucorhoa*, change "Kurile" to "Kuril"; change "Indonesia, New Guinea" to "Japan, Bonin Is."

330 *Oceanodroma markhami*, change range to "**Peru**. Ranges at sea in e Pacific off American coasts from Clipperton I. (off s Mexico) to Chile."

330 *Xenicus lyalli*, change English name to STEPHENS ISLAND WREN (not "STEPHENS WREN"); change Stewart I., **s** to "Stephens I., **c**"; in comments change "STEPHENS ISLAND" to "STEPHENS"

331 *Pitta oatesi*, change end of range to "...Laos, n,c Vietnam (...) and n Malaya."

331 *Pitta superba*, change English name to SUPERB PITTA (not BLACK-BACKED); in comments change "SUPERB" to "BLACK-BACKED"

332 *Pitta angolensis*, after "s Cameroon" add "and sw C. African Rep."

332 *Pitta reichenowi*, after "s Cameroon" add "and sw C. African Rep."; in comments after "212-213)" add "and southwestern Central African Republic"

333 *Pitta anerythra*, at beginning of comments add "(MASKED PITTA)."

333 *Smithornis capensis*, change range to "...Sierra Leone, Liberia and n Ivory Coast E to s Cameroon, sw C. African Rep. and Gabon;..."

334 *Philepitta castanea*, change "e Madagascar" to "**nw,e Madagascar**"

334 *Philepitta schlegeli*, change "cw,nw Madagascar" to "**w,nw Madagascar**"

334 *Neodrepanis coruscans*, change English name to SUNBIRD ASITY (not WATTLED); change "**e Madagascar**" to "**nw,e Madagascar**"; in comments after "affinities." add "(WATTLED ASITY/THE SUNBIRD-ASITY)."

334 *Neodrepanis hypoxantha* (not *hypoxanthus*); change English name to YELLOW-BELLIED ASITY (not SMALL-BILLED); change "known only from two old specimens" to "rare"; add comments "(SMALL-BILLED ASITY). AG: SUNBIRD-ASITY."

334 *Mionectes olivaceus*, change end of range to "...n Puno) and n Bolivia (n La Paz)."

334 *Mionectes macconnelli*, change English name to MACCONNELL'S FLYCATCHER (not MCCONNELL'S)

335 *Poecilotriccus albifacies*, in heading change "Blake 1959" to "(Blake 1959)"

335 *Taenotriccus andrei*, in heading change "(Berlepsch and Hartert)" to "Berlepsch and Hartert"

335 *Hemitriccus minor*, change range to "...Grosso) and ne Bolivia (ne Beni, ne Santa Cruz)..."

336 *Hemitriccus obsoletus*, change "Lowlands" to "Highlands"

336 *Hemitriccus aenigma*, change range to "**C S. America** in nc Brazil (e bank of lower r. Tapajós in w Pará) and ne Bolivia (ne Beni, ne Santa Cruz)."

336 *Hemitriccus iohannis*, in comments after "considerably" add "; Traylor (1982: 15-18) treated *iohannis* as a separate species"

336 *Hemitriccus spodiops*, in habitat after "second growth" add ", bamboo"; in range before "La Paz," add "Beni,"

337 *Hemitriccus mirandae*, change "Lowlands" to "Highlands"

337 *Hemitriccus kaempferi*, in heading change "(Zimmer) 1953" to "(Zimmer 1953a)"; in range change "type from" to "type locality in"

337 *Todirostrum sylvia*, at beginning of comments add "*Todirostrum hypospodium* Berlepsch 1907 is regarded as a variant."

337 *Todirostrum cinereum*, after "Santa Cruz)" add ", n Paraguay"

338 *Phyllomyias fasciatus*, change beginning of range to "**Se S. America** in n Bolivia (Beni, ne Santa Cruz), Brazil..."

338 *Phyllomyias burmeisteri*, change beginning of range to "**Sc,se S. America** in nc,e,se Bolivia (Beni, Santa Cruz,...)"; change comments to "...morphology suggest treatment..."

338 *Phyllomyias virescens*, change range to "Highlands of **se S. America** in se Brazil (...), e Paraguay and ne Argentina (Misiones)."; change end of comments to "See *P. reiseri* and *P. sclateri*."; sequence *virescens* after *reiseri*

338 *Phyllomyias reiseri*, in heading change "(Temminck) 1824" to "Hellmayr 1905"; change habitat and range to "Dry forest, cerrado. Mts., 900-1100 m, of **ne Venezuela** (Sucre, n Monagas, n Anzoátegui) ¶*urichi* (Chapman) 1899, URICH'S TYRANNULET [4559.1]; highlands of **se S. America** in se Brazil (s Piauí, Goiás, s Mato Grosso) and ne Paraguay) ¶*reiseri*, REISER'S TYRANNULET [5614.1]." Change comments to "*Reiseri* is a separate species differing in ecology and morphology (Zimmer 1955; Stotz 1990). The Venezuelan form *urichi* is poorly known and probably more closely related to *P. reiseri* than to *P. virescens* (Stotz 1990)."

339 *Zimmerius vilissimus*, change range to "Locally in hills and mts., 500-2600 m, of **nc Middle America** in e Chiapas, Guatemala (incl. Petén) and El Salvador ¶*vilissimus*, PALTRY TYRANNULET [1493]; lowlands to 1500 m of **C. and nw S. America** in Honduras (below 500 m), Nicaragua, Costa Rica (except nw), Panama and nw Colombia (nw Chocó) ¶*parvus* (Lawrence) 1862, MISTLETOE TYRANNULET [1493.1]."; in comments after "usage of *Zimmerius*." add "There is an abrupt change in habitat (elevational) and morphology (size) in northern Central America, suggesting possible species status for *parvus* (Traylor 1982: 2-4)."

339 *Zimmerius improbus,* in heading change "[1493.1.]" to "[4563.1.]"

340 *Ornithion inerme,* change range to "...e Peru, n,e Bolivia (Pando, Beni, La Paz, Santa Cruz) and Amazonian,e..."

340 *Phaeomyias murina,* change habitat and range to "Savanna, mangroves, thickets, forest edge (¶*murina*); arid scrub, thornbush (¶*tumbezana*). Lowlands...Guianas S, E of Andes, through Brazil...Tucumán} ¶*murina,* MOUSE-COLORED TYRANNULET [1497]; **cw S. America** in sw Ecuador (N to Guayas) and w Peru (S to Ancash) ¶*tumbezana* (Taczanowski) 1877, TUMBES TYRANNULET [4565.2]."; at beginning of comments add "The two groups differ vocally and morphologically (R. S. Ridgely, pers. comm.)."

340 *Sublegatus arenarum,* habitat and range in one paragraph; in comments after "*S. modestus*" add ", but Traylor (1982: 4-10) treated *arenarum* as a separate species."

340-341 Split *Sublegatus modestus* into the following two species:

Sublegatus [modestus] obscurior Todd 1920. AMAZONIAN SCRUB-FLYCATCHER. [4566.1.]

Scrub, open woodland, savanna. Lowlands to 500 m of **wc,n S. America** E of Andes from se Colombia (N to Putumayo and Meta), c,ne Venezuela (Bolívar, Sucre, Delta Amacuro, possibly as a migrant only) and Guianas S to e Peru, nw Bolivia and Amazonian Brazil (mostly N of Amazon E to Pará).

Obscurior is a species separate from *modestus,* vocally as well as morphologically distinct (Traylor, in Peters 1979b: 20; R. S. Ridgely, pers. comm.), although the apparent sympatry in Peru may be due to migratory movements (Traylor 1982: 4-10). (TODD'S SCRUB-FLYCATCHER).

Sublegatus [modestus] modestus (Wied) 1831. SOUTHERN SCRUB-FLYCATCHER. [4566.2.]

Scrub, open woodland, savanna. Lowlands of **sc S. America** from se Peru (N at least to r. Urubamba drainage), n,e Bolivia, Paraguay and e,s Brazil (from Piauí, Pernambuco, Bahia and Minas Gerais S to Rio Grande do Sul) S to Uruguay and c Argentina (S to Mendoza, La Pampa and Buenos Aires, but not recorded from Misiones). Winters N to e Peru and Amazonian Brazil, probably to Venezuela.

(SHORT-BILLED FLYCATCHER). [SCRUB FLYCATCHER]. See *S. arenarum* and *S. obscurior.*

341 *Myiopagis gaimardii,* at beginning of comments add "Includes *Serpophaga berliozi* Dorst (1957)."

341 *Myiopagis caniceps,* change "(D. F. Stotz, pers. comm.)" to "(Cardoso da Silva 1990)"

342-343 *Elaenia cristata,* after "(Cuzco)" add "and ne Bolivia (ne Santa Cruz)"

344 *Serpophaga cinerea,* change "**Middle**" to "s C."; delete "and Colombia (incl. Santa Marta Mts.)"

344 *Serpophaga subcristata,* change beginning of range to "**Sc,se S. America** in c,se Bolivia (except sw), Paraguay,..."

344 *Serpophaga munda,* in comments change "1959" to "(1959c)"

345 Change **Anairetes** *[agilis] agilis* and **Anairetes** *[agilis] agraphia* to **Uromyias** *[agilis] agilis* and **Uromyias** *[agilis] agraphia*; sequence before *Anairetes alpinus*

345 *Uromyias agilis,* change comments to "Lanyon (1988a) presented evidence for generic recognition of *Uromyias.* [<*Anairetes* (+N)]. See *U. agraphia.*"

345 *Uromyias agraphia,* in heading change "Chapman" to "(Chapman)"; in comments change "*A. agilis*" to "*U. agilis*"

345 *Tachuris rubrigastra,* before "La Paz," add "Cochabamba,"

345 *Culicivora caudacuta,* after "Beni," add "n La Paz,"

346 *Euscarthmus meloryphus,* change "Corrientes" to "n Buenos Aires"

346 *Euscarthmus rufomarginatus,* change range to "...**cn,sc,se S. America**: Surinam; ne Bolivia (ne Santa Cruz) and e,s Brazil..."

346 *Phylloscartes ophthalmicus,* after "Cochabamba" add ", w Santa Cruz"

346 *Phylloscartes nigrifrons,* in heading change "(Sclater and Salvin)" to "(Salvin and Godman)"

347 *Lophotriccus pileatus,* change end of range to "...n Puno); a record from Brazil is erroneous."

348 Move *Ramphotrigon megacephala, R. fuscicauda* and *R. ruficauda* to p. 364 and sequence after *Deltarhynchus flammulatus*

348 *Ramphotrigon megacephala,* change comments to "Lanyon (1985: 373-374) presented evidence for relationship of *Ramphotrigon* to *Deltarhynchus* and its placement within the assemblage of myiarchine flycatchers. [≠*Tolmomyias*]."

348 *Ramphotrigon fuscicauda,* after "La Paz" add ", ne Santa Cruz"

348 *Rhynchocyclus brevirostris,* change range to "...Costa Rica (except nw) and w,e Panama (E to w Panamá prov.; e Darién) ¶*brevirostris*...1100 m of **nw S. America** in w Colombia..."; add comments "Ridgely and Gwynne (1989: 294) regarded *pacificus* as a separate species."

349 *Tolmomyias flaviventris,* after "La Paz" add ", ne Santa Cruz"

350 *Onychorhynchus coronatus,* change range to "...[4626.2]; **c,e S. America**...Amazonian Brazil...[4626.1]; **se Brazil** (from e Minas Gerais, Rio de Janeiro and São Paulo S to Paraná) ¶*swainsoni,* SWAINSON'S ROYAL-FLYCATCHER [4626.3]."

350 *Myiophobus roraimae,* change "Carriker 1832" to "Carriker 1932"

350 *Myiophobus lintoni,* in heading change "1951" to "(1951a)"

350 *Myiophobus fasciatus,* in heading delete "*[fasciatus]*"; in range change "w Peru (to Piura)" to "nw Peru (to Piura)"; in comments delete "[BRAN-COLORED FLYCATCHER]."

350 *Myiophobus cryptoxanthus,* in heading delete "*[fasciatus]*"

352 *Lathrotriccus euleri,* change range to "...Pará} ¶*flaviventris* (Lawrence) 1887 [= *lawrencei* (Allen) 1889], LAWRENCE'S..."; change comments to "...genus *Lathrotriccus.* With treatment of *euleri* in *Lathrotriccus, Blacicus flaviventris* Lawrence 1887 is no longer preoccupied by *Tyrannula flaviventris* Baird 1843 [= *Empidonax flaviventris*]. [≠*Empidonax*]. See *L. griseipectus.*"

352 *Contopus borealis,* change English name from "BOREAL PEWEE" to "OLIVE-SIDED FLYCATCHER"; change end of comments to "...[>*Nuttallornis*]. (BOREAL PEWEE)."

353 *Contopus nigrescens*, after "s Guyana" add "; ce Brazil (n Pará, n Maranhão)"

353 *Contopus albogularis*, in heading change "(Berlioz) 1962" to "(Berlioz 1962)"

353 Change "***Empidonax griseipectus*** Lawrence" to "***Lathrotriccus griseipectus*** (Lawrence)" and move to p. 352, sequence after *Lathrotriccus euleri*; change comments to "Vocalizations of *L. griseipectus* are nearly identical to those of *L. euleri*; thus the former belongs in *Lathrotriccus* as previously suspected (R. S. Ridgely, pers. comm.)."

353 *Empidonax flaviventris*, add comments "See *Lathrotriccus euleri*."

354 *Empidonax traillii*, after "s Quebec" add ", Prince Edward Island"; after "n Georgia," add "w S. Carolina,"

354 *Empidonax affinis*, at end of range add "Winters S to c Guatemala."

355 *Empidonax fulvifrons*, change end of range to "Zacatecas, w Nuevo León and San Luis Potosí S to c Honduras."

355 *Sayornis phoebe*, change range to "...Gulf states, and w,ne S. Carolina. Winters..."

357 *Neoxolmis rufiventris*, change comments to "AG: MONJITA."

358 *Muscisaxicola macloviana*, after "Entre Rios" add ", Buenos Aires"

358 *Muscisaxicola juninensis*, after "La Paz," add "Cochabamba,"

359 *Knipolegus signatus*, change "**sc S. America**" to "**sw S. America**"; change "1959" to "(1959c)"

360 *Alectrurus tricolor*, after "Beni," add "La Paz,"

360 *Gubernetes yetapa*, after "Beni," add "La Paz,"

361 *Attila phoenicurus*, after "do Sul)" add ", ne Bolivia (ne Santa Cruz)"

361 *Attila rufus*, change "Rio Grando do Sul" to "Rio Grande do Sul"

362 *Laniocera rufescens*, before "Chiapas" add "n Oaxaca and"

363 *Myiarchus cephalotes*, in heading change "Hellmayr 1925" to "Taczanowski 1879"

363 *Myiarchus cinerascens*, after "w Kansas" add ", c Oklahoma"

363 *Myiarchus nuttingi*, change range to "**Middle America** from c Sonora and sw Chihuahua S along Pacific slope of Mexico (also int. in México, Morelos and Puebla, and the Gulf drainage in s San Luis Potosí and Hidalgo), and in the Pacific lowlands and int. valleys of Guatemala, El Salvador, Honduras, Nicaragua and nw Costa Rica."

363 *Myiarchus crinitus*, change range to "...s Canada to Prince Edward Island and s Nova Scotia, and S (E of Rockies) to c,se Texas..."

364 After *Deltarhynchus flammulatus*, sequence *Ramphotrigon* spp. from p. 348

364 *Tyrannus melancholicus*, in comments change "David "(1979d)" to "Davis (1979b)"

364 *Tyrannus vociferans*, after "se Montana," add "sw S. Dakota,"

364 *Tyrannus crassirostris*, after "sw Chihuahua," add "w Texas,"

365 *Tyrannus forficatus*, change range to "...s Texas, with isolated breeding in c Iowa, ne Mississippi, nc Tennessee, nw Alabama and S. Carolina. Winters..."

366 *Conopias parva*, change range to "...Andes in se Colombia (Vaupés), s Venezuela (...), Guianas and n Brazil (...)."

371 *Zaratornis stresemanni*, in heading change "(Koepcke 1964)" to "Koepcke (1964)"

372 *Lipaugus subalaris*, before "e Ecuador" add "se Colombia (Putumayo),"

372 *Lipaugus unirufus*, delete comments"

375 *Oxyruncus cristatus*, after "Junín)" add "wc Bolivia (La Paz),"

376 Split *Pipra serena* into the following two species:

Pipra [serena] suavissima Salvin and Godman 1882. TEPUI MANAKIN. [4728.1.]
Humid forest, edge. Lowlands and slopes of Pantepui, 500-1800 m, of **n S. America** in s Venezuela (nw,se Bolívar and s Amazonas above *P. coronata*), Guyana, and adjacent nw Brazil (n Amazonas, n Roraima).
Prum (1988b, 1990) recognized *P. suavissima* as a species distinct from *P. serena*.

Pipra [serena] serena Linnaeus 1766. WHITE-FRONTED MANAKIN. [4728.]
Humid forest, edge. Lowlands to 1000 m of **n S. America** in Surinam, French Guiana and adjacent n Brazil (Amapá, n Pará).
See *P. suavissima*.

376 *Pipra isidorei*, in comments change "*P. [coronata]*" to "*P. [serena]*"

378 *Xenopipo atronitens*, after "Heath)" add ", ne Bolivia (ne Santa Cruz)"

378 *Heterocercus aurantiivertex*, change "**Amreica**" to "**America**"

379 *Neopelma pallescens*, change range to "Lowlands of **c,e S. America** in e,c Brazil (...) and ne Bolivia (ne Santa Cruz)."

379 *Cymbilaimus lineatus*, change range to "...(La Paz, Beni, ne Santa Cruz) and Amazonian..."

379-380 *Frederickena unduligera*, after "e Peru" add ", n Bolivia (n La Paz)"

380 *Thamnnophilus doliatus*, add comments "*Zarumae* differs in vocalizations, plumage and size, and is treated as a full species by M. and P. Isler (pers. comm.)."

380 *Thamnophilus multistriatus*, change range to "Andes, 1500-2650 m (...), of **nw S. America** in Colombia (except...upper Dagua v., upper r. San Juan and upper Patía v...Boyacá) and extreme nw Venezuela (Sierra de Perijá)."

380 *Thamnophilus palliatus*, change range to "... Cajamarca and San Martín) ¶*tenuepunctatus*...upper r. Madeira and w Pará S to w,n Mato Grosso; e Pará and Maranhão; from Paraíba S coastally to Minas Gerais and..."; change comments to "Males of *tenuepunctatus* are morphologically distinct, showing no intergradation where the range of *tenuepunctatus* approaches that of *palliatus* in eastern Peru (M. and P. Isler, pers. comm.)."

381 *Thamnophilus nigrocinereus*, change habitat to "River island forest, mangroves, humid forest."

381 *Thamnophilus cryptoleucus*, before "ne Peru" add "ne Ecuador (Napo),"; change end of range to "...(E to r. Solimões)."

381 *Thamnophilus schistaceus*, in heading change "(d'Orbigny)" to "d'Orbigny"; change range to "...w Amazonian Brazil (from Acre, r. Purús and r. Solimões E, generally S of Amazon, to r. Tocantins..."; at beginning of comments add "Records from Argentina are questionable (M. and P. Isler, pers. comm.)."

381 *Thamnophilus aroyae*, in habitat after "second growth" add ", bamboo"; change end of range to "...(Puno) and c Bolivia (Beni, La Paz, Cochabamba)."

381 *Thamnophilus amazonicus*, add comments "*T. ruficollis* Spix 1825 has been suppressed and *T. amazonicus* validated (I.C.Z.N. 1981)."

382 *Clytoctantes alixii*, at end of comments add "See *C. atrogularis*."

382 Change *Clytoctantes alixii* to *Clytoctantes [alixii] alixii*, and add a new species following:

Clytoctantes [alixii] atrogularis Lanyon, Stotz and Willard (1990). RONDONIA BUSHBIRD. [4458.2.]
Humid forest undergrowth. Known only from the type from **sw Brazil** (r. Jiparaná, in Rondônia).
Apparently a distinct species related to *C. alixii* (Lanyon, Stotz and Willard 1990).

383 *Dysithamnus plumbeus*, change comments to "Schulenberg (1983: 518) recommended that this superspecies be removed from *Thamnomanes* and suggested that relationships were with *Dysithamnus*, a treatment followed by Hilty and Brown (1986: 387). [PLUMBEOUS..."

383 *Dysithamnus occidentalis*, change English name to BICOLORED ANTVIREO (not WESTERN); change comments to "Schulenberg (1983: 518) suggested that *occidentalis* be removed from *Thamnomanes*, although it is placed in that genus by Hilty and Brown (1986: 388) with a statement that its true taxonomic position remains unknown. Whitney (1992) recommended that it be placed in *Dysithamnus*. [≠*Thamnophilus/Thamnomanes*]. (WESTERN/CHAPMAN'S ANTVIREO). AG: ANTSHRIKE."

383 *Thamnomanes ardesiacus*, delete "Guianas,"; in comments after "*Thamnomanes*" add ", a treatment also recommended by Schulenberg (1983: 516)"

383 *Thamnomanes caesius*, change range to "...Loreto), Amazonian,n,e Brazil (...) and ne Bolivia (ne Santa Cruz)."

384 *Myrmotherula sclateri*, change range to "...Dios), n,e Bolivia (Pando, n La Paz, e Santa Cruz) and sw Amazonian..."

385 *Myrmotherula schisticolor*, change "**nw S. America**" to "**w S. America**"

385 *Myrmotherula sunensis*, change end of range to "...e Ecuador, ne,c Peru (...) and wc Brazil (middle r. Juruá)."

386 *Myrmotherula assimilis*, after "Pando" add ", Beni"

386 *Herpsilochmus longirostris*, after "Beni" add ", ne Santa Cruz"

387 *Microrhopias quixensis*, after "Chiapas" add ", s Campeche"

387 Split *Formicivora melanogaster* into the following two species:

Formicivora [melanogaster] melanogaster Pelzeln 1868. BLACK-BELLIED ANTWREN. [5548.]
Riparian thickets, brush, dense woodland. Plateau of **sc S. America** in e,se Bolivia and sw,c Brazil (from Piauí, Ceará and Alagoas S to Mato Grosso, w São Paulo, Goiás and Bahia, except for area occupied by *F. serrana*).
[BLACK-BELLIED ANTWREN]. See *F. serrana*.

Formicivora [melanogaster] serrana (Hellmayr) 1929. SERRA ANTWREN. [5547.]
Serra woodland, scrub, coastal restinga. Lowlands to 1000 m of **se Brazil** (se Minas Gerais, Espirito Santo, Rio de Janeiro).
Often considered conspecific with *melanogaster* but differs in morphology and ecology; treated as a species by Gonzaga and Pachecho (1990).

387 *Formicivora grisea*, change range to "...Tobago, n,e Bolivia (Beni, Santa Cruz) and Amazonian..."

387 *Drymophila devillei*, change range to "Locally in lowlands of **w S. America** E of Andes in cs Colombia (Putumayo), se Ecuador,...Cochabamba, ne Santa Cruz) and s Amazonian..."

388 *Terenura callinota*, in heading change "1955" to "1855"; in comments change "*Hylophilus puella*" to "*Hylophilus puellus*"

388 *Terenura humeralis*, after "Pando" add ", n La Paz"

389 After *Cercomacra carbonaria*, add:

Cercomacra manu Fitzpatrick and Willard (1990). MANU ANTBIRD. [5561.1.]
Bamboo thickets, dense riparian vegetation. Lowlands to 1200 m of **sw S. America** in se Peru (Cuzco) and extreme nw Bolivia (nw Pando).
Probably most closely related to *C. melanaria* (Fitzpatrick and Willard 1990).

389 *Cercomacra melanaria*, change range to "...Santa Cruz), w Brazil (...) and n Paraguay"; change comments to "See *C. ferdinandi* and *C. manu*."

389 *Pyriglena leuconota*, after "n Bolivia" add ", n Paraguay"

390 *Gymnocichla nudiceps*, change "**Middle**" to "C."

390 *Percnostola lophotes*, after "Pando" add ", n La Paz"

390 Replace accounts of *Sipia berlepschi* and *S. rosenbergi* with the following:

Myrmeciza berlepschi (Hartert) 1898. STUB-TAILED ANTBIRD. [4488.]
Forest. Pacific lowlands to 400 m of **nw S. America** in w Colombia (from upper r. Atrato S) and nw Ecuador (Esmeraldas).
Sipia is not distinct as a genus from *Myrmeciza* (Robbins and Ridgely 1991). For disposition of *Sipia rosenbergi*, see *M. nigricauda*.

391 *Myrmeciza exsul*, change "s C,. and" to "s C. and"

391 Split *Myrmeciza laemosticta* into the following two species:

Myrmeciza [laemosticta] laemosticta Salvin 1865. DULL-MANTLED ANTBIRD. [1474.]
Humid forest undergrowth, dense second growth. Lowlands to 1100 m of **s C. and nw S. America** in Costa Rica (Caribbean slope), Panama (both slopes), n Colombia (from Antioquia E through Caribbean lowlands to Norte de Santander, and S in Magdalena v. to Caldas) and nw Venezuela (w Zulia, w Mérida, s Táchira).
(SALVIN'S ANTBIRD). [DULL-MANTLED ANTBIRD]. See *M. nigricauda*.

Myrmeciza [laemosticta] nigricauda Salvin and Godman 1892. ESMERALDAS ANTBIRD. [4489.]

Humid forest undergrowth, dense second growth. Lowlands to 1000 m of **nw S. America** in w Colombia (Pacific lowlands north to southern Chocó) and nw Ecuador (S to El Oro).

Sipia rosenbergi (Hartert) 1898 was based on the male *M. nigricauda*, and the latter is specifically distinct from *M. laemosticta* (Robbins and Ridgely 1991).

391 *Myrmeciza goeldii*, after "Pando" add ", n La Paz"

391 *Myrmeciza fortis*, after "Pando" add ", n La Paz"

392 *Myrmeciza atrothorax*, delete superspecies; change comments to "Includes *M. stictothorax* (Todd) 1972, SPOT-BREASTED ANTBIRD [5574], known only from two specimens from rio Tapajós, now regarded as aberrant *M. atrothorax* (Schulenberg and Stotz 1991). [>*Myrmophylax*]."

392 Delete *Myrmeciza stictothorax* entry

393 *Phlegopsis barringeri*, in heading change "1951" to "(1951c)"; change beginning of comments to "May be a hybrid..."

393 *Geobates poecilopterus* (not *poeciloptera*); change range to "Lowlands of **sc S. America** in s Brazil (...) and ne Bolivia (ne Santa Cruz)."

394 *Geositta rufipennis*, after "Potosí" add ", Chuquisaca"

394 *Upucerthia certhioides*, in heading change "1892" to "1838"; before "w Paraguay" add "se Bolivia (se Santa Cruz),"

395 *Upucerthia validirostris*, change range to "Andes, 2700-5000 m, of **sw S. America** in sw Bolivia (Potosí) and nw Argentina (from Jujuy to Mendoza)."

394 *Upucerthia dumetaria*, change range to "...w Argentina (from Jujuy and Salta S to Neuquén, and E to w Córdoba and La Pampa), thence E to coastal lowlands of Argentina (N to Río Negro and S to Santa Cruz...n Argentina (N to Santiago del Estero, Santa Fe and Entre Ríos)"

395 *Cinclodes comechingonus*, in heading after "*comechingonus*" add "Zotta and Gavio 1944"

395 *Cinclodes excelsior*, change "(Carriker 1932)" to "(Carriker) 1932"

396 *Furnarius leucopus*, change end of comments to "...See *F. torridus* and *F. cristatus*."

396 *Furnarius cristatus*, in heading change "1878" to "1888"; add comments "*Furnarius tricolor* Cabanis 1878, applicable to this species, is preoccupied by *F. tricolor* Giebel 1868, a subspecies of *F. leucopus*."

397 *Schizoeaca moreirae*, in heading delete "Miranda"

398 *Synallaxis azarae*, in comments change "(J. V. Remsen, in press)" to "(Remsen, Schmitt and Schmitt 1989: 367)"

400 *Cranioleuca curtata*, before "La Paz," add "Beni,"

401 *Cranioleuca obsoleta*, in comments after "*C. pyrrhophia*" add "inasmuch as vocalizations are closely similar (Belton 1984: 183-185)"

402 *Asthenes pyrrholeuca*, change comments to "[<*Thripophaga* (~*Asthenes*)]."

402 *Asthenes baeri*, before "Tarija" add "Santa Cruz,"

402 *Asthenes modesta*, change end of comments to "...*cactorum* and *A. luizae*."

402 After *Asthenes modesta*, add:

Asthenes luizae Vieillard (1990). CIPO CANASTERO. [5453.1.]

Scrub and thickets on rocky slopes. **Se Brazil** (s Serra do Espinaço, sc Minas Gerais).

Ecology, vocalizations and behavior were noted by Pearman (1990) and the species described by Vieillard (1990b). *A. luizae* is probably related to *A. modesta*, *A. dorbignyi*, or possibly *A. patagonica*.

402 *Asthenes dorbignyi*, change comments to "...(Fjeldså 1985, R. Ridgely, pers. comm.). See *A. berlepschi*, *A. steinbachi* and *A. luizae*."

402 *Asthenes patagonica*, add comments "See *A. luizae*."

403 *Asthenes punensis*, change habitat to "Open rocky slopes, meadows, arid scrub, bushes."; change end of range to "...[5459.3]; Andes, 2000-2900 m, of **nc Argentina** (Sierra de Córdoba in w Córdoba) ¶*sclateri* (Cabanis) 1878, CORDOBA CANASTERO [5460]."; change end of comments to "...*A. punensis* as a separate species. *Sclateri* is conspecific with *A. punensis* (Vaurie 1980: 183; Navas and Bo 1982; R. S. Ridgely, pers. comm.), not *A. anthoides*, contrary to the opinion of Hoy and Stresemann (1965)."

403 delete *Asthenes sclateri* entry

403 *Siptornopsis hypochondriacus*, change comments to "[<*Thripophaga*...]."

404 *Phacellodomus sibilatrix*, before "c Paraguay," add "se Bolivia (se Santa Cruz),"

404 *Phacellodomus ruber*, after "Beni," add "La Paz,"

404 *Phacellodomus erythrophthalmus*, change range to "Coastal lowlands of **e Brazil** (from se Bahia to extreme ne São Paulo) ¶*erythrophthalmus*, RED-EYED THORNBIRD [5472]; **se Brazil** (from central São Paulo south to Rio Grande do Sul) ¶*ferrugineigula* (Pelzeln) 1858, ORANGE-EYED THORNBIRD [5472.1]."; change comments to "E. Willis (pers. comm.) suggests that *ferruginegula* deserves specific rank. [>*Drioctistes*]."

405 *Xenerpestes singularis*, change comments to "Parker and Parker (1980) discussed rediscovery and status of this species. See *X. minlosi*."

406 *Lochmias nematura*, in comments after "(1972: 684)" add "and refuted by Rudge and Raikow (1992)"

406 *Pseudocolaptes lawrencii*, change range to "Mts., 800-2500 m, of **s C. America** in c,s Costa Rica and w Panama (Chiriquí, w Bocas del Toro, Veraguas) ¶*lawrencii*, BUFFY TUFTEDCHEEK [1415]; **nw S. America** in w Colombia (w slope of W. Andes from Valle to Nariño) and w Ecuador ¶*johnsoni* Lönnberg and Rendahl 1922, PACIFIC TUFTEDCHEEK [4407.1]."

406 *Berlepschia rikeri*, after "Pando" add ", Beni, n La Paz"

407 *Syndactyla rufosuperciliata*, add comments "See *S. ruficollis*."

407 *Philydor fuscipennis*, in heading change "[1419.1.] to "[1419.]; in range change "[1419.1]" to "[1419]" and "[4411.1]" to "[1419.1]"; in comments after "(Hilty and Brown 1986: 370)." add "*P. fulvescens* Todd (1951) is a synonym of *P. (fuscipennis) erythronotus*."

407 *Philydor erythrocercus*, in heading change "[1419.]" to "[4411.1.]"

407 *Philydor ochrogaster*, change comments to "Usually considered conspecific with *P. erythrocercus* because of similar vocalizations, but there are no specimens that can be considered intergrades despite extensive latitudinal parapatry (Parker, Bates and Cox 1992: 176)."

408 *Philydor novaesi*, in heading change "(1983)" to "(1983b)"

408 *Simoxenops striatus*, change range to "Andean foothills, 650-1000 m, of **wc,c Bolivia** (La Paz, Cochabamba, w Santa Cruz)."; change comments to "Parker, Bates and Cox (1992: 174) discussed the history and rediscovery of this species."

408 *Thripadectes ignobilis*, change "Chimborazo" to "El Oro"

408 *Thripadeactes virgaticeps*, change end of range to "...Táchira) and w,ne Ecuador (S to El Oro and Napo)."

409 Change *Automolus ruficollis* to *Syndactyla ruficollis*; change comments to "Parker, Schulenberg et al. (1985: 177-178) suggested relationships with *Syndactyla rufosuperciliata*, supported by more recent studies (R. S. Ridgely, pers. comm.)."; move to p. 407 and sequence after *Syndactyla rufosuperciliata*

409 *Automolus dorsalis*, change end of range to "...Ecuador, e Peru (...) and n Bolivia (La Paz)."

409 *Automolus infuscatus*, after "Pando" add ", n La Paz"

409 *Automolus roraimae*, in comments change "1956" to "(1956)"

409 *Automolus rubiginosus*, change range to "...**Neotropical** from Guerrero, Hidalgo, s San Luis Potosí, Veracruz..."

409 *Hylocryptus rectirostris*, change range to "**Sc S. America** in sc Brazil (...) and Paraguay."

410 *Sclerurus mexicanus*, change range to "...**Neotropical** from Hidalgo, e Puebla, Veracruz, Oaxaca..."

410 *Xenops milleri*, after "Madre de Dios)" add ", n Bolivia (n La Paz)"

411 *Megaxenops parnaguae*, change "Highlands" to "Lowlands"

411 *Dendrocincla tyrannina*, in heading after "(Lafresnaye)" add "1851"; change end of comments to "...CREEPER/WOODHEWER."

411 *Dendrocincla fuliginosa*, change "**Middle**" to "**C.**"

411 *Dendrocincla merula*, change range to "...n Bolívar) S through w Amazonian Brazil (Amazonas W to r. Uaupés and r. Negro, and S of Amazon E to r. Tapajós and S to upper r. Purús, r. Cururu and Serra do Cachimbo) and e Peru to n,e Bolivia (...) ¶*castanoptera* Ridgway 1888, BLUE-EYED WOODCREEPER [4429.1]; **ne S. America** in Guianas and ne Brazil (Pará N of Amazon) ¶*merula*, WHITE-CHINNED WOODCREEPER [4429]."

412 *Glyphorynchus* (not *Glyphorhynchus*)

412 *Drymornis bridgesii*, before "w Paraguay" add "se Bolivia (se Santa Cruz),"

412 *Hylexetastes stresemanni*, in heading change "*[perrottii]*" to "*[perrotii]*"

412 *Hylexetastes perrotii*, in heading change "*[perrottii]*" to "*[perrotii]*"; change range to "...Lowlands to 300 m of **nc S. America**...Guianas and n Amazonian Brazil (N of Amazon from r. Negro E to Óbidos) *perrotii*, RED-BILLED WOODCREEPER [4433]; **c S. America** in Amazonian Brazil (S of Amazon from r. Madeira E to r. Tapajós) and extreme ne Bolivia (ne Santa Cruz) ¶*uniformis* Hellmayr 1909, UNIFORM WOODCREEPER [4433.2]."

412 *Xiphocolaptes promeropirhynchus*, before "Veracruz," add "Hidalgo,"

412 *Xiphocolaptes albicollis*, change end of comments to "...See *X. falcirostris*."

412 Delete *Xiphocolaptes franciscanus* entry

412 *Xiphocolaptes falcirostris*, change range to "**Ne Brazil** (Maranhão, Piauí, Ceará, Paraíba, w,n Bahia) ¶*falcirostris*, MOUSTACHED WOODCREEPER [5504]; **e Brazil** (cn Minas Gerais) ¶*franciscanus* Snethlage 1927, SNETHLAGE'S WOODCREEPER [5503]."; change comments to "Meyer de Schauensee (1966: 231) suggested that *franciscanus* may be conspecific with *X. albicollis*, but it appears to be simply a southern race of *X. falcirostris* (Teixeira, Nacinovic and Luigi 1989: 154; R. S. Ridgely, pers. comm.)."

413 *Dendrocolaptes certhia*, change range to "Lowlands to 1400 m of **Middle America and nw S. America** from Veracruz,...region), w,n Colombia (E to Santa Marta Mts., Norte de Santander and nw Santander, and on Pacific slope), w Venezuela (nw Zulia, n Mérida) and nw Ecuador ¶*sanctithomae* (Lafresnaye) 1852, NORTHERN BARRED-WOODCREEPER [1437]; **n,c,e S. America** from se Colombia (N to Meta and Vichada), s,se Venezuela (Amazonas, Bolívar, Delta Amacuro) and Guianas S, E of Andes, through e Ecuador and e Peru to n,e Bolivia and n,Amazonian,e Brazil (S to s Amazonas and nw Mato Grosso, and E to Maranhão, Pernambuco and Alagoas) ¶*certhia*, AMAZONIAN BARRED-WOODCREEPER [5506]."; change comments to "Although *D. concolor* Pelzeln 1868, CONCOLOR WOODCREEPER, of Amazonian Brazil south of the Amazon, is regarded as a species by Peters (1951: 33) and Meyer de Schauensee (1966: 231), it has identical vocalizations to and appears to be a race of *D. certhia*, not even recognizable as a group (R. Ridgely, E. Willis, pers. comm.). *Sanctithomae* differs in vocalizations from *certhia* and probably represents a distinct species (R. Ridgely, pers. comm.)."

413 *Dendrocolaptes hoffmannsi*, change English name to HOFFMANNS'S WOODCREEPER (not HOFFMANNS')

414 *Xiphorhynchus erythropygius*, before "Veracruz" add "Hidalgo,"

415 *Formicarius analis*, change "Caribbean slop" to "Caribbean slope"

416 ***Chamaeza [campanisoma] campanisoma***, add superspecies; at end of comments add "Willis (1992) discussed relationships among *Chamaeza [campanisoma]* superspecies, *C. [meruloides]* superspecies, and *C. ruficauda*."

416 ***Chamaeza [campanisoma] nobilis***, add superspecies; after "Pando" add ", n La Paz"; add comments "See *C. campanisoma*."

416 After *Chamaeza nobilis*, add the following two accounts:

Chamaeza [meruloides] turdina (Cabanis and Heine) 1859. SCHWARTZ'S ANTTHRUSH. [4522.]
Humid forest floor. Mts., 1500-2600 m, of **nw,n S. America** in Colombia (w slope of C. Andes in Valle, head of Magdalena v. in Huila) and n Venezuela (from Yaracuy and Carabobo E to Miranda).
(SCALLOPED ANTTHRUSH). See *G. campanisoma*.

Chamaeza [meruloides] meruloides Vigors 1825. SUCH'S ANTTHRUSH. [5581.5.]
Humid forest floor. Mts., 1000-1500 m, of **se Brazil** (Espírito Santo, Rio de Janeiro).
See *G. campanisoma*.

416 *Chamaeza ruficauda*, in heading change "[4522.]" to "[5581.4.]"; change range to "Mts., 1200-2000 m, of **se Brazil** (from Minas Gerais and Espírito Santo S to Rio Grande do Sul)."; add comments "(BRAZILIAN ANTTHRUSH). See *G. campanisoma*."

416 *Grallaria gigantea*, change range to "...Huila) and e Ecuador ¶*gigantea*, GIANT ANTPITTA [4527]; **nw Ecuador** ¶*hylodroma* Wetmore 1945, PICHINCHA ANTPITTA [4527.1]."; add comments "See *G. excelsa*."

416 *Grallaria excelsa*, add comments "*G. (gigantea) gigantea* may be conspecific with *G. excelsa*, with *G. hylodroma* as a separate species (R. S. Ridgely, pers. comm.)."

416 *Grallaria guatimalensis*, before "Veracruz" add "Hidalgo,"

417 After *Grallaria eludens*, add the following species:

Grallaria kaestneri Stiles (1992). CUNDINAMARCA ANTPITTA. [4534.1.]
Humid forest undergrowth. E. Andes, 1800-2300 m, of **c Colombia** (Cundinamarca).
Most closely similar to *G. bangsi* (Stiles 1992).

417 *Grallaria bangsi*, at end of comments add "See *G. kaestneri*."

417 *Grallaria albigula*, change range to "...(Puno), c Bolivia (...) and nw Argentina (Jujuy)."

418 Split *Hylopezus fulviventris* into the following two species:

Hylopezus [fulviventris] dives Salvin 1865. FULVOUS-BELLIED ANTPITTA. [1486.]
Humid forest undergrowth, edge, second-growth woodland. Lowlands to 1000 m of **C. and nw S. America** on Caribbean slope of ne Honduras (Olancho), e Nicaragua and Costa Rica; e Panama (Darién), w Colombia (Pacific lowlands from Gulf of Urabá and upper Sinú v. S), w Ecuador ¶*dives* (Salvin) 1865, FULVOUS-BELLIED ANTPITTA (DIVES ANTPITTA) [1486]; **w Panama** (Bocas del Toro) ¶*flammulatus* (Griscom) 1928, FLAMMULATED ANTPITTA [1486.1].
Vocalizations of *H. dives* and *H. fulviventris* are different; these two taxa represent distinct species (R. G. Ridgely, pers. comm.).

Hylopezus [fulviventris] fulviventris (Sclater) 1858. WHITE-LORED ANTPITTA. [4542.1.]
Humid forest undergrowth, edge. Lowlands to 1000 m of **nw S. America** E of Andes in se Colombia (N to Caquetá) and e Ecuador.
[FULVOUS-BELLIED ANTPITTA]. See *H. dives* and *H. berlepschi*.

418 *Hylopezus ochroleucus*, change "**Se Brazil**" to "**Ne Brazil**"

418 *Hylopezus nattereri*, in heading change "Pinto 1973" to "(Pinto) 1937"; at end of comments add "(NATTERER'S ANTPITTA)."

419 *Conopophaga peruviana*, after "Dios)" add ", n Bolivia (n La Paz)"

420 *Pteroptochos tarnii*, change beginning of range to "Lowlands to 1500 m of **c,s Chile** (from..."

421 *Scytalopus novacapitalis*, in comments change "Orig. descr." to "Originally described"

421 Split *Scytalopus indigoticus* into two species:

Scytalopus [indigoticus] psychopompus Teixeira and Carnevalli (1989). CHESTNUT-SIDED TAPACULO. [5612.1.]
Undergrowth in flooded forest. Coastal lowlands of **se Brazil** (e Bahia).
This species is closest morphologically to *S. indigoticus* (Teixeira and Carnevalli 1989).

Scytalopus [indigoticus] indigoticus (Wied) 1831. WHITE-BREASTED TAPACULO. [5612.]
Undergrowth, second growth, bracken, riparian woodland. **Se Brazil** (from Espírito Santo, s Minas Gerais and Rio de Janeiro S to Rio Grande do Sul).
[WHITE-BREASTED TAPACULO]. See *S. novacapitalis* and *S. psychopompus*.

422 *Climacteris picumnus*, in comments change "Bordekin-Lynd" to "Burdekin-Lynd"

422 *Menura alberti*, in heading change "1851" to "1850"

423 *Amblyornis macgregoriae*, in heading change "MACGREGOR'S" to "MACGREGOR'S"

423 *Sericulus chrysocephalus*, change end of range to "...ce New S. Wales (to Sydney area)."

424 *Chlamydera nuchalis*, after "Mackay" add ")"

424 *Chlamydera cerviniventris*, change "Fly r." to "Kumbe r."

424 *Malurus campbelli*, change range to "Lowlands to 1000 m of **sc New Guinea** (middle Strickland r., Mt. Bosavi region)."; change end of comments to "...pl. 3); for additional description and comments, see Schodde and Weatherly (1983) and Schodde (1984)."

425 *Malurus elegans*, change range to "Coastal **sw W. Australia** (...)."

426 *Amytornis dorotheae*, change range to "...ne N. Terr. (W to McArthur r.) and extreme nw Queensland."

427 *Myzomela sanguinolenta*, in comments before "(SANGUINEOUS MYZOMELA)." add "The correct name for *M. sanguinolenta* may be *M. dibapha* (Latham) 1801 (McAllan 1990)."

427 *Myzomela cardinalis*, in range after "Banks is.)" add ", Loyalty Is.,"; in comments change "*chloropterus*" to "*chloroptera*"

428 *Timeliopsis griseigula*, change "nw,se New Guinea" to "**nw,se New Guinea**"

429 *Lichmera lombokia*, in heading change "1863" to "1926"

430 *Meliphaga mimikae*, in comments after "LARGE SPOT-BREASTED" add "/GREATER SPOT-BREASTED"

430 *Meliphaga orientalis*, in comments after "SMALL SPOT-BREASTED" add "/LESSER SPOT-BREASTED"

430 *Meliphaga analoga*, in comments after "ALLIED" add "/MIMETIC"

430 *Meliphaga vicina*, change "sw New Guinea" to "**se New Guinea**"

431 *Lichenostomus frenatus*, change end of range to "...ne Queensland (Atherton Tableland)."

431 *Lichenostomus hindwoodi*, change end of range to "...ce Queensland (Clarke Range)."

432 *Lichenostomus penicillatus*, change end of range to "...se Australia (from Eyre pen. E to se New S. Wales)."

432 *Oreornis chrysogenys*, in heading change "Van Oort" to "van Oort"

432 *Apalopteron familiare,* change comments to
"Relationships uncertain, no DNA-DNA hybridization
data. Deignan (1958: 133-136) placed this species in the
Meliphagidae, but recent suggestions have included it as
a relative of timaliines or zosteropids (H. D. Pratt, pers.
comm.). (WHITE-EYED HONEYEATER)."

433 *Melitograis gilolensis,* in heading change "1851" to
"1850"

434 *Philemon buceroides,* change end of range to "...1912,
MELVILLE ISLAND FRIARBIRD (MELVILLE FRIARBIRD)
[8506.1]."

435 *Melidectes nouhuysi,* in heading change "Van Oort" to
"van Oort"

435 *Melidectes princeps,* in heading change "1951" to
"(1951)"

435 *Melipotes gymnops,* change comments to "*M. gymnops,
M. fumigatus* and *M. ater* are allopatric, and the first two
may be conspecific. (LARGE ..."

435 *Melipotes ater,* remove superspecies

436 *Moho nobilis,* change range to "Probably extinct (last
definite record in 1898, reported heard in 1934);
formerly..."

438 *Acanthagenys rufogularis,* in heading change "1858" to
"1838"

438 *Anthochaera lunulata,* in heading change "1832" to
"1838"

438 **Epthianura tricolor** (not **Ephthianura**); change
comments to "...indicates that *Epthianura* and
Ashbyia..."; also change *Ephthianura* to *Epthianura* in
headings for *E. aurifrons, E. crocea* and *E. albifrons,* and
twice in comments under *Ashbyia lovensis.*"

438 *Pardalotus punctatus,* in range change "¶*xanthopygos*" to
"¶*xanthopygus*" twice

439 *Pardalotus striatus,* change range to "...¶*melanocephalus*
Gould 1838, BLACK-HEADED PARDALOTE...¶*striatus,*
YELLOW-TIPPED PARDALOTE..."

439 *Crateroscelis murina,* delete "*C. nigrorufa* and"

439 *Crateroscelis nigrorufa,* change "between" to
"overlapping both"; in comments after "BLACK-
HEADED" add "/BLACK-BACKED"

439 *Crateroscelis robusta,* change "both preceding species"
to "*C. murina*"

440 *Sericornis arfakianus,* change comments to
"(DUSKY/OLIVE SCRUBWREN)."

440 *Sericornis papuensis,* change "c,e New Guine" to "c,e
New Guinea"

441 *Acanthiza pusilla,* in range change "North 1847" to
"North 1904"; change end of comments to "...above).
[BROWN THORNBILL]. See *A. katherina.*"

443 *Gerygone ruficollis,* in comments after "TREEFERN" add
"/RUFOUS-BREASTED"

444 *Gerygone insularis,* change English name to LORD HOWE
ISLAND GERYGONE (not LORD HOWE GERYGONE); at end
of comments add "(LORD HOWE GERYGONE)."

444 *Gerygone modesta,* change English name to NORFOLK
ISLAND GERYGONE (not NORFOLK GERYGONE); in
comments delete "ISLAND"

444 *Gerygone albofrontata,* delete superspecies entry
"*[igata]*"; change English name to CHATHAM ISLANDS
GERYGONE (not CHATHAM GERYGONE); change
comments to "[>*Hapolorhynchus*]. (CHATHAM
GERYGONE)."

444 **Petroicidae,** *not* **Eopsaltriidae;** add comments
"Petroicidae Mathews 1919-1920 has priority over
Eopsaltriidae Mathews 1946."

452 *Eurocephalus anguitimens,* in comments change
"*rueppellii*" to "*rueppelli*"

452 *Vireolanius pulchellus,* change range to "...Nicaragua,
locally on Pacific slope of El Salvador, and on both
slopes..."

453 *Vireo pallens,* change beginning of comments to "The
two groups may represent distinct species (Parkes
1989b). *V. pallens* and the following four..."

453 *Vireo crassirostris,* change "**Providencia**" to "**I.
Providencia**"

454 *Vireo cassinii,* in heading change "1866" to "1858"

454 *Vireo solitarius,* change English name to BLUE-HEADED
VIREO; in comments, delete "(BLUE-HEADED VIREO)."

454 *Vireo philadelphicus,* change range to "...n Michigan, n
New England and Prince Edward I. Winters..."

455 *Vireo gilvus,* after "New Brunswick" add "and s Nova
Scotia"; after "sw Tennessee," add "w S. Carolina,"

455 *Vireo leucophrys,* after "Tamaulipas S" add "locally"

455 Split *Hylophilus poicilotis* into two species:

Hylophilus amaurocephalus (Nordmann) 1835. GREY-EYED
GREENLET. [5810.2.]
Dry woodland, scrubby pastures, forest edge. Lowlands
to 1800 m of **e Brazil** (from Piauí, Ceará, Paraíba and Bahia S
to ne São Paulo and c Minas Gerais).
AG (~GREENLET): VIREO. See *H. poicilotis.*

Hylophilus poicilotis Temminck 1822. RUFOUS-CROWNED
GREENLET. [5810.]
Humid forest, second growth. Lowlands to 1800 m of
sc,se S. America in n Bolivia (Beni), e Paraguay, n Argentina
(Misiones) and s Brazil (sw Mato Grosso, s Minas Gerais, São
Paulo, Paraná, Santa Catarina, n Rio Grande do Sul).
H. amaurocephalus and *H. poicilotis* differ in morphol-
ogy (including eye and bill color) and vocalizations, and are
sympatric in southern Minas Gerais and northeastern São
Paulo (Willis 1991).

455 *Hylophilus muscicapinus,* change range to "...[4778]; **wc
S. America** in c Brazil (...) and ne Bolivia (ne Santa
Cruz) ¶*griseifrons*..."

456 *Hylophilus hypoxanthus,* delete "(S to r. Marañón)"

456-457 *Psophodes olivaceus,* change "**e Australia**" to "**ne
Australia**"; before "from se Queensland" add "**e,se
Australia**"

458 Under Tribe Mohouini, change comments to: "Olson
(1990c) presented osteological evidence to support his
argument that *Mohoua* is not a member of the Corvida
but did not specify to which of the Passerida he thought it
to be related. We retain *Mohoua* in the Corvida on the
basis of the DNA hybridization evidence presented in
Sibley and Ahlquist (1990, figs. 229, 230)."

458 *Mohoua albicilla,* change comments to "...*ochrocephala,*
although Olson (1990c) presented evidence that the two
are specifically distinct."

458 *Mohoua ochrocephala,* change end of comments to
"...See *M. albicilla* and *M. novaeseelandiae.*"

458 *Mohoua novaeseelandiae,* change comments to
"...between '*Finschia*' *novaeseelandiae* and the *Mohoua
[ochrocephala]* superspecies (Sibley and Ahlquist
1987a), supported also by the osteological studies of
Olson (1990c). [>*Finschia*]..."

459 *Pachycephala grisola,* before "Lombok" add "Bali,"; in
comments change "1989" to "1989a" in two places

459 *Pachycephala albiventris,* change beginning of range to "Lowlands to 2000 m of **n,nc**..."; in comments change "1989" to "1989a"

459 *Pachycephala homeyeri,* change range to "**C,s Philippines** (Tablas, Sibuyan, Masbate, Ticao, Panay, Negros, Cebu, Sulu Arch.)."

459 *Pachycephala phaionotus,* in heading change "1851" to "1850"

460 *Pachycephala philippensis,* after "Luzon," add "Catanduanes,"

460 *Pachycephala griseiceps,* change English name to GREY-HEADED WHISTLER (not GREY); in comments change "GREY-HEADED" to "GREY"

460 *Pachycephala pectoralis,* change end of range to "...1838, NORFOLK ISLAND WHISTLER (NORFOLK WHISTLER) [0624.3]."

460 *Pachycephala soror,* change "discusssed" to "discussed"

461 *Pachycephala implicata,* change English name to HOODED WHISTLER (not MOUNTAIN); in comments before "SOLOMONS MOUNTAIN" add "MOUNTAIN"

461 *Pachycephala leucogastra,* in heading change "d'Albertis" to "D'Albertis"

462 *Pitohui kirhocephalus,* in comments change "WOOD-SHRIKE" to "WOODSHRIKE"

463 *Platylophus galericulatus,* in heading change "1817" to "1816"; in range change "1851" to "1850"

463 *Aphelocoma californica,* delete "s Wyoming,"

463 *Aphelocoma unicolor,* after "México," add "Hidalgo,"

464 *Cyanolyca cucullata,* before "Veracruz," add "Hidalgo,"

464 *Cyanocorax violaceus,* after "Pando" add ", n La Paz"

464 *Cyanocorax cristatellus,* after "Paulo)" add ", ne Bolivia (ne Santa Cruz)"

466 *Urocissa caerulea,* change English name to "FORMOSAN MAGPIE"; change comments to "(TAIWAN MAGPIE)."

466 Split *Cissa thalassina* into the following two species:

Cissa hypoleuca Salvadori and Giglioli 1885. YELLOW-BREASTED MAGPIE. [3458.1.]
Dense woodland. Lowlands to 1500 m of **se Asia** in s China (s Szechwan, Kwangsi, Hainan), se Thailand, s Laos and s Vietnam.
Although often considered a race of *C. thalassina, C. hypoleuca* may be more closely related to *C. chinensis;* recognized as a species by Goodwin (1976: 190, 202-203). (EASTERN MAGPIE). AG (+N): GREEN-MAGPIE.

Cissa thalassina (Temminck) 1826. SHORT-TAILED MAGPIE. [3458.]
Dense woodland. Mts. of **n Borneo** ¶*jefferyi* Sharpe 1888, BORNEAN MAGPIE [3458.2]; **Java** ¶*thalassina,* SHORT-TAILED MAGPIE [3458].
See *C. hypoleuca.*

467 *Pica pica,* change range to "...Kamchatka) and S to n Mediterranean region (...), Turkey,...Taiwan, and **w N. America**...w Kansas ¶*pica,* BLACK-BILLED MAGPIE [475]; nw Africa (from ne Mauritania to Tunisia) ¶*mauritanica* Malherbe 1845, NORTH AFRICAN MAGPIE [2445.1]. Winters (¶*pica*) to lower...Intro. (¶*pica*) Japan (n Kyushu)."; at beginning of comments add "The unique area of bare skin behind the eye, which is turquoise in life, suggests possible species status for *mauritanica* (L. Larson, pers. comm.)."

468 *Ptilostomus afer,* change range to "...s Mali, Burkina Faso, s Niger, n Ivory Coast, Ghana, Benin and Nigeria to Cameroon, C. African Rep., s Sudan, ne Zaire, sw Ethiopia, Uganda and w Kenya."

469 Ranges of *Corvus woodfordi* and *C. meeki* are reversed; after exchanging range accounts only (but not comments), sequence *C. meeki* before *C. woodfordi.*

469 *Corvus woodfordi,* in comments change "[SOLOMON CROW]" to "[SOLOMON ISLANDS CROW]"

469 *Corvus capensis,* change range to "...e Uganda, w,c Kenya and ce Tanzania; from wc,ne Angola..."

470 *Corvus brachyrhynchos,* before "nc British Columbia," add "se Alaska (E of *C. caurinus*),"

470 **Corvus [ossifragus] ossifragus, Corvus [ossifragus] imparatus** and **Corvus [ossifragus] sinaloae,** including sequence change

470 *Corvus imparatus,* change range to "...1000 m of **cs U.S. and ne Mexico** from Nuevo León, Tamaulipas and s Texas (lower Rio Grande v.) S to..."; change comments to "(MEXICAN CROW). See *C. ossifragus* and *C. sinaloae.*"

470 *Corvus sinaloae,* in heading change "Davis 1958" to "Davis (1958)"; change comments to "Formerly considered conspecific with *imparatus* (as the MEXICAN CROW), but *sinaloae* appears to be a distinct species (Davis 1958; Hardy 1990). See *S. ossifragus.*"

470 *Corvus ossifragus,* add comments "Hardy (1990) discussed relationships in the *C. [ossifragus]* superspecies."

470 *Corvus corone,* before "Ireland" add "Faroe Is.,"; in comments remove "southern Scotland,"; after "allospecies" add "(e.g., Stepanyan 1990c)"

470 *Corvus levaillantii,* change end of range to "...n Burma, n Thailand and Andaman Is."

471 *Corvus boreus,* change habitat and range to "Wet sclerophyll woodland. Locally in **se Australia** (ne New S. Wales)."

472 *Melampitta lugubris,* in comments after "...1987b)" add ", probably closest to *Cnemophilus macgregorii* (Frith and Frith 1990)."

*472 **Loboparadisea** (not **Loboparadisaea**)

472 *Cnemophilus macgregorii,* at end of comments add "See *Melampitta lugubris.*"

472 *Macgregoria pulchra,* in heading change "MACGREGOR'S" to "MACGREGOR'S"

472 *Lycocorax pyrrhopterus,* in heading change "1851" to "1850"

473 *Semioptera wallacii,* in comments after "*Semeioptera wallacei*" add "; the former has now been conserved by the I.C.Z.N. (1990)."

473 *Parotia sefilata,* in comments change "BIRD-OR-PARADISE" to "BIRD-OF-PARADISE"

474 Split *Ptiloris magnificus* into the following two species:

Ptiloris [magnificus] magnificus (Vieillot) 1819. MAGNIFI-CENT RIFLEBIRD. [8263.]
Forest. Lowlands to 1450 m of **Australian region** in w,c New Guinea (E to Sepik r. and Kratke Mts.), and ne Australia in ne Queensland (Cape York pen. S to Albatross Bay and Chester r.).
[=*Craspedophora* (~*Ptiloris*)]. (PRINCE ALBERT RIFLE-BIRD). [MAGNIFICENT RIFLEBIRD]. See *P. intercedens.*

Ptiloris [magnificus] intercedens Sharpe 1882. EASTERN
          RIFLEBIRD. [8263.1.]

Forest. Lowlands to 1000 m of **e New Guinea** (W to
Astrolabe Bay and Hall Sound).

Beehler and Swaby (1991) gave evidence for the specific
distinctness of *P. intercedens*.

474 *Ptiloris victoriae*, change to *P. [paradiseus] victoriae*;
change comments to "Sometimes considered conspecific
with *P. paradiseus*. (VICTORIA/...). [PARADISE
RIFLEBIRD]."

474 *Ptiloris paradiseus*, change to *P. [paradiseus]
paradiseus*; add comments "See *P. victoriae*."

474 *Astrapia mayeri*, at end of comments add *"Astarchia
barnsei* Iredale (1954) is an apparent hybrid *Astrapia
mayeri* x *A. stephaniae*."

474 *Paradisaea apoda*, in comments before "[GREATER
BIRD-OF-PARADISE]" add "*P. bloodi* Iredale (1954) is an
apparent hybrid *P. apoda* x *P. rudolphi*."

475 *Paradisaea rudolphi*, at end of comments add "See *P.
apoda*."

475 *Cracticus mentalis*, in heading change "d'Albertis" to
"D'Albertis"

475 *Cracticus cassicus*, change "Numfoor" to "Numfor"

475 *Cracticus nigrogularis*, change end of range to
"...Victoria; Tasmania)."

475 *Gymnorhina tibicen*, after "(Taveuni)" add "and New
Zealand"

476 *Strepera graculina*, after "extreme se S. Australia)" add
", also **Lord Howe I.**"

476-477 Change "WOOD-SWALLOW" to "WOODSWALLOW" in
all cases

476 *Artamus leucorynchus*, after "Andaman Is.," add "Malay
pen.,"

477 *Pityriasis gymnocephala*, change comments to
"...*Pityriasis* is artamine (Ahlquist,...BALD-HEADED
WOODSHRIKE)."

477 *Oriolus forsteni*, in heading change "1851" to "1850"

478 *Oriolus xanthonotus*, after "adjacent is.)" add ", Java";
change "See *O. albiloris*." to "See *O. steerii*."

478 *Oriolus steerii*, before "**Philippines**" add "**c,s**"; at end of
comments add "See *O. albiloris*."

478 *Oriolus albiloris*, change comments to "May be
conspecific with *O. steerii*, although B. King..."

478 *Oriolus auratus*, before "s Niger," add "sw Mali,"

478 *Oriolus larvatus*, after "Angola," add "sw C. African
Rep.,"

479 *Oriolus xanthornus*, before "n,e Sumatra," add
"Andaman Is.,"

479-485 Change "CUCKOO-SHRIKE" to "CUCKOOSHRIKE" in
all cases

479 *Coracina javensis*, JAVAN CUCKOOSHRIKE (not
MALAYSIAN CUCKOO-SHRIKE)

480 *Coracina novaehollandiae*, change range to "Lowlands
of **Australian region** in se New Guinea and Australia
(incl. Tasmania). Winters..."

480 *Coracina leucopygia*, in heading change "1851" to
"1850"

480 *Coracina papuensis*, in comments change "*papuensiS*" to
"*papuensis*"

481 *Coracina pectoralis*, change range to "**Africa** from
Senegal, Guinea-Bissau and s Mali E to Nigeria,..."

481 *Coracina caesia*, change range to "...**Africa** from se
Nigeria, sw Cameroon (incl. Bioko), n C. African Rep.,
se Sudan, Ethiopia and n Somalia S through ne,ce Zaire,
Kenya,..."

481 *Coracina azurea*, change range to "...Ghana, Nigeria, s
Cameroon, sw C. African Rep. and n,ne Zaire, and S to
Gabon, Congo Rep., sw,c,ce Zaire and sw Uganda."

481 *Coracina graueri*, change range to "Mts. above 1500 m
of **ec Africa** in ne,ce Zaire (...) and sw Uganda."

481 *Coracina cinerea*, ASHY CUCKOOSHRIKE (not
MADAGASCAR); at end of comments add
"(MADAGASCAR CUCKOO-SHRIKE)."

482 *Coracina schisticeps*, in comments after "SLATY" add
"BLACK-TIPPED"

482 *Coracina holopolia*, change English name to SOLOMON
ISLANDS CUCKOOSHRIKE (not SOLOMON CUCKOO-
SHRIKE); in comments before "CICADA" add
"SOLOMON/"

482 *Coracina melaschistos*, change "from of" to "of"

483 *Lalage tricolor*, change range to "**Australian region** in
drier parts of Australia and se New Guinea (Port
Moresby area). Winters..."

483 *Lalage leucomela*, change range to "...Duke of York,
Tabar and Lihir...Newcastle area) ¶*leucomela*, VARIED
TRILLER [8308]; **n Bismarck Arch.** (Mussau I., in St.
Matthias Is.) ¶*conjuncta* Rothschild and Hartert 1924,
MUSSAU TRILLER [8308.1]."; at beginning of comments
add "Coates (1990: 47-48) suggested that *conjuncta* may
represent a distinct species."

483 *Lalage leucopyga*, before "Norfolk I." add "(formerly)"

483 *Campephaga petiti*, change range to "**C Africa** from se
Nigeria, s Cameroon, C. African Rep., ne Zaire, w
Uganda and w Kenya S to nw Angola and se,ce Zaire."

484 *Campephaga quiscalina*, after "s Cameroon," add "sw C.
African Rep.,"

484 *Campephaga lobata*, change range to "**W Africa** in
Sierra Leone, Liberia, Ivory Coast and s Ghana."

487 *Rhipidura phasiana*, before "Beehler," add "Ford (1981)
and"

487 *Rhipidura fuliginosa*, change range to "...New Caledonia,
Loyalty Is. (Lifou), Vanuatu (incl. Banks Is.) and s
Solomon Is...."

487 *Rhipidura lepida*, change "Pepeliu" to "Peleliu"

488 *Rhipidura rufifrons*, change "**Melanesia**" to
"**Micronesia**"

488 *Dicrurus ludwigii*, change range to "**N,c Africa** from
Senegambia, Guinea-Bissau and Sierra Leone E to s
Cameroon, C. African Rep., n,ne Zaire,...w Kenya, and S
to sw Zaire..."

488 *Dicrurus atripennis*, after "s Cameroon" add ", C.
African Rep."

489 *Dicrurus hottentottus*, before "n Borneo" add "Java,
Bali,"

490 *Dicrurus megarhynchus*, in comments after "NEW
IRELAND" add "/PARADISE"

490 *Erythrocercus mccallii*, after "s Cameroon," add "sw C.
African Rep.,"

490 *Erythrocercus holochlorus*, change "Ehrlanger" to
"Erlanger"

490 *Elminia longicauda*, change range to "...Sierra Leone,
sw Mali and Burkina Faso E to Cameroon,...Uganda, w
Kenya and nw Tanzania."; in comments after
"NORTHERN" add "/BLUE"

490 *Trochocercus nigromitratus*, change range to "Lowlands to 1500 m of **w,c Africa** from Liberia, Ivory Coast, Ghana, s Nigeria, s Cameroon, sw C. African Rep., n,ne Zaire, extreme s Sudan, Uganda and w Kenya S to Gabon and c,ce Zaire."

491 *Trochocercus nitens*, after "s Cameroon," add "sw C. African Rep.,"

491 *Trochocercus cyanomelas*, change range to "...Uganda, c,se Kenya and s Somalia S through..."

491 *Hypothymis helenae*, change range to "...1000 m of **Philippines** (Luzon, Polillo Is., Catanduanes, Samar, Dinagat, Siargao, ne Mindanao) ¶*helenae*..."

491 *Hypothymis coelestis*, delete "Camiguin Sur,"

491 *Terpsiphone rufiventer*, change range to "...s Cameroon (incl. Bioko), s C. African Rep.,...sw,cs,ce Zaire and extreme nw Tanzania ¶*rufiventer*, BLACK-HEADED PARADISE-FLYCATCHER [7514]; **Pagalu** (in Gulf of Guinea) ¶*smithii* (Fraser) 1843, ANNOBON PARADISE-FLYCATCHER [7514.1]."

491 *Terpsiphone rufocinerea*, change "**wc,sc,cn,ne Zaire**" to "**wc Africa** in w,se Cameroon, sw C. African Rep., ne Gabon and wc,sc,cn,ne Zaire"

491 *Terpsiphone viridis*, change "from s Niger," to "through Burkina Faso, s Niger,"

492 *Terpsiphone paradisi*, change "Andaman and Nicobar is.," to "Nicobar Is.,"

492 *Terpsiphone atrocaudata*, after "Luzon," add "Palawan,"

492 *Terpsiphone cinnamomea*, before "Mindanao," add "Dinagat, Siargao, Camiguin Sur,"

493 *Mayrornis versicolor*, change English name to OGEA MONARCH (not VERSICOLORED); in comments before "FIJI" add "VERSICOLORED/"

493 *Neolalage banksiana*, change range to "**Se Melanesia** in Vanuatu (S to Éfaté, incl. Banks Is.)."

493 *Clytorhynchus pachycephaloides*, change range to "**Melanesia** in Vanuatu (incl. Banks and Torres is.) and New Caledonia."

493 *Clytorhynchus nigrogularis*, change range to "Mts. of **Melanesia and sw Polynesia** in Santa Cruz Is. and Fiji (...)."

495 *Monarcha verticalis*, change "1964" to "(1964)"; at beginning of comments, add "*M. ateralba* was used originally by Salomonsen (1964), but the genus is masculine."

495 *Myiagra erythrops*, change English name to MANGROVE FLYCATCHER (not PALAU); in comments change "MANGROVE" to "PALAU"

496 *Myiagra caledonica*, change English name to MELANESIAN FLYCATCHER (not NEW CALEDONIAN); change range to "...Vanuatu (incl. Banks and Torres is.) and s Solomon is. (Rennell)."; in comments change "MELANESIAN" to "NEW CALEDONIAN"

496 *Myiagra vanikorensis*, change range to "Lowlands of **Melanesia and sw Polynesia** in Santa Cruz Is. (Vanikoro) and Fiji."

497 *Aegithina viridissima*, in heading change "1851" to "1850"

497 *Nilaus afer*, after "se Zaire," add "Rwanda,"

497 *Dryoscopus gambensis*, change range to "...s Mali, Burkina Faso, Nigeria,...Ethiopia and n Somalia, and S (except..."

498 *Dryoscopus angolensis*, before "se Sudan," add "n C. African Rep.,"

498 *Dryoscopus sabini*, after "s Cameroon" add ", sw C. African Rep."

498 *Tchagra senegala*, after "**African region**" add "S of Sahara"

498 *Tchagra australis*, change range to "...n,c Angola and nw Zimbabwe ¶*souzae* (Barboza du Bocage)..."

498 *Tchagra ruficeps*, after "¶*rufinuchalis*" add "(Sharpe) 1895"

499 *Laniarius luehderi*, change range to "**C. Africa** from e Nigeria and s Cameroon S to sw Zaire, and E across sw C. African Rep. and n Zaire..."

499 After *Laniarius amboimensis*, add the following new species:

Laniarius liberatus Smith, Arctander, Fjeldså and Amir (1991). BULO BURTI BOUBOU. [6595.1.]
Acacia thickets. **C Somalia** (known from a single individual).

This species was described by Smith et al. (1991) from a captive individual. In addition to extensive photographs, blood samples (from which DNA sequencing was done on the mtDNA gene cyt-b) and molted feathers were collected as type material.

499 *Laniarius aethiopicus*, place habitat and range in one paragraph, comments in second, breaking paragraphs between "Transvaal)." and "(BOUBOU"

499 *Laniarius bicolor*, change English name to GABON BOUBOU (not GABOON); in comments change "GABON" to "GABOON"

499 *Laniarius erythrogaster*, change range to "**C Africa** from Nigeria and c,n Cameroon E to Sudan, Eritrea and w,s Ethiopia, and S to C. African Rep., ne,se Zaire, Uganda, Rwanda, nw Kenya and nw Tanzania."

499 *Laniarius mufumbiri*, change end of range to "...Uganda, nw Kenya and nw Tanzania."

500 *Telophorus bocagei*, change range to "...s Cameroon, C. African Rep., n,ne Zaire, Uganda and w Kenya..."

500 *Telophorus sulphureopectus*, before "s Niger," add "sw Mali,"

500 *Telophorus multicolor*, change range to "Locally in **w,c Africa** from sw Mali, Sierra Leone and Liberia E to s Cameroon, C. African Rep. and ne Zaire,..."

500 *Telophorus nigrifrons*, before "Zambia," add "extreme e Angola,"

500 *Telophorus kupeensis*, in heading change "(Serle) 1951" to "(Serle 1951)"

500 *Telophorus viridis*, in comments change "*Calophoneuss*" to "*Calophoneus*"

501 *Telophorus dohertyi*, after "w Uganda" add ", Rwanda"

501 *Malaconotus cruentus*, after "s Cameroon," add "sw C. African Rep.,"

501 *Malaconotus lagdeni*, change range to "Locally in lowlands and mts. to 3800 m of **w,ec Africa** in Sierra Leone, Liberia, Ivory Coast, s Ghana and ce Zaire."

501 *Malaconotus gladiator*, change range to "Mts., 1300-2000 m, of **wc Africa** in se Nigeria and s Cameroon."

501 *Malaconotus blanchoti*, change range to "**Africa** from Senegambia, sw Mali and Sierra Leone E through Burkina Faso, n Ghana,..."

501 *Malaconotus monteiri*, change end of range to "...(Cameroon Mt., one specimen); and questionably w Kenya (Kakamega Forest, one specimen that has been lost)."

501 *Prionops plumatus*, change range to "...Nigeria, Cameroon and s Chad ¶*plumatus*..."

501 *Prionops caniceps*, in heading change "1851" to "1850"

501 *Prionops rufiventris*, change English name to GABON HELMETSHRIKE (not GABOON); in comments change "GABON" to "GABOON"

502 *Bias flammulatus*, change end of range to "...nw Angola, s Zaire (...) and extreme nw Tanzania."

502 *Bias musicus*, before "Uganda" add "sw Sudan,"

502 *Batis diops*, at beginning of comments add "The gender of the genus *Batis* is feminine (Clancey 1989; Dowsett 1990)."

503 *Batis senegalensis*, before "Ghana," add "Ivory Coast, Burkina Faso,"

503 *Batis orientalis*, change range to "C,ne Africa in n Nigeria, c,s Chad, C. African Rep., s Sudan, ne Uganda, Ethiopia, Somalia and nw,ne Kenya."

503 *Batis perkeo*, after "extreme se Sudan," add "ne Uganda,"

503 *Batis occulta*, in heading change "[7597.]" to "[7497.]"

503 *Platysteira cyanea*, change range to "W,c Africa from Senegambia, sw Mali and Guinea-Bissau...Uganda (incl. is in L. Victoria), w Kenya and nw Tanzania; occurs..."; at beginning of comments add "(SCARLET-SPECTACLED WATTLE-EYE)."

504 *Platysteira castanea*, change range to "...s Cameroon, C. African Rep., n,ne Zaire,...sw,cs,ce Zaire, ne Zambia and extreme nw Tanzania."

504 *Platysteira tonsa*, after "Gabon" add ", sw C. African Rep.,"

504 *Platysteira jamesoni*, change end of range to "...Uganda, w Kenya and extreme nw Tanzania."

504 *Platysteira concreta*, change range to "...Liberia, Ivory Coast, Ghana,...ne,ce Zaire, w Uganda and w Kenya ¶*concreta*..."

504 *Tephrodornis gularis*, in comments change "prionopine" to "vangine"

504 **Calicalicus madagascariensis** (not *Calicalius*)

504 *Schetba rufa*, change range to "Locally in lowlands to 2000 m of **w,n Madagascar** (...)."

504 *Vanga curvirostris*, change range to "Lowlands to 1800 m of **Madagascar.**"

504 *Xenopirostris xenopirostris*, change range to "Lowlands of **sw,s Madagascar** (...)."

504 *Xenopirostris damii*, change range to "Lowlands of **nw Madagascar** (...)."

505 *Xenopirostris polleni*, change range to "Lowlands to 1000 m of **nw coastal,e Madagascar** (...)."

505 *Falculea palliata*, change range to "Lowlands to 900 m of **w,n,s Madagascar** (...)."

505 *Artamella viridis*, change range to "Lowlands to 2000 m of **Madagascar.**"

505 *Leptopterus chabert*, change English name to CHABERT'S VANGA (not CHABERT); change range to "Lowlands to 1800 m of **Madagascar.**"; add comments "(CHABERT VANGA)."

505 *Cyanolanius madagascarinus*, change "Madagascar" to "n,e Madagascar"

505 *Oriolia bernieri*, change range to "Lowlands to 900 m of **ne Madagascar** (...)."

505 *Euryceros prevostii*, change English name to HELMET VANGA (not the HELMETBIRD); add comments "(THE HELMETBIRD)."

505 *Tylas eduardi*, change English name to TYLAS VANGA (not KINKIMAVO); change end of comments to "...Vangini. (THE KINKIMAVO/THE KINKIMANO)."

505 *Hypositta corallirostris*, change English name to NUTHATCH VANGA (not CORAL-BILLED NUTHATCH); in comments before "MADAGASCAR NUTHATCH" add "CORAL-BILLED/"

505 *Callaeas cinerea*, change "1851" to "1850"

505 Change *Creadion carunculatus* to **Philesturnus carunculatus**; at end of range add "Intro. Little Barrier I."; change comments to "The genus *Creadion* Vieillot 1816 was established for the Australian wattlebirds (now known as *Anthochaera* in Meliphagidae); however, the New Zealand species *carunculatus* was included as a 'wattlebird' at that time. The subsequent designation of the type-species for *Creadion* by Vigors and Horsfield 1827 unfortunately set the type as *carunculatus*. Because of the confusion surrounding *Creadion*, the S.C.O.N. (Standing Committee on Ornithological Nomenclature) of the International Ornithological Congress voted in December 1990 to suppress *Creadion* for purposes of synonymy, thus validating *Philesturnus* Geoffroy Saint-Hilaire 1832. The matter is awaiting plenary action by the International Zoological Commission, but it is felt advisable to adopt *Philesturnus* at this time. (THE TIEKO)."

*505 **Heteralocha acutirostris** (not **Heterolocha**)

505 *Picathartes gymnocephalus*, change range to "Locally in **w Africa** in Guinea, Liberia, Sierra Leone, Ivory Coast and Ghana."

506 *Bombycilla cedrorum*, change range to "...s Illinois, ec Mississippi, n Alabama, n Georgia and South Carolina. Winters..."

507 *Cinclus mexicanus*, in comments after "DIPPER" add "/WATER OUZEL"

507 *Neocossyphus fraseri*, change end of range to "...cs,ce Zaire, nw Zambia and extreme nw Tanzania."

507 *Neocossyphus rufus*, change range to "...s Cameroon, Rio Muni, Gabon, sw C. African Rep., nc,ne Zaire,..."

507 *Pseudocossyphus sharpei*, change English name to FOREST ROCK-THRUSH (not EASTERN ROBINCHAT); change "n,e,se Madagascar" to "**n,e Madagascar**"; change end of comments to "...EASTERN/SHARPE'S ROCK-THRUSH. AG (~*Pseudocossyphus*): ROBINCHAT. See *P. imerinus*."

507 *Pseudocossyphus bensoni*, change English name to BENSON'S ROCK-THRUSH (not FARKAS'S ROBINCHAT); change range to "Mts. of **sc Madagascar**."; change comments to "(FARKAS'S ROCK-THRUSH). See *P. imerinus*."

507 *Pseudocossyphus imerinus*, change English name to LITTORAL ROCK-THRUSH (not MADAGASCAR ROBINCHAT); change "n,e,se Madagascar" to "**n,e Madagascar**"; change comments to "...*Pseudocossyphus* were considered...(1964: 134). (MADAGASCAR ROCK-THRUSH). [MADAGASCAR ROCK-THRUSH]."

508 *Monticola brevipes*, in heading change "1938" to "1838"

508 *Monticola saxatilis*, change range to "...s Europe (N to se France, Switzerland and Poland), Mediterranean... Turkey, Near and Middle East, s Russia (...) and s S.S.R...Manchuria) and Afghanistan. Winters..."

508 *Monticola gularis*, change comments to "...with *M. cinclorhynchus*. (SWINHOE'S..."

509 *Myiophonus insularis*, change English name to
FORMOSAN WHISTLING-THRUSH (not TAIWAN); in
comments change "FORMOSAN" to "TAIWAN"

510 *Zoothera sibirica*, change end of range to "...se Asia and
w Indonesia."

510 *Zoothera tanganjicae*, change "*G. piaggiae*" to "*Z.
piaggiae*"

511 *Zoothera princei*, after "s Cameroon" add ", sw C.
African Rep."

511 *Zoothera guttata*, change range to "Locally in **se,s Africa**
in extreme se Zaire, s Tanzania, s Malawi and se S.
Africa (coastal Natal, se Cape prov.). Winters N to
coastal Kenya and Tanzania."; change end of comments
to "...(NATAL/FISCHER'S GROUND-THRUSH)."

512 *Zoothera heinei*, in heading change "1851" to "1850"

512 *Zoothera talaseae*, change range to "Mts., 550-1500 m,
of **Melanesia** in cs Bismarck Arch. (Umboi, New
Britain) and nw Solomon Is. (Bougainville)."; change
comments to "(BLACK-BACKED/TALASEA THRUSH). See
Z. margaretae."

512 *Zoothera margaretae*, add comments "Sometimes
considered conspecific with *Z. talaseae* (e.g., Coates
1990: 57) and called NORTHERN MELANESIAN GROUND-
THRUSH. (WHITE-BELLIED THRUSH)."

512 *Sialia mexicana*, after "s Alberta," add "cw
Saskatchewan,"

512 *Sialia currucoides*, change range to "...c Saskatchewan,
w Manitoba and nw Minnesota S in mts..."

513 *Myadestes lanaiensis*, in comments after "LANAI" add
"/MOLOKAI"

513 *Cichlopsis leucogenys*, in heading change "1851" to
"1850"

514 *Catharus aurantiirostris*, change range to "Mts, 600-
2900 m, of **Middle**...Guanacaste); n Colombia..."

515 *Turdus pelios*, in heading change "1851" to "1850";
change range to "...w Kenya, and S to c Angola,...¶*pelios*,
AFRICAN..."

516 *Turdus unicolor*, change English name to TICKELL'S
THRUSH (not INDIAN GREY); change comments to
"(INDIAN GREY THRUSH). [TICKELL'S THRUSH]."

516 *Turdus torquatus*, in comments delete "See *T.
viscivorus*."

516-517 *Turdus merula*, before "British Isles" add "Iceland,";
at end of range after "e Australia" add ", New Zealand"

517 *Turdus pallidus*, in comments after "Siberia" add "; the
two taxa are treated as full species by Stepanyan
(1990c)."

517 *Turdus chrysolaus*, in comments after "*celaenops*" add
"but considered a full species by Stepanyan (1990c)"

517 *Turdus ruficollis*, in comments after "river." add "Stepanyan (1990c) considered the two groups full species."

518 *Turdus naumanni*, at beginning of comments add
"Stepanyan (1990c) treated the two groups as full
species."

518 *Turdus philomelos*, at end of range after "se Australia"
add ", New Zealand"

518 *Turdus aurantius*, at end of comments add "(THE
HOPPING-DICK)."

519 *Turdus infuscatus*, after "México," add "Hidalgo,"

520 *Turdus amaurochalinus*, in heading change "1851" to
"1850"

520 *Turdus lawrencii*, after "Pando" add ", n La Paz"

520 *Turdus hauxwelli*, before "e Peru," add "e Ecuador,"

521 *Turdus jamaicensis*, add comments "(THE GLASS-EYE)."

521 *Turdus migratorius*, after "Tehuantepec)" add "and wc
Veracruz"

521 *Turdus rufitorques*, change "w Honduras" to "c
Honduras"

522 *Heinrichia calligyna*, in heading change "(Stresemann)"
to "Stresemann"

522 *Alethe poliocephala*, in heading change "1851" to
"1850"; in range change "**w Africa**" to "**w,c Africa**"

522 *Alethe diademata*, in heading change "1851" to "1850";
in range change "Gambia" to "Senegal"

522 *Alethe castanea*, before "n,ne Zaire" add "sw C. African
Rep. and"

523 *Melaenornis edolioides*, change range to "...sw Mali,
Burkina Faso and Sierra Leone...Uganda, w,c Kenya and
nw Tanzania."

523 *Melaenornis annamarulae*, change English name to
WEST AFRICAN BLACK-FLYCATCHER (not LIBERIAN);
change range to "Foothills of **w Africa** in e Guinea,
Sierra Leone, Liberia and wc,sw Ivory Coast."; change
comments to "(LIBERIAN/MRS. FORBES-WATSON'S
BLACK-FLYCATCHER)."

523 *Fraseria ocreata*, after "s Cameroon" add "(incl. Bioko)"

523 *Fraseria cinerascens*, change range to "**W,c Africa** from
Guinea-Bissau, Guinea, Liberia and Sierra Leone..."

524 *Rhinomyias brunneata*, in comments change "WHITE-
GORGETTED" to "WHITE-GORGETED"

524 *Rhimomyias albigularis*, in heading change "Sharpe
1888" to "Bourns and Worcester 1894"

524 *Muscicapa gambagae*, before "n Ghana" add "n Ivory
Coast and"

525 *Muscicapa randi*, change beginning of comments to
"Dickinson, Kennedy and Parkes (1991: 345-346)
recognized *randi*..."

525 *Muscicapa segregata*, in heading change "[773.1.]" to
"[9494.1.]"

525 *Muscicapa ruficauda*, before "n Pakistan" add "s S.S.R.
(e Uzbek, Tadzikistan), e Afghanistan,"

525 *Muscicapa muttui*, at end of range add "Winters in sw
India and Ceylon."

525 *Muscicapa ussheri*, delete superspecies entry; change
end of range to "...Ivory Coast, Ghana and Nigeria."

525 *Muscicapa infuscata*, delete superspecies entry; after "s
Cameroon," add "sw C. African Rep.,"; in comments
change "this superspecies in" to "*ussheri* and *fuliginosa*
[= *infuscata*] in"

525 *Muscicapa aquatica*, before "s Niger," add "sw Mali,"

525 *Muscicapa olivascens*, change range to "Locally in **w,c
Africa** from Liberia, Ivory Coast, s Ghana and s Nigeria
E to s Cameroon, C. African Rep. and n,ne Zaire,..."

526 *Muscicapa epulata*, change range to "Locally in **w,c
Africa** in Liberia, Ivory Coast, Ghana, Cameroon, Rio
Muni, sw C. African Rep., Gabon,..."

526 *Muscicapa sethsmithi*, change range to "Locally in **c
Africa** in s Nigeria, s Cameroon (incl. Bioko), sw C.
African Rep., Gabon..."

526 *Muscicapa comitata*, after "s Cameroon," add "sw C.
African Rep.,"

526 *Muscicapa tessmanni*, in heading change English name
to TESSMANN'S FLYCATCHER (not TESSMAN'S); change
range to "Locally in **w,c Africa** in Liberia, Ivory Coast,
Ghana, Nigeria, s Cameroon, Congo Rep. and sw,ne
Zaire.

526 *Muscicapa cassini*, change range to "**W,c Africa** from sw Mali, Liberia, Ivory Coast and Ghana E through s Nigeria, s Cameroon and C. African Rep. to n,ne Zaire,...cs,se,ce Zaire, extreme n Zambia and extreme nw Tanzania."

526 *Myioparus griseigularis*, change range to "Locally in **w,c Africa** in Liberia, Ivory Coast, Ghana, s Nigeria, s Cameroon, sw C. African Rep., nw Angola, Zaire (except se), w Uganda and extreme nw Tanzania."

526 *Humblotia flavirostris*, add comments "[<*Muscicapa* (≈*Muscicapella*)]."

526 *Ficedula hypoleuca*, change comments to "(PIED/ WESTERN PIED FLYCATCHER)."

526 *Ficedula albicollis*, change range to "...Moscow) S to Italy (incl. Sicily), Yugoslavia,..."

527 *Ficedula semitorquata*, in comments after "*albicollis*" add "(e.g., Stepanyan 1990c)"

527 *Ficedula parva*, change range to "**W Eurasia** from Denmark...Romania E to ec Russia (southern Ural Mts., Ukraine), and S locally to sc Europe (Balkans), s Russia (Caucasus, Transcaucasus), n Turkey and n Iran (s Caspian region) ¶*parva*, RED-BREASTED FLYCATCHER [2629.1]; and **e Eurasia** in c,s Siberia (from Ural Mts. and Altai E to Anadyrland, Kamchatka, n Ussuriland and Transbaicalia) and n Mongolia, possibly also e Tibet ¶*albicilla* (Pallas) 1811, RED-THROATED FLYCATCHER [771]. Winters (¶*parva*) in Pakistan and w India, rarely in ne Africa; and (¶*albicilla*) in c,e India, se Asia and Borneo."; at beginning of comments add "Svensson (1987) suggested that the two groups may represent separate species, based on morphology, vocalizations, and migration patterns."

527-528 *Ficedula hyperythra*, in comments change "))" to ")"

528 *Ficedula basilanica*, after "Leyte," add "Dinagat,"

528 *Ficedula crypta*, in heading change "(Vaurie) 1951" to "(Vaurie 1951b)"

528 *Ficedula westermanni*, delete "Culion,"

528 *Ficedula tricolor*, in comments remove parentheses around "Hodgson"

530 *Cyornis sanfordi*, at end of range add "."

530 *Cyornis concretus*, change English name to WHITE-TAILED FLYCATCHER (not WHITE-TAILED BLUE-FLYCATCHER)

531 *Cyornis rufigaster*, before "Malaya" add "**se Asia and Malay Arch. in**"

531 before *Horizorhinus dohrni*, insert two species of *Culicicapa* from p. 444

531 *Pogonocichla stellata*, after "Kenya," add "Rwanda, Burundi,"

531 *Stiphrornis erythrothorax*, change end of range to "...Gabon, sw C. African Rep., nw,n,nc,ne Zaire, extreme s Sudan, Uganda and extreme nw Tanzania."

531 *Sheppardia poensis*, before "sw Cameroon" add "se Nigeria,"

531 *Sheppardia cyornithopsis*, change range to "...Sierra Leone, Liberia and Ivory Coast, and from..."; in comments before "*Vibrissosylvia*" add ">"

532 *Sheppardia gunningi*, change range to "...Forest), ne,s Tanzania and..."

532 *Erithacus rubecula*, in comments remove "[]."

532 *Erithacus akahige*, in comments change "(~*Erithacus*)" to "(+N)"

532 *Luscinia luscinia*, after "n Yugoslavia" add ", Romania"

533 *Luscinia ruficeps*, after "w Shensi" add ", Szechwan"

533 *Luscinia obscura*, in heading and comments, change "Berezowsky" to "Berezowski"; in comments change "*E. pectardens*" to "*L. pectardens*"

533 *Luscinia pectardens*, at beginning of comments add "Includes *L. daulias* Koelz (1954)."

533 *Irania gutturalis*, at end of range add "Winters in Arabia and ne Africa."

534 *Cossypha roberti*, before "cw,s Cameroon" add "se Nigeria,"

534 *Cossypha anomala*, after "s Tanzania" add ", ne Zambia"

534 *Cossypha cyanocampter*, change range to "...s Cameroon, Gabon, C. African Rep., ne Zaire, s Sudan, Uganda, w Kenya and nw Tanzania."

534 *Cossypha polioptera*, after "e Sierra Leone," add "Liberia, Ivory Coast,"

534 *Cossypha heuglini*, change range to "...**c,s,e Africa** from Gabon, C. African Rep. and s Chad E to s Sudan, s Ethiopia and s Somalia, and S through Zaire, Uganda, Kenya, Malawi,..."

534 *Cossypha natalensis*, before "s Cameroon," add "e Nigeria,"

535 *Cossypha niveicapilla*, change range to "**W,c Africa** from Senegambia and sw Mali E to Ghana, Nigeria, Cameroon, C. African Rep., s Sudan..."

535 *Cossypha albicapilla*, change "Senegal" to "Senegambia"

535 *Xenocossyphus ansorgei*, in heading change "(Hartert)" to "Hartert"

535 *Cercotrichas hartlaubi*, change range to "Locally in **c Africa** in Cameroon, sw C. African Rep., cn,ne,ce Zaire, Uganda, c,s Kenya, Rwanda and nw Tanzania."

535 *Cercotrichas leucophrys*, change "**Ec Africa** in c,s Africa" to "**C,s Africa**"

536 *Cercotrichas podobe*, after "L. Chad area," add "C. African Rep.,"

537 *Phoenicurus alaschanicus*, in heading change "Przevalski" to "Przewalski"

537 *Phoenicurus erythronota*, change end of range to "...Winters S to ne Arabia and Middle East."

537 *Phoenicurus phoenicurus*, change range to "...Iran, n Iraq, s Russia (...), s S.S.R. (...) and nw Afghanistan (probably). Winters..."

539 *Enicurus schouleri*, change end of range to "...1910, FORMOSAN FORKTAIL (TAIWAN FORKTAIL) [2714.1]."

540 *Saxicola dacotiae*, change English name to CANARY ISLANDS CHAT (not CANARY CHAT); in comments delete "ISLAND"

540 *Saxicola torquata*, at end of habitat add "...trees, scrub, arid steppes."; change range to "...w,n Iran, and **African region**...Cameroon (incl. Bioko) and w Sudan, from Gabon,...S. Africa, and in sw Arabia, Comoro Is. (Grand Comoro) and Madagascar ¶*torquata*, COMMON STONECHAT [2709.1]; **c,e Eurasia** from nw,c Russia (W to White Sea and middle Volga r., and S to e Caucasus and e Transcaucasus) E across Siberia to w Anadyrland, Sea of Okhotsk and Sakhalin, and S to ne Iran, s S.S.R. (Transcaspia, e Turkestan, e Kazakhstan), Afghanistan, n Pakistan (Gilgit), n India (Himalayas from Kashmir E to Arunachal Pradesh, and S to Megahalaya, Assam and Nagaland), ne Burma, n Laos, China, Korea, Japan (Hokkaido, n,c Honshu) and Kuril Is. ¶*maura* (Pallas) 1773, SIBERIAN STONECHAT [765.1]; **ne**

Africa...[7552.1]. Winters (¶*torquata*) from British Isles, w,s Europe and Near East S to s Africa; (¶*maura*) S to ne Africa, Arabia, s Asia and Borneo."; change comments to "Although Vaurie (1959: 335) was unaware of any intergradation between *torquata* and *maura* where they meet in the Caucasus and Transcausus of southern Russia, the two forms intergrade freely there, producing many intermediates (M. Beaman, pers. comm.). (COLLARED...BUSHCHAT. [COMMON STONECHAT]. See *S. dacotiae* and *S. tectes*."

540 Delete *Saxicola maura* account

540 *Saxicola caprata*, change range to "...Philippines ¶*caprata*...se ranges) and Bismarck Arch. (Long I., e New Britain, Watom, s New Ireland) ¶*aethiops*..."

541 *Oenanthe monacha*, change "**ne Africa**" to "**ne Africa and sc Palearctic**"

541 *Oenanthe oenanthe*, delete "Spitsbergen,"; after "Iran," add "n Afghanistan,"

541 *Oenanathe lugens*, after "Middle East" add "and nw Arabia"

542 *Oenanthe finschii*, after "w,n Iran" add ", n Afghanistan"

542 *Oenanthe picata*, change end of range to "...Winters S to s Iran, e Arabia and c India."

542 *Oenanthe pleschanka*, in heading change superspecies to "*Oenanthe [hispanica] pleschanka*"; change comments to "...*O. hispanica* because of limited hybridization in the Caspian Sea area, but generally treated as a full species (e.g., Stepanyan 1990c). *Pleschanka*.../PLESCHANKA'S WHEATEAR). See..."

542 *Oenanthe cypriaca*, in heading change superspecies to "*Oenanthe [hispanica] cypriaca*"; in comments before "van den Berg" add "Sluys and"

542 *Oenanthe [hispanica] hispanica*, add superspecies and sequence before *O. pleschanka*; change range to "...Yugoslavia, w,s Romania and Greece...n Iraq, w,s Iran and s Russia (Transcaucasus); nw Africa..."; in comments after "WHEATEAR)." add "[PIED WHEATEAR]."

543 *Oenanthe heuglini*, change end of range to "...Chad, n C. African Rep., Sudan and sw Ethiopia to n Uganda and Kenya."

543 *Cercomela familiaris*, in heading change "(Stephens) 1826" to "(Wilkes) 1817"; change range to "**C,s Africa** from n Ghana, sw Mali, Ivory Coast, Benin, n Nigeria"; at beginning of comments add "Clancey and Brooke (1990) discussed the original citation."

543 *Cercomela sordida*, after "Ethiopia," add "e Uganda,"

543 *Myrmecocichla tholloni*, after "Gabon" add ", C. African Rep."

543 *Myrmecocichla nigra*, before "ne Zaire," add "C. African Rep.,"

544 *Myrmecocichla arnotti*, in comments after "not *arnoti*." add "Winterbottom and Skead (1965) claimed the spelling *arnotti* was a *lapsus calami* for *arnoti*, but it is not, even though Tristram may have spelled the man's name incorrectly. Not only does Tristram spell the name *arnotti* in the text as well as on the plate, but he also spelled the man's name "Arnott" in the text."

544 *Thamnolaea cinnamomeiventris*, change range to "...1200-2450 m, of **ne Africa** in extreme e Sudan and n,c Ethiopia...Uganda, s Ethiopia, Kenya..."

544 *Thamnolaea coronata*, change range to "**Subsaharan w,nc Africa** from Liberia, Ghana, n Togo,...E to C. African Rep. and sc Sudan."

544 *Aplonis atrifusca*, change range to "Lowlands to mt. tops of **Samoa.**"

545 *Aplonis striata*, change end of range to "...1859, LOYALTY ISLANDS STARLING (LOYALTY STARLING) [9673.1]."

545 *Aplonis fusca*, before "*Aplonis fusca*" add "†"; change range to "Extinct (before 1928); formerly **Lord Howe and Norfolk is.**"

546 *Onychognathus walleri*, before "Cameroon" add "se Nigeria and"

546 *Onychognathus tristramii*, change range to "...Near East, ne Egypt (Sinai pen.) and w,s Arabia (S to Yemen and s Oman)."

546 *Onychognathus morio*, change range to "...e Senegal and s Mali E through n,c Nigeria to sw C. African Rep., Sudan and Ethiopia, and S through e Uganda, Kenya,..."

546 *Onychognathus blythii*, change range to "**Ne Africa** in n Ethiopia and n Somalia (...)."

546 *Onychognathus fulgidus*, change habitat and range to "Forest clearings. **W,c Africa**...Cameroon (incl. Bioko and São Tomé), sw C. African Rep., n,ne Zaire..."

546 *Onychognathus tenuirostris*, after "ne,ce Zaire," add "w Uganda,"

547 *Lamprotornis purpureiceps*, change range to "...s Nigeria E to sw C. African Rep., n,ne Zaire, Uganda and nw Kenya, and S to sw Congo Rep. and sw,sc,ce Zaire."

547 *Lamprotornis purpureus*, change "Senegal" to "Senegambia"

547 *Lamprotornis nitens*, after "Botswana" add ", extreme s Mozambique"

547 *Lamprotornis chalcurus*, change range to "**Subsaharan Africa** from Senegambia E to Cameroon, s Sudan, Uganda and ne Kenya."

547 *Lamprotornis chalybaeus*, change range to "**Africa** from Senegambia E to Sudan and n Somalia, and S through..."

547 *Lamprotornis chloropterus*, change "Senegal" to "Senegambia"

547 *Lamprotornis splendidus*, change "extreme nw Tanzania" to "w Tanzania"

547 *Lamprotornis australis*, after "se Angola" add ", sw Zambia"

548 *Lamprotornis caudatus*, change "Senegal" to "Senegambia"

548 *Lamprotornis purpuropterus*, change range to "...ec,s Sudan, Ethiopia and s Somalia S through Kenya, Rwanda and Burundi to sw,ne Tanzania."

548 *Lamprotornis pulcher*, change "Senegal" to "Senegambia"

548 *Cinnyricinclus sharpii*, after "e Zaire" add ", Rwanda, Burundi"

548 *Spreo albicapillus*, change end of range to "...e,s Ethiopia, n Somalia and n Kenya."

549 *Creatophora cinerea*, delete "Zambia,"

549 *Necropsar rodericanus*, after "Extinct" add "(ca. 1750)"

549 *Sturnus vulgaris*, after "Turkey," add "Near East,"

550 *Sturnus melanopterus*, add comments "Feare and Nee (1992) presented evidence that *melanopterus* should be placed in *Acridotheres*, but an analysis of other species in *Sturnus* (especially *burmannicus*) and *Acridotheres* should be made before such action."

550 *Acridotheres grandis*, in heading change *Acridotheres [javanicus] grandis* to *Acridotheres [cinereus] grandis*; in range after "Bangladesh," add "Arunachal Pradesh,"; in comments change "*javanicus*" to "*cinereus*"

550 *Acridotheres javanicus*, change heading to "*Acridotheres [cinereus] cinereus* Bonaparte 1851. PALE-BELLIED MYNA. [3889.1.]"; change comments to "*A. cinereus* (Bonaparte), dated 1850 but published before 3 February 1851 (Browning and Monroe 1991: 382), antedates *A. javanicus* (Cabanis) 1851, also dated 1850 but published in October 1851 (Wolters 1982: 434). (WHITE-VENTED/JAVAN MYNA)..."

552 *Buphagus erythrorhynchus*, before "se Angola," add "sw C. African Rep.,"

552 *Mimus polyglottos*, after "e Oregon," add "c Washington,"

553 *Nesomimus trifasciatus*, in comments after "SANTA MARIA" add "/FLOREANA"

553 *Mimodes graysoni*, change habitat and range to "Scrub, woodland, thickets. **Revillagigedo Is.** (Socorro)."

553 *Toxostoma rufum*, after "s Florida" add "(incl. Florida Keys)"

554 *Toxostoma bendirei*, delete comments "See *T. cinereum*."

554 *Toxostoma cinereum*, in comments delete "Possibly conspecific with *T. bendirei*."

554 *Toxostoma curvirostre*, change "extreme w Oklahoma" to "w Oklahoma"

554 *Cinclocerthia gutturalis*, change beginning of comments to "Storer (1989) treated..."

554 *Sitta europaea*, after "Turkey," add "Near East,"

555 *Sitta cashmirensis*, before "n Pakistan" add "e Afghanistan,"

555 *Sitta villosa*, change range to "...e Tsinghai, Kansu and Szechwan, and from..."

556 Change page heading to "(Sitta-Certhiidae)"

556 *Sitta neumayer*, before "Greece," add "Albania,"

556 *Sitta tephronota*, after "Iran" add ", Afghanistan"

556 *Sitta frontalis*, delete ", Hainan"

556 *Sitta solangiae*, change range to "Mts. of **se Asia** in n,c Vietnam (...) and s China (Hainan)."; at end of comments add "The resident Hainan population of this complex is yellow-billed rather than red-billed, and better associated with *S. solangiae* than with *S. frontalis*, where it has traditionally been placed (Harrap 1991)."

556 *Tichodroma muraria*, before "ne Iran" add "Near East,"

556-557 *Certhia familiaris*, change end of range to "...ne Burma, Korea and Japan."

557 *Salpornis spilonotus*, after "Sierra Leone," add "Ivory Coast,"

557 *Campylorhynchus gularis*, in heading change "1859" to "1861"

558,560,562,564 Change page headings to "(Certhiidae)"

558 *Campylorhynchus rufinucha*, change range to "...**sc Mexico** in c Veracruz and e Puebla ¶*rufinucha*..."

558 *Campylorhynchus turdinus*, after "(Santa Cruz)" add ", n Paraguay"

558 *Campylorhynchus megalopterus*, in heading change *Campylorhynchus megalopterus* to *Campylorhynchus [zonatus] megalopterus*; change "c Oaxaca" to "n Oaxaca"; in comments delete ", but their ranges overlap"

558 *Campylorhynchus zonatus*, change range to "...n Puebla, e Oaxaca, Tabasco, Chiapas and s Campeche S to nc Nicaragua;..."

559 *Odontorchilus cinereus*, change range to "Lowlands of **wc S. America** in Amazonian Brazil (...) and ne Bolivia (ne Santa Cruz)."

559 *Catherpes mexicanus*, change comments to "[<*Salpinctes*)]. See *Hylorchilus sumichrasti*."

559 *Catherpes sumichrasti*, in heading change *Catherpes sumichrasti* to *Hylorchilus sumichrasti*; change range to "...wc Veracruz and extreme nw Oaxaca ¶*sumichrasti*, SUMICHRAST'S WREN [1649]; **sw Mexico** in se Oaxaca and w Chiapas ¶*navai* Crossin and Ely (1973), NAVA'S WREN [1649.1]."; change comments to "Although J. W. Hardy (pers. comm.) suggests that on the basis of song this species is congeneric with *Catherpes mexicanus* despite striking morphological differences, such differences in this case seem to warrant generic separation. The two groups differ vocally as well as morphologically and probably represent distinct species (S. Howell, pers. comm.). [<*Catherpes*]. (SUMI-CHRAST'S WREN)."

559 *Cistothorus platensis*, after "c Guatemala," add "Belize,"

560 *Thryothorus fasciatoventris*, after "Tolima" add ")"

561 *Thryothorus leucopogon*, in comments change "*leucopogon*" to "*thoracicus*"

562 *Thryothorus modestus*, change range to "...Guatemala, Belize and Honduras; Mosquitia of ne Honduras) and Panama (both slopes,..."

562 *Thryothorus guarayanus*, change "possibly Paraguay" to "n Paraguay"

562 *Troglodytes troglodytes*, after "Japan" add ", Korea"

563 *Uropsila leucogastra*, change "**w Mexico**" to "**Middle America**"

563 *Henicorhina leucosticta*, change range to "...c Peru (Huánuco) and n Brazil (...)."

564 *Henicorhina leucophrys*, before "Puebla" add "Hidalgo,"

564 *Cyphorhinus thoracicus*, change end of range to "...Puno) and wc Bolivia (La Paz)."

565 *Polioptila caerulea*, after "sw Wyoming," add "Colorado,"

565 *Polioptila melanura*, change range to "...s Nevada, s Utah, w,c Arizona, sw Colorado, c New Mexico..."

565 *Polioptila albiloris*, change range to "...Chiapas (also n Yucatán) S to nw Costa Rica (to Gulf of Nicoya area)."

565-566 *Polioptila plumbea*, change "1851" to "1850"

566 Change page heading to "(Certhiidae-Paridae)"

566 *Polioptila guianensis*, change end of range to "...Guianas and n,wc Brazil (S locally to Rondônia, upper r. Urucu, r. Tapajós and n Pará)."

566 *Remiz pendulinus*, change "(Severtzov)" to "(Severtsov)"; at beginning of comments add "Stepanyan (1990c) treated the two groups as full species."

566 *Remiz coronatus*, in heading change "(Severtzov)" to "(Severtsov)"

567 *Anthoscopus parvulus*, change range to "...*A. punctifrons*) from Senegambia E through s Mali, n Ivory Coast, s Niger, n Nigeria and C. African Rep..."

567 *Anthoscopus flavifrons*, before "s Ghana," add "Liberia, s Ivory Coast,"

567 *Anthoscopus caroli*, in comments after "species" add "Includes *A. pygmaea* Horniman (1956), a synonym of *A. (caroli) caroli*."

567 *Pholidornis rushiae*, change "Uganda" to "s Uganda"

567 *Parus lugubris*, change end of range to "...(sw Transcaucasus) and w,s Iran ¶*lugubris*, SOMBRE TIT [2465]; **n Iran** ¶*hyrcanus* (Zarudny and Loudon) 1905, HYRCANIAN TIT [2465.1]."; add comments "Stepanyan (1990c) considered the two groups separate species."

567 *Parus montanus*, change range to "...Sakhalin, n Korea, Japan...¶*songarus* Severtsov 1873..."; at end of comments add "Stepanyan (1990c) treated the two groups as distinct species."

568 *Parus melanolophus*, at beginning of range add "Considered conspecific with *P. ater* by Haffer (1989) because of a hybrid population in Nepal, but the two species appear to be sympatric without interbreeding elsewhere in the range of overlap."

569 *Parus ater*, after "Taiwan," add "Korea,"; at end of comments add "See *P. melanolophus*."

569 *Parus elegans*, change range to "**Philippines.**"

569 *Parus amabilis*, before "Palawan," add "Calamian Is.,"

569 *Parus guineensis*, change English name to WHITE-SHOULDERED TIT (not BLACK-TIT); at end of comments add "AG: BLACK-TIT."

569 *Parus leucomelas*, change English name to WHITE-WINGED TIT (not BLACK-TIT); change range to "**C,se Africa** S of...Ethiopia S to c Angola, Zambia, Malawi and n Mozambique ¶*leucomelas*, WHITE-WINGED TIT [7303]; **sw Africa** in s Angola and ne Namibia (S to Damaraland) ¶*carpi* Macdonald and Hall (1967), CARP'S TIT [6386]."; change end of comments to "...233). Clancey (1972b: 236-244) and Eck (1988) considered *carpi* a race of *P. leucomelas*. (BLACK TIT/COMMON/WHITE-WINGED BLACK-TIT). See *P. guineensis* and *P. albiventris*."

569 *Parus niger*, change English name to BLACK TIT (not SOUTHERN BLACK-TIT); change range to "**Se Africa** from s,e Zambia and Malawi...Natal, e Cape prov.)."; change beginning of comments to "(SOUTHERN BLACK-TIT). [BLACK TIT]..."

569 *Parus leuconotus*, change English name to WHITE-BACKED TIT (not BLACK-TIT); change comments to "AG: BLACK-TIT."

569 *Parus funereus*, in heading change "1885" to "1855"; change range to "Locally in **w,c Africa** in Liberia, Ivory Coast, Ghana, Cameroon...nw Kenya; a questionable old record exists for Gabon."

570 *Parus pallidiventris*, change comments to "...(including brown rather than yellow eyes)..."

570 *Parus cinerascens*, before "Namibia," add "sw Angola,"

570 *Parus major*, change comments to "...appropriate, although Stepanyan (1990c) treated them as distinct species. (GREY TIT). See *P. bokharensis*."

570 *Parus nuchalis*, change English name to WHITE-NAPED TIT (not WHITE-WINGED); change comments to "(WHITE-NAPED BLACK/COLLARED/WHITE-WINGED TIT)."

571 *Parus flavipectus*, in heading change "Severtzov" to "Severtsov"; change range to "...¶*flavipectus*, YELLOW-BREASTED TIT [2476.1]; **nw China** (e Tsinghai) ¶*berezowskii* (Pleske) 1893, CHINESE..."; in comments after "1957)" add "; treated as a full species by Stepanyan (1990c)"

571 *Parus inornatus*, change range to "...¶*inornatus*, PLAIN..."; change comments to "...*Parus* (Gill and Slikas 1992). AG:..."

572 Change range of *Aegithalos iouschistos* to "...Arunachal Pradesh) and s Tibet ¶*iouschistos*, BLACK-BROWED TIT [2483]; **se Asia** in sw China (Szechwan, n Yunnan) and w,ne Burma ¶*bonvaloti* (Oustalet) 1891, BLACK-HEADED TIT [2483.1]."

573 *Pseudochelidon sirintarae*, in citation change "Thonglongya" to "Kitti"; change comments to "...(1978b). Although Dickinson (1986) presented evidence that this species breeds in China, Parkes (1987) suggested that the evidence pertained instead to a species of pratincole *(Glareola)*. [>*Eurochelidon*]."

573 *Tachycineta bicolor*, delete "(formerly)"

573 *Tachycineta thalassina*, after "c Montana," add "w N. Dakota,"

575 *Neochelidon tibialis*, after "Pando" add ", La Paz"

575 *Stelgidopteryx fucata*, before "Cochabamba," add "Beni,"

575 *Stelgidopteryx serripennis*, after "Veracruz" add "and Belize"

575 *Stelgidopteryx ridgwayi*, change comments to "Often considered conspecific with *S. serripennis* (or *S. ruficollis*) but distinct morphologically and treated as a species by Phillips (1986: 24-25); it probably overlaps with *S. serripennis* in Chiapas and Belize. (YUCATAN ROUGH-WINGED SWALLOW)."

575 *Riparia riparia*, change range to "...Turkey, Near East, ne Egypt (incl. Nile v.), Iraq, w Iran, sw Russia (Transcaucasus), s Siberia (from Altai E to Ussuriland and Sakhalin), n Manchuria (Heilungkiang, Kirin) and n Japan (Hokkaido), and **N. America**...e Virginia ¶*riparia*, COMMON SAND-MARTIN [616]; **c,s Asia** in n Iran, s S.S.R. (N to Kirghiz steppes), Afghanistan, Pakistan, n India (from Kashmir, Himachal Pradesh and Haryana E to s Nepal, Bhutan and n W. Bengal) and w,n,sc China (from Sinkiang E to Heilungkiang, and S to Yunnan, Hupeh and Fukien) ¶*diluta* (Sharpe and Wyatt) 1893, EASTERN SAND-MARTIN [2422.1]. Winters (¶*riparia*) from Mediterranean...Philippines, and in Panama and S. America; and (¶*diluta*) in Pakistan and India."

576 *Riparia paludicola*, change range to "...s Chad, C. African Rep. and s Sudan...500-1800 m of nw,e Madagascar; **s Asia**..."

576 *Hirundo griseopyga*, change beginning of range to "**Africa** from Sierra Leone and Liberia E through Nigeria,..."; in comments change "(1966)" to "(1966a)"

576 *Hirundo rupestris*, after "Iran," add "Afghanistan,"

576 *Hirundo fuligula*, change range to "...Senegal, s Mali, Sierra Leone and Liberia E to Cameroon,..."

577 *Hirundo rustica*, change range to "...¶*rustica*, EURASIAN SWALLOW (EUROPEAN SWALLOW) [613.1];...se Georgia, also **ne Argentina** ¶*erythrogaster*..."; at end of comments add "See *H. lucida*, *H. domicola* and *H. tahitica*."

577 *Hirundo aethiopica*, change range to "**Subsaharan Africa** from s Niger, Ivory Coast, Ghana, Nigeria and Cameroon E to n C. African Rep., Sudan,...*H. lucida* or *H. angolensis*..."

577 **Hirundo domicola** (not *dumicola*); in comments change "*H. javanica*" to "*H. tahitica*" twice

577 *Hirundo tahitica*, change end of comments to "...See *H. rustica*, *H. angolensis*, *H. domicola* and *H. neoxena*."

577 *Hirundo neoxena*, at end of range after "Tasmania)" add "; **New Zealand** (since 1958)."

577 *Hirundo smithii*, after "s Mali," add "n Ivory Coast,"

578 *Hirundo nigrita*, after "s Cameroon" add ", sw C. African Rep."

578 *Hirundo leucosoma*, change "Senegal" to "Senegambia"

578 *Hirundo semirufa*, change "Senegal" to "Senegambia"; before "nc Namibia," add "coastal Ivory Coast and Ghana,"

578 *Hirundo daurica*, change range to "...**e Africa** from C. African Rep., e Zaire, extreme se Sudan, s Ethiopia and n Somalia S through Uganda..."

579 *Hirundo domicella*, change range to "...**Africa** from Senegambia and Guinea E across s Mali,..."

579 *Hirundo striolata,* change end of range to "...Timor) and Philippines (except from Mindanao to Sulu Arch.)."

579 *Hirundo preussi,* change range to "...Mali E to n Ivory Coast, Burkina Faso, n Ghana, Benin, Nigeria,..."

579 *Hirundo pyrrhonota,* change range to "...s Texas, s Louisiana, s Alabama, c Georgia, w S. Carolina..."

579 *Hirundo fulva,* change range to "...s **Mexico** (c Chiapas, Yucatán, Quintana Roo), **s Florida,** and **Greater Antilles...** (Chapman) 1924, ECUADORIAN..."

580 *Hirundo ariel,* change range to "...extreme sw W. Australia). Ranges..."

580 *Delichon dasypus,* in heading change "1851" to "1850"; in comments after "treatment" add "(e.g., Stepanyan 1990c)"

581 *Psalidoprocne holomelas,* after "Uganda," add "Rwanda, Burundi,"

581 *Psalidoprocne obscura,* change range to "**W Africa** from Senegambia E to e Nigeria, sw Cameroon and C. African Rep."

581 *Regulus regulus,* remove superspecies and change English name to GOLDCREST (not COMMON GOLDCREST); in range after "n Mediterranean region" add "(incl. Corsica, Sardinia and Sicily)"; change beginning of comments to "(COMMON/EUROPEAN GOLDCREST). See..."

581 *Regulus teneriffae,* remove superspecies and change English name to CANARY ISLANDS KINGLET (not TENERIFE GOLDCREST); change comments to "Löhrl and Thaler (1980) treated *teneriffae* as a race of *R. regulus* but it may be more closely related to *R. ignicapillus* (J. T. R. Sharrock, pers. comm.). (TENERIFE GOLD-CREST/TENERIFE FIRECREST)."

581 *Regulus ignicapillus,* change beginning of range to "**W Palearctic** from s England, cont. Europe (E to c Poland) and s Russia..."

582 *Regulus satrapa,* change range to "...n,ec Minnesota, n Illinois, c Indiana, n Ohio, s Ontario, New York and c New England, and S in Appalachians to e Tennessee and w N. Carolina. Winters..."

582 *Pycnonotus atriceps,* before "Palawan" add "Calamian Is.,"

583 *Pycnonotus nigricans,* change range to "Arid regions of **sw Africa** from s Angola, Botswana and sw Zimbabwe S to Namibia..."

585 *Andropadus montanus,* after "Togo" add "(questionably), Nigeria"; in comments change "[MOUNTAIN GREENBUL]" to "[MONTANE GREENBUL]"

585 *Andropadus kakamegae,* in comments change "regard" to "regarded"

585 *Andropadus masukuensis,* change end of comments to "See *A. kakamegae* and *A. nigriceps.*"

585 *Andropadus hallae,* in comments change "1985" to "1985a"

585 *Andropadus gracilis,* after "s Cameroon," add "C. African Rep.,"

585 *Andropadus ansorgei,* change range to "...**w,c Africa** from Sierra Leone and Liberia E to s Cameroon...w Kenya, and S to n Angola..."

585 *Andropadus curvirostris,* after "Liberia E" add "to"

586 *Andropadus gracilirostris,* before "n,ne Zaire," add "sw C. African Rep.,"

586 *Andropadus latirostris,* change "Senegal," to "Sierra Leone,"

586 Split *Andropadus tephrolaemus* into the following two species:

Andropadus tephrolaemus (Gray) 1862. GREY-THROATED GREENBUL. [7330.]
     Forest. Mts. of **wc Africa** in se Nigeria and sw Cameroon (incl. Bioko).
     A. tephrolaemus, A. nigriceps and *A. chlorigula* are sometimes considered conspecific and often placed in the same superspecies, but relationships are controversial. [>*Arizelocichla* (≈*A. miljanensis*)]. (OLIVE-BREASTED MOUNTAIN/OLIVE-BREASTED/MOUNTAIN GREENBUL). See *A. nigriceps.*

Andropadus nigriceps (Shelley) 1890. MOUNTAIN GREENBUL. [7330.2.]
     Locally in mts. of **e Africa** in s Kenya, w,ce, sw Tanzania, extreme e Zambia, Malawi and ne Mozambique.
     A. nigriceps differs vocally and morphologically from *A. tephrolaemus* and may be more closely related to *A. masukuensis* (Short, Horne and Muringo-Gichuki 1990: 150). (KILIMANJARO GREENBUL). See *A. tephrolaemus.*

586 Change *Andropadus [tephrolaema] chlorigula* to *Andropadus chlorigula*

586 *Calyptocichla serina,* change range to "...s Cameroon (incl. Bioko), sw C. African Rep. and nc,ne,ce Zaire,..."; change comments to "(SERINE GREENBUL)."

586 *Baeopogon indicator,* after "s Cameroon," add "C. African Rep.,"

586 *Ixonotus guttatus,* after "s Cameroon," add "sw C. African Rep.,"

586 *Chlorocichla simplex,* after "s Cameroon," add "s C. African Rep.,"

586 *Chlorocichla falkensteini,* after "s Cameroon" add ", s C. African Rep.,"

587 *Thescelocichla leucopleura,* after "Cameroon," add "sw C. African Rep.,"

587 *Phyllastrephus baumanni,* change comments to "AG (≈*P. hypochloris*): GREENBUL. [OLIVE GREENBUL]. See *P. poensis, P. hypochloris* and *P. lorenzi.*"

587 Sequence *Phyllastrephus poensis* before *P. hypochloris*

588 *Phyllastrephus albigularis,* after "s Cameroon," add "s C. African Rep.,"

588 *Phyllastrephus icterinus,* before "n,ne Zaire" add "sw C. African Rep.,"

588 *Phyllastrephus madagascariensis,* change English name to LONG-BILLED GREENBUL (not COMMON TETRAKA); in range change "w,n,e Madagascar" to "**Madagascar** (except s)"; change end of comments to "...MADAGASCAR GREENBUL/COMMON TETRAKA. AG (≈*P. cinereiceps*): TETRAKA."

588 *Phyllastrephus zosterops,* change English name to SPECTACLED GREENBUL (not SHORT-BILLED TETRAKA); in range change "**Madagascar**" to "**nw,e Madagascar**"; add comments "(SHORT-BILLED GREENBUL)."

588 *Phyllastrephus apperti,* change English name to APPERT'S GREENBUL (not TETRAKA); in range delete "(known from two specimens)"; change comments to "COLSTON'S GREENBUL."

588 *Phyllastrephus tenebrosus,* change English name to DUSKY GREENBUL (not TETRAKA)

588 *Phyllastrephus cinereiceps,* change English name to GREY-CROWNED GREENBUL (not TETRAKA)

588 *Bleda syndactyla*, after "s Cameroon," add "s C. African Rep.,"

588 *Bleda eximia*, change range to "s Cameroon (incl. Bioko), s C. African Rep., n,ne Zaire,..."

588 *Bleda canicapilla*, before "Sierra Leone" add "Gambia,"

589 *Nicator chloris*, change "Senegal" to "Senegambia"

589 *Nicator vireo*, after "s Cameroon," add "s C. African Rep.,"

589 *Criniger calurus*, change range to "...s Cameroon (incl. Bioko), n,ne Zaire," add "sw C. African Rep.,"

589 *Criniger olivaceus*, change range to "**W Africa** in sw Senegal, se Guinea, Sierra Leone, Liberia, Ivory Coast and s Ghana."

590 *Alophoixus affinis*, in comments change "<" to "≠"

590 *Ixos rufigularis*, in heading change "Sharpe" to "(Sharpe)"; change end of comments to "...ranges marginally overlap."

590 *Ixos malaccensis*, in heading change "Blyth" to "(Blyth)"

591 *Hemixos flavala*, in heading change "(Blyth)" to "Blyth"

591 *Hemixos castanonotus*, in heading change "(Swinhoe)" to "Swinhoe"

591 *Hypsipetes leucocephalus*, change range to "...1000-3050 m, of n Afghanistan,...Nagaland), c,s China..."

592 *Malia grata*, change "Affinties" to "Affinities"

592 *Hypocolius ampelinus*, in heading change "1851" to "1850"; in range before "Iraq" add "sw Arabia,"

592 *Cisticola cantans*, after "Cameroon," add "C. African Rep.,"

592 *Cisticola lateralis*, change range to "...s Sudan, Uganda and w Kenya, and S to..."

592 *Cisticola woosnami*, before "Rwanda," add "sw Kenya,"

592 *Cisticola discolor*, change range to "Mts., 1000-3350 m, of **wc Africa** in se Nigeria and Cameroon."

593 *Cisticola emini*, change habitat to "Bare rocky areas, sometimes extensively overgrown with grasses, bushes and small trees."; change range to "...sw Mali, Ivory Coast and Ghana E to n,e Nigeria, ne Chad, C. African Rep., ne Zaire, w Uganda, Kenya and Tanzania (except sw), and S to e Malawi and n Mozambique, also in w Angola."; at end of comments add "Stronach (1990) discussed habitat and distribution."

593 *Cisticola ruficeps*, after "n Ghana," add "Benin,"

593 After *Cisticola mongalla*, add:

Cisticola dorsti Chappuis and Erard (1991). DORST'S CISTICOLA. [7385.2.]

Grass steppe, old fields. **Wc Africa** in nw Nigeria, n Cameroon and s Chad.

Vocally distinct from and sympatric with *C. ruficeps;* also occupies a different habitat (Chappuis 1974: 479-481; Chappuis and Erard 1991).

594 *Cisticola carruthersi*, change end of range to "...w Kenya, Rwanda and nw Tanzania."

594 *Cisticola tinniens*, delete ", Uganda"

594 *Cisticola natalensis*, at end of comments add "(STRIPED CISTICOLA)."

594 *Cisticola melanurus*, change English name to BLACK-TAILED CISTICOLA (not SLENDER-TAILED); change comments to "...an *Apalis*, but see Irwin (1991) for a discussion of its probable relationships with *Cisticola*. [≠*Apalis*]. (SLENDER-TAILED/ANGOLA/PEARSON'S CISTICOLA)..."

594 *Cisticola brachypterus*, change "Senegal" to "Senegambia"

595 *Cisticola juncidis*, change range to "**Sw Palearctic** from w Europe (N to w,s France, Belgium and Netherlands), n Mediterranean region (incl. most is.) and n Africa...n Nigeria, C. African Rep., Sudan...Ryukyu is. S through Nicobar Is., se Asia (...) and Indonesia (except Borneo) to Philippines and Lesser Sunda Is (E to Tanimbar Is.); locally **Australian region** in cs new Guinea, and in coastal n Australia in N. Terr. (Darwin area)..."

597 *Prinia flaviventris*, after "Nias)" add "and Java"

597 *Prinia inornata*, change end of range to "...Taiwan S to se Asia; Java."

597 *Prinia maculosa*, after "DRAKENSBURG PRINIA" add "(SAFFRON-BREASTED PRINIA)"; in comments delete "(+N)"

597 Change *Prinia substriata* and WHITE-BREASTED PRINIA to ***Phragmacia substriata*** and NAMAQUA WARBLER, and sequence after *P. melanops* (p. 598); change comments to "The genus *Phragmacia* Brooke and Dean (1990) was recently erected for *substriata;* although Clancey (1991a) expressed caution concerning adoption of *Phragmacia*, he (1991b) subsequently accepted the validity of *Phragmacia* based on morphology, breeding biology, and molt. [<*Prinia* (≈*Malcorus*); ≠*Drymoica*]. (WHITE-BREASTED/NAMAQUA PRINIA)."

597 Change *Prinia robertsi* entry to "***Oreophilais robertsi*** (Benson) 1946. BRIAR WARBLER..." and sequence after *Phragmacia substriata* (p. 598); change comments to "The genus *Oreophilais* Clancey (1991b) was recently erected for *robertsi*. (ROBERTS'S/FOREST PRINIA)."

598 *Prinia leontica*, change range to "...e Sierra Leone, s Guinea, Liberia and sw Ivory Coast."

598 *Prinia leucopogon*, before "Cameroon" add "e Nigeria and"

598 *Prinia bairdii*, change range to "Lowlands of **c Africa** from se Nigeria, Cameroon and sw C. African Rep. S to n Angola,..."

598 Change *Prinia erythroptera* and RED-WINGED PRINIA to ***Heliolais erythroptera*** and RED-WINGED WARBLER; change range to "...Ivory Coast, Burkina Faso, Ghana, Nigeria, Cameroon, C. African Rep. and n Zaire..."; change comments to "Analysis by Clancey (1991b) indicated this species was neither a *Prinia* nor closely related to any species in that genus. (REDWING WARBLER). AG: PRINIA."

598 *Malcorus pectoralis*, in heading change "(Smith)" to "Smith"; change comments to "...Maclean (1974) and Clancey (1991b) retained it in *Malcorus*. AG: PRINIA."

598 *Urolais epichlora*, before "sw Cameroon" add "se Nigeria and"

598 *Spiloptila clamans*, change comments to "...problem. [>*Prinia*]...(SCALY/SCALY-FRONTED LONGTAIL). AG:..."

598 *Apalis pulchra*, change range to "...**c,e Africa** in e Nigeria, Cameroon, sw C. African Rep., se Sudan, ne,se Zaire, sw Uganda and w,c Kenya."

598 *Apalis nigriceps*, in range after "Sierra Leone" add ", Liberia, Ivory Coast"; add comments "Irwin (1987) discussed affinities of *A. nigriceps*."

599 *Apalis jacksoni*, change end of range to "...extreme se Sudan, w,c Kenya (...) and nw Tanzania."

599 *Apalis flavida*, change beginning of range to "**Africa** from Gambia, n Ivory Coast, Burkina Faso, s Ghana..."

599 *Apalis sharpei,* change beginning of range to "**W Africa...**"

599 *Apalis goslingi,* after "s Cameroon," add "C. African Rep.,"

600 *Apalis melanocephala,* after "c,se Kenya" add "and s Somalia"

600 *Apalis cinerea,* change range to "**c,e Africa** in se Nigeria, s Cameroon (incl. Bioko), cw Angola,..."

600 *Apalis alticola,* change "sw Tanzania" to "n,sw Tanzania"

600 *Hypergerus atriceps,* change "Senegal" to "Senegambia and sw Mali"

600 *Camaroptera brevicaudata,* change "Senegal" to "Senegambia, sw Mali"

600 *Camaroptera superciliaris,* after "s Cameroon," add "sw C. African Rep.,"

600 *Camaroptera chloronota,* change range to "...s Cameroon, sw C. African Rep., ne,ce Zaire,...Gabon, c Zaire and extreme nw Tanzania."

601 *Calamonastes fasciolatus,* after "Transvaal" add ", Orange Free State"

601 *Zosterops senegalensis,* in heading change "1851" to "1850"; in range after "s Niger," add "Benin,"; change end of comments to "...*Z. vaughani, Z. poliogaster* and *Z. maderaspatanus.*"

601 Delete *Zosterops kirki*

601-602 *Zosterops poliogaster,* change "se Kenya" to "**se Kenya**"

602 *Zosterops maderaspatanus,* change English name to "MALAGASY WHITE-EYE"; change range to "Lowlands to 2300 m of **Comoro Is.** (Grand Comoro) ¶*kirki* Shelley 1880, KIRK'S WHITE-EYE (GRAND COMORO WHITE-EYE) [6641.1]; **Madagascar region** in Comoro...Madagascar ¶*maderaspatanus,* MALAGASY WHITE-EYE [6643]."; change comments to "...*Z. maderaspatanus* (Langrand 1990: 288). The form *kirki* appears to be conspecific with *Z. maderaspatanus,* not *Z. senegalensis* as treated in the past (Louette 1988c: 80-84). (MADAGASCAR WHITE-EYE)."

603 *Zosterops meyeni,* in heading change "1851" to "1850"

603 *Zosterops salvadorii,* in heading change "1892" to "1894"

603 *Zosterops conspicillatus,* change range to "**Sc Mariana Is.** (Saipan, Tinian, Agiguan) ¶*saypani* Dubois 1902, SAIPAN WHITE-EYE [9791.3]; **cs Mariana Is.** (Rota) ¶*rotensis* Takatsukasa and Yamashina 1931, ROTA WHITE-EYE [9791.4]; **s Mariana Is.** (Guam) ¶*conspicillatus,* BRIDLED WHITE-EYE [9791]."; change comments to "Pratt, Bruner and Berrett (1987: 283-284) treated *Z. hypolais* and *Z. semperi* as allospecies of *Z. conspicillatus,* but H. D. Pratt (pers. comm.) now believes *Z. semperi* is unrelated to this complex. [BRIDLED WHITE-EYE]."

603 *Zosterops semperi,* change English name to CAROLINE ISLANDS WHITE-EYE (not CAROLINE WHITE-EYE); remove superspecies and sequence after *Z. hypolais*; change comments to "(CAROLINE WHITE-EYE). See *Z. conspicillatus.*"

603 *Zosterops everetti,* change end of range to "...and c,s Philippines (N to Negros, Cebu, Leyte and Samar)."

603 *Zosterops nigrorum,* change English name to GOLDEN-GREEN WHITE-EYE (not YELLOWISH); in range change "Highlands (primarily)" to "Lowlands to 1000 m"; in comments before "WHITE-EYE" add "/YELLOWISH"

603 *Zosterops montanus,* in heading change "1851" to "1850"

603 *Zosterops natalis,* change English name to CHRISTMAS ISLAND WHITE-EYE (not CHRISTMAS WHITE-EYE); in comments delete "ISLAND"

603 *Zosterops flavus,* delete comments

604 *Zosterops chloris,* in heading change "1851" to "1850"

604 *Zosterops citrinellus,* in heading change "1851" to "1850"

604 *Zosterops grayi,* change "(Kai Cecil)" to "(Kai Besar)"

604 *Zosterops uropygialis,* change "(Kai Besar)" to "(Kai Cecil)"

605 *Zosterops kulambangrae,* change English name to SOLOMON ISLANDS WHITE-EYE (not SOLOMON WHITE-EYE); in comments delete "ISLANDS"

606 *Zosterops lateralis,* change "SILVER-EYE" to "SILVEREYE" in five places; in range change "1851" to "1850";

606 *Zosterops tephropleurus,* change English name to LORD HOWE ISLAND WHITE-EYE (not LORD HOWE WHITE-EYE); change end of comments to "...1964: 94). (LORD HOWE WHITE-EYE). AG: SILVEREYE."

606 *Zosterops tenuirostris,* before "***Zosterops tenuirostris***" add "†"; change range to "Extinct (before 1928); formerly **Norfolk I.**"

607 *Zosterops cinereus,* change English name to GREY-BROWN WHITE-EYE (not GREY); change range to "...1876, GREY-brown WHITE-EYE (POHNPEI/ PONAPE...)"; change comments to "(GREY WHITE-EYE). [GREY-brown/CAROLINE..."

607 *Rukia ruki,* sequence after *R. longirostra*; change comments to "Related to and perhaps congeneric with *Cleptornis marchei* (H. D. Pratt, pers. comm.). (LARGE TRUK/GREAT TRUK/TRUK GREATER WHITE-EYE)."

607 *Rukia longirostra,* change comments to "*R. longirostra* is related to *Zosterops* but perhaps worthy of recognition in a monotypic genus *Cinnyrorhyncha* (H. D. Pratt, pers. comm.). If *Rukia* is merged in *Zosterops, longirostra* becomes preoccupied by *Zosterops longirostra* Ramsay, 1879, a form considered to be a subspecies of *Z. griseotinctus.* [<*Zosterops* (+N); >*Cinnyrorhyncha*]..."

607 *Cleptornis marchei,* change "[9475.]" to "[9745.]"; at end of comments add "See *Rukia ruki.*"

607 *Lophozosterops javanicus,* change comments to "...(GREY-THROATED/JAVAN GREY-FRONTED/JAVAN WHITE-EYE)...See *Speirops melanocephalus.*"

607 *Lophozosterops squamiceps,* in heading change "1903" to "1896"

607 *Heleia muelleri,* change English name to SPOT-BREASTED WHITE-EYE (not SPOT-BREATED)

608 *Urosphena subulata,* change comments to "[<*Tesia* (~*Urosphena*).] (SUNDA..."

609 *Cettia canturians,* at end of range add "Winters in se Asia and Philippines."

609 *Cettia seebohmi,* change "[746.1.]" to "[3584.2.]"

609 *Cettia [fortipes] carolinae,* include in superspecies and sequence after *C. [fortipes] vulcania.*

609 *Cettia fortipes,* change end of comments to "See *C. vulcania* and *C. acanthizoides.*"

609 *Cettia vulcania,* change end of range to "...Timor) and sw Philippines (Palawan)."

609 ***Cettia acanthizoides*** (Verreaux) 1871 (not ***Cettia robustipes*** (Swinhoe) 1866; change end of range to "...e Burma ¶*acanthizoides,* YELLOWISH-BELLIED BUSH-WARBLER [2531.1]; **Taiwan** ¶*concolor* (Ogilvie-Grant) 1912 [= *robustipes* auct.], FORMOSAN BUSH-WARBLER (TAIWAN BUSH-WARBLER) [2531]."; change comments to "Although Watson, in Peters...*acanthizoides,* the name *C. robustipes* (Swinhoe) 1866 pertains to a race of *C. fortipes;* the treatment by Meyer de Schauensee (1984: 402-403) is correct. (VERREAUX'S..."

610 *Bradypterus carpalis,* change end of range to "...c Uganda, w Kenya, Rwanda and nw Tanzania."

610 *Bradypterus lopezi* (not *lopesi*), also change spelling of group; change beginning of comments to "The original spelling *'lopezi'* was *not* a *lapsus calami* in Alexander's January 1903 article; there are many other new species in this article with the patronym *'lopezi,'* including what is now *Poliolais lopezi,* and all are spelled this way. The 'correction' published by Alexander in July 1903 was an unjustified emendation. [>*Cryptillas...*"

610 *Bradypterus mariae,* change range to "...Tanzania, n Zambia, Malawi..."

610 *Bradypterus cinnamomeus,* before "s Cameroon" add "se Nigeria and"

610 *Bradypterus thoracicus,* change range to "...Himalayas of sw Siberia (from Altai to w Amurland), ne,c,s China (...), se Tibet, n India (...) and n Burma. Winters..."

611 *Bradypterus taczanowskius,* before "se Tibet" add "n Mongolia,"

611 *Bradypterus seebohmi,* in comments after "(1952)." add "Rozendaal (1989) treated *montis* as a race of *seebohmi* on the basis of similarity in vocalizations."

611 *Bradypterus caudatus,* change end of range to "...(n Luzon; Mindanao)."

611 *Dromaeocercus brunneus,* in comments after "*Bradypterus.*" add "The separation of *D. brunneus* and *Amphilais seebohmi* is supported by Olson (1990a)."

611 *Bathmocercus cerviniventris,* after "se Guinea" add ", Liberia, Ivory Coast"

611 *Bathmocercus rufus,* change end of range to "...Gabon, sw C. African Rep., ne,ce Zaire, extreme se Sudan, Uganda, w Kenya and nw Tanzania."

611 *Nesillas aldabrana,* change English name to ALDABRA BRUSH-WARBLER (not TSIKIRITY); change range to "**Aldabra Is.**; possibly extinct..."; change comments to "...was as *N. aldabranus,* but the...AG (~*Nesillas*): TSIKIRITY/WARBLER. See *N. typica.*"

611 After *Nesillas aldabrana,* add the following species:

Nesillas [typica] longicaudata Newton (1877). ANJOUAN BRUSH-WARBLER. [6422.1.]
Forest undergrowth. **Comoro Is.** (Anjouan).
See *N. typica.*

611 *Nesillas typica,* change English name to MALAGASY BRUSH-WARBLER (not MADAGASCAR TSIKIRITY); change range to "...2000 m of **Madagascar region** in Comoro Is. (Mohéli) and Madagascar."; change comments to "Relationships in *Nesillas* were discussed by Louette (1988c: 78-80). [MALAGASY BRUSH-WARBLER]. (COMMON TSIKIRITY/TSIKIRITY WARBLER/MADAGASCAR BRUSH-WARBLER)."

611 After *Nesillas typica,* add the following species:

Nesillas brevicauda (Milne-Edwards and Oustalet) 1888. GRAND COMORO BRUSH-WARBLER. [6422.2.]
Forest undergrowth. **Comoro Is.** (Grand Comoro).
See *N. typica.*

612 *Nesillas mariae,* change English name to MOHELI BRUSH-WARBLER (not TSIKIRITY); in heading change "1960" to "(1960)"; change comments to "(COMORO BRUSH-WARBLER). See *N. typica.*"

612 *Thamnornis chloropetoides,* change English name to THAMNORNIS WARBLER (not KIRITIKA); change comments to (THE KIRITIKA/THE THAMNORNIS)."

612 *Melocichla mentalis,* change "Senegal" to "Senegambia, sw Mali"

612 *Locustella naevia,* change English name to COMMON GRASSHOPPER-WARBLER (not GRASSHOPPER WARBLER); after "Kirghiz steppes)" add ", w China (w Sinkiang)"; in comments before "PALE" add "GRASSHOPPER WARBLER/"

612 *Locustella certhiola,* change English name to PALLAS'S GRASSHOPPER-WARBLER (not PALLAS'S WARBLER); change comments to "(GREY-NAPED GRASSHOPPER-WARBLER). [GREY-NAPED GRASSHOPPER-WARBLER]. AG (~*L. pleskei*): WARBLER. See *L. ochotensis...*"

612 *Locustella ochotensis,* change English name to MIDDENDORFF'S GRASSHOPPER-WARBLER (not MIDDENDORFF'S WARBLER)

612 *Locustella pleskei,* change English name to PLESKE'S GRASSHOPPER-WARBLER (not PLESKE'S WARBLER); change end of comments to "...STYAN'S GRASSHOPPER-WARBLER)."

613 *Locustella fasciolata,* in heading delete superspecies and change English name to GRAY'S GRASSHOPPER-WARBLER (not GRAY'S WARBLER); change range to "...Amurland and Ussuriland), n Manchuria...and Korea ¶*fasciolata,* GRAY'S GRASSHOPPER-WARBLER [2550]; **e Asia** in extreme se Siberia (Sakhalin) and s Kuril Is. ¶*amnicola* Stepanyan (1972), SAKHALIN GRASSHOPPER-WARBLER (SAKHALIN LARGE/STEPANYAN'S GRASSHOPPER-WARBLER) [2550.1]. Winters (¶*fasciolata*) in Philippines..."; change comments to "*Amnicola* has been reported to be sympatric with *fasciolata* on Sakhalin and to differ in wing formula (Mayr and Vuilleumier 1983: 219-220; Stepanyan 1990c), but songs as well as the type and paratype of *amnicola* are identical with *fasciolata* (K. Mild, pers. comm.). (LARGE GRASSHOPPER-WARBLER). AG: WARBLER."

613 Delete *Acrocephalus amnicola* entry

613 *Acrocephalus melanopogon,* change range to "...w Turkestan), cn Arabia (cn Saudi Arabia) and Near and Middle East to w Pakistan...Kumaon); also se British Isles. Winters..."

613 *Acrocephalus paludicola,* change "Europe" to "**Europe**"

613 Combine *Acrocephalus tangorum* and *A. agricola* under one species, as follows:

Acrocephalus [agricola] agricola (Jerdon) 1895. PADDY-FIELD WARBLER. [2558.]
Open reedbeds, sedges, rank grass, scrubby growth in swamps. **C Eurasia** in s,se Russia (n shore region of Black

Sea, and n Caspian Sea area), sw Siberia (upper Ob r., upper
Yenesei r., Tuva), s S.S.R. (except Turkestan), ne Iran, n
Afghanistan and nw China (Sinkiang, n Tsinghai) ¶*agricola*,
PADDYFIELD WARBLER [2558]; **Manchuria** ¶*tangorum* La
Touche 1912, MANCHURIAN REED-WARBLER [2556.1].
Winters (¶*agricola*) in s Asia, and (¶*tangorum*) in se Asia
(Thailand); recorded in migration (¶*tangorum*) in ne China
(Hopeh).

[>*Notiocichla*]. The conspecificity of *tangorum* and
agricola has been demonstrated by Alström, Olsson and
Round (1991). (JERDON'S REED-WARBLER).

614 *Acrocephalus baeticatus*, change range to "...**African
     region** in Senegambia and Niger;...c Ethiopia, s Somalia
     and w,c,se Kenya..."
614 *Acrocephalus dumetorum*, before "n Afghanistan" add "e
     Iran,"
614 *Acrocephalus arundinaceus*, change range to "...Turk-
     menia) ¶*arundinaceus*, GREAT REED-WARBLER [2564];
     e Asia in c,e China (from Kansu, Ningsia, Shensi and s
     Heilungkiang S to e Tsinghai, Hunan and Fukien), se
     Siberia (s Transbaicalia, Amurland, Ussuriland, Sak-
     halin), Korea and Japan (Hokkaido, Honshu, Shikoku,
     Kyushu) ¶*orientalis* (Temminck and Schlegel) 1847,
     ORIENTAL REED-WARBLER (ORIENTAL GREAT/EASTERN
     GREAT REED-WARBLER) [2564.1]. Winters
     (¶*arundinaceus*) in trop.,s Africa; and (¶*orientalis*) in s
     Asia, E. Indies and Philippines."; change comments to
     "*Orientalis* is considered conspecific with *arundinaceus*
     by Stepanyan (1990c), a treatment supported by K. Mild
     (pers. comm.), U. Olsson (pers. comm.) and others.
     [GREAT REED-WARBLER]."
614 Delete *Acrocephalus orientalis* entry
614 *Acrocephalus stentoreus*, change range to "**S Palearctic,
     Malay Arch. and Australasian region** from n,c
     Egypt,...Ceylon), s China (...) and c,e Burma; w
     Java,...Buru) and Philippines (Luzon,...Mindanao)
     ¶*stentoreus*..."; change comments to "...probably
     represents a molting individual of *A. stentoreus*...See *A.
     griseldis* and *A. australis*."
614 *Acrocephalus griseldis*, change comments to "May be
     conspecific with *A. stentoreus*."
614 *Acrocephalus australis*, change range to "**Australian
     region** in Australia (incl. Tasmania), New Guinea, Bis-
     marck Arch. and Solomon Is. Southernmost populations
     winter to N."; add comments "Usually considered a race
     of *A. stentoreus*, but Coates (1990: 79-80) recommended
     it be treated as a 'semispecies.'"
615 *Acrocephalus syrinx*, change English name to CAROLINE
     ISLANDS REED-WARBLER (not CAROLINE REED-
     WARBLER); at beginning of comments add "(CAROLINE
     REED-WARBLER)."
615 *Acrocephalus aequinoctialis*, change "Tahuaeran," to
     "Tabuaeran,"; at end of comments add "AG (≈*A.
     vaughani*): WARBLER."
615 *Acrocephalus [caffer] caffer* and *Acrocephalus [caffer]
     mendanae* (not "*[cafer]*"); in comments delete "AG (≈*A.
     vaughani*): WARBLER."
615 Split *Acrocephalus vaughani* into the following three
     species:

Acrocephalus [vaughani] rimatarae (Murphy and Mathews)
         1929. RIMATARA REED-WARBLER [9478.1.]
     Brushy forest, reedbeds. **Tubuai Is.** (Rimatara).
     See *A. vaughani*.

Acrocephalus [vaughani] vaughani (Sharpe) 1900. PITCAIRN
         REED-WARBLER [9478.]
     Brushy forest, reedbeds. **C Pitcairn Is.** (Pitcairn I.).
     Graves (1992: 37-40) recognized species status for *A.
     rimatarae, A. vaughani* and *A. taiti* based on differences in
     subadult plumages, extent of leucism in adults, color of mouth-
     linings, and vocalizations. [POLYNESIAN REED-WARBLER].

Acrocephalus [vaughani] taiti Ogilvie-Grant 1913. HENDER-
         SON ISLAND REED-WARBLER [9478.2.]
     Brushy forest, reedbeds. **Sw Pitcairn Is.** (Henderson I.).
     See *A. vaughani*.

615 *Acrocephalus rufescens*, change range to "...Senegal;
     from Ghana, s Nigeria, s Cameroon, C. African Rep., n,e
     Zaire,...; change end of comments to "...Swamp-
     Warbler. [>*Calamocichla* (≈*A. newtoni*)]. (RUFOUS
     SWAMP-WARBLER). AG (+N): CANE-WARBLER."
615 *Acrocephalus brevipennis*, in comments delete "AG:
     CANE-WARBLER."
615 *Acrocephalus gracilirostris*, change range to "...c
     Angola, se,e,ne Zaire, C. African Rep., se Sudan,..."
615-616 Split *Hippolais caligata* into the following two
     species:

Hippolais [caligata] caligata (Lichtenstein) 1823. BOOTED
         WARBLER. [2567.]
     Gardens, hedgerows, canebrakes, scrub, bushes,
     generally near water. **C,e Eurasia** from nw,c Russia E to w
     Siberia (upper Yenisei r.) and nw Mongolia, and S to s S.S.R.
     (E of Caspian Sea and N of range of *rama*) and extreme w
     China (w Sinkiang). Winters in Pakistan and c,s India.
     [>*Iduna* (+N)]. [BOOTED WARBLER].

Hippolais [caligata] rama (Sykes) 1823. SYKES'S WARBLER.
         [2567.1.]
     Gardens, hedgerows, canebrakes, scrub, bushes,
     generally near water. **Sc Eurasia** in ne Arabia (nw Oman), s,e
     Iran, Afghanistan, s S.S.R. (from Transcaspia E to Turkestan)
     and probably Pakistan. Winters in s India and Ceylon.
     K. M. Bauer and J. Haffer, in Glutz von Blotzheim
     (1991: 541, 556), discussed reasons for regarding *H. rama* as a
     species distinct from *H. caligata*, a treatment supported by
     Stepanyan (1990c).

616 *Hippolais polyglotta*, change range to "...sw Switzerland,
     n Italy (incl. Sicily) and Corsica; nw Africa..."
616 *Chloropeta natalensis*, change range to "...**Africa** from se
     Nigeria, s Cameroon, sw C. African Rep., s,e,ne Zaire,..."
616 *Chloropeta gracilirostris*, after w Uganda" add ", w
     Kenya"
616 *Phyllolais pulchella*, change range to "**C,ec Africa** from
     n Nigeria, n Cameroon and L. Chad area E to ne Zaire,..."
617 *Orthotomus sutorius*, change end of range to "...Hainan)
     S to se Asia; Java."
617 *Orthotomus frontalis*, change "Calicaon," to "Calicoan,"
617 *Orthotomus sericeus*, before "Palawan," add "Calamian
     Is.,"
617 *Orthotomus [nigriceps] samarensis*, add superspecies;
     in comments delete ", but it is closer to *O. cinereiceps*."
617 *Orthotomus [nigriceps] nigriceps*, add superspecies
617 *Orthotomus cinereiceps*, delete comments

617 *Poliolais lopezi* (not *lopesi*); change range to "Mts. of
wc Africa in se Nigeria and s Cameroon (incl. Bioko).";
change comments to "...341-342). [<*Camaroptera/*
Orthotomus). (CAMEROON WARBLER). See *Bradypterus*
lopezi."

618 *Graueria vittata*, after "ce Zaire" add ", extreme sw
Uganda"

618 *Eremomela pusilla*, change range to "**W Africa** from
Senegambia, Guinea-Bissau, Sierra Leone, s Mali and
Burkina Faso E to extreme s Niger, Nigeria, Cameroon,
L. Chad area and n C. African Rep."

618 *Randia pseudozosterops*, change English name to
RAND'S WARBLER (not MAROANTSETRA); change
comments to "(MAROANTSETRA WARBLER)."

618 *Newtonia amphichroa*, change English name to DARK
NEWTONIA (not TULEAR); add comments "(TULEAR
NEWTONIA)."

618 *Newtonia archboldi*, change English name to
ARCHBOLD'S NEWTONIA (not TABITY); change "**sw**
Madagascar" to "**sw,s Madagascar**"; change comments
to "(TABIKY NEWTONIA)" [note correct spelling of name]

619 *Newtonia fanovanae*, change English name to RED-
TAILED NEWTONIA (not FANOVANA); change range to
"**E,se Madagascar**."; change comments to "Known
from a single specimen taken in 1931 until rediscovered
in 1989 (Evans 1991). (FANOVANA NEWTONIA)."

619 *Sylvietta virens*, change range to "...Liberia E to sw
Nigeria ¶*flaviventris*...**c Africa** from se Nigeria, s
Cameroon,...nw,cw Angola, sw,sc,ce Zaire and extreme
nw Tanzania ¶*virens*..."

619 *Sylvietta denti*, change range to "Locally in **w,c Africa** in
Liberia, Ivory Coast, s Ghana, Nigeria, s Cameroon, sw
C. African Rep. and n,sc,ne,ce Zaire."

619 *Sylvietta leucophrys*, change end of range to "...Uganda,
w,c Kenya and w Tanzania."

619 *Sylvietta brachyura*, change range to "...s Mali E through
Burkina Faso, s Niger, Ghana, Nigeria,..."

619 *Hemitesia neumanni*, change "**ce Zaire**" to "**ec Africa** in
ce Zaire and extreme sw Uganda"

619 *Macrosphenus kempi*, change "s Nigeria" to "sw
Nigeria"

619 *Macrosphenus flavicans*, change range to "**C Africa** in se
Nigeria, s Cameroon (incl. Bioko), Gabon, nw Angola,
Zaire (except se), extreme s Sudan, Uganda and extreme
nw Tanzania."

619 *Macrosphenus concolor*, after "s Cameroon," add "sw C.
African Rep.,"

620 *Hylia prasina*, before "Guinea-Bissau" add "Gambia,"

620 *Phylloscopus [ruficapillus] laetus, Phylloscopus*
[ruficapillus] laurae and *Phylloscopus [ruficapillus]*
ruficapillus (genus masculine, *ruficapillus* adjectival)

620 *Phylloscopus laurae*, before "c Angola," add "Gabon,"

620 *Phylloscopus herberti*, change range to "Mts. of **wc**
Africa in se Nigeria and Cameroon (incl. Bioko)."

620 *Phylloscopus budongoensis*, change end of range to
"...Uganda, w Kenya and extreme nw Tanzania."

620 Change accounts of *Phylloscopus collybita* and *P.*
sindianus to the following two species:

Phylloscopus [collybita] collybita (Vieillot) 1817. EURASIAN
CHIFFCHAFF. [2592.]
Open forest, edge, towns, scrub. **Eurasia** from British
Isles... nw Mongolia, also locally w,nw Turkey...e Afghanistan
¶*collybita*, EURASIAN CHIFFCHAFF [2592]; **Siberia** from

Yenisei r. E to Kolyma r. and L. Baikal ¶*tristis* Blyth 1843,
SIBERIAN CHIFFCHAFF [2592.1]; Himalayas, 2000-4400 m, of
s Asia in extreme w China (sw Sinkiang), n Pakistan (Gilgit)
and n India (E to Ladakh) ¶*sindianus* Brooks 1879, MOUNTAIN
CHIFFCHAFF [2593]. Winters (¶*collybita*) from Mediterranean
region and n,ne Africa E to India; (¶*tristis*) in India; and
(¶*sindianus*) S to Middle East and c Pakistan.
The form *sindianus* is apparently a close relative of the
tristis group despite wide allopatry (K. Mild, pers. comm.). If
these two forms are regarded as a single species distinct from
P. collybita, *P. tristis* (MOUNTAIN CHIFFCHAFF) would have
priority. (COMMON CHIFFCHAFF / THE CHIFFCHAFF). [CHIFF-
CHAFF]. See *P. lorenzii*.

Phylloscopus [collybita] lorenzii (Lorenz) 1887. CAUCASIAN
CHIFFCHAFF. [2593.1.]
Open forest, edge, towns, scrub. Mts., 1000-3000 m, of
sw Asia in ne Turkey and extreme s Russia (Caucasus, Trans-
caucasia, occurring at altitudes below *collybita*).
Often considered conspecific with *P. (collybita) sindi-*
anus but *lorenzii* replaces it altitudinally in southwestern
Russia without any sign of hybridization; *P. lorenzii* differs in
morphology and vocalizations, importance of the latter con-
firmed by playback experiments (K. Mild, pers. comm.).
Stepanyan (1990c) considered *P. lorenzii* a full species. (SIND
CHIFFCHAFF/LORENZ'S WARBLER).

621 *Phylloscopus bonelli*, change range to "...**sw Palearctic**
from France...w Austria and Czechoslovakia S to nw
Africa (...) and n Mediterranean region E to Italy and w
Yugoslavia (incl. Corsica and Sicily) ¶*bonelli*, WESTERN
BONELLI'S-WARBLER [2595]; **e Mediterranean region**
in e Yugoslavia, Romania, Bulgaria, Greece, w,s Turkey,
Near East (to Israel) and extreme w Iran ¶*orientalis*
(Brehm) 1855, EASTERN BONELLI'S-WARBLER [2595.1].
Winters (¶*bonelli*) in n Africa E to L. Chad; and (¶*ori-*
entalis) in Sudan and Egypt."; at beginning of comments
add "Playback experiments of song and call of *orientalis*
to *bonelli* suggest that these two allopatric groups may be
separate species (L. Larsson, pers. comm.)."

621 *Phylloscopus subaffinis*, at end of range add "...Winters
in se Asia."; in comments after "*P. affinis*" add ", but
vocalizations are distinct and the two taxa are sympatric
in central China (Alström and Olsson 1992)"

621 Split *Phylloscopus proregulus* into the following two
species:

Phylloscopus [proregulus] proregulus (Pallas) 1811. LEMON-
RUMPED WARBLER. [2603.]
Coniferous forest, taiga. **E Asia** in s Siberia (from Altai
E through L. Baikal region and Transbaicalia to Amurland,
Ussuriland and Sakhalin, Mongolia and ne China (from Kansu,
Inner Mongolia and Heilungkiang S to Shensi and Hopeh).
Winters in se Asia, ranging rarely to w Europe.
[>*Reguloides* (≈*P. inornatus*)]. (YELLOW-RUMPED
WARBLER). AG (≈*P. amoenus*): LEAF-WARBLER. [PALLAS'S
WARBLER]. See *P. chloronotus*.

Phylloscopus [proregulus] chloronotus (Gray and Gray)
1846. PALE-RUMPED WARBLER. [2603.1.]
Coniferous forest. **S Asia** in the Himalayas, 2400-4000
m, of n Pakistan (W to border of Afghanistan), ne India (from
Kashmir E to Arunachal Pradesh; n Cachar Hills), se Tibet and

sc China (s Tsinghai, sw Kansu, Szechwan). Winters to lower elevations and se Asia.

Vocalization studies indicate that *P. chloronotus* is a distinct species (Alström and Olsson 1990).

622 *Phylloscopus inornatus*, change range to 'Taiga of **e Eurasia** from...S to sw Siberia (n Sayan Mts.), n China (Heilungkiang), se Siberia (Ussuriland) and (possibly) n Korea ¶*inornatus*, YELLOW-BROWED WARBLER [2601]; mts. of **sc Asia** in sw Siberia (s Sayan Mts., Altai), s S.S.R. (Turkestan, s,e Kazakhstan), w,c China (...), ne Afghanistan and n India (...) ¶*humei* (Brooks) 1878, BUFF-BROWED WARBLER [2601.1]. Winters (¶*inornatus*) from Near East,...w Europe; and (¶*humei*) in India and se Asia."; change comments to "*Humei* may be a distinct species, differing in vocalizations and habitat as well as slightly in morphology (Svennson 1984, 1987). (YELLOW-BROWED WARBLER)."

622 *Phylloscopus borealis*, change range to "...(n Heilungkiang), Kuril Is. and Japan (mts.); **w Alaska**..."

622 *Phylloscopus trochiloides*, change range to "...se Tibet ¶*trochiloides*, GREENISH WARBLER (DULL-GREEN WARBLER) [2607]; **e Asia** in s Siberia (from Yenisei r. E to Kolyma r. region, Amurland, Ussuriland and Sakhalin), s Kuril Is., Mongolia and Manchuria (Heilungkiang, Kirin) ¶*plumbeitarsus* Swinhoe 1861, TWO-BARRED WARBLER (TWO-BARRED GREENISH / GREY-LEGGED WARBLER) [2608]; mts., 900-3000 m, of **sc Asia** in extreme s Russia (Caucasus, Transcaucasus), s S.S.R. (s Transcaspia), n Turkey, n Iran and nw Afghanistan ¶*nitidus* Blyth 1843, BRIGHT-GREEN WARBLER (GREEN/YELLOWISH-BREASTED WARBLER) [2609]. Winters (¶*trochiloides*) in s Asia; (¶*plumbeitarsus*) in se Asia; and (¶*nitidus*) in India."; change comments to "K. M. Bauer and J. Haffer, in Glutz von Blotzheim (1991: 1024, 1045), discussed reasons for regarding *trochiloides* and *plumbeitarsus* as conspecific, strongly supported by playback experiments (K. Mild, pers. comm.). Vaurie (1954a: 20-21) and Stepanyan (1990c) treated *nitidus* as a separate species, but K. Mild (pers. comm.) indicates that vocalizations are identical and that playback experiments show *nitidus* to be conspecific with *trochiloides*. See *P. nitidus*."

622 Delete *Phylloscopus plumbeitarsus* and *P. nitidus* entries

622 Split *Phylloscopus tenellipes* into the following two species:

Phylloscopus [tenellipes] tenellipes Swinhoe 1860. PALE-LEGGED LEAF-WARBLER. [2612.]
Forest undergrowth in river valleys. **E Asia** in se Siberia (Ussuriland), Manchuria (e Heilungkiang) and n Korea. Winters in se Asia.
[PALE-LEGGED LEAF-WARBLER]. See *P. borealoides*.

Phylloscopus [tenellipes] borealoides Portenko 1950. SAK-HALIN LEAF-WARBLER. [2612.1.]
Forest undergrowth in river valleys. **E Asia** in se Siberia (Sakhalin), s Kuril Is. and Japan (Hokkaido, Honshu). Winters in se Asia.
A species distinct from *P. tenellipes* differing in territorial songs and calls (Martens 1988).

622 *Phylloscopus coronatus*, change range to "...Ussuriland), nc,ne China (...), Korea and Japan. Winters..."

623 *Phylloscopus davisoni*, at end of comments change "WARBLER." to "WARBLER."

623 *Phylloscopus ricketti*, change end of range to "...Kwangtung). Winters in se Asia."

623 *Phylloscopus trivirgatus*, change end of range to "...**se Asia and Malay Arch.** in Malaya, Greater Sunda Is., w Lesser Sunda Is. (Lombok, Sumbawa) and Philippines (Luzon, Mindoro, Palawan, Camiguin Sur, Mindanao)." [i.e., delete all from "Moluccas" to end, which range applies to *P. poliocephalus*]

624 *Seicercus xanthoschistos* (not *xanthoschistus*)

624 *Hyliota australis*, change end of range to "...Uganda, w Kenya and ne Tanzania."

624 *Hyliota violacea*, change range to "Locally in **c Africa** in Liberia, Ghana, Cameroon, Gabon, C. African Rep. and sw,nc,ce Zaire."

625 *Amphilais seebohmi*, change English name to GREY EMU-TAIL (not SEEBOHM'S); change "**c Madagascar**" to "**c,e Madagascar**"; change comments to "...*Amphilais*, a generic allocation supported by Olson (1990a). [≠*Dromaeocercus*]. (SEEBOHM'S EMU-TAIL)..."

625 *Megalurus palustris*, after "Java," add "Bali,"

625 *Megalurus gramineus*, change "one record," to "isolated population,"

625 Split *Megalurus punctatus* into the following two species:

Megalurus [punctatus] punctatus (Quoy and Gaimard) 1830. NEW ZEALAND FERNBIRD. [8311.]
Swamps, fernland, scrub. **New Zealand region** in New Zealand (incl. Stewart, Codfish, and smaller adjacent is.) and Snares Is.
DNA-DNA hybridization data indicate that this superspecies is closely related to and probably congeneric with the Australian members of *Megalurus* (Sibley and Ahlquist 1987a), although Olson (1990b) regarded it as more closely related to *Amphilais*. [>*Bowdleria* (+N)]. (THE MATA). [FERNBIRD]. See *M. rufescens*.

†***Megalurus [punctatus] rufescens*** (Buller) 1869. CHATHAM ISLANDS FERNBIRD. [8311.1.]
Scrub. **Chatham Is.** (formerly, now probably extinct).
Olson (1990b: 168-171) gave evidence for recognition of *M. rufescens* as a species distinct from *M. punctatus*. (CHATHAM FERNBIRD). See *M. punctatus*.

626 *Megalurulus whitneyi*, in comments change "(1985)" to "(1985b)"

626 *Trichocichla rufa*, in comments change "(1985)" to "(1985b)"

626 *Schoenicola brevirostris*, before "s Cameroon," add "se Nigeria,"

628 *Garrulax poecilorhynchus*, in comments after "uncertain" add "."

630 *Arcanator orostruthus*, after "DAPPLE-THROAT" add "."; change beginning of range to "Locally in **e Africa**..."

630 *Trichastoma rostratum*, move statement in comments "Relationships,...(1985)." forward to position under "Tribe Timaliini"

631 *Malacocincla malaccensis*, change range to "...N. Natuna Is.) ¶*malaccensis*, SHORT-TAILED BABBLER [3729]; **ne Sarawak** (Mt. Mulu) ¶*feriatum* (Chasen and Kloss) 1931, OCHRACEOUS-THROATED BABBLER [3729.1]."

631 *Pellorneum tickelli,* before "Arunachal Pradesh" add "from"; in comments change "(Vuilleumier and Mayr 1987: 138)" to "(Ripley 1985a)"

632 *Illadopsis rufescens,* change range to "...w Africa in e Guinea, Sierra Leone, Liberia, Ivory Coast and Ghana."

632 *Illadopsis puveli,* after "Sierra Leone," add "Liberia, Ivory Coast, Ghana,"; add comments: "See *Ptyrticus turdinus.*"

632 *Kakamega poliothorax,* before "s Cameroon" add "se Nigeria,"

634 *Pnoepyga albiventer,* after "w Yunnan)", add "Taiwan"; in comments after "rejected." add "The Taiwan population is referable to *P. albiventer,* not *P. pusilla* (Harrap 1989)."; at end of comments add "See *P. immaculata.*"

634 After *Pnoepyga albiventer,* add:

Phoepyga immaculata Martens and Eck (1991). NEPAL WREN-BABBLER. [2748.1.]
Wet forest undergrowth. **Nepal.**
Described by Martens and Eck (1991) on the basis of vocalizations and morphological differences.

634 *Pnoepyga pusilla,* change range to "...Tenasserim) and c,se China (...) S through..."

634 *Spelaeornis troglodytoides,* after "se Tibet," add "extreme e India (se Arunachal Pradesh),"

634 *Spelaeornis formosus,* in heading change "1845" to "1874"

635 *Spelaeornis chocolatinus,* change range to "...(from Cachar Hills, Nagaland and se Arunachal Pradesh S to..."

635 *Neomixis tenella,* change English name to COMMON JERY (not NORTHERN); in comments change "COMMON" to "NORTHERN"

635 *Stachyris dennistouni,* change comments to "...conspecific, but Dickinson, Kennedy and Parkes (1991: 307-309) treated them as allospecies. AG..."

636 *Stachyris capitalis,* delete "Panaon,"

636 After *Stachyris striata,* add:

Stachyris [striata] latistriata Gonzales and Kennedy (1990). PANAY STRIPED-BABBLER. [3779.1.]
Forest. Mountains above 1000 m of **c Philippines** (Panay).

636 *Stachyris nigrorum,* delete ", Panay"

636 *Stachyris oglei,* after "ne Assam" add ", se Arunachal Pradesh"

637 *Dumetia hyperythra,* change "Andrha" to "Andhra"

637 *Macronous striaticeps,* change end of range to "...se **Philippines** (N to Bohol, Leyte and Samar)."

637 *Timalia pileata,* change end of range to "...Kwangtung), S to se Asia (...); Java."

637 *Chrysomma altirostre,* in heading change "(Jerdon)" to "Jerdon"

639 *Turdoides reinwardtii,* change "Senegal" to "Senegambia, sw Mali"

639 *Turdoides tenebrosus,* before "ne Zaire," add "n C. African Rep.,"

639 Sequence *Turdoides plebejus* before *Turdoides leucocephalus*

639 *Turdoides plebejus,* change range to "**Subsaharan Africa** from Senegambia and sw Mali E to Nigeria,...and S to C. African Rep., ne Zaire,..."

641 *Actinodura [egertoni] egertoni* and *Actinodura [egertoni] ramsayi,* add superspecies

641 *Actinodura morrisoniana,* change English name to FORMOSAN BARWING (not TAIWAN); change comments to "(TAIWAN BARWING)."

642 Split *Alcippe cinereiceps* into the following two species:

Alcippe [cinereiceps] cinereiceps (Verreaux) 1870. STREAK-THROATED FULVETTA. [2795.]
Forest thickets, bamboo. Himalayas, 650-4600 m, of **s Asia** in ne India (from e Bhutan E to Arunachal Pradesh, and S to n Assam, Manipur and Nagaland), ne Burma, s China (from s Kansu, s Shensi and Hupeh S to, se Szechwan, Yunnan and Hunan; nw Fukien), Taiwan, ne Laos and n Vietnam (nw Tonkin).
(GREY-HEADED FULVETTA). See *A. ludlowi.*

Alcippe [cinereiceps] ludlowi (Kinnear) 1935. LUDLOW'S FULVETTA. [2795.1.]
Forest thickets, bamboo. Himalayas of **s Asia** in se Tibet, sw China (sw Szechwan), e Bhutan and extreme ne India (se Arunachal Pradesh). Winters to lower elevations.
A. cinereiceps and *A. ludlowi* are morphologically distinct and marginally sympatric in Arunachal Pradesh (Ripley et al. 1991: 23-24). (BROWN-HEADED FULVETTA).

643 *Kupeornis gilberti,* change range to "Mts., 1500-1800 m, of **wc Africa** in se Nigeria and sw Cameroon."

643 *Phyllanthus atripennis,* change end of range to "...s Nigeria, sw Cameroon, sw C. African Rep. and cn,ne Zaire."

644 *Yuhina brunneiceps,* change English name to FORMOSAN YUHINA (not TAIWAN); change comments to "(TAIWAN YUHINA)."

644 *Oxylabes madagascariensis,* change "**e Madagascar**" to "**nw,e Madagascar**"

645 *Crossleyia xanthophrys,* change "**ce Madagascar**" to "**n,ce Madagascar**"

645 *Panurus biarmicus,* change range to "...Balkan states, c Turkey and Syria. Winters..."

646 *Paradoxornis zappeyi,* in comments before "ZAPPEY'S" add "CRESTED/"

645 *Paradoxornis brunneus,* change end of range to "...nw Yunnan) and ne,c,e Burma."

646 **Rhabdornis mystacalis** (not *mysticalis*); change range to "Lowlands to 1200 m of **Philippines** (Luzon, Catanduanes, Masbate,...Negros, Leyte, Calicoan, Bohol, Dinagat, Mindanao, Basilan)."; change comments to "...tentative); *Rhabdornis* is placed by Dickinson, Kennedy and Parkes (1991: 302) in a separate family, Rhabdornithidae. (STRIPE-HEADED..."

646 *Rhabdornis grandis,* in heading change "1953" to "(1953)"; in comments change "1952" to "(1952)" and "*mysticalis*" to "*mystacalis*"

647 *Sylvia lugens,* in heading change "1804" to "1840"

647 *Sylvia borin,* after "n Turkey" add ", n Iran"

647 Split *Sylvia curruca* into the following three species:

Sylvia [curruca] curruca (Linnaeus) 1758. LESSER WHITETHROAT. [2585.]
Woodland, thickets, bushes, steppes. **Palearctic** from s British Isles and Scandinavia (N to Arctic Circle) E across n Russia to w Siberia (upper Lena r., Transbaicalia), n Mongolia

and n Manchuria (nw Heilungkiang), and S to c,se France, n Italy, Balkan states, Turkey, Near East, nw,s Iran and s S.S.R. (Kazakhstan, n Turkestan). Winters from trop.,e Africa E to India.

There is controversy about the treatment of the three groups as races or as separate species; Watson, in Peters (1986: 275, footnote), summarized the arguments, and Haffer (1989) gave reasons for consideration of *curruca, minula* and *althaea* as distinct species, a treatment followed by Glutz von Blotzheim (1991: 642, 795, 1236). [>*Curruca* (≈*S. althaea*)]. [LESSER WHITETHROAT].

Sylvia [curruca] minula Hume 1873. SMALL WHITETHROAT. [2585.1.]
Desert scrub, thorn bushes, semi-desert, often near water in oases. **Sc Asia** in ne Iran, s S.S.R. (Transcaspia, s,e Turkestan) and nw,nc China (from Sinkiang E through n Tsinghai, n Kansu and Ningsia to ne Inner Mongolia). Winters in s Asia.
(DESERT WHITETHROAT/DESERT LESSER-WHITETHROAT). See *S. curruca*.

Sylvia [curruca] althaea Hume 1878. HUME'S WHITE-THROAT. [2585.2.]
Open barren slopes with scattered scrub, thorn bushes, thorny thickets, juniper. Mts., 1500-3700 m, of **s Asia** in Afghanistan, n Pakistan (n Baluchistan) and n India (Kashmir, Ladakh). Winters from Iraq E to India and Ceylon.
S. affinis, based on *Curruca affinis* Blyth 1845 and applicable to this species, has been suppressed by the I.C.Z.N. (1975). (HUME'S LESSER-WHITETHROAT). See *S. curruca*.

648 *Sylvia hortensis*, in heading change "[2585.]" to "[2583.]"; change range to "...Turkey, Near East, Iran, Afghanistan, s Russia..."
648 *Sylvia rueppelli*, after "w,sw Turkey" add ", Near East"
648 *Sylvia cantillans*, after "w Turkey" add "and Syria"
649 *Mirafra cantillans*, change range to "...s Mali, Burkina Faso, s Niger, n Nigeria and s Chad to n C. African Rep., s Sudan,..."
649 *Mirafra hova*, change English name to MADAGASCAR LARK (not HOVA); in comments change "MADAGASCAR" to "HOVA"
649 *Mirafra williamsi*, in heading change "1956" to "(1956)"
649 *Mirafra africana*, change range to "Locally in **Africa** in sw Mali, se Guinea, c Nigeria, Cameroon, Gabon, sw C. African Rep. and n Sudan;..."
652 *Ammomanes cincturus*, in comments change "1951" to "1951a"
652 *Ammomanes deserti*, before "Pakistan" add "s S.S.R. (Transcaspia),"
653 *Calandrella brachydactyla*, change range to "...Turkey, Near East, Iran, Afghanistan, s Russia..."
653 *Calandrella cinerea*, change range to "**Wc,e,s Africa** in n Nigeria, and from sw,s,ne Zaire,..."
653-654 *Calandrella rufescens*, change "s,e Spain," to "Iberian pen.,"; after "Iran," add "Afghanistan,"
654 *Calandrella cheleensis*, change end of range to "Winters S to c China."
654 *Calandrella raytal*, change "s,e Pakistan," to "s,e Afghanistan,"
654 *Eremalauda dunni*, before "n,c Sudan" add "s Egypt and"

655 *Galerida cristata*, change range to "...s Mauritania, Gambia and Sierra Leone across Mali, Niger, Ghana and n Nigeria to n Sudan,..."
655 *Galerida modesta*, after "s Niger," add "Benin,"
655 *Pseudalaemon fremantlii*, in heading change "(Phillips)" to "(Lort Phillips)"
655 *Alauda japonica*, at end of comments after "separate species" add "(e.g., Stepanyan 1990c)"
656 *Eremophila alpestris*, before "c,n Norway," add "Franz Josef Land,"; after "n Russia" add (incl. Novaya Zemlya)"
656 *Promerops cafer*, move sentence under comments "Has been included...142-144)." forward to position under Subfamily Promeropinae.
657 *Prionochilus plateni*, change "Culion," to "Calamian Is.,"
657 *Dicaeum aeruginosum*, change "Romblen," to "Romblon,"
657 *Dicaeum anthonyi*, change English name to FLAME-CROWNED FLOWERPECKER (not FLAME-CROWED); change range to "Mts., 800-2100 m, of **n Philippines** (n Luzon) ¶*anthonyi*, YELLOW-CROWNED FLOWERPECKER [3922]; **s Philippines** (Mindanao) ¶*kampalili* Manuel and Gilliard (1953), RED-CROWNED FLOWERPECKER [3922.1]."; at beginning of comments, add "*D. rubricapilla* Manuel and Gilliard (1952), originally proposed for the form known now as *kampalili*, is pre-occupied."
658 *Dicaeum hypoleucum*, after "Luzon," add "Catanduanes,"
659 *Dicaeum hirundinaceum*, change range to "...[8452.1]; nomadic in **Australian**...Torres Strait ¶*hirundinaceum*..."
660 *Anthreptes malacensis*, change range to "...sw Philippines (Calamian Is., Palawan, Balabac) ¶*malacensis*,...**Philippines** (Luzon, Catanduanes, Mindoro, Samar, Leyte, Dinagat, Siargao, Camaguin Sur, ne Mindanao)..."
660 *Anthreptes longuemarei*, change "Senegal" to "Senegambia,"
660 *Anthreptes orientalis*, in comments before "KENYA" add "EASTERN VIOLET-BACKED/"
660 *Anthreptes aurantium*, change range to "**C Africa** from Cameroon E to sw C. African Rep. and ne Zaire,..."
661 *Anthreptes rectirostris*, change range to "...s Cameroon (incl. Bioko), sw C. African Rep., n,ne Zaire,...nw Angola, sw,cs,ce Zaire and extreme nw Tanzania ¶*tephrolaema*..."; in comments change "1958" to "(1959b)"
661 *Anthreptes collaris*, before "Guinea-Bissau," add "Gambia,"
661 *Anthreptes platurus*, change range to "...across s Mali, Burkina Faso, s Niger, Benin, n,c Nigeria,..."
661 *Nectarinia seimundi*, change range to "...Cameroon (incl. Bioko), sw C. African Rep., n,ne Zaire,..."
661 *Nectarinia batesi*, change range to "**W,c Africa** in Ivory Coast, Ghana, s Nigeria, s Cameroon (incl. Bioko), Rio Muni,..."
661 *Nectarinia olivacea*, change range to "**Africa** from sw Mali, Guinea-Bissau,...extreme s Sudan, sw,c Ethiopia and s Somalia, and S to..."
662 *Nectarinia oritis*, change range to "Mts., 1200-2100 m, of **wc Africa** in se Nigeria and Cameroon (incl. Bioko)."
662 *Nectarinia verticalis*, change "Senegal" to "Senegambia,"

662 *Nectarinia cyanolaema,* change end of range to "...n,ne Zaire, w,c Uganda and w Kenya, and S to nw,ne Angola, sw,cs,ce Zaire and nw Tanzania."

662 *Nectarinia rubescens,* change range to "**C Africa** from s Cameroon (incl. Bioko), C. African Rep., n,ne Zaire, extreme se Sudan, Uganda and w Kenya S to nw,cn Angola,..."

662 *Nectarinia hunteri,* after "Sudan," add "ne Uganda,"

663 *Nectarinia sperata,* change range to "...Babuyan Is., Camiguin Norte, n Luzon).../PHILIPPINE SUNBIRD [3943.2]; **s Philippines**..."

663 *Nectarinia aspasia,* under comments change "*coccinogastra*" to "*coccinigastra*"

664 *Nectarinia venusta,* change range to "**W,c,e Africa** from Senegambia, sw Mali, Sierra Leone,...L. Chad, C. African Rep., s Sudan..."

664 *Nectarinia bouvieri,* change range to "...*N. osea*), w,s Uganda and w Kenya S (except..."

665 *Nectarinia prigoginei,* in heading change "(Macdonald) 1958" to "(Macdonald 1958)"

665 *Nectarinia preussi,* before "se Cameroon" add "se Nigeria,"

665 *Nectarinia chloropygia,* change range to "...Cameroon (incl. Bioko), C. African Rep., ne Zaire,..."

665 *Nectarinia loveridgei,* change comments to "See *N. moreaui*."

665 After *Nectarinia loveridgei,* add:

Nectarinia moreaui (Sclater) 1933. MOREAU'S SUNBIRD. [7714.1.]
Forest. Mountains above 1200 m in **ce Tanzania**.
Although Stuart and van der Willigen (1980) considered *N. moreaui* to be a hybrid *N. loveridgei* x *N. mediocris*, a nest (with two nestlings) was reported by Fuggles-Couchman (1987: 24), and Short, Horne and Muringo-Gichuki (1990: 202) treated *moreaui* as a species.

665 *Nectarinia cuprea,* change beginning of range to "**C. Africa** from Senegambia, sw Mali, Sierra Leone..."

666 *Nectarinia tacazze,* after "se Sudan," add "ne Uganda,"

666 *Nectarinia johnstoni,* in comments after "MALACHITE-SUNBIRD" delete ")"

667 *Nectarinia notata,* LONG-BILLED GREEN SUNBIRD (not MADAGASCAR); in comments after "MADAGASCAR GREEN" add "/MADAGASCAR"

667 *Nectarinia coccinigastra* (not *coccinogastra*); change range to "**C Africa** from Senegambia, sw Mali, Burkina Faso and Sierra Leone..."

667 *Nectarinia superba,* change range to "...Cameroon, sw C. African Rep., n,ne Zaire,...cw,nw Angola, sw,cs,ce Zaire and extreme nw Tanzania."

667 *Nectarinia pulchella,* change range to "**Subsaharan, ne Africa** from...s Mali, Burkina Faso, s Niger,...Kenya (except ne) and Tanzania."

667 *Aethopyga shelleyi,* change range to "Lowlands to 2000 m of **Philippines.**"

668 *Aethopyga mystacalis,* change range to "...Sumatra and Borneo ¶*temminckii* (Müller) 1843, SCARLET SUNBIRD [3956]; **Java** ¶*mystacalis,* JAVAN SUNBIRD [3956.1]."

669 *Paramythia montium,* at end of range add "."

670 *Passer domesticus,* change range to "...Intro. (¶*domesticus*) Iceland, e Atlantic is. (Azores, Cape Verde), w,s,e Africa, c,e Australia,...and c,s S. America (from w Colombia, Curaçao and e Brazil..."; change end

of comments to "...Massa 1989). Although the *domesticus* and *indicus* groups are reported to intergrade where their ranges meet, Stepanyan (1990c) considered them as full species. See *P. motitensis* and *P. castanopterus*."

670 *Passer castanopterus,* remove superspecies; add comments "J. D. Summers-Smith (pers. comm.) believes this species to be more closely related to *P. domesticus* than to *P. rutilans*."

670 *Passer rutilans,* remove superspecies; at end of comments add "See *P. castanopterus*."

670 *Passer iagoensis,* change English name to IAGO SPARROW (not CAPE VERDE SPARROW); in comments before "RUFOUS-BACKED" add "CAPE VERDE/"

671 *Passer griseus,* change "Senegal" to "Senegambia and sw Mali"

671 *Passer simplex,* after "e Iran" add "(probably extirpated)"

671 *Passer montanus,* change range to "...Taiwan, Korea, Japan and Ryukyu Is. Intro. Canary Is., Pescadores...Bermuda (now extirpated)."

671 *Passer eminibey,* change range to "**Ne Africa** from w,s Sudan, c,s Ethiopia and s Somalia S through..."

671 *Petronia pyrgita,* before "sc,e,se Sudan," add "n C. African Rep.,"

672 *Petronia dentata,* change range to "...s Mali, n Ivory Coast, Burkina Faso, s Niger,..."

672 *Carpospiza brachydactyla,* change range to "...Saudi Arabia and s S.S.R. (Armenia, s Turkmenia). Winters..."

672 *Montifringilla davidiana,* in comments after "Neufeldt, 1986" add "; Stepanyan 1990a"

673 *Motacilla alba,* in range change "[2928.2]" to "[2829.2]"; in comments after "Lobkov 1979)." add "*M. personata* is considered a full species by Stepanyan (1990c)."

673 *Motacilla lugens,* after "(n Honshu)" add "; **sw Alaska** (Attu in Aleutian Is.)"

674 *Motacilla citreola,* change English name to CITRINE WAGTAIL (not YELLOW-HOODED); in range after "Transbaicalia)" add "and n Mongolia"; change comments to "[>*Budytes* (+N)]. YELLOW-HOODED/ YELLOW-HEADED WAGTAIL). See *M. flava*."

674 *Motacilla flava,* change range to "...¶*lutea* (Gmelin) 1774, YELLOW-HEADED WAGTAIL (YELLOW-BROWED WAGTAIL/EASTERN YELLOW-WAGTAIL)...¶*taivana* (Swinhoe) 1863, GREEN-HEADED WAGTAIL (GREEN-CROWNED WAGTAIL/KURILE YELLOW-WAGTAIL)...; in comments after "unclear" add "; Stepanyan (1990c) treated this complex as four species, *M. feldegg* (with *melanogrisea*), *M. lutea, M. taivana* and *M. flava* (including all remaining groups)."

674 *Motacilla clara,* change beginning of range to "Locally in **Africa** in Sierra Leone, Ivory Coast, se Nigeria, Cameroon, sw C. African Rep. and Gabon;..."

675 *Macronyx grimwoodi,* in heading change "1955" to "(1955)"

675 *Anthus cinnamomeus,* in comments after "Prigogine" add "1981b;"

676 *Anthus hoeschi,* in comments after "species" add ", supported by Dowsett-Lemaire (1989)"

676 *Anthus richardi,* change end of comments to "...related forms and are regarded as conspecific; we here treat all other groups as allospecies. *A. richardi* is considered a species separate from *A. novaeseelandiae* by Stepanyan (1990c)."

676 *Anthus campestris,* change range to "...and S to n Africa (from Morocco E to Tunisia, and in Somalia), n Mediterranean..."

676 *Anthus godlewskii,* in comments after "subspecies of *A. campestris*" add "but considered a full species by Stepanyan (1990c)"

677 *Anthus similis,* change range to "**African region** in c Niger, se Ghana, e,se Nigeria, Cameroon and cw Sudan...LONG-BILLED PIPIT [2838]; mts. of **cw Angola** (Mt. Moco) ¶*moco* Traylor (1962), MOCO PIPIT [6578.2].'; change comments to "...Dowsett and Dowsett-Lemaire (1980: 188-191; 1987) and Clancey (1987c) discussed this complex..."

677 *Anthus nyassae,* change end of range to "...Angola, Zambia and Zimbabwe."

677 *Anthus pratensis,* after "Iceland," add "Faroe Is.,"

678 *Anthus petrosus,* in comments change "1988" to "1988b"

678 *Anthus rubescens,* change range to "..Kamchatka, and Kuril and Commander is.); **N. America**...se Quebec, n New Hampshire and n Maine..."

679 *Anthus hellmayri,* in comments delete "See *A. lutescens.*"

679 *Anthus lutescens,* in comments after "species" add "(e.g., Zimmer 1953b: 18-20)"; at end of comments add "See *A. chacoensis.*"

679 *Anthus chacoensis,* in heading change "1952" to "(1952a)"; add comments "*A. chacoensis* is a good species, distinct from *A. lutescens* (Zimmer 1953b: 19)."

679 *Prunella ocularis,* change English name to RADDE'S ACCENTOR (not SPOT-THROATED); in comments change "RADDE'S" to "SPOT-THROATED"

680 *Prunella fulvescens,* in heading change "(Severtzov)" to "(Severtsov)"

680 *Prunella atrogularis,* change end of range to "...Winters S to Transcaspia and Middle East."

680 *Bubalornis albirostris,* change range to "**Subsaharan Africa** from Senegambia and Guinea-Bissau E across s Mali, Burkina Faso, s Niger, n Ghana, n Nigeria..."

680 *Sporopipes frontalis,* change range to "...s Mali, Burkina Faso, s Niger, n Ghana, n Nigeria, s Chad and n C. African Rep. to c,s Sudan..."

681 *Plocepasser superciliosus,* change range to "...s Mali, n Ivory Coast, Burkina Faso, n Ghana,..."

681 **Philetairus socius** (not **Philetarius**)

681 *Ploceus bannermani,* change range to "Mts. above 1500 m of **wc Africa** in se Nigeria and Cameroon."

681 *Ploceus baglafecht,* change beginning of range to "Highland areas of **c Africa** in e Nigeria, sw Cameroon, sw C. African Rep., w,nw Ethiopia,..."

681 *Ploceus bertrandi,* after "ce,sc Tanzania," add "ne Zambia,"

681 *Ploceus pelzelni,* change range to "Locally in **w,c Africa** from Senegal, s Ivory Coast and Ghana E to..."

681 *Ploceus luteolus,* change range to "...s Mali, Burkina Faso, s Niger, n Ghana, Nigeria,..."

682 *Ploceus intermedius,* change "Zambia," to "C. African Rep.,"

682 *Ploceus melanogaster,* change range to "Locally in mts. of **c Africa** in se Nigeria, Cameroon (incl. Bioko), ne,ce Zaire, extreme se Sudan, w Uganda, w Kenya and w Tanzania."

682 *Ploceus princeps,* in comments after "subgenus *Deleplectes.*" add "(PRINCIPE WEAVER)."

682 *Ploceus aurantius,* change "**Africa**" to "**w,c Africa**"

682 *Ploceus bojeri,* change range to "**E Africa** in s Somalia, c,e Kenya and ne Tanzania."

683 *Ploceus castanops,* after "Uganda," add "w Kenya,"; at end of comments add "See *P. burnieri.*"

683 After *Ploceus castanops,* add:

Ploceus burnieri Baker and Baker (1990). KILOMBERO WEAVER. [7777.1.] Riverside swamp. **Ec Tanzania** (Ifakara region). Relationships uncertain; may be intermediate between *P. castanops* and the "masked-weaver" group (Baker and Baker 1990).

683 *Ploceus galbula,* after "extreme ne Kenya" add "(formerly)"

683 *Ploceus heuglini,* change range to "**Subsaharan Africa** from extreme sw Mauritania and Senegambia E through s Mali, n Ivory Coast, Burkina Faso, s Niger, n Ghana, n Nigeria,..."

683 *Ploceus victoriae,* change comments to "The validity of this form as a species has been questioned by Louette (1987); possibly a subspecies...'masked weaver,' or a hybrid."

683 *Ploceus vitellinus,* change range to "...s Mali, Burkina Faso, s Niger, n Ghana, ne Nigeria, L. Chad area, n C. African Rep. and c,s Sudan...Somalia, and S (incl. São Tomé) through..."

683 *Ploceus cucullatus,* change range to "...s Mali, Burkina Faso, s Niger,...Intro. (¶*cucullatus*) Hispaniola (incl. Saona I.); (¶*nigriceps*) São Tomé; (¶*spilonotus*) Mascarene Is."

684 *Ploceus nigerrimus,* before "n,ne Zaire," add "C. African Rep.,"

684 *Ploceus melanocephalus,* change range to "...s Mali, Burkina Faso, s Niger, n Ghana and n Nigeria..."

684 *Ploceus sakalava,* change range to "Lowlands to 700 m of **n,w,s Madagascar.**"

685 *Ploceus preussi,* change range to "Locally in lowlands of **w,c Africa** from Sierra Leone and Liberia E through Ivory Coast and Ghana to s Cameroon, sw C. African Rep. and n,ne Zaire, and S to Congo r. mouth."

685 *Ploceus insignis,* after "cw Angola," add "sw C. African Rep.,"

685 *Pachyphantes superciliosus,* change range to "...Cameroon, C. African Rep., s Sudan...Rwanda, Burundi and nw Tanzania."

686 *Malimbus coronatus,* after "Rio Muni" add ", sw C. African Rep."

686 *Malimbus cassini,* change range to "Lowlands of **wc Africa** from s Ghana and s Cameroon S to...forest to sw C. African Rep. and c,cn,ne,ce Zaire."

686 *Malimbus ballmani,* change English name to BALLMANN'S MALIMBE (not BALLMAN'S); in comments change "Field (1979)" to "(Field 1979)" and "1981" to "1981a"

686 *Malimbus ibadanensis,* in heading change "1958" to "(1958)"; at end of comments add "(ELGOOD'S MALIMBE)."

686 *Malimbus erythrogaster,* before "n,ne Zaire," add "sw C. African Rep.,"

686 *Malimbus nitens,* change range to "Lowlands of **c Africa** from Senegambia, sw Mali and Guinea-Bissau E to s Cameroon, sw C. African Rep., n,ne Zaire..."

686 *Malimbus malimbicus*, after "Cameroon," add "sw C. African Rep.,"

686 *Malimbus rubricollis*, change range to "...Cameroon (incl. Bioko), sw C. African Rep., n,ne Zaire,...nw Angola, sc,se Zaire and extreme nw Tanzania."

686 *Anaplectes rubriceps*, in range after "Senegal," add "n Ivory Coast,"

686 *Quelea cardinalis*, before "ne,ce Zaire," add "sw C. African Rep.,"

687 *Foudia madagascariensis*, change English name to MADAGASCAR RED FODY (not RED); change beginning of comments to "(RED/CARDINAL..."

687 *Foudia omissa*, change English name to FOREST FODY (not ROTHSCHILD'S); in comments before "RED FOREST" add "ROTHSCHILD'S/"

687 *Euplectes franciscanus*, change range to "...s Mali, Ivory Coast and Ghana E through Burkina Faso, s Niger,..."; at beginning of comments add "Includes *E. zavattarii* Moltoni 1943, regarded as a synonym of a race of *E. franciscanus*."

688 *Euplectes axillaris*, change range to "...Niger r.; from n Nigeria, sw Cameroon, Gabon, C. African Rep., sw,sc,ce,ne Zaire,..."

688 *Euplectes macrourus*, change "Senegal" to "Senegambia, sw Mali"

688 *Euplectes albonotatus*, after "Tomé)" add "and sw C. African Rep."

689 *Parmoptila rubrifrons*, change range to "Locally in **w,c Africa** in ne Liberia, s Ivory Coast and sc Ghana...[7819.1]; **ec Africa** in n,ne,c,ce Zaire, w Uganda and extreme nw Tanzania ¶*jamesoni*..."

689 *Nigrita fusconota*, change range to "Locally in **c Africa** from se Guinea, Liberia, Ivory Coast, Ghana, s Benin, s Nigeria..."

689 *Nigrita bicolor*, change range to "...n,ne Zaire, w Uganda and w Kenya, and S to..."

689 *Nigrita luteifrons*, change range to "**C Africa** from e Guinea, Sierra Leone, Ivory Coast, se Ghana, s Nigeria, Cameroon (incl. Bioko), C. African Rep. and n,ne Zaire S to nw Angola, sw,c,ce Zaire and w Uganda."

689 *Nigrita canicapilla*, change range to "...Cameroon (incl. Bioko), C. African Rep., n,ne Zaire,..."

689 *Nesocharis shelleyi*, change range to "Mts., 1200-1500 m, of **wc Africa** in se Nigeria and Cameroon (incl. Bioko, where ranging to sea level)."

689 *Nesocharis ansorgei*, in heading change "1861" to "1899"

689 *Nesocharis capistrata*, after "Cameroon," add "C. African Rep.,"

690 Change *Pytilia [afra] phoenicoptera* to *Pytilia [phoenicoptera] phoenicoptera*; change range to "...s Mali, n Ivory Coast, Burkina Faso and Ghana to n Nigeria, c Cameroon, C. African Rep., s Sudan,..."; change comments to "*Pytilia* Swainson (before May) 1837 antedates *Pytelia* Swainson (after June) 1837. (CRIMSON-WINGED/... WAXBILL. [RED-WINGED PYTILIA]. See *P. lineata*."

690 Change *Pytilia [afra] lineata* to *Pytilia [phoenicoptera] lineata*

690 *Pytilia afra*, remove superspecies; in comments delete "[YELLOW-BACKED PYTILIA]."

690 *Pytilia melba*, remove superspecies

690 *Pytilia hypogrammica*, remove superspecies

690 *Cryptospiza reichenovii*, before "Cameroon" add "se Nigeria,"

690 *Pyrenestes ostrinus*, change range to "**C Africa** from Ivory Coast E to C. African Rep., ne Zaire...Malawi, nw,s Tanzania and se,ce Zaire."

690 *Pyrenestes minor*, in comments before "(NYASA" add "Includes *P. vincenti* Benson (1955)."

691 *Clytospiza monteiri*, change range to "...Congo forest from e Nigeria and Cameroon E through...s Sudan, Uganda and extreme w Kenya, and in Gabon..."

691 *Euschistospiza dybowskii*, in comments after "333)." add "[<*Clytospiza* (+N)]."

691 *Lagonosticta rufopicta*, change range to "**W,c Africa** from Gambia and Sierra Leone E...ne Zaire, nw Uganda and w Kenya."

692 *Lagonosticta vinacea*, change range to "Locally in **w Africa** in Senegambia, sw Mali and Guinea...**nc Africa** from n Ivory Coast, Burkina Faso, Ghana..."

692 *Uraeginthus angolensis*, change range to "...Zambia and s,c,ne Tanzania S (incl. São Tomé) to n Namibia,..."; at beginning of comments add "[<*Estrilda* (~*Uraeginthus*)]."

692 *Estrilda caerulescens*, change range to "...s Mali, n Ivory Coast, Burkina Faso, n Ghana, n Togo, n Benin and n Nigeria to n Cameroon, sw Chad and C. African Rep. Intro..."

693 *Estrilda paludicola*, after "c,n,ne Angola," add "C. African Rep.,"

693 *Estrilda melpoda*, change "Senegal" to "Senegambia, sw Mali,"

693 *Estrilda rhodopyga*, change range to "...e,se Sudan, w,c Ethiopia and s Somalia S through..."

693 *Estrilda troglodytes*, change range to "...s Mali, Burkina Faso, s Niger, n Ghana, Nigeria,...extreme ne Zaire, n,e Uganda and w Kenya. Intro..."

693 *Estrilda astrild*, change range to "**C,s Africa** from sw Mali, Sierra Leone, s Guinea and Liberia E to s Cameroon (incl. Bioko and São Tomé), c C. African Rep., n,ne Zaire, c,s Sudan, w,c Ethiopia and s Somalia, and S (...) to s S. Africa. Intro. Portugal, se Spain, Cape Verde Is., Hawaiian Is..."

693 *Estrilda nonnula*, change beginning of range to "**C Africa** from se Nigeria and Cameroon (incl. Bioko) E across..."

693 *Estrilda atricapilla*, after "Cameroon" add "and sw C. African Rep."

693 *Estrilda kandti*, change end of range to "...ce Zaire, sw Uganda and w,c Kenya."

694 *Amandava amandava*, change end of range to "...Hawaiian is. (Kauai, Oahu, Hawaii)."

694 *Ortygospiza gabonensis*, change end of range to "...n Zambia, Rwanda and nw Tanzania."

694 *Stagonopleura oculata*, change "sw Australia" to "sw W. Australia"

695 *Oreostruthus fuliginosus*, change comments to "(ALPINE FIRETAIL/CRIMSON-SIDED/RED-SIDED MOUNTAIN-FINCH). AG (+N): FINCH."

695 *Neochmia temporalis*, change end of comments to "...(SYDNEY FIRETAIL). AG (+N): WAXBILL."

695 *Neochmia phaeton*, in comments delete "AG: WAXBILL."

696 *Lonchura cantans*, after "s Niger," add "n Ghana,"

697 *Lonchura cucullata,* change beginning of range to "**Africa** from Senegambia, sw Mali and Burkina Faso E to Cameroon (incl. Bioko, São Tomé and Príncipe), C. African Rep., Sudan..."

697 *Lonchura striata,* boldface "**s Asia**"; in comments after "MUNIA" add "/BENGALESE FINCH"

697 *Lonchura kelaarti,* change "Andrha" to "Andhra"

698 *Lonchura punctulata,* after "Mindoro," add "Calamian Is.,"

698 *Lonchura malacca,* change world numbers of groups, ¶*malacca* [3982.2] and ¶*atricapilla* [812]; change "Intro. (group uncertain)" to "Intro. (mostly ¶*atricapilla*)"

698 *Lonchura ferruginosa,* change English name to WHITE-CAPPED MUNIA (not CHESTNUT); in comments before "BLACK-THROATED" add "CHESTNUT/"

699 *Lonchura montana,* change "3700-3600 m," to "2100-4150 m,"

700 *Vidua chalybeata,* change range to "**W Africa** from Senegambia, sw Mali and Sierra Leone...Chad and C. African Rep. E to c,s Sudan, w,c Ethiopia and s Somalia ¶*ultramarina*..."; in comments change "(1982)" to "(1982, 1985)"; at end of comments add "See *V. codringtoni.*"

700 Split *Vidua funerea* into the following two species:

Vidua funerea (Tarragon) 1847. VARIABLE INDIGOBIRD. [6754.]
Moist savanna. Locally in **w,c,s Africa** in sw Mali, Sierra Leone, Nigeria, Cameroon, C. African Rep., s,sc,ce,ne Zaire, extreme se Sudan, and se Kenya S through e,c,s Tanzania, Zimbabwe, ne Botswana, c,n Angola, extreme ne Namibia (Caprivi) and Mozambique to S. Africa (Transvaal, Natal, e Cape prov.).
Includes *V. nigerrima* (Sharpe) 1871, BLACK INDIGOBIRD, sometimes regarded as a separate species but now considered a race of *V. funerea* (Payne 1973: 248-250). *V. nigeriae* (Alexander) 1908, ALEXANDER'S INDIGOBIRD, and *V. camerunensis* (Grote) 1922, CAMEROON INDIGOBIRD, usually associated with birds now considered to be *V. wilsoni* and formerly treated as separate species, are considered *nomina dubia* by Payne (1982: 50-53). *V. funerea* interbreeds with *V. purpurascens* in southeastern Zaire. Parasitizes *Lagonosticta rubricata.* See *V. chalybeata* and *V. codringtoni.*

Vidua codringtoni (Neave) 1907. TWINSPOT INDIGOBIRD. [6754.1.]
Moist savanna. Locally in **se Africa** in Zambia, sw Tanzania, Malawi and Zimbabwe.
Sympatric with *V. chalybeata, V. funerea* and *V. purpurascens,* and parasitizes *Hypargos niveoguttatus* (R. B. Payne, pers. comm.). (CODRINGTON'S INDIGOBIRD).

700 *Vidua purpurascens,* remove superspecies; change comments to "Parasitizes *Lagonosticta rhodopareia.* See *V. chalybeata, V. funerea* and *V. codringtoni.*"

700 *Vidua wilsoni,* in comments change "Nicolai (1972)" to "(Nicolai 1972)"

700 *Vidua macroura,* change range to "**Africa** from Senegambia and Guinea-Bissau...s Somalia, and S (incl. São Tomé) to s S. Africa..."

701 *Vidua orientalis,* after "Chad" add ", C. African Rep."

701 *Vidua interjecta,* change range to "**W,c Africa** in Mali, Ivory Coast, Ghana, s Nigeria,..."

701 *Vidua obtusa,* after "extreme sw Uganda" add ", s Kenya"

701 *Fringilla coelebs,* before "Madeira," add "Azores,"

701 *Fringilla montifringilla,* after "Sakhalin)" add "and n Mongolia"

702 *Serinus serinus,* before "Morocco" add "from"

702 *Serinus citrinella,* change habitat to "...forest edge; also (¶*corsicana* only) dry scrub."; change range to "...n Italy and Balearic Is. ¶*citrinella,* EUROPEAN CITRIL [2950]; mts. of **Corsica and Sardinia** ¶*corsicana* (Koenig) 1899, CORSICAN CITRIL [2950.1]. Winters..."

702 *Serinus koliensis,* in heading change "1952" to "(1952)"

703 *Serinus leucopygius,* change range to "...s Niger, Ghana, n Nigeria, s Chad, n Cameroon, n C. African Rep. and c,s Sudan..."

703 After *Serinus rothschildi,* add:

Serinus flavigula Salvadori 1888. YELLOW-THROATED SEEDEATER. [7742.3.]
Dry open areas, scattered trees. Highlands, 1400-1500 m, of **c Ethiopia.**
S. flavigula was thought to be based on variants of *S. xanthopygius* (Rand 1968) or hybrids (Hall and Moreau 1970: 272-273), but recent data indicate *S. flavigula* is a distinct species sympatric with *S. xanthopygius* (Ash and Gullick 1990).

703 *Serinus xanthopygius,* change end of comments to "...See *S. flavigula* and *S. atrogularis.*"

703 *Serinus mozambicus,* after "Ethiopia, and S" add "(incl. São Tomé)"

703 *Serinus dorsostriatus,* in comments after "Baars 1980)." add "Includes *S. xantholaema* Salvadori 1896, now regarded as a synonym of a race of *S. dorsostriatus* (Erard 1986)."

704 *Serinus canicapillus,* before "Ghana" add "sw Mali, n Ivory Coast and"

704 *Serinus whytii,* after "cs Tanzania" add ", ne Zambia"

704 *Serinus burtoni,* before "Cameroon" add "se Nigeria and"

704 *Serinus symonsi,* change English name to DRAKENSBERG SISKIN (not DRAKENSBURG)

705 *Carduelis sinica,* before "Bonin" add "Ryukyu,"

705 *Carduelis spinoides,* change range to "...Nagaland), sc Tibet and wc Burma. Winters to lower elevations and to n Thailand and sc Vietnam (s Annam)."

705 **Carduelis [spinoides] ambigua,** add superspecies and sequence before *C. monguilloti*

706 **Carduelis [spinus] atriceps** (not *[pinus]*)

706 *Carduelis crassirostris,* change range to "...Puno) and c,sw Bolivia (Cochabamba, Oruro,..."

706 *Carduelis olivacea,* change end of range to "...Peru to c Bolivia (La Paz, Cochabamba, ne Santa Cruz)."

706 *Carduelis notata,* in heading after "de Gisignies" add "1847"

706 *Carduelis xanthogastra,* change range to "...Sucre), sw Ecuador (El Oro), se Peru (Puno) and c Bolivia (...)."

707 *Carduelis psaltria,* change "n Utah," to "s Idaho,"

707 *Carduelis carduelis,* in comments after "Russia" add "; Stepanyan (1990c) treated them as full species"

707 *Carduelis hornemanni,* in comments change "1988" to "1988a"

709 *Rhodopechys githaginea,* after "Canary Is.;" add "se Spain;"

709 *Rhodopechys obsoleta,* change range to "...1000-3000 m, of **sw,c Asia** in s Turkey, Near East,..."

709 *Carpodacus erythrinus,* change range to "...**Eurasia** from s Scandinavia, ne Germany, Poland and Switzerland E across..."

709-710 *Carpodacus mexicanus,* after "Gulf states" add "and n Florida"

711 *Loxia scotica,* change end of comments to "...*L. curvirostra* but represents a distinct species (Knox 1990)."

711 *Loxia curvirostra,* before "England" add "s Scotland,"

712 *Loxia leucoptera,* change "sw Norway, ne Finland" to "Scandinavia (locally)"

712 *Pyrrhula pyrrhula,* change range to "...Kamchatka, the Sea of Okhotsk and n Kuril Is., and S to...Balkans, n Turkey, nw Iran...[2961.1]; **e Asia** in c,s Kuril Is., se Siberia (Amurland, Ussuriland), Sakhalin and Japan (Hokkaido, c Honshu) ¶*griseiventris* Lafresnaye 1841, GREY-BELLIED BULLFINCH [2961.3]; **Azores** (São...Winters (¶*pyrrhula*) S to n Mediterranean region, s Russia, w,c,ne China and Japan; (¶*cineracea*) S to se Siberia and Manchuria; (¶*griseiventris*) in c,e China, n Korea and Japan (lower elevations)."; in comments after "659-660)" add "; Stepanyan (1990c) recognized *P. pyrrhula, P. cineracea* and *P. griseiventris* as species."

712 *Coccothraustes coccothraustes,* before "Manchuria" add "n Mongolia,"

713 *Dysmorodrepanis munroi,* change "James, Olson and Zusi" to "James, Zusi and Olson"

713 *Rhodacanthis flaviceps,* in heading change "(Rothschild)" to "Rothschild"

714 *Rhodacanthis palmeri,* in heading change "(Rothschild)" to "Rothschild"

714 *Chloridops kona,* in heading change "(Wilson)" to "Wilson"

714 *Viridonia stejnegeri,* in heading change "Wilson" to "(Wilson)"; change habitat to "Mountain koa and ohia forest."; change comments to "...species. [=*Hemignathus kauaiensis* Pratt (1989a)]..."

714 *Viridonia virens,* in comments change "(1987)" to "(1988)"

714 *Viridonia sagittirostris,* in heading change "(Rothschild)" to "Rothschild"

714 *Hemignathus obscurus,* change beginning of comments to "The form from Kauai..."

714 *Oreomystis bairdi,* change comments to "*O. bairdi* and *O. mana* were formerly considered...[HAWAIIAN CREEPER], but neither is closely related to...[BAIRD'S CREEPER]."

714 *Oreomystis mana,* change comments to "See *O. bairdi.*"

714 *Paroreomyza montana,* in range change "¶*montana*" to "¶†*montana*"; in comments before "ALAUWAHIO" add "ALAUAHIO/"

714-715 *Paroreomyza maculata,* in comments before "ALAUWAHIO" add "ALAUAHIO/"

715 *Loxops caeruleirostris,* change habitat to "Forest, primarily ohia."

715 *Himatione sanguinea,* in comments after "LAYSAN HONEYCREEPER" add "(LAYSAN HONEYEATER/APAPANE)"

715 *Melamprosops phaeosoma,* change comments to "Pratt (1992) discussed relationships of *Melamprosops,* indicating that its affinities remain unknown but probably are not drepanidine. (BLACK-FACED HONEYCREEPER)."

715 *Urocynchramus pylzowi,* change comments to "...B. King, P. Alström and U. Olsson (pers. comm.) are convinced..."

715 *Latoucheornis siemsseni,* change "s Asia" to "c Asia"

715 After *Emberiza leucocephalos,* add *E. stewarti* from p. 716

716 *Emberiza cia,* change range to "...Sardinia, Sicily and Cyprus) and nw Africa..."

716 *Emberiza godlewskii,* in comments after "*E. cia*" add ", but Stepanyan (1990c) treated them as full species"

716 *Emberiza stewarti,* move to p. 715 and sequence after *E. leucocephalos*

717 *Emberiza tahapisi,* change "Sierra Leona" to "Sierra Leone"

717 *Emberiza capensis,* change "n Mozambique" to "s Tanzania"

717 *Emberiza yessoensis,* move to p. 718 and sequence after *E. schoeniclus;* in comments delete "(+N)"

717 *Emberiza tristrami,* add comments "[>*Christemberiza*]."

717 After *Emberiza aureola,* add *E. rutila* from p. 718

717 *Emberiza affinis,* change end of range to "...n C. African Rep., n Uganda and (formerly) w Kenya."

718 *Emberiza rutila,* move to p. 715 and sequence after *E. aureola*

718 After *Emberiza schoeniclus,* add *E. yessoensis* from p. 717

718-719 *Miliaria calandra,* change beginning of comments to "Voous (1977: 398) suggested that..."

719 *Calcarius lapponicus,* delete ", n Baja Calif."

719 *Plectrophenax nivalis,* before "Prince Patrick," add "Banks,"; change "s U.S.," to "c (rarely s) U.S.,"

719 *Passerella iliaca,* change "n Sonora" to "n Baja Calif."

720 *Zonotrichia leucophrys,* sequence after *Z. albicollis;* add comments "*Z. leucophrys* and *Z. atricapilla* are sister taxa within the genus, as evidenced by mtDNA studies (Zink, Dittman and Rootes 1991)."

720 *Zonotrichia atricapilla,* add comments "See *Z. leucophrys.*"

721 Split *Passerculus sandwichensis* into the following two species:

Passerculus [sandwichensis] sandwichensis (Gmelin) 1789. SAVANNAH SPARROW. [542.]
Grasslands, tundra, meadows, bogs, farmlands, marshes; salt marshes (¶*beldingi*). **Nearctic** from w,n Alaska, n Yukon, n Mackenzie, n Keewatin, n Ontario, is. in James Bay, n Quebec, n Labrador and Newfoundland S to sw,s Alaska (W to Amukta in Aleutians; Nunivak I.), in coastal regions to wc Calif., in int. to c Calif., s Nevada, s Utah, ec Arizona, n New Mexico, c Colorado, Nebraska, Missouri, Kentucky, e Tennessee, w N. Carolina, w Virginia, w Maryland, se Pennsylvania and n New Jersey, and locally in int. highlands of Mexico S to Guerrero and Puebla; highlands of sw Guatemala ¶*sandwichensis,* SAVANNAH SPARROW [542]; **Nova Scotia** (Sable I. and adjacent mainland) ¶*princeps* Maynard 1872, IPSWICH SPARROW [541.]; salt marshes of **coastal s Calif.** (N to Monterey region, incl. Channel Is.) **and Baja Calif.** (incl. Todos Santos Is.) ¶*beldingi* Ridgway 1885, BELDING'S SPARROW [543]. Winters in N. America from s British Columbia and n U.S. S to n C. America, Bahamas, Cuba and w Caribbean is. (¶*sandwichensis*); Atlantic coast from Nova Scotia S to ne Florida (¶*princeps*).
[<*Ammodramus* (+N)]. [SAVANNAH SPARROW]. See *P. rostratus.*

Passserculus [sandwichensis] rostratus (Cassin) 1852.
LARGE-BILLED SPARROW. [544.]

Salt marshes. **Nw Mexico** from ne Baja Calif. S along coast of Sonora to n Sinaloa, and San Benito Is. off Pacific coast. Winters in coastal salt marshes from s Calif. (formerly incl. Salton Sea) S around both coasts of Baja Calif. to Sonora and n Sinaloa.

Studies of mtDNA variation between *P. sandwichensis* and *P. rostratus* indicated specific status of these two forms (Zink et al. 1991).

721 *Ammodramus maritimus*, before "Massachusetts" add "s New Hampshire and"

721 *Ammodramus caudacutus*, delete "nw Baja Calif. and"

721 *Ammodramus savannarum*, delete "Oaxaca,"

722 *Spizella pallida*, change "s Ontario," to "s,ne Ontario,"

722 *Spizella pusilla*, before "w Kansas," add "e Colorado,"

722 *Spizella atrogularis*, before "c Calif.," add "cs Oregon,"

723 *Amphispiza bilineata*, delete "sw Wyoming,"

723 *Amphispiza belli*, change habitat and range to "Sagebrush, salt-bush brushland (¶*nevadensis*); chaparral (¶*belli*). **Wc N. America** from c int. Washington, e Oregon, s Idaho, sw Wyoming and nw Colorado S to ce Calif., s Nevada, sw Utah, ne Arizona and nw New Mexico ¶*nevadensis* (Ridgway) 1873, SAGE SPARROW [574.1]; **sw N. America** in w,c,sw Calif. (incl. San Clemente I., but absent from nw Calif.) and n,c Baja Calif. ¶*belli*, BELL'S SPARROW [574]. Winters (¶*nevadensis*) in sw U.S. and nw Mexico."; add comments "The two groups differ in morphology, ecology and genetics, and generally behave as reproductively isolated species in areas where both are found (Johnson and Marten 1992)."

723 *Aimophila quinquestriata*, not *Amphispiza*; change comments to "The transfer of *quinquestriata* from *Aimophila* to *Amphispiza* by A.O.U. (1983: 703-705) had no strong foundation; most recent workers suggest that the species is better retained in *Aimophila* (K. Groschupf, pers. comm.). [>*Amphispizopsis* (≈*A. humeralis*); ≠*Amphispiza*]."

723 *Aimophila mystacalis*, change "c Oaxaca" to "Oaxaca (W of Isthmus of Tehuantepec)"

723 *Aimophila strigiceps*, change range to "Lowlands to 1000 m of **sc S. America** in se Bolivia (se Santa Cruz), n Argentina (...) and sw Paraguay."

723 *Aimophila cassinii*, after "c,ne Colorado," add "s Wyoming,"

724 *Pipilo crissalis*, delete [*fuscus*] superspecies designation; change comments to "See *P. fuscus*."

724 *Pipilo fuscus*, delete [*fuscus*] superspecies designation; change comments to "...studies indicated that...*crissalis* as species is warranted. Furthermore, mtDNA studies demonstrated that *P. aberti* and *P. crissalis* are sister taxa, with the relationship of *P. fuscus* and *P. albicollis* less strongly supported (Zink and Dittman 1991). (BROWN TOWHEE). See *P. albicollis*."

725 *Pipilo aberti*, sequence on p. 724 before *P. crissalis*; add comments "[≠*Melozone* (≈*P. fuscus*). See *P. fuscus*."

725 *Melozone kieneri*, in heading change "1851" to "1850"

725 *Arremonops chloronotus*, in heading after "(Salvin)" add "1861"

726 *Arremonops conirostris*, in heading change "1851" to "1850"

726 *Atlapetes schistaceus*, change English name to "SLATY BRUSH-FINCH" (not BUSH-FINCH)

727 *Atlapetes rufigenis*, boldface "**s Peru**"

727 *Atlapetes brunneinucha*, add comments "[>*Buarremon* (≈*A. torquatus*)]."

727 *Atlapetes virenticeps*, in comments delete "[>*Buarremon* (≈*A. torquatus*)]."

728 *Paroaria gularis*, after "n Bolívar)" add "and Trinidad"

729 *Vermivora crissalis*, change range to "...(Chisos Mts.), Coahuila, w,c Nuevo León, ne Zacatecas, n San Luis Potosí and sw Tamaulipas..."

730 *Dendroica coronata*, before "nw Virginia" add "W. Virginia and"

730 *Dendroica townsendi*, change "W N. America" to "**W N. America**"

731 *Dendroica virens*, change "N Indiana," to "n Indiana,"

731 *Dendroica dominica*, change range to "**Se U.S.** from ne N. Dakota, se Iowa, s Wisconsin, c Indiana, c Ohio, c Pennsylvania, c New Jersey and Connecticut S to..."

731 *Dendroica pinus*, change range to "...sw Quebec, c Maine and New Brunswick S to..."

731 *Dendroica castanea*, after "New England" add "; isolated breeding in Colorado and West Virginia"

732 *Dendroica cerulea*, before "se Nebraska," add "se S. Dakota,"

732 *Dendroica pharetra*, change English name to ARROWHEAD WARBLER (not ARROW-HEADED)

732 *Mniotilta varia*, after "S. Carolina" add "; c Arizona"

733 *Oporornis philadelphia*, change "nw Virginia" to "w N. Carolina"

733 *Oporornis tolmiei*, change comments to "Sometimes considered conspecific with *O. philadelphia*, but see Pitocchelli (1990)."

735 *Euthlypis lachrymosa*, in heading change "1851" to "1850"; in range change "Nigaragua" to "Nicaragua"; at beginning of comments add "This species appears to be a typical *Basileuterus* in nest, eggs, vocalizations and juvenal plumage (S. Howell, pers. comm.). [<*Basileuterus*]."

736 *Basileuterus hypoleucus*, in heading change "1851" to "1850"

737 *Basileuterus flaveolus*, before "c,e Brazil" add "s Guyana,"

737 *Granatellus venustus*, in heading change "1851" to "1850"

738 *Coereba flaveola*, change range to "...n Oaxaca, Chiapas and is. off Yucatán pen. (Holbox, Cancun, Cozumel, Cayo Culebra, but absent from mainland) S in Caribbean..."

739 *Schistochlamys ruficapillus* and *Schistochlamys melanopis* (not *Schistoclamys*)

739 *Conothraupis speculigera*, change range to "...s Pichincha), n,e Peru (...), n Bolivia (n La Paz) and wc Brazil (upper r. Jurúa)."

739 *Lamprospiza melanoleuca*, before "r. Madeira" add "r. Urucu,"

740 *Chlorospingus tacarcunae*, change range to "...(e Panamá prov.), and on Cerro Tacarcuna in extreme e Panama (e Darién) and nw Colombia (nw Chocó)."

741 *Hemispingus parodii*, change range to "Andes, 2750-3500 m, of **se Peru** (...Vilcanota in Cuzco)."

741 *Hemispingus superciliaris*, in range before "c,s Colombia" add "of **w S. America**"

742 *Phaenicophilus palmarum*, in comments after "suggested" add ", but gene flow is low (McDonald and Smith 1990)"

743 *Chlorothraupis carmioli*, after "Cochabamba" add ", w Santa Cruz"

745 *Tachyphonus phoenicius*, after "Ucayali)" add ", ne Bolivia (ne Santa Cruz)"

745 *Habia rubica*, in heading change "1819" to "1817"

746 *Piranga rubra*, change range to "...W. Virginia, Maryland, New Jersey and se New York S to ne Baja..."

746-747 *Ramphocelus nigrogularis*, after "Pando" add ", n La Paz"

747 *Ramphocelus passerinii*, change end of range to "..w Panama (Bocas del Toro, Chiriquí, sw Veraguas)."

748 *Thraupis sayaca*, in comments change ").)." to ")."

748 *Thraupis palmarum*, remove "se Honduras and"

748 *Cyanicterus cyanicterus*, change end of range to "...Guianas and n,wc Brazil (S to n bank of Amazon near mouth of r. Negro, and in upper r. Urucu)."

749 *Stephanophorus diadematus*, change range to "...ne Argentina (from..."

751 *Euphonia saturata*, habitat and range in one paragraph

751 *Euphonia cyanocephala*, in heading change "[4854.]" to "[4854.1.]"

753 *Tangara cabanisi*, in heading change "1866" to "1868"

756 *Tangara cyanicollis*, change range to "...e Peru to c Bolivia (La Paz, Cochabamba, ne Santa Cruz) and sw..."

756 *Tangara larvata*, after "Oaxaca," add "s Veracruz,"

757 *Tangara callophrys*, after "Pando" add ", n La Paz"

758 *Cyanerpes lucidus*, after "Nicaragua," add "Pacific slope in El Salvador,"

759 *Charitospiza eucosma*, change range to "Lowlands to 1200 m of int. **sc,se S. America** in c,e Brazil (...), ne Bolivia (ne Santa Cruz) and ne Argentina (Misiones)."

761 *Incaspiza ortizi*, in heading change "1952" to "(1952b)"

763 *Sicalis lutea*, change range to "...Tacna), wc,sw Bolivia (La Paz, Oruro,..."

764 *Sporophila schistacea*, add comments "Includes *S. subconcolor* Berlioz (1959a), regarded as a subspecies of *S. schistacea*."

765 *Sporophila americana*, change range to "...(Bonaparte) 1850, VARIABLE SEEDEATER (HICK'S SEEDEATER/ NORTHERN VARIABLE-SEEDEATER)..."

765 *Sporophila torqueola*, in heading change "1851" to "1850"; change range to "...Tamaulipas S on Gulf-Caribbean slope...(Bonaparte) 1850, WHITE-COLLARED..."

767 *Sporophila insulata*, change end of range to "...sw Nariño); possibly extinct."

767 *Oryzoborus atrirostris*, in heading change "[5903.1.]" to "[5903.7.]"

768 *Amaurospiza moesta*, change "se Paraguay (formerly)" to "Paraguay"

769 *Loxigilla portoricensis*, change "1926" to "1929"

769 *Diglossa baritula*, in comments change "1969" to "1969a"

769 *Diglossa lafresnayii*, in comments change "1969" to "1969a"

771 *Geospiza fuliginosa*, change comments to "Vagvolgyi and Vagvolgyi (1989, 1991) placed...*G. difficilis*, but see Schluter, Ratcliffe and Grant (1991) for a contrary opinion."

771 *Spiza americana*, after "c Colorado," add "e New Mexico,"

771 *Pheucticus chrysopeplus*, change "nw Oaxaca" to "Guerrero"

772 *Pheucticus aureoventris*, in heading change "d'Orbigny and Lafresnaye" to "(d'Orbigny and Lafresnaye)"

772 *Pheucticus ludovicianus*, change range to "...n Ohio, Maryland and Delaware, and S in..."

773 *Pitylus grossus*, after "La Paz" add ", ne Santa Cruz"

774 *Saltator cinctus*, change range to "Locally in Andes, 1650-3100 m, of **w S. America** in c Colombia (Caldas, Quíndio), e Ecuador and n Peru (Cajamarca, Amazonas, Huánuco)."; change end of comments to "...*Saltator* and *Pitylus;* Renjifo (1991) discussed ecology and behavior."

774 *Cyanocompsa parellina*, in heading change "1851" to "1850"

774 *Guiraca caerulea*, change "c Illinois" to "c,ne Illinois"

775 *Passerina ciris*, change range to "**Sc U.S. and nc Mexico** from se New Mexico,...nw Florida) ¶*pallidior* Mearns 1911, WESTERN PAINTED-BUNTING [601.1]; **se U.S.** along Atlantic coast from...to c Florida ¶*ciris*, EASTERN PAINTED-BUNTING [601]. Winters (¶*pallidior*) in Middle America, rarely s Texas and s Louisiana; and (¶*ciris*) in Florida, Bahama Is., Cuba and Jamaica."; add comments "Although not conforming to the limits of the currently recognized subspecies of the same name, the two groups differ dramatically in their timing and pattern of molt and migration, as well as in certain morphological parameters, suggesting differences at the species level (Thompson 1991)."

775 *Porphyrospiza caerulescens*, change range to "...**sc S. America** in n,e Bolivia (Beni, ne Santa Cruz, questionably Chuquisaca)..."

775 *Psarocolius oseryi*, change end of range to "...e Ecuador, e Peru (...) and n Bolivia (n La Paz)."

775 *Psarocolius angustifrons*, after "n,e Bolivia" remove ")"

776 *Gymnostinops guatimozinus*, change range to "...nw Colombia (from..."

777 *Cacicus chrysonotus*, change "1844" to "1845"

777 *Cacicus sclateri*, after "n Amazonas" add ", Loreto"

777 *Icterus cayanensis*, change "La Rioja," to "San Juan, San Luis,"

777 *Icterus chrysater*, in comments after "1981)." add "Appears to be closely related to *I. graduacauda* S. Howell, pers. comm.)."

777 *Icterus auratus*, in heading change "1851" to "1850"

778 *Icterus pustulatus*, change range to "...(Guanacaste), also arid int..."

778 *Icterus cucullatus*, move to p. 779 and sequence after *I. galbula;* change comments to "[>*Pendulinus* (≈*I. oberi*); >*Icterioides*]."

779 **Icterus wagleri** (remove from superspecies)

779 *Icterus graduacauda*, move to p. 777 and sequence after *I. cayanensis;* at end of comments add "See *I. chrysater*."

780 *Agelaius cyanopus*, change end of range to "...Paraguay and nw,ne Argentina (Jujuy, and from Formosa E to Misiones and S to n Río Negro)."

780 *Agelaius phoeniceus*, in comments change "including" to "especially"

780 *Leistes militaris*, in comments change "Remsen and Parker" to "Parker and Remsen"; change end of comments to "...See *L. superciliaris*."

781 *Sturnella bellicosa*, in heading change "Filippi" to "de Filippi"

781 **Sturnella [militaris] militaris** (add superspecies name)

781 *Sturnella loyca*, in heading change "(Bonaparte) 1851" to "(Molina) 1782"; after "s La Pampa" add ", s Córdoba"

781 *Sturnella magna*, change end of comments to "See *S. lilianae* and *S. neglecta.*"

781 *Sturnella lilianae*, at end of comments add "See *S. neglecta.*"

781 *Sturnella neglecta*, change range to "...sw Tennessee, sw Kentucky, s Illinois, n Indiana, c Ohio..."

781 *Amblyramphus holosericeus*, change range to "...Uruguay and nw,ne Argentina (Jujuy, and from Misiones,..."

782 *Dives dives*, after "nc Nicaragua" add "; Pacific slope in El Salvador"

782 *Quiscalus mexicanus*, change "se Colorado," to "c Colorado,"

783 *Quiscalus nicaraguensis*, change end of range to "...n Costa Rica."

783 *Molothrus bonariensis*, change end of range to "...Florida, thence W to s Louisiana and N to S. Carolina."

783-784 *Molothrus aeneus*, change range to "...wc,s Arizona, s New Mexico, w,wc,s Texas and..."; in comments before "conspecific" add "as"

784 *Molothrus ater*, change "c Florida" to "sc Florida"

WORLD NUMBERS

Correct number entries are listed below. If the number already exists on pp. 785-848, the new entry should replace the old one; if the entry is an entirely new number, it should be added in the appropriate numerical sequence.

50　　*Larus fuscus* (¶*graellsi*).
51　　*Larus argentatus* (¶*argentatus*).
52　　*Larus argentatus* (¶*vegae*).s
79.2　*Procelsterna cerulea* (¶*cerulea*).
83　　*Diomedea chlororhynchos.*
88　　*Calonectris diomedea* (¶*diomedea*).
98.2　*Pterodroma arminjoniana* (¶*arminjoniana*).
98.6　*Pterodroma arminjoniana* (¶*heraldica*).
119　　*Phalacrocorax carbo* (¶*carbo*).
126　　*Pelecanus occidentalis.*
134.1　*Anas poecilorhyncha* (¶*poecilorhyncha*).
143　　*Anas acuta.*
171.1　*Anser fabalis* (¶*fabalis*).
176　　*Anser canagica.*
195　　*Ardea cinerea* (¶*cinerea*).
196　　*Casmerodius albus* (¶*egretta*).
296.1　*Numida meleagris* (¶*galeata*).
315.1　*Streptopelia chinensis* (¶*chinensis*).
372　　*Aegolius acadicus* (¶*acadicus*).
374.1　*Otus scops* (¶*sunia*).
380　　*Glaucidium brasilianum* (¶*brasilianum*).
388　　*Coccyzus erythropthalmus.*
475　　*Pica pica* (¶*pica*).
527.1　*Carduelis hornemanni* (¶*hornemanni*).
544　　*Passerculus rostratus.*
574　　*Amphispiza belli* (¶*belli*).
574.1　*Amphispiza belli* (¶*nevadensis*).
574.2　*Aimophila quinquestriata.*
601　　*Passerina ciris* (¶*ciris*).
601.1　*Passerina ciris* (¶*pallidior*).
616　　*Riparia riparia* (¶*riparia*).
621.1　*Lanius cristatus* (¶*cristatus*).

629.2　*Vireo cassinii.* [not "629.12"]
746.1　*Cettia diphone.*
765.1　*Saxicola torquata* (¶*maura*).
771　　*Ficedula parva* (¶*albicilla*).
812　　*Lonchura malacca* (¶*atricapilla*).
1087　*Neocrex colombianus.*
1123.2　*Aratinga holochlora* (¶*brevipes*).
1183　*Otus kennicottii* (¶*seductus*).
1183.1　*Otus kennicottii* (¶*lambi*).
1184　*Otus kennicottii* (¶*cooperi*).
1185　*Otus atricapillus* (¶*guatemalae*).
1202　*Aegolius acadicus* (¶*ridgwayi*).
1220.1　*Cypseloides storeri.*
1237　*Phaethornis superciliosus* (¶*longirostris*).
1237.1　*Phaethornis superciliosus* (¶*griseoventris*).
1237.2　*Phaethornis superciliosus* (¶*mexicanus*).
1239　*Phaethornis longuemareus* (¶*adophi*).
1242　*Doryfera ludovicae.*
1260.1　*Lophornis brachylopha.*
1264　*Chlorostilbon canivetii* (¶*canivetii*).
1264.1　*Chlorostilbon canivetii* (¶*auriceps*).
1264.2　*Chlorostilbon canivetii* (¶*forficatus*).
1264.3　*Chlorostilbon canivetii* (¶*salvini*).
1271　*Thalurania ridgwayi.*
1271.2　*Thalurania fannyi* (¶*fannyi*).
1291　*Amazilia viridifrons* (¶*viridifrons*).
1291.1　*Amazilia viridifrons* (¶*wagneri*).
1399.1　xCeleus immaculatus.
1415　*Pseudocolaptes lawrencii* (¶*lawrencii*).
1419　*Philydor fuscipennis* (¶*fuscipennis*).
1419.1　*Philydor fuscipennis* (¶*erythronotus*).
1435　*Glyphorynchus spirurus.*
1437　*Dendrocolaptes certhia* (¶*sanctithomae*).
1486　*Hylopezus dives* (¶*dives*).
1486.1　*Hylopezus dives* (¶*flammulatus*).
1493　*Zimmerius vilissimus* (¶*vilissimus*).
1493.1　*Zimmerius vilissimus* (¶*parvus*).
1497　*Phaeomyias murina* (¶*murina*).
1649　*Hylorchilus sumichrasti* (¶*sumichrasti*).
1649.1　*Hylorchilus sumichrasti* (¶*navai*).
2006　*Pterodroma rostrata.*
2006.1　*Pterodroma becki.*
2010.4　*Calonectris diomedea* (¶*edwardsii*).
2021　*Phalacrocorax pygmeus.*
2030　*Dupetor flavicollis.*
2034　*Mesophoyx intermedia* (¶*intermedia*).
2034.1　*Casmerodius albus* (¶*albus*).
2045　*Threskiornis aethiopicus* (¶*aethiopicus*).
2059.1　*Anser fabalis* (¶*serrirostris*).
2076　*Milvus migrans* (¶*migrans*).
2093.3　*Spilornis cheela* (¶*perplexus*).
2111　*Aquila rapax* (¶*rapax*).
2111.1　*Aquila nipalensis* (¶*nipalensis*).
2111.2　*Aquila rapax* (¶*vindhiana*).
2111.3　*Aquila nipalensis* (¶*orientalis*).
2126　xFalco altaicus.
2127　*Perdix dauurica.*
2253.2　*Larus argentatus* (¶*heuglini*).
2254　*Larus cachinnans* (¶*cachinnans*).
2254.1　*Larus cachinnans* (¶*atlantis*).
2254.2　*Larus fuscus* (¶*fuscus*).
2304　*Cuculus fugax* (¶*fugax*).
2304.1　*Cuculus fugax* (¶*hyperythrus*).
2314　*Otus bakkamoena* (¶*bakkamoena*).

2314.2	*Otus bakkamoena (¶lempiji).
2314.3	*Otus bakkamoena (¶semitorques).
2316	*Otus scops (¶scops).
2324	Ninox scutulata (¶scutulata).
2324.1	*Ninox scutulata (¶obscura).
2377	Dendrocopos leucotos (¶leucotos).
2377.1	*Dendrocopos leucotos (¶lilfordi).
2387.1	*Picus viridis (¶sharpei).
2388	Picus vaillantii.
2422.1	*Riparia riparia (¶diluta).
2445.1	*Pica pica (¶mauritanica).
2465	Parus lugubris (¶lugubris).
2465.1	*Parus lugubris (¶hyrcanus).
2483	Aegithalos iouschistos (¶iouschistos).
2483.1	*Aegithalos iouschistos (¶bonvaloti).
2527	Cettia canturians.
2585	Sylvia curruca.
2585.1	Sylvia althaea.
2585.2	Sylvia minula.
2592	Phylloscopus collybita (¶collybita).
2592.1	*Phylloscopus collybita (¶tristis).
2593	*Phylloscopus collybita (¶sindianus).
2593.1	Phylloscopus lorenzii.
2595	Phylloscopus bonelli (¶bonelli).
2595.1	*Phylloscopus bonelli (¶orientalis).
2601	Phylloscopus inornatus (¶inornatus).
2601.1	*Phylloscopus inornatus (¶humei).
2603.1	Phylloscopus chloronotus.
2607	Phylloscopus trochiloides (¶trochiloides).
2608	*Phylloscopus trochiloides (¶plumbeitarsus).
2609	*Phylloscopus trochiloides (¶nitidus).
2612.1	Phylloscopus borealoides.
2629.1	*Ficedula parva (¶parva).
2700.1	Oenanthe lugubris.
2700.2	Oenanthe lugentoides.
2709	*Saxicola torquata (¶torquata).
2709.1	delete entry
2748.1	Pnoepyga immaculata.
2795	Alcippe cinereiceps.
2795.1	Alcippe ludlowi.
2847.1	*Lanius cristatus (¶superciliosus).
2950	Serinus citrinella (¶citrinella).
2950.1	*Serinus citrinella (¶corsicana).
2961.3	*Pyrrhula pyrrhula (¶griseiventris).
3022.2	*Anas poecilorhyncha (¶zonorhyncha).
3060	Coturnix coromandelica. [not a second 3059]
3075	Arborophila hyperythra (¶hyperythra).
3075.1	*Arborophila hyperythra (¶erythrophrys).
3091.1	Lophura hoogerwerfi.
3092	Lophura erythrophthalma.
3092.1	Lophura hatinhensis.
3109.1	xArgusianus bipunctatus.
3145.1	*Streptopelia chinensis (¶suratensis).
3183	Ducula bicolor.
3198	Loriculus philippensis (¶philippensis).
3198.1	*Loriculus philippensis (¶bonapartei).
3209.1	*Cuculus fugax (¶pectoralis).
3244.3	xOtus stresemanni.
3244.4	*Otus spilocephalus (¶hambroecki).
3244.5	*Otus spilocephalus (¶luciae).
3246.1	*Otus magicus (¶enganensis).
3249.2	*Otus megalotis (¶nigrorum).
3249.3	*Otus megalotis (¶everetti).
3312.1	Penelopides manillae.

3337	Alcedo cyanopecta.
3445.1	Hirundo domicola.
3497	Rhabdornis mystacalis.
3584.2	Cettia seebohmi.
3729	Malacocincla malaccensis (¶malaccensis).
3729.1	*Malacocincla malaccensis (¶feriatum).
3779.1	Stachyris latistriata.
3922	Dicaeum anthonyi (¶anthonyi).
3922.1	*Dicaeum anthonyi (¶kampalili).
3956	Aethopyga mystacalis (¶temminckii).
3956.1	*Aethopyga mystacalis (¶mystacalis).
3982.2	*Lonchura malacca (¶malacca).
4015.1	Pelecanus thagus.
4120.1	Nannopsittaca dachilleae.
4140	Coccyzus euleri.
4145	Otus ingens (¶ingens).
4145.1	*Otus ingens (¶colombianus).
4146	Otus watsonii (¶watsonii).
4146.1	*Otus watsonii (¶usta).
4147.1	Glaucidium bolivianum.
4147.2	Glaucidium peruanum.
4151.1	Lurocalis rufiventris.
4172.1	*Phaethornis superciliosus (¶superciliosus).
4178.2	*Phaethornis longuemareus (¶longuemareus).
4178.3	*Phaethornis longuemareus (¶striigularis).
4202.3	*Thalurania fannyi (¶hypochlora).
4407.1	*Pseudocolaptes lawrencii (¶johnsoni).
4411.1	Philydor erythrocercus.
4429	Dendrocincla merula (¶merula).
4429.1	*Dendrocincla merula (¶castanoptera).
4433	Hylexetastes perrotii (¶perrotii).
4433.2	*Hylexetastes perrotii (¶uniformis).
4458.1	*Thamnistes anabatinus (¶rufescens).
4458.2	Clytoctantes atrogularis.
4460	Dysithamnus occidentalis.
4488	Myrmeciza berlepschi.
4489	Myrmeciza nigricauda.
4522	Chamaeza turdina.
4527	Grallaria gigantea (¶gigantea).
4527.1	*Grallaria gigantea (¶hylodroma).
4534.1	Grallaria kaestneri.
4542.1	Hylopezus fulviventris.
4559.1	*Phyllomyias reiseri (¶urichi).
4563.1	Zimmerius improbus.
4565.2	*Phaeomyias murina (¶tumbezana).
4566.1	Sublegatus obscurior.
4566.2	Sublegatus modestus.
4585	Uromyias agilis.
4626.3	*Onychorhynchus coronatus (¶swainsoni).
4728.1	Pipra suavissima.
4854	Euphonia violacea.
4854.1	Euphonia cyanocephala. [not a second 4854]
4906	Schistochlamys melanopis.
5039.1	Pagodroma nivea (¶nivea).
5039.2	*Pagodroma nivea (¶confusa).
5041.1	Pterodroma brevirostris.
5077	Anas specularioides.
5082	Netta peposaca.
5215.1	Amazona kawalli.
5222	Otus roboratus (¶roboratus).
5222.3	*Otus roboratus (¶pacificus).
5223	*Otus atricapillus (¶atricapillus).
5223.1	Otus marshalli (¶marshalli).
5223.2	*Otus marshalli (¶petersoni).

5224.2	*Glaucidium hardyi.*
5225	**Glaucidium brasilianum (¶nanum).*
5270	*Aphantochroa cirrochloris.*
5291	*Polyonymus caroli.*
5373	*Geobates poecilopterus.*
5453.1	*Asthenes luizae.*
5460	**Asthenes punensis (¶sclateri).*
5472	*Phacellodomus erythrophthalmus (¶erythrophthal-mus).*
5472.1	**Phacellodomus erythrophthalmus (¶ferrugine-igula).*
5491	*Syndactyla ruficollis.*
5498	*Pygarrhichas albogularis.*
5503	**Xiphocolaptes falcirostris (¶franciscanus).*
5504	*Xiphocolaptes falcirostris (¶falcirostris).*
5506	**Dendrocolaptes certhia (¶certhia).*
5547	*Formicivora serrana.*
5548	*Formicivora melanogaster.*
5561.1	*Cercomacra manu.*
5581.4	*Chamaeza ruficauda.*
5581.5	*Chamaeza meruloides.*
5612.1	*Scytalopus psychopompus.*
5614.1	*Phyllomyias reiseri (¶reiseri).*
5633	*Uromyias agraphia.*
5678	*Lathrotriccus griseipectus.*
5810.2	*Hylophilus amaurocephalus.*
5856	*Schistochlamys ruficapillus.*
5903.7	*Oryzoborus atrirostris.* [not a second 5903.1]
6001	*Tachybaptus rufolavatus.*
6004	*Pterodroma aterrima.*
6008	**Phalacrocorax carbo (¶lucidus).*
6012.1	**Ardea cinerea (¶monicae).*
6013.1	**Mesophoyx intermedia (¶brachyrhyncha).*
6020.1	**Threskiornis aethiopicus (¶bernieri).*
6038.1	**Milvus migrans (¶aegyptius).*
6069	*Hieraaetus spilogaster.*
6070	*Hieraaetus ayresii.*
6083	*Falco cuvierii.*
6181	*Treron australis.*
6232	**Otus scops (¶senegalensis).*
6233.2	*Otus pauliani.*
6233.3	**Otus rutilus (¶capnodes).*
6244.1	*Caprimulgus prigoginei.*
6253	*Telacanthura ussheri.*
6275	*Bucorvus leadbeateri.*
6288	*Merops hirundineus.*
6332	*Neodrepanis hypoxantha.*
6386	**Parus leucomelas (¶carpi).*
6387	*Parus niger.*
6422.1	*Nesillas longicaudata.*
6422.2	*Nesillas brevicaudata.*
6458	*Phragmacia substriata.*
6459	*Oreophilais robertsi.*
6460	*Heliolais erythroptera.*
6487	*Phylloscopus ruficapillus.*
6595.1	*Laniarius liberatus.*
6608	*Calicalicus madagascariensis.*
6696	*Philetairus socius.*
6747	*Ortygospiza locustella (¶locustella).*
6748	*Lemuresthes nana.*
6749	*Lonchura bicolor (¶bicolor).*
6749.1	*Lonchura nigriceps.*
6750	*Lonchura fringilloides.*
6751	*Amadina erythrocephala.*
6752	*Amadina fasciata.*

6753	*Vidua chalybeata (¶chalybeata).*
6753.1	**Vidua chalybeata (¶amauropteryx).*
6754	*Vidua funerea.*
6754.1	*Vidua codringtoni.*
6755	*Vidua purpurascens.*
6756	*xVidua incognita.*
6757	*Vidua regia.*
6758	*Vidua paradisaea.*
6759	*Vidua obtusa.*
7043.1	**Numida meleagris (¶meleagris).*
7077	*Treron pembaensis.*
7093	*Corythaixoides personatus.*
7139	*Telacanthura melanopygia.*
7209.3	**Lybius leucocephalus (¶leucogaster).*
7303	*Parus leucomelas (¶leucomelas).*
7330	*Andropadus tephrolaemus.*
7330.2	*Andropadus nigriceps.*
7368.2	*Bradypterus lopezi (¶lopezi).*
7368.3	**Bradypterus lopezi (¶camerunensis).*
7385.2	*Cisticola dorsti.*
7431	*Poliolais lopezi.*
7514	*Terpsiphone rufiventer (¶rufiventer).*
7514.1	**Terpsiphone rufiventer (¶smithii).*
7637.1	**Lanius excubitor (¶leucopygos).*
7714.1	*Nectarinia moreaui.*
7723	*Nectarinia coccinigastra.*
7742.3	*Serinus flavigula.*
7777.1	*Ploceus bernieri.*
8030.1	**Mesophoyx intermedia (¶plumifera).*
8069	*Falco novaeseelandiae.*
8076	*Coturnix ypsilophora (¶australis).*
8077	**Coturnix ypsilophora (¶ypsilophora).*
8107	*Thinornis novaeseelandiae.*
8125.1	**Procelsterna cerulea (¶albivitta).*
8145	*Ducula spilorrhoa.*
8145.1	*Ducula constans.*
8207	*Geopsittacus occidentalis.*
8238	*Todirhamphus pyrrhopygius.*
8240	*Tanysiptera sylvia (¶sylvia).*
8290	*Philesturnus carunculatus.*
8291	*Heteralocha acutirostris.*
8302	*Cormobates leucophaeus (¶leucophaeus).*
8302.1	**Cormobates leucophaeus (¶minor).*
8308	*Lalage leucomela (¶leucomela).*
8308.1	**Lalage leucomela (¶conjuncta).*
8311	*Megalurus punctatus.*
8311.1	*Megalurus rufescens.*
8387	*Epthianura albifrons.*
8388	*Epthianura tricolor.*
8389	*Epthianura aurifrons.*
8390	*Epthianura crocea.*
9003	*Pterodroma macgillivrayi.*
9049.1	*Gallirallus rovianae.*
9065	*Rhynochetos jubatus.*
9168.1	*Ducula subflavescens.*
9282	**Otus magicus (¶albiventris).*
9304.1	*Caprimulgus celebensis.*
9334.1	**Todirhamphus cinnamominus (¶reichenbachii).*
9353.1	**Tanysiptera sylvia (¶nigriceps).*
9368	*Loboparadisea sericea.*
9478.1	*Acrocephalus rimatarae.*
9478.2	*Acrocephalus taiti.*
9791	*Zosterops conspicillatus (¶conspicillatus).*
9791.3	**Zosterops conspicillatus (¶saypani).*
9791.3	**Zosterops conspicillatus (¶rotensis).*

page #

MAPS

852 Africa—change "Upper Volta" to "Burkina Faso", "Fernando Po" to "Bioko", and "Annobón" to "Pagalu"

859 New Guinea—change "Orinomo r." to "Oriomo r.", "Squally I." label to "Tench I.", "Rooke I." to "Umboi", and "Vuatom" to "Watom"; "Aroa r." label should be by river near Hall Sound; dot for "Port Moresby" should be about 50 km NW of position on map; add "Wuvulu I." label for small island halfway between "Humboldt Bay" and "Ninigo Is."

860 Australia—"Sydney" label omitted next to city dot just south of Newcastle, New South Wales

862 South Pacific—"Nuguria Is." label should be in is. group due north of Buka

865 Alaska—"Bristol Bay" label omitted on bay just north of Alaska pen.

GAZETTEER

875 Agiguan—Mariana Is., just SW of Tinian; *Aguijan

875 Aguijan—[=Agiguan]

875 **Amberpon I.**—i., Geelvink Bay, nw New Guinea [002S-134E] *(N.G.)*

875 Amukta—Aleutian Is., just E of Seguam, Alaska

876 Annobón—[=Pagalu]

876 **Aroa r.**—se New Guinea, mouth near Hall Sound [009S-147E] *(N.G.)*

876 Astrolabe Mts.—se New Guinea, coastal foothills of Owen Stanley Mts. E of Port Moresby

877 **Attu**—i, w Aleutian Is., Alaska [053N-173E] *(Alaska)*

878 Bavo I.—off Port Moresby, sc New Guinea

878 **Bioko**—i., Gulf of Guinea, off wc Africa; *Fernando Po, *Fernando Póo [003N-009E] *(Africa)*

878 delete Bolod Is. entry

878 after "**Borodino Is.**" add "Bosavi, Mt.—sc New Guinea SW of Mt. Giluwe"

878 Botel Tobago—[= Lan Yü Is.]

878 delete Bovasi, Mt. entry

879 **Burkina Faso**—country, wc Africa; *Upper Volta [013N-002W] *(Africa)*

879 **Cabinda**—small country, cw Africa, formerly part of Angola [005S-012E] *(Africa)*

879 **Cameroon**—country, wc Africa; *Cameroun [005N-012E] *(Africa)*

879 Canlaon, Mt. (not "Canloan")

881 after "**Clarión**" add "Clarke Range—mts., se Queensland W of Mackay"

882 **D'Entrecasteaux Arch.**—off se New Guinea (Goodenough + Fergusson + Normanby is.) [009S-151E] *(N.G.)*

882 after "**Desertas, Ilhas**" add "Desolación, I.—between I. Diego del Almagro and I. Dawson, s Chile"

883 after "**Ellice Is.**" add "Emira I.—St. Matthias Is. SE of Mussau; *Emirau I., *Squally I." and "Emirau I.—[=Emira I.]"

883 after "**Esperance Bay**" add "Espinaço, Serra do—e Brazil from cs Bahia S to sc Minas Gerais"

883 Eungella Range—erroneous name for Clarke Range

883 after "**Farallon Is.**" add "Farilhões, Is.—off coast of c Portugal"

883 Fernando Po—[=Bioko]

883 Fernando Póo—[=Bioko]

884 **Florida**—state, se U.S. [028N-082W] *(N.A.)*

884 delete Fort Albany entry

884 after "**Ghana**" add "Gibraltar—cs Spain at mouth of Mediterranean Sea"

884 **Giluwe, Mt.**—c New Guinea, SW of Mt. Hagen [006S-144E] *(N.G.)*

885 after "**Goulburn r.**" add "Gower Mts.—Lord Howe I."

886 after "**Himachal Pradesh**" add "Himalayas—high mt. range along border of India (including Nepal and Bhutan) and Tibet"

886 after "**Honan**" add "Hondo—[=Honshu]"

886 **Honshu**—main i., Japan; *Hondo [035N-138E] *(Asia)*

886 Hydrographer Mts.—e New Guinea, just NE of Owen Stanley Mts.

886 delete "Idihi I." entry

886 after "**Idenburg r.**" add "Ifakara—town, ec Tanzania S of Uluguru Mts."

886 delete "Illawarra" entry

888 **Kanaga**—i., c Aleutian Is., Alaska [052N-177W] *(Alaska)*

888 **Kilimanjaro, Mt.** (not "**Kiliminjaro**")

888 **Kiska**—i., Aleutian Is., Alaska [052N-177E] *(Alaska)*

889 Kubor Mts.—ec New Guinea, SW of Bismarck Mts.

889 after "**Kumawa Mts.**" add "Kumbe r.—cs New Guinea, mouth NW of Merauke"

889 **Lan Yü I.**—i., se Taiwan; *Botel Tobago [022N-121E] *(China)*

889 **La Palma**—i., nw Canary Is. [029N-018W] *(Africa)*

889 delete Las Palmas entry

889 after "**Libya**" add "Lidgbird Mts.—Lord Howe I."

890 Lobo Bay—head of Triton Bay, s New Guinea coast

890 delete "Loran I." entry

891 after "**Mangole**" add "Mangsi—islet, sw Philippines between Balabac and Cagayan Sulu"

891 Manim—small i. off w Numfor I., Geelvink Bay, w New Guinea

892 after "**Matuku**" add "Maturin—islet, ec Philippines off ne Catanduanes"

892 Micronesia—w Pacific O. area, from Mariana and Wake is. S to Palau, Caroline Is. and Kiribati

892 after "**MIDDLE AMERICA**" add "Middle East—[=Iran + Iraq + Afghanistan]"

893 delete "Morehead r." entry

893 Narcondam I. (not "Narcodam")

895 after "**Nuevo León**" add "Nuguria Is.—sw Pacific E of Tanga Is. and NNE of Green Is. [003S-155E] *(s.Pac.)*"

895 **Onin pen.**—part of Bomberai pen., w New Guinea [003S-132E] *(N.G.)*

895 **Orizaba, Mt.**—wc Veracruz

896 after "**Pagai Utara**" add "Pagalu—i., Gulf of Guinea, off wc Africa; *Annobón [001S-006E] *(Africa)*"

896 after "**Pará**" add "Paracel Is.—S. China Sea, between c Vietnam and Palawan"

897 **Queen Charlotte Is.**—off cw British Columbia, Canada [053N-132W] *(N.A.)*

898 Rook I. [=Umboi]

898 Rooke I. [=Umboi]

898 delete "St. Aignan Is." entry

899 Samarai—small i., off se tip of New Guinea

900 after "Sapo, Serrania del" add "Sarawaget Mts.
[=Saruwaged Mts.]

900 **Saruwaged Mts.**—ne New Guinea; *Sarawaget Mts.
[006S-147E] *(N.G.)*

900 Schildpad Is.—w Papuan is., between Misool and
Salawati [not "Schilpad"]

900 Schrader Mts.—nc New Guinea, just NW of Bismarck
Mts.

900 **Shemya**—i, w Aleutian Is., Alaska [053N-174E]
(Alaska)

901 **Squally I.**—[=Emira I.]

902 Supiori—i., Geelvink Bay off nw coast of Biak, nw
New Guinea

902 after "Tehuantepec, Isthmus of" entry, add "Teita
hills—s Kenya, just E of Mt. Kilimanjaro; *Taita
hills"

903 after "**Tenasserim**" add "**Tench I.**—Easternmost of St.
Matthias Is. [002S-150E] *(N.G.)*"

904 after "Tuangku" add "Tubbataha reef—in Sulu Sea
between Cagayan Is. and Cagayan Sulu"

904 Uatom—[=Watom]

904 **Umboi**—w Bismarck Arch.; *Rook I., *Rooke I. [005S-
148E] *(N.G.)*

904 Upper Volta—[=Burkina Faso]

904 after "Urubamba, r." add "Urucu, r.—trib. of r.
Solimões, Amazonas, wc Brazil, between r. Juruá
and r. Purús"

905 Vuatom—[=Watom]

905 **Watom**—i., off New Britain, Bismarck Arch.; *Uatom,
*Vuatom [004S-152E]

905 Western Papuan Is.—continental shelf is. W of New
Guinea from Gebe and Waigeo S to Misool

905 after "**Wrangell Mts.**" add "**Wuvulu I.**—w Bismarck
Arch. [002S-143E] *(N.G.)*"

906 Yunaska—i., Aleutian Is., between Seguam and Umnak,
Alaska

REFERENCES

907 after ALLEN ET AL. entry, add "ALSTRÖM, P., AND U.
OLSSON. 1990. Taxonomy of the *Phylloscopus pro-
regulus* complex. Bull. Brit. Ornithol. Club 110: 38-
43." and "ALSTRÖM, P., U. OLSSON, AND P. D.
ROUND. 1991. The taxonomic status of
Acrocephalus agricola tangorum. Forktail 6: 3-13."

907 under ALSTRÖM AND OLSSON entries, add "1992. On
the taxonomic status of *Phylloscopus affinis* and
Phylloscopus subaffinis. Bull. Brit. Ornithol. Club
112: 111-125."

907 under AMADON, D. entries, add "1987. Comments on
eagles of the genus *Hieraaetus.* Gabar 2: 18-19."

907 after ASH, J. S. entry, add "ASH, J. S., AND T. M.
GULLICK. 1990. *Serinus flavigula* rediscovered.
Bull. Brit. Ornithol. Club 110: 81-83."

907 after ATWOOD, J. L. entry, add "AUBURN, J. 1988. Why
Wahlberg's Eagle is not a *Hieraaetus* eagle. Gabar
3: 15-18."

908 after AVISE AND ZINK entry, add "BAKER, N. E., AND E.
M. BAKER. 1990. A new species of weaver from
Tanzania. Bull. Brit. Ornithol. Club 110: 51-58."

908 under BANKS, R. C. entries, add "1990a. Taxonomic
status of the coquette hummingbird of Guerrero,
Mexico. Auk 107: 191-192." and "1990b.
Taxonomic status of the Rufous-bellied Chachalaca
(Ortalis wagleri). Condor 92: 749-753."

908 after BARLOW AND NASH entry, add "BARROWCLOUGH,
G. F., AND R. J. GUTTIÉRREZ. 1990. Genetic
variation and differentiation in the Spotted Owl
(Strix occidentalis). Auk 107: 737-744."

908 after BAUER entry, add "BECKER, J. J. 1987. Revision
of *'Falco' ramenta* Wetmore and the Neogene
evolution of the Falconidae. Auk 104: 270-276."

908 after BEEHLER, PRATT AND ZIMMERMAN entry, add
"BEEHLER, B. M. AND R. J. SWABY. 1991.
Phylogeny and biogeography of the *Ptiloris*
riflebirds (Aves: Paradisaeidae). Condor 93: 738-
745."; and "BELTON, W. 1984. Taxonomy of
certain species of birds from Rio Grande do Sul,
Brazil. Natl. Geogr. Soc. Res. Repts. 17: 183-188."

908 under BENSON, C. W. entries, add "1955. New forms of
pipit, longclaw, robin-chat, grass-warbler, sunbird,
quail-finch and canary from central Africa. Proc.
Biol. Soc. Washington 75: 101-109."

908 in entry for BERGER, A. J. 1957, change "the the" to
"from the"

908 under BERLIOZ, J. entries, add "1959a. Un oiseau
nouveau de Mexique. Oiseau 29: 40-42."; "1959b.
Étude d'une collection d'oiseaux de Guinée
française. Bull. Mus. Hist. Nat. Paris 30 (1958):
490-497."; "1959c. Description de deux espèces
nouvelles de Guinée française. Bull. Mus. Hist. Nat.
Paris 31: 271-219."; and "1962. Étude d'une
collection d'oiseaux de Guyane française. Bull.
Mus. Hist. Nat. Paris 35: 131-143."

908 after BHUSAN, B. entry, add "BIBBY, C. J., AND A. J. DEL
NEVO. 1991. A first record of *Pterodroma feae*
from the Azores. Bull. Brit. Ornithol. Club 111:
183-186."

909 under BISWAS, B. entries, change "1951" to "1951b" and
add "1951a. Revision of Indian birds. Am. Mus.
Novit., no. 1500."

909 under BLAKE, E. R. entries, add "1959. A new species
of *Todirostrum* from Peru. Nat. Hist. Misc., no.
171."

909 under BOURNE, W. R. P. entries, change "1987" to
"1987a" and add "1987b. The classification and
nomenclature of the petrels. Ibis 129: 404."

910 after BRAZIL AND IKENAGA entry, add "BRETAGNOLLE,
V. 1990. Behavioural affinities of the Blue Petrel,
Halobaena caerulea. Ibis 132: 102-105." and
"BRETAGNOLLE, V., R. ZOTIER, AND P. JOUVENTIN.
1990. Comparative population biology of four
prions (Genus *Pachyptila*) from the Indian Ocean
and consequences for their taxonomic status. Auk
107: 305-316."

910 after BROOKE AND CLANCEY entry, add "BROOKE, R. K.,
AND W. R. J. DEAN. 1990. On the biology and taxonomic position of *Drymoica substriata* Smith, the
so-called Namaqua Prinia. Ostrich 61: 50-55."

910 after BROOKE, OATLEY ET AL. entry, add "BROOKE, R.
K., AND C. J. VERNON. 1981. Early names and
records of two small Hieraaetus eagles (Aves:
Accipitridae) in the Cape Province of South Africa.
Ann. Cape Prov. Mus. (Nat. Hist.) 13: 133-137."

910 after BROWN, L. H. entry, add "BROWN, L. H., E. K. URBAN AND K. NEWMAN. 1982. The birds of Africa. Vol. I. Academic Press, London."

910 under BROWNING, M. R. entries, add "1992. Comments on the nomenclature and dates of publication of some taxa in Bucerotidae. Bull. Brit. Ornithol. Club 112: 22-27."

910 after BROWNING, M. R. entries, add "BROWNING, M. R., AND B. L. MONROE, JR. 1991. Clarifications and corrections of the dates of issue of some publications containing descriptions of North American birds. Arch. Nat. Hist. 18: 381-405."; and "BRUCE, M. D. 1989. A reappraisal of species limits in the Pied Imperial Pigeon *Ducula bicolor* (Scopoli, 1786) superspecies. Riv. Ital. Ornitol. 59: 218-222."

910 after BRUNEL, CHAPPUIS AND ERARD entry, add "BUCKLEY, P. A. 1990. The world's first known juvenile Cox's Sandpiper. British Birds 81: 253-257."

910 after CAIN AND GALBRAITH entry, add "CARDOSO DA SILVA, J. M. 1990. A reavaluation [sic] of *Serpophaga araguayae* Snethlage, 1928 (Aves: Tyrannidae). Goeldiana, Zoologia, no. 1."

910 after CASEY AND JACOBI entry, add "CHAPIN, J. P. 1958. A new honey-guide from the Kivu District, Belgian Congo. Bull. Brit. Ornithol. Club 78: 46-48."

911 under CLANCEY, P. A. entries, change "1965ba" entry to "1965a"; change "1972" entry to "1972a"; add "1972b. Miscellaneous taxonomic notes on African birds XXXV. Durban Mus. Novit. 9: 233-250."; "1987c. Longbilled Pipit systematics. Ostrich 58: 45-46."; "1991a. On the generic status and geographical variation of the Namaqua Prinia. Bull. Brit. Ornithol. Club 111: 101-104."; and "1991b. The generic status of Roberts' Prinia of the south-eastern Afrotropics. Bull. Brit. Ornithol. Club 111: 217-222."

911 after CLANCEY, P. A. entries, add "CLANCEY, P. A., AND R. K. BROOKE. 1990. Avian nomenclatural issues arising from the publication of Rookmaker's 'The zoological exploration of southern Africa 1650-1790.' Ostrich 61: 143-145."

911 in entry for CLARK, G. A., JR. change "Jr."to "JR."; change 'Neogropical" to "Neotropical"

911 after CLARK, G. A., JR. entry, add "COATES, B. J. 1985. The birds of Papua New Guinea including the Bismarck Archipelago and Bougainville. Vol. I. Non-passerines. Dove Publications, Alderley, Queensland, Australia." and "1990. The birds of Papua New Guinea including the Bismarck Archipelago and Bougainville. Vol. II. Passerines. Dove Publications, Alderley, Queensland, Australia."; and "COLEBROOK-ROBJENT, J. F. R. 1986. On the validity of the genus *Micronisus*. Gabar 1: 7-8."

911 after COLEBROOK-ROBJENT AND ASPINWALL entry, add "COLLAR, N. J., AND S. N. STUART. 1985. Threatened birds of Africa and related islands. I.C.B.P. and I.U.C.N., Cambridge."

912 under COURTNEY, J. entry, change "*Calyptorhynchus funereus* funereus" to "*Calyptorhynchus funereus funereus*"

912 under COX, J. B. entries, add "1989. Notes on the affinities of Cooper's and Cox's Sandpipers. S. Austr. Ornithol. 30: 169-181." and "1990. The enigmatic Cooper's and Cox's Sandpipers. Dutch Birding 12: 53-64."

912 after CROOK, J. H. entry, add "CROSSIN, R. S., AND C. A. ELY. 1973. A new race of Sumichrast's Wren from Chiapas, México. Condor 75: 137-139."

912 after CROWE AND CROWE entry, add "CROWE, T. M., E. H. HARLEY, M. B. JAKUTOWICZ, J. KOMEN, AND A. A. CROWE. 1992. Phylogenetic, taxonomic and biogeographical implications of genetic, morphological, and behavioral variation in francolins (Phasianidae: *Francolinus*). Auk 109: 24-42."

912 under DAVIS, L. I. entries, add "1958. Acoustic evidence of relationships in North American crows. Wilson Bull. 70: 151-167."

912 after DEAN, W. R. J. entry, add "DEBUS, S. J. S. 1986. The small *Hieraaetus* eagles on four continents: a superspecies? Gabar 1: 36-39."

912 under DEIGNAN, H. G. entries, add "1955. The races of the swiftlet, *Collocalia brevirostris* (McClelland). Bull. Brit. Ornithol. Club 75: 116-118."

913 under 1966 DE NAUROIS, R. entry, change "Héron" to "Héron"; under 1988 entry, change "VAert" to "Vert"

913 under DEVILLERS, P. entries, add "1978. Distribution and relationships of South American skuas. Gerfaut 68: 374-417."

913 under DIAMOND, J. M. entries, change "1969. 1972." to "1972."; add "1969. Preliminary results of an ornithological expedition of the North Coastal Range, New Guinea. Am. Mus. Novit., no. 2362."; "1971. Bird records from west New Britain. Condor 73: 481-483."; and "1991. A new species of rail from the Solomon Islands and convergent evolution of insular flightlessness. Auk 108: 461-470."

913 under DICKINSON, E. C. entries, add "1989a. A review of the larger Philippine swiftlets of the genus *Collocalia*. Forktail 4: 19-53." and "1989b. A review of the smaller Philippine swiftlets of the genus *Collocalia*. Forktail 5: 23-34."

913 after DICKINSON entries, add "DICKINSON, E. C., R. S. KENNEDY, AND K. C. PARKES. 1991. The birds of the Philippines. B.O.U. Check-list No. 12. Dorset Press, Dorchester."

913 delete second entry for DILGER, W. C., 1956

913 under DORST, J. entries, add "1957. Description d'une espèce nouvelle de Tyran du genre *Serpophaga* du Pérou septentrional. Bull. Mus. Hist. Nat. Paris 29: 207-209."

913 after DORST entries, add "DORST, J., AND C. JOUANIN. 1952. Description d'une espèce nouvelle de francolin d'Afrique orientale. Oiseau 22: 71-74."

913 under DOWSETT, R. J. entry, add "1990. The gender of the avian genus *Batis*. Bull. Brit. Ornithol. Club 109: 180-181."

913 under DOWSETT AND DOWSETT-LEMAIRE entry, add "1987. Longbilled Pipit systematics. Ostrich 58: 46."

914 under DOWSETT-LEMAIRE, F. entry, add "1989. On the voice of the Mountain Pipit. Ostrich 60: 85-87."; move these entries ahead of those for DOWSETT-LEMAIRE AND DOWSETT.

914   under 1985 entry for DUBOIS, P., change "sue" to "sur"

914   after DUBOIS, P. entry, add "DUFF, D. G., D. N.
       BAKEWELL, AND M. D. WILLIAMS. 1991. The Relict
       Gull *Larus relictus* in China and elsewhere. Forktail
       6: 43-65."

914   after EARLÉ, R. A. entry, add "ECK, S. 1988.
       Geschichtspunkte zur Art-Systematik der Meisen
       (Paridae) (Aves). Zool. Abh. Staatliches Mus.
       Tierkunde Dresden 43: 101-134."

914   under EISENMANN AND LEHMANN entry, change "1962"
       to "1963"; after "no. 2117" add "(1962)"

914   under ELGOOD, J. H. entries, add "1958. A new species
       of *Malimbus*. Ibis 100: 621-624."

914   under ERARD, C. entries, add "1986. Taxonomie des
       serins a gorge jaune d'Ethiopie. Oiseau 44: 308-
       323."

914   after ERARD, C., entries, add "ERARD, C., J. J. GUILLOU,
       AND N. MAYAUD. 1986. Le héron blanc du Banc
       d'Arguin *Ardea monicae,* ses affinités
       morphologiques, son histoire. Alauda 54: 161-169."

914   after ERISE, F. entry, add "ESCALANTE-PLIEGO, P., AND
       A. T. PETERSON. 1992. Geographic variation and
       species limits in Middle American woodnymphs
       (Thalurania). Wilson Bull. 104: 205-219."

914   after ESKEL AND GARNETT entry, add "EVANS, M. I.
       1991. The Red-tailed Newtonia Newtonia
       fanovanae in the Ambatovaky Reserve, north-east
       Madagascar. Bird Conserv. Int. 1: 33-45."

914   after FARKAS entries, add "FARRAND, J., AND S. L.
       OLSON. 1973. The correct spelling of Scopoli's
       specific name for the Malaysian Crested Wood
       Partridge *(Rollulus)*. Bull. Brit. Ornithol. Club 93:
       53-54."

914   after FAVALORO AND MCEVEY entry, add "FEARE, C. J.,
       AND K. NEE. 1992. Allocation of *Sturnus
       melanopterus* to *Acridotheres*. Bull. Brit. Ornithol.
       Club 112: 125-129."

915   after FITZPATRICK, TERBORGH AND WILLARD entry, add
       "FITZPATRICK, J. W., AND D. E. WILLARD. 1990.
       Cercomacra manu, a new species of antbird from
       southwestern Amazonia. Auk 107: 239-245."

915   under FORD, J. entries, add "1981. Evolution,
       distribution and stage of speciation in the *Rhipidura
       fuliginosa* complex in Australia. Emu 81: 128-144."

916   under FRITH AND FRITH entry, add "1990. Nesting
       biology and relationships of the Lesser Melampitta
       Melampitta lugubris. Emu 90: 65-73."

916   under 1973 entry for GERMAIN, M., ET AL., change "der"
       to "de"

916   after GILL, FUNK AND SILVERIN entry, add "GILL, F. B.,
       AND B. SLIKAS. 1992. Patterns of mitochondrial
       DNA divergence in North American crested titmice.
       Condor 94: 20-28."

917   after GILLIARD, E. T., entries, add "GLUTZ VON
       BLOTZHEIM, U. N. 1991. Handbuch der Vögel
       Mitteleuropas, Band 12/II. AULA-Verlag, Wies-
       baden."

917   after GONZAGA entry, add "GONZAGA, L. P., AND J. F.
       PACHECO. 1990. Two new subspecies of
       Formicivora serrana (Hellmayr) from southeastern
       Brazil, and notes on the type locality of *Formicivora
       deluzae* Ménétries. BBOC 110: 187-193."

917   after GONZALEZ ET AL. entry, add "GONZALES, P. C.,
       AND R. C. KENNEDY. 1990. A new species of
       Stachyris babbler (Aves: Timaliidae) from the island
       of Panay, Philippines. Wilson Bull. 102: 367-379."

917   after GOULD entry, add "GRANT, C. H. B., AND C. W.
       MACKWORTH-PRAED. 1952. A new race of serin
       from eastern Africa. Bull. Brit. Ornithol. Club 72: 1-
       2."

917   after GRANTSAU entries, add "GRANTSAU, R., AND H. F.
       DE A. CAMARGO. 1989. Nova espécie Brasileira de
       Amazona (Aves, Psittacidae). Rev. Brasil. Biol. 49:
       1017-1020."

917   under GRAVES, G. R. entries, in 1998 entry CHANGE
       "*Phylloscopus*" to "*Phylloscartes*"; add "1990.
       Systematics of the "Green-throated Sunangels"
       (Aves: Trochilidae): valid taxa or hybrids? Proc.
       Biol. Soc. Wash. 103: 6-25." and "1992. The
       endemic land birds of Henderson Island,
       southeastern Polynesia: notes on natural history and
       conservation. Wilson Bull. 104: 32-43."

917   under HAFFER, J. entries, add "1989. Parapatrische
       Vogelarten der paläarktischen Region. J. Ornithol.
       130: 475-512."

918   under HARDY, J. W. entries, add "1990. The Fish Crow
       (Corvus ossifragus) and its Mexican relatives: vocal
       clues to evolutionary relationships? Fla. Field Nat.
       18: 74-80."

918   after HARDY AND DICKERMAN entry, add "HARDY, J.
       W., AND R. STRANECK. 1989. The Silky-tailed
       Nightjar and other neotropical caprimulgids:
       unraveling some mysteries. Condor 91: 193-197."

918   after HARPER entry, add "HARRAP, S. 1989.
       Identification, vocalisations, and taxonomy of
       Pnoepyga wren-babblers. Forktail 5: 61-70." and
       "1991. The Hainan Nuthatch. Bull. Oriental Bird
       Club, no. 13."

918   under 1970 entry for HEIM DE BALSAC, H., change
       "Unfacheux" to "Un facheux"

918   after HEPP ET AL. entry, add "HERREMANS, M., M.
       LOUETTE, AND J. STEVENS. 1991. Conservation
       status and vocal and morphological description of
       the Grand Comoro Scops Owl *Otus pauliani*. Bird
       Cons. Int. 1: 123-133."

918   after HINKELMANN, C. entries, add "HINKELMANN, C.,
       B. NICOLAI, AND R. C. DICKERMAN. 1991. Notes on
       a hitherto unknown specimen of *Neolesbia nehrkorni*
       (Berlepsch, 1887; Trochilidae) with a discussion of
       the hybrid origin of this 'species.' Bull. Brit.
       Ornithol. Club 111: 190-199."

918   under HOCKEY AND BROOKE entry, "1987" (not "1983")

919   after HOLYOAK AND THIBAULT entries, add
       "HORNIMAN, R. B. Preliminary descriptions of some
       new birds. Ann. Mag. Nat. Hist. 12: 366-368."

919   after HUNT, J. H. entry, add "HUNTER, L. A. 1988.
       Status of the endemic Atitlan Grebe of Guatemala:
       is it extinct? Condor 90: 906-912."

919   under I.C.Z.N. entries, add "1990. Bull. Zool. Nomencl.
       47: 169-170." and "1991. Bull. Zool. Nomencl. 48:
       187-188."

919   after I.C.Z.N. entries, add "IREDALE, T. 1948. A check
       list of the birds of paradise and bower-birds. Austr.
       Zool. 11: 161-189."

920 under IRWIN, M. P. S., entries, add "What are the
affinities of the Black-capped Apalis *Apalis
nigriceps?* The need for field studies. Malimbus 9:
130-131." and "1991. The specific characters of the
Slender-tailed Cisticola *Cisticola melanura*
(Cabanis). Bull. Brit. Ornithol. Club 111: 228-236."

920 under JAMES, ZUSI AND OLSON entry, change "JAMES,
A. H." to "JAMES, H. F."; change
"Desmorodrepanis" to *"Dysmorodrepanis"*

920 after JIMÉNEZ AND JAKSIĆ entries, add "JOHNSGARD, P.
A. 1978. Ducks, geese, and swans of the world.
Univ. Nebraska Press, Lincoln."

920 after JOHNSON AND JOHNSON entry, add "JOHNSON,
N.K., AND R. E. JONES. 1990. Geographic
differentiation and distribution of the Peruvian
Screech-Owl. Wilson Bull. 102: 199-212."

920 under JOHNSON AND MARTEN entry, add "1992.
Macrogeographic patterns of morphometric and
genetic variation in the Sage Sparrow complex.
Condor 94: 1-19."

921 under JOUANIN, C. entries, add "1959. Les emeus de
l'expedition Baudin. Oiseau 29: 169-203."

921 after JOUANIN AND GILL entry, add "JOUANIN, C., AND
F. ROUX. 1963. Une race nouvelle de Héron cendré
Ardea cinerea monicae. Oiseau 33: 103-106."

921 under KEMP, A. C. entry, add "1986. The Gabar
Goshawk: taxonomy, ecology, and further research.
Gabar 1: 4-6."

921 after KITSON, A. R., entry, insert KITTI, T., entry from p.
935

921 under KNOX entries, change "1988" to "1988b" and add
"1988a. The taxonomy of redpolls. Ardea 76: 1-
26." and "1990. The sympatric breeding of
Common and Scottish crossbills *Loxia curvirostra*
and *L. scotica* and the evolution of crossbills. Ibis
132: 454-466."

921 after KNOX, A. entries, add "KOELZ, W. N. 1954.
Ornithological Studies. I. New birds from Iran,
Afghanistan, and India. Contrib. Inst. Reg. Explor.,
no. 1."

921 after KOEPCKE entries, add "KÖNIG, C. 1991.
Taxonomical and ecological studies of pygmy owls
(*Glaucidium* spp.) of the Andean region. Ökol.
Vögel 13: 15-76."

921 under KROODSMA AND CANADY entry, change "439-
436" to "439-446"

921 sequence KROGMAN entries before KROODSMA entry

922 after LALAS AND HEATHER entry, add "LANGRAND, O.
1990. Guide to the birds of Madagascar. Yale Univ.
Press, New Haven." and "LANNING, D. V. 1991.
Distribution and breeding biology of the Red-fronted
Macaw. Wilson Bull. 103: 357-365."

922 after LANYON, S. M., AND W. E. LANYON entry, add
"LANYON, S. M., D. F. STOTZ, AND D. E. WILLARD.
1990. *Clytoctantes atrogularis,* a new species of
antbird from western Brazil. Wilson Bull. 102: 571-
580."

922 under LA TOUCHE, J. D. entry, change "J. D.." to "J. D."

922 after LEHMANN AND HAFFER entry, add "LIVEZEY, B. C.
1986. A phylogenetic analysis of recent anseriform
genera using morphological characters. Auk 103:
737-754." and "1991. A phylogenetic analysis and
classification of recent dabbling ducks (Tribe
Anatini) based on comparative morphology. Auk
108: 471-507."

922 Reverse sequence of LONGMORE AND BOLES and
LONGMORE entries

922 under LOUETTE, M. entries, add "1987. A new weaver
from Uganda? Ibis 129: 405-406."; "1988c.
Double invasions of birds on the Comoro Islands.
Proc. Sixth Pan-African Ornith. Congr., pp. 77-86.";
"1990a. The nightjars of Zaïre. Bull. Brit. Ornithol.
Club 110: 71-77."; and "1990b. A new species of
nightjar from Zaïre. Ibis 132: 349-353."

923 after LOUETTE AND HERREMANS entry, add "LOWE, K.
W., AND G. C. RICHARDS. 1991. Morphological
variation in the Sacred Ibis *Threskiornis aethiopicus*
superspecies complex. Emu 91: 41-45."

923 after LUDLOW entry, add "MCALLAN, I. A. W. 1990.
The Cochineal Creeper and the Fascinating
Grosbeak: a re-examination of some names of John
Latham. Bull. Brit. Ornithol. Club 110: 153-159."

923 after MCALLAN entry, insert MCALLAN AND BRUCE
entry from p. 924

923 after MCALLAN AND BRUCE entry, add "MACDONALD, J.
D. 1956. A new species of lark from Kenya. Bull.
Brit. Ornithol. Club 76: 70-72."; and "1958. Note
on *Cinnyris manoensis* Reichenow. Bull. Brit.
Ornithol. Club 78: 7-9."; "MACDONALD, J. D., AND
B. P. HALL. 1967. Ornithological results of the
Bernard Carp/Transvaal Museum expedition to the
Kaokoveld, 1951. Ann. Transvaal Mus. 23: 1-39.";
and "MCDONALD, M. A., AND M. H. SMITH. 1990.
Speciation, heterochrony, and genetic variation in
Hispaniolan palm-tanagers. Auk 107: 707-717."

923 after MANN ET AL. entry, add "MANUEL, C. G., AND E.
T. GILLIARD. 1952. Undescribed and newly
recorded Philippine birds. Am. Mus. Novit., no.
1545." and "1953. A new name for a flowerpecker
from the Philippines. Auk 70: 90-91."

923 under MARION, L., entry, change "côtes atlantique" to
"côtes atlantiques"

923 under MARSHALL, J. T. entry, add "1978. Systematics
of smaller Asian night birds based on voice.
Ornithol. Monogr., no. 25."

923 after MARSHALL, J. T. entries, add "MARSHALL, J. T., R.
A. BEHRSTOCK, AND CLAUS KÖNIG. 1991. 'Voices
of the New World nightjars and their allies
(Caprimulgiformes: Steatornithidae, Nyctibiidae,
and Caprimulgidae),' by J. W. Hardy, B. B. Coffey,
Jr., and G. B. Reynard (review). Wilson Bull. 103:
311-315."

923 under MARTENS, J. entry, add "1988. *Phylloscopus
borealoides* Portenko—ein verkannter Laubsänge
der Ost-Paläarktis. J. Ornithol. 129: 343-351."

923 after MARTENS entry, add "MARTENS, J., AND C. ECK.
1991. *Pnoepyga immaculata* n. sp., eine neue
bodenbewohnende Timalie aus dem Nepal –
Himalaya. J. Ornithol. 132: 179-198."

923 under MAYR, E. entries, add "1963. *Gallinago* versus
Capella. Ibis 105: 402-403."

923 after MAYR entries, add "MAYR, E., AND E. T.
GILLIARD. 1951. New species and subspecies of
birds from the highlands of New Guinea. Am. Mus.
Novit., no. 1524."

924 Move MCALLAN AND BRUCE entry to p. 923 and
sequence after LUDLOW entry

924   under MEYER DE SCHAUENSEE, R. entries, change
       "1951a" to "1951c"; add "1951a. Notes on
       Ecuadorian birds. Not. Nat., no. 234."; "1967.
       Eriocnemis mirabilis, a new species of hummingbird
       from Colombia. Not. Nat., no. 402."; and "1959.
       Additions to the 'Birds of the Republic of
       Colombia.' Proc. Acad. Nat. Sci. Philadelphia 111:
       53-75."

924   under MILLER ET AL. entries, the 1964 reference should
       be listed separately under "MILLER, A. H." preceding
       the other MILLER ET AL. entry

924   after MONROE, B. L., JR. entries, add "MONROE, B. L.,
       JR., AND M. R. BROWNING. 1992. A re-analysis of
       Butorides. Bull. Brit. Ornithol. Club 112: 81-85."

925   after MOORE AND KOENIG entry, add "MOORE, W. S.,
       AND J. T. MARSHALL, JR. 1959. A new race of
       screech owl from Oaxaca. Condor 61: 224-225."

925   after NAROSKY entry, add "NAROSKY, T., AND D.
       YZURIETA. 1987. Guía para la identificación de las
       aves de Argentina y Uruguay. Assoc. Ornit. del
       Plata, Buenos Aires." and "NAVARRO S., A. G., A. T.
       PETERSON, B. P. ESCALANTE P., AND H. BENÍTEZ D.
       1992. *Cypseloides storeri,* a new species of swift
       from Mexico. Wilson Bull. 104: 55-64."

925   under NAVAS AND BO entry, change "Posicion" to
       "posicion"

925   after OBERHOLSER, H. C. entry, add "OLIVER, W. R. B.
       1953. The crested penguins of New Zealand. Emu
       53: 185-187."; "OLROG, C. C. 1958. Notas
       ornitologica sobre la coleccion del Instituto Miguel
       Lillo Tucuman. III. Acta Zool. Lilloana 15: 5-19.";
       and "1979. Notas ornitologica sobre la coleccion del
       Instituto Miguel Lillo Tucuman. XI. Acta Zool.
       Lilloana 33(2): 5-7."; and "OLROG, C. C., AND F.
       CONTINO. 1966. Dos nuevos tiranidos para la fauna
       Argentina. Neotropica 12: 113-114."

925   under OLSON, S. L. entries, add "1976. The affinities of
       the falconid genus *Spiziapteryx.* Auk 93: 633-636.";
       "1990a. Remarks on the osteology of the
       Madagascan warblers *Dromaeocercus* and
       Amphilais. Bull. Brit. Ornithol. Club 110: 9-10.";
       "1990b. Comments on the osteology and
       systematics of the New Zealand passerines of the
       genus *Mohoua.* Notornis 37: 157-160."; and
       "1990c. Osteology and systematics of the fernbirds
       (*Bowdleria:* Sylviidae). Notornis 37: 157-160."

926   after O'NEILL AND GRAVES entry, add "O'NEILL, J. P.,
       C. A. MUNN, AND I. FRANKE J. 1991. *Nannopsittaca
       dachilleae,* a new species of parrotlet from eastern
       Peru. Auk 108: 225-229."

926   after PARKER, T. A., III entries, add "PARKER, T. A., III,
       J. M. BATES, AND G. COX. 1992. Rediscovery of the
       Bolivian Recurvebill with notes on other little-
       known species of the Bolivian Andes. Wilson Bull.
       104: 173-178."; and "PARKER, T. A., III, A.
       CASTILLO U., M. GELL-MANN AND O. ROCHA O.
       1991. Records of new and unusual birds from
       northern Bolivia. Bull. Brit. Ornithol. Club 111:
       120-138."

926   after PARKER AND O'NEILL entries, add "PARKER, T. A.,
       III, AND S. A. PARKER. 1980. Rediscovery of
       Xenerpestes singularis (Furnariidae). Auk 97: 203-
       204."

926   after PARKER AND REMSEN entry, add "PARKER, T. A.,
       III, AND O. ROCHA O. 1991. Notes on the status and
       behaviour of the Rusty-necked Piculet *Picumnus
       fuscus.* Bull. Brit. Ornithol. Club 111: 91-92."

927   under PARKES, K. C. entries, in 1980 entry change
       "Spiney-cheeked" to "Spiny-cheeked"; change
       "1989" entry to "1989a"; and add "1987. Letter:
       Was the 'Chinese' White-eyed River-Martin an
       Oriental Pratincole? Forktail 3: 68-69."; "1989b. A
       revision of the Mangrove Vireo (*Vireo pallens*)
       (Aves: Vireonidae). Ann. Carnegie Mus. 59: 49-
       60."; and "1992. Distribution and taxonomy of birds
       of the world (book review). J. Field Ornithol. 63:
       228-235."

927   under PAYNE, R. B. entries, add "1985. The species of
       parasitic finches in West Africa. Malimbus 7: 103-
       113."

927   after PAYNTER entries, add "PEARMAN, M. 1990.
       Behaviour and vocalizations of an undescribed
       Canastero *Asthenes* sp. from Brazil. Bull. Brit.
       Ornithol. Club 110: 145-153."

927   under PETERS, J. L. entries, delete "1979a. vol. 1 (rev.)."

927   under PHILLIPS, A. R. entries, change "1964" entry to
       "1965" and change end of this citation to "...Nat. 25
       (1964): 217-242."

928   after PINTO AND CAMARGO entry, add "PITOCCHELLI, J.
       1990. Plumage, morphometric, and song variation in
       Mourning (*Oporornis philadelphia*) and
       MacGillivray's (*O. tolmiei*) Warblers. Auk 107:
       161-171."

928   under PRATT, H. D. entries, add "1992. Is the Poo-uli a
       Hawaiian honeycreeper (Drepanidinae)? Condor 94:
       172-180."

928   under PRATT, BRUNER AND BERRETT entry, change
       "field-guide" to "fieldguide"

928   under PRIGOGINE, A. entries, add "1960. Un nouveau
       Martinet du Congo. Rev. Zool. Bot. Afr. 62: 103-
       105."

928   under PRUM, R. O. entries, change "1988" to "1988a";
       add "1988b. Historical relationships among avian
       forest areas of endemism in the Neotropics. Acta
       19th Int. Ornithol. Congr. Ottawa, 1986, pp. 2562-
       2572." and "1990. Phylogenetic analysis of the
       evolution of display behavior in the Neotropical
       manakins (Aves: Pipridae). Ethology 84: 202-231."

928   after PRUM AND LANYON entries, add "QUINN, T. W., G.
       F. SHIELDS, AND A. C. WILSON. 1991. Affinities of
       the Hawaiian Goose based on two types of
       mitochrondial DNA data. Auk 108: 585-593."

929   after RAND AND RABOR entry, add "RANDI, E., A.
       MERIGGI, R. LORENZINI, G. FUSCO, AND P. U.
       ALKON. 1992. Biochemical analysis of relationships
       of Mediterranean *Alectoris* partridges. Auk 109:
       358-367."

929   after RATTI, J. T. entry, add "RAXWORTHY, C. J., AND P.
       R. COLSTON. 1992. Conclusive evidence for the
       continuing existence of the Madagascar Serpent-
       Eagle *Eutriorchis astur.* Bull. Brit. Ornithol. Club
       112: 108-111."

929   after REMSEN ET AL. entry, add "REMSEN, J. V., JR., C.
       G. SCHMITT, AND D. C. SCHMITT. 1989. Natural
       history notes on some poorly known Bolivian birds.
       Gerfaut 78: 363-381."; and "RENJIFO, L. M. 1991.

Discovery of the Masked Saltator in Colombia, with notes on its ecology and behavior. Wilson Bull. 103: 685-690."

929 after RIDGELY, R. S. entry, add "RIDGELY, R. S., AND J. A. GWYNNE. 1989. A guide to the birds of Panama with Costa Rica, Nicaragua, and Honduras. 2nd ed. Princeton Univ. Press, Princeton, New Jersey."

929 after RIDGELY AND ROBBINS entry, add "RIDGELY, R. S., AND G. TUDOR. 1989. The birds of South America, vol. 1. The Oscine Passerines. Univ. of Texas Press, Austin."

929 under RIPLEY, S. D. entries, change "1985" entry to "1985b" and add "1985a. A note on the status of *Brachypteryx cryptica*. J. Bombay Nat. Hist. Soc. 81: 700-701."

930 after RIPLEY AND RABOR entries, add "RIPLEY, S. D., S. S. SAHA, AND B. M. BEEHLER. 1991. Notes on birds from the Upper Noa Dihing, Arunachal Pradesh, Northeastern India. Bull. Brit. Ornithol. Club 111: 19-28."

930 after ROBBINS ET AL. entry, add "ROBBINS, M. B., AND R. S. RIDGELY. 1991. *Sipia rosenbergi* (Formicariidae) is a synonym of *Myrmeciza [laemosticta] nigricauda*, with comments on the validity of the genus *Sipia*. Bull. Brit. Ornithol. Club 111: 11-18."

930 under ROUX, MOUGIN AND BARTLE entry, change "Prior" to "Prion"; change "taxinomiques" to "taxonomiques"

930 under ROWLEY, I. entry, add "1970. The genus *Corvus* (Aves: Corvidae) in Australia. CSIRO Wildl. Res. 15: 27-71."

930 under ROZENDAAL, F. G. entry, add "1989. Taxonomic affinites of *Bradypterus montis*. Dutch Birding 11: 164-167." and "1990. Vocalizations and taxonomic status of *Caprimulgus celebensis*. Dutch Birding 12: 79-81."

930 after ROZENDAAL, F. G. entries, add "RUDGE, D. W., AND R. J. RAIKOW. 1992. The phylogenetic relationships of the *Margarornis* assemblage (Furnariidae). Condor 94: 760-766."

930 under SALOMONSEN, F. entries, add "1952. Systematic notes on some Philippine birds. Vidensk. Medd. Dansk. Naturh. Foren. 114: 341-364."; "1953. Et nyt navn for *Rhabdornis longirostris* Salomonsen. Dansk. Ornithol. Foren. Tidsskr. 47: 138-139."; and "1964. Some remarkable new birds from Dyaul Island, Bismarck Archipelago, with zoogeographical notes. Biol. Skr. Dansk. Vid. Selsk. 14: 9-14."

930 after SALOMONSEN, F., entries add "SANE, S. R., P. KANNAN, C. G. RAJENDRAN, S. T. INGLE, AND A. M. BHAGWAT. 1986. On the taxonomic status of *Psittacula intermedia* (Rothschild). J. Bombay Nat. Hist. Soc. 83 (suppl.): 127-134."

930 after SCHIFTER, H. entries, add "SCHLUTER, D., L. M. RATCLIFFE, AND P. R. GRANT. 1991. The taxonomic status of the small Genovesa ground-finch in the Galápagos. Auk 108: 201-204."

931 under 1978 SCHUCHMANN, K.-L. entry, change "artbildung" to "Artbildung"; change "Kolibriggattung" to "Kolibrigattung"

931 under SCHUCHMANN AND WOLTERS entry, change "K. L.," to "K.-L.,"

931 after SCHULENBERG AND PARKER entry, add "SCHULENBERG, T. S., AND D. F. STOTZ. 1991. The taxonomic status of *Myrmeciza stictothorax* (Todd). Auk 108: 731-733."

931 after SELANDER AND GILLER entry, add "SERLE, W. 1951. A new species of shrike and a new race of apalis from West Africa. Bull. Brit. Ornithol. Club 71: 41-43."

932 after SHORT, HORNE AND CHAPIN entry, add "SHORT, L. L., J. F. M. HORNE, AND C. MURINGO-GICHUKI. 1990. Annotated check-list of the birds of East Africa. Proc. W. Found. Vert. Zool. 4: 61-246."

933 under SIBLEY AND AHLQUIST entries, change title of 1990 entry to "Phylogeny and classification of birds: a study in molecular evolution."

933 under SIEGEL-CAUSEY, D. entries, add "1991. Systematics and biogeography of North Pacific shags, with a description of a new species. Occas. Papers Mus. Nat. Hist., Univ. Kansas, no. 140."

934 after SLUYS AND VAN DEN BERG entry, add "SMEENK, C., AND N. SMEENK-ENSERINK. 1975. Observations of the Pale Chanting Goshawk *Melierax poliopterus*, with comparative notes on the Gabar Goshawk *Micronisus gabar*. Ardea 63: 93-115." and "SMITH, E.F.G. , P. ARCTANDER, J. FJELDSÅ AND O. G. AMIR. 1991. A new species of shrike (Laniidae: *Laniarius*) from Somalia, verified by DNA sequence data from the only known individual. Ibis 133: 227-235."

934 under STAGER, K.E. entries, change "1961" to "1962", and change end of this entry to "...no. 46 (1961)."

934 under STEPANYAN, L. S. entries, add "1990a. Remarks on four names of Palaearctic birds. Zool. Zh. 69: 73-85."; "1990b. A new hypothesis of the origin of Cox's Sandpiper *Calidris paramelanotos* (Scolopacidae, Aves). Zool. Zh. 69: 148-151."; and "1990c. [Conspectus of the ornithological fauna of the USSR]. Moscow."

934 under STILES, F. G. entries, add "1992. A new species of antpitta (Formicariidae: *Grallaria*) from the Eastern Andes of Colombia. Wilson Bull. 104: 389-399."

935 after STORER entry, add "STOTZ, D. F. 1990. The taxonomic status of *Phyllomyias reiseri*. Bull. Brit. Ornithol. Club 110: 184-187."

935 after STRESEMANN entry, add "STRONACH, N. 1990. Habitat and distribution of the Rock-loving Cisticola *Cisticola aberrans* in Serengeti National Park, Tanzania. Bull. Brit. Ornithol. Club 110: 32-34."

935 after SUTTER entry, add "SVENNSON, L. 1984. Identification guide to European passerines, 3rd ed. Stockholm." and "1987. More about Phylloscopus taxonomy. Brit. Birds 80: 580-581."

935 after TEIXEIRA, D. M., entry, add "TEIXEIRA, D. M., AND N. CARNEVALLI. 1989. Nova espécie de *Scytalopus* Gould, 1837, do nordeste do Brasil (Passeriformes, Rhinocryptidae). Bol. do Mus. Nac., n.s., Rio de Janeiro, Zool., no. 331."

935 after TEIXEIRA AND SNOW entry, add and "THOMPSON, C. W. 1991. Is the Painted Bunting actually two species? Problems determining species limits between allopatric populations. Condor 93: 987-1000."

935 change entry for "THONGLONGYA, K." to "KITTI, T." and move to p. 921 following KITSON, A. R. entry

935   after TODD, D. entry, add "TODD, W. E. C. 1951. Two apparently new oven-birds from Colombia. Proc. Biol. Soc. Washington 63: 85-87." and "TOMKINS, R. J., AND B. J. MILNE. 1991. Differences among Dark-rumped Petrel *(Pterodroma phaeopygia)* populations within the Galapagos Archipelago. Notornis 38: 1-35."

935   under TRAYLOR, M. A. entries, change "1961b" to "1951b"; add "1952. A new race of *Otus ingens* (Salvin) from Colombia. Nat. Hist. Misc., no. 99."

936   after TROY AND BRUSH entry, add "TURNER, D. A., D. J. PEARSON, AND D. A. ZIMMERMAN. 1991. Taxonomic notes on some East African birds. Part I—Non-passerines. Scopus 14: 84-91."

936   after URBAN, FRY AND KEITH entry, add "URBAN, E. K., AND T. G. JEFFORD. 1974. The status of cormorants *Phalacrocorax carbo lucidus* and *Phalacrocorax carbo patricki.* Bull. Brit. Ornithol. Club 94: 104-107."

936   under VAGVOLGYI AND VAGVOLGYI entry, add "1991. Response to Schluter, Ratcliffe, and Grant. Auk 108: 204-206."

936   under VAURIE, C. entries, change "1951" entry to "1951a"; add "1951b. A new species of flycatcher from Mindanao, Philippine Islands. Am. Mus. Novit., no. 1543."

937   under VIELLIARD, J. entries, add "1990a. Uma nova espécie de *Glaucidium* (Aves, Strigidae) da Amazônia. Rev. Bras. Zool. 6 (1989): 685-693." and "1990b. Uma nova espécie de *Asthenes* da Serra do Cipó, Minas Gerais, Brasil. Ararajuba (Rio de Janeiro) 1: 121-122."

937   under VUILLEUMIER, F. entries, change "1969" to "1969a" and add "1969b. Field notes on some birds from the Bolivian Andes. Ibis 111: 599-608."

937   under WALTERS 1987 entry, change *"conditicus"* to *"conditicius"*

938   under WETMORE, A. entries, add "1957. The birds of Isla Coiba, Panamá. Smithson. Misc. Collect., vol. 134, no. 9." and "1963. Additions to records of birds known from the Republic of Panamá. Smithson. Misc. Collect., vol. 145, no. 6."

938   after WHITE AND BRUCE entry, add "WHITNEY, B. M. 1992. Observations on the systematics, behavior, and vocalizations of *'Thamnomanes' occidentalis* (Formicariidae). Auk 109: 302-308."

938   under WILLIAMS, J. G. entries, change "1966" to "1966a" and add "1966b. A new cormorant from Uganda. Bull. Brit. Ornithol. Club 86: 48-50."

938   under WILLIS, E. O. entries, add "1991. Sibling species of greenlets (Vireonidae) in southern Brazil. Wilson Bull. 103: 559-567." and "1992. Three *Chamaeza* antthrushes in eastern Brazil (Formicariidae). Condor 94: 110-116."

939   after WINKER AND RAPPOLE entry, add "WINTERBOTTOM, J. M., AND C. J. SKEAD. 1965. On the correct spelling of *Saxicola arnotti* Tristram. Ostrich 36: 147."

939   after YAMASHINA AND MANO entry, add "YÉSOU, P. 1991. The sympatric breeding of *Larus fuscus, L. cachinnans* and *L. argentatus* in western France. Ibis 133: 256-263."

939   under ZIMMER, J. T. entries, add "1952a. A new subspecies of pipit from Argentina and Paraguay.

Proc. Biol. Soc. Washington 65: 31-34"; "1952b. A new finch from northern Perú. J. Washington Acad. Sci. 42: 103."; "1953a. Notes on tyrant flycatchers (Tyrannidae). Am. Mus. Novit., no. 1953."; and "1953b. Studies in Peruvian birds. No. 65. The jays (Corvidae) and pipits (Motacillidae). Am. Mus. Novit., no. 1649."

939   after ZINK, R. M. entry, add "ZINK, R. M., AND D. L. DITTMAN. 1991. Evolution of Brown Towhees: mitochondrial DNA evidence. Condor 93: 98-105."; "ZINK, R. M., D. L. DITTMAN, S. W. CARDIFF, AND JAMES D. RISING. 1991. Mitochondrial DNA variation and the taxonomic status of the Large-billed Savannah Sparrow. Condor 93: 1016-1019."; and "ZINK, R. M., D. L. DITTMAN, AND W. L. ROOTES. 1991. Mitochondrial DNA variation and the phylogeny of *Zonotrichia.* Auk 108: 578-584."

INDEX

Correct index entries are listed below. If the entry already exists on pp. 940-1111, the new entry should replace the old one; if the entry is an entirely new one, it should be added where indicated.

964 *carbo, Phalacrocorax,* **300,** *300*
964 CARDINAL, 772 (before BLACK-EARED entry)
964 CARDINAL, NORTHERN, 772, *772*
964 CARDINAL, RED-CAPPED, 728, *728, 728*
964 delete CARDINAL, RED-EARED entry
964 *caroli, Polyonymus,* **161** (not *Polyonomus*)
965 *Carphibis,* **313** (not *Carphibi*)
964 CASIORNIS, RUFOUS, 361, *361*
965 *castaniceps, Seicercus,* **624** (after *castaneus* entries)
965 *castaniceps, Yuhina,* **644,** *644* (not *castaneus*)
965 *castanonotum, Glaucidium,* **179** (not *castanonotus*);
      move "*castanonotus,*" to precede "*Hemixos,* 591"
965 *castanoptera, Dendrocincla,* **411** (after *castanops*
      entries)
965 *Catherpes,* **559**
965 *caucasicus, Tetraogallus,* **11** (not *caucasius*)
965 *cayanensis, Icterus,* **777** (after *cayana, Tityra* entry);
      "*Leptodon,* 266" and "*Myiozetetes,* 366" should
      be placed under "*cayanensis*"
965 *celebensis, Caprimulgus,* **190** (after *Basilornis* entry)
965 *cerulea, Procelsterna,* **263,** *263*
966 CHACHALACA, CHESTNUT-WINGED, 5, *6*
966 CHACHALACA, RUFOUS-BELLIED, **6**
966 CHACHALACA, WAGLER'S, *6*
966 *Chapinortyx,* **13** (after *chapini* entries)
966 CHAT, 531, 534, 536, 537, 539, 543, 544
966 CHAT, CANARY, 540
966 CHAT, CANARY ISLANDS, 540
966 CHAT, MOUNTAIN, 543 (after MOORLAND entry)
966 CHAT, RED-TAILED, 543 (not RED-TAILE)
966 CHAT, WHITE-FOREHEADED, 544
966 CHAT, WHITE-FRONTED, **438,** 544
967 *cheriway, Polyborus,* **289**
967 delete CHICKEN, PRAIRIE entry
967 CHIFFCHAFF, CAUCASIAN, 620 (before COMMON entry)
967 CHIFFCHAFF, COMMON, **620**
967 CHIFFCHAFF, EURASIAN, *620*
967 CHIFFCHAFF, MOUNTAIN, *620*
967 CHIFFCHAFF, SIBERIAN, *620* (after MOUNTAIN entry)
967 *chinchipensis, Synallaxis,* **400** (not *chinchipaensis*)
967 *chinensis, Streptopelia,* **197,** *197*
967 Chionidae, 243 (not Chionididae)
967 Chionoidea, 243 (not Chionidoidea)
967 *chlororhynchos, Diomedea* (not *chlorohynchos*);
      sequence after *chloropygia* entry
967 *chloronotus, Phylloscopus,* **621** (after *Gerygone* entry)
967 *chlorotis, Anas,* **35**
967 CHOUGH, ALPINE, 468
967 CHOUGH, YELLOW-BILLED, **468**
968 *chrysolaema, Zosterops,* *604*
968 CINCLODES, CORDOBA, 395 (not CORADOBA)
968 Cinclosomatinae, 456 (not Cinclosomatidae)
969 *cinerea, Ardea,* 303, 304, *304*
969 *cinereiceps, Alcippe,* **642**
969 *cinereus, Acridotheres,* **550** (before *Artamus* entry)
969 *ciris, Passerina,* **775,** *775*
969 *cirrochloris, Aphantochroa,* **156** (not *Aphanotochroa*)
969 CISTICOLA, BLACK-TAILED, **594,** 595
969 CISTICOLA, DORST'S, **593** (after DESERT entry)
969 CISTICOLA, GREATER BLACK-BACKED, 594 (after
      GOLDEN-HEADED entry)
969 CISTICOLA, RED-FACED, **592,** *592*
969 CISTICOLA, SLENDER-TAILED, 594
969 CISTICOLA, STRIPED, 594 (after STREAKED entry)

970 CITRIL, CORSICAN, *702* (after AFRICAN entry)
970 CITRIL, EUROPEAN, *702* (after EASTERN entry)
970 *clamosa, Rhipidura,* *486*
970 CLIFF-CHAT, MOCKING, **544,** *544*
970 CLIFF-SWALLOW, AMERICAN, 579
970 *coccinigastra, Nectarinia,* 663, 667 (not *coccinogastra*)
970 COCHOA, INDONESIAN, 539
970 COCHOA, SUNDA, *539* (after SUMATRAN entry)
970 COCKATOO, 111 (before BLACK entry)
970 COCKATOO, SOLOMON, 112 (after SALMON-CRESTED
      entry)
970 *codringtoni, Vidua,* **700**
970 COLASISI, **120,** *120*
970 COLLARED-DOVE, 197, 198
970 COLLARED-DOVE, JAVAN, 198 (not JAVA)
971 *collybita, Phylloscopus,* **620,** *620, 620*
971 COMET, PURPLE-TAILED, 161
971 *conditicius, Gallirallus,* 222, **223** (not *conditicus*)
971 *confusa, Pagodroma,* *321*
971 *conirostris, Spizocorys,* **654** (not *Calandrella*);
      sequence after *Indicator*
971 *conjuncta, Lalage,* **483** (after *Conirostrum* entry)
971 *conspicillatus, Zosterops,* **603,** *603*
971 *constans, Ducula,* **214** (after *conspicillatus* entries)
971 *cookii, Cyanorhamphus,* **117** (before *Pterodroma* entry)
971 *cooperi, Calidris,* **241** (before *Otus* entry)
971 *cooperi, Otus,* **172**
971 COQUETTE, FESTIVE, **148,** *148*
971 COQUETTE, SHORT-CRESTED, 148 (after RUFOUS-
      CRESTED entry)
972 CORDONBLEU, 692
972 CORDONBLEU, ANGOLA, 692
972 CORDONBLEU, BLUE-BREASTED, **692**
972 CORMORANT, BLACK-FACED, **300** (after BLACK entry)
972 CORMORANT, GREAT, 300, *300*
972 CORMORANT, INDIAN, 300 (after GUANAY entry)
972 CORMORANT, WHITE-BREASTED, *300*
972 *corsicana, Serinus,* **702** (after *corruscus* entry)
972 COTINGA, RED, *370* [→RED-COTINGA]
973 COUA, DELALANDE'S, 102
973 COUA, OLIVE-CAPPED, 102
973 COUA, RED-CAPPED, **102** (after RED-BREASTED entry)
973 COUA, RED-FRONTED, **102**
973 COUA, REYNAUD'S, 102
973 COUA, SNAIL-EATING, **102** (after RUNNING entry)
973 COUCAL, BLACK-THROATED, **104,** *104*
973 delete COUCAL, GREATER entry
973 COUCAL, MENBEKI, 103 (after MARSH entry)
973 COUROL, 85
973 change "COURSER, AUSTRALIAN, 253" to "COURSER,
      253"
973 CRAKE, HENDERSON, 228
973 CRAKE, HENDERSON ISLAND, **228**
973 CRAKE, OLIVIER'S, 226
974 CRAKE, WHITE-THROATED, **222**
974 CRANE, 218
974 *Creadion,* 505
974 CREEPER, BAIRD'S, *714*
974 CREEPER, HAWAIIAN, 714, *715*
974 CRESTED-TINAMOU, 5 (before ELEGANT entry)
974 *cristatus, Lanius,* 449, *449,* 450
974 CROCIAS, MOUNT LANG BIAN, 643 (not BIANG)
975 delete CROW, RELICT entry
975 CROW, SOLOMON, 469

983 EMERALD, SIMON'S, 149 (after SHORT-TAILED entry)
983 *emmae, Aglaiocercus*, 162
983 EMU-TAIL, GREY, **625**
983 EMU-TAIL, SEEBOHM'S, 625
983 EMUWREN, *425* (before MALLEE entry)
983 *enganensis, Otus*, *171*
983 Eopsaltriidae, 444
983 *Ephthianura*, 438
983 *Epthianura*, **438** (after *epops* entry)
984 *erythronotos, Formicivora*, **387** (not *Myrmotherula*)
984 *erythrophrys, Arborophila*, **17** (before *Poospiza* entry)
984 *erythrophthalma, Lophura*, **19** (before *Netta* entry)
984 *erythrophthalmus, Phacellodomus*, *404, 404*
984 *erythroptera, Heliolais*, **598** (not *Prinia*); sequence after *Gallicolumba*
984 *erythrophthalma*, delete *Lophura* entry
984 *erythrorhyncha, Anas*, **37**
984 *esculenta, Collocalia*, *134*
984 *euchloris, Chlorostilbon*, *150*
984 *euleri, Coccyzus*, **105**
984 EUPHONIA, GOLDEN-SIDED, **752**, *752*
985 Eurostopodidae, 185 (not Eurystopodidae)
985 Eurostopodoidea, 185 (not Eurystopodoidea)
985 *everetti, Otus*, *172* (after *Monarcha* entry)
985 *fabalis, Anser*, **29**, *29*
985 FAIRY-FLYCATCHER, BLUE, 490 (after FAIRY-BLUEBIRD entries)
985 FAIRY-FLYCATCHER, NORTHERN, 490 (not FAIRY-FLYCATCHER)
985 FAIRYWREN, BLACK-BACKED, *425*
985 FAIRYWREN, TURQUOISE, *425*
985 *falcirostris, Xiphocolaptes*, **412**, *412*
985 FALCON, ALTAI, 293
986 FALCON, GYR, 294
986 FALCON, PALLID, 294 (after ORANGE-BREASTED entry)
986 FALCON, RED-NECKED, **292**
986 *fannyi, Thalurania*, *150*, *150*
986 FANTAIL, GREY-BREASTED, 487, 488
986 FANTAIL, HEINROTH'S, 488
986 FANTAIL, RUFOUS, **488**, *488* [→RUFOUS-FANTAIL]
986 *fasciolata, Locustella*, *613*, *613*
986 *feriatum, Malacocincla*, **631** (after *ferdinandi* entries)
987 FERNBIRD, *625*
987 FERNBIRD, CHATHAM, 625
987 FERNBIRD, CHATHAM ISLANDS, 625
987 FERNBIRD, NEW ZEALAND, **625**
987 *ferrugineigula, Phacellodomus*, *404* (after *ferrugineifrons* entry)
987 *fervidus, Caprimulgus*, *191*
987 FIG-PARROT, COXEN'S, *113* (after BLUE-FACED entry)
987 FIG-PARROT, DOUBLE-EYED, 113, *113*
987 under FINCH entry, add "689," before "690,"
987 FINCH, BENGALESE, 697 (after BARRANCA entry)
987 FINCH, BLACK-THROATED, **695**, *695*, 760
987 delete FINCH, CUCKOO entry
987 FINCH, LOCUST [→LOCUST-FINCH]
987 FINCH, ROSY, *708* [→ROSY-FINCH]
987 FINCH, SAFFRON, *763*, *763*
987 FINCH, SPARROW [→SPARROW-FINCH]
987 FINCH, STAR, **695**
987 FINCH, YELLOW-THIGHED, **728**, *728*
988 *finschii, Neocossyphus*, **507** (not *Stizorhina*); sequence after *Micropsitta*)
988 FIREFINCH, AFRICAN, **691**, *691*

988 under FIREFINCH change entries for BLACK-FACED, BLACK-THROATED, CHAD, ETHIOPIAN, JAMESON'S, KULIKORO, LANDANA, MALI, MASKED, REICHENOW'S and VINACEOUS from "691" to "692" preserving fonts
988 FIRETAIL, ALPINE, 695 (before BEAUTIFUL entry)
988 *fischeri, Zoothera*, 511
988 FISH-EAGLE, SANFORD'S, **270**
988 FISH-EAGLE, SOLOMON, 270
988 FISH-EAGLE, VULTURINE, 271
988 change FISHING-HAWK, 282 to FISHING-HAWK, COLLARED, 282
988 FLAMEBACK, BLACK-RUMPED, **61** (not BLACK-NAPED)
988 FLAMINGO, AMERICAN, *311*
988 FLATBILL, 348, 497
988 *flavibuccalis, Tricholaema*, **66**
989 *flavicollis, Dupetor*, **310** (not *Ixobrychus*); sequence after *Chlorocichla*
989 *flavigula, Serinus*, **703**
989 *flaviventris, Blacicus*, 352 (before *Brachypteryx* entry)
989 *flaviventris, Empidonax*, 352, **353**
989 *flaviventris, Lathrotriccus*, 352 (after *Hylophilus* entry)
989 *flaviventris, Tyrannula*, 352 (after *Tolmomyias* entry)
989 FLOWER-PIERCER, CARBONATED, 770
989 FLOWER-PIERCER, COAL-BLACK, *770*
989 FLOWER-PIERCER, HIGHLAND, *769*
989 FLOWERPECKER, BORNEAN FIRE-BREASTED, 659 (after BORNEAN entry)
989 FLOWERPECKER, FLAME-CHESTED, *657* (not FLAME-CRESTED)
990 FLOWERPECKER, INDONESIAN, *658*
990 FLOWERPECKER, RED-CROWNED, *657* (after RED-COLLARED entry)
990 FLOWERPECKER, YELLOW-CROWNED, *657*
990 FLUFFTAIL, SLENDER-BILLED, **220** (after RED-TAILED entry)
990 FLUFFTAIL, WATERS'S, 220
990 FLYCATCHER, AFRICAN DUSKY, 526
990 FLYCATCHER, AFRICAN SOOTY, 525
990 FLYCATCHER, ASIAN BROWN, **525**, *525*, 525
990 FLYCATCHER, BOAT-BILLED, 365, 497
990 FLYCATCHER, BRAN-COLORED, 350, *350*, *350*
990 FLYCATCHER, BROWN, 525
990 FLYCATCHER, BROWNISH, **348** (after BROWN-STREAKED entry)
990 after FLYCATCHER, BUFF-RUMPED add "FLYCATCHER, BURU, 528" and "FLYCATCHER, CANARY, 531 [→CANARY-FLYCATCHER]"
990 FLYCATCHER, CLIFF, **351**
990 FLYCATCHER, COLLARED, **526**, *526*
990 FLYCATCHER, DARK-SIDED, **525**, *525*
991 FLYCATCHER, MANGROVE, *495*
991 FLYCATCHER, MACCONNELL'S, *495* (not MCCONNELL'S); sequence after LUZMIN entry
991 FLYCATCHER, MELANESIAN, **496**
991 FLYCATCHER, NEW CALEDONIAN, 496
991 FLYCATCHER, OCEANIC, **495**
991 FLYCATCHER, OLIVE-SIDED, **352**
991 FLYCATCHER, PALAU, 495
991 FLYCATCHER, PALE-THROATED, 363
991 FLYCATCHER, RED-BREASTED, **527**, *527*, *527*, 528
991 FLYCATCHER, RED-THROATED, *527*
991 FLYCATCHER, SHRIKE, 502 [→SHRIKE-FLYCATCHER]
991 delete extra FLYCATCHER, SOOTY entry
991 FLYCATCHER, SULPHUR-RUMPED, **351**, *351*

1044 OYSTERCATCHER, CANARY ISLANDS, **244**
1044 OYSTERCATCHER, CHATHAM, 244
1044 OYSTERCATCHER, CHATHAM ISLANDS, *244*
1044 OYSTERCATCHER, SPECTACLED, *245*
1044 *pacificus, Otus,* 173 (after *Larus* entry)
1045 PADDYFIELD-WARBLER, 613 (delete BLUNT-WINGED)
1045 after *Pagophila* entry, add:
    PAINTED-BUNTING, EASTERN, *775*
        WESTERN, *775*

1045 *pallidior, Passerina, 775* (after *pallidinucha* entry)
1045 *Panychlora,* 149 (after *Panurus* entry)
1045 PARADISE-FLYCATCHER, AFRICAN, **491**, *491*
1045 PARADISE-FLYCATCHER, ANNOBON, *491* (after AFRICAN entry)
1045 PARADISE-FLYCATCHER, BLACK-HEADED, **491**, *491*
1045 PARADISE-KINGFISHER, BLACK-HEADED, *92* (after BIAK entry)
1046 PARADISE-KINGFISHER, BUFF-BREASTED, *92, 92*
1046 PARADISE-KINGFISHER, COMMON, *92, 92*
1046 PARADISE-KINGFISHER, LESSER, 92 (after KOFIAU entry)
1046 PARAKEET, GOLDEN-PLUMED, **125**
1046 PARAKEET, GREY-HEADED, **121**, 127
1046 PARAKEET, LORD HOWE, 117
1046 PARAKEET, LORD HOWE ISLAND, *117*
1046 PARAKEET, MAROON-TAILED, **126**, *126, 126*
1046 PARAKEET, NORFOLK, 117
1046 PARAKEET, NORFOLK ISLAND, **117** (after NORFOLK entry)
1046 PARAKEET, RAIATEA, *117*
1046 PARAKEET, RED-CHEEKED, 122 (after RED-BREASTED entry)
1046 PARAKEET, SANTA MARTA, **126** (after RUFOUS-FRONTED entry)
1046 PARAKEET, SOCIETY, 117
1046 PARAKEET, SOCORRO, *123* (after SOCIETY entry)
1046 PARAKEET, SUN, **124**, *124*
1047 PARROT, AFRICAN ORANGE-BELLIED, 119 (before AFRICAN YELLOW-FACED entry)
1047 PARROT, BROWN-HOODED, **129**, *129*
1047 PARROT, FIG [→FIG-PARROT]
1047 PARROT, KAWALL'S, **132** (after JARDINE'S entry)
1047 PARROT, MUSK [→MUSK-PARROT] (after MULGA entry)
1047 PARROT, PARADISE, **117**, *117*
1047 PARROT, PLUM-CROWNED, *130*
1047 PARROT, PRETRE'S, 131
1047 PARROT, PUERTO RICAN, 131 (after PRINCESS entry)
1047 PARROT, RED-CROWNED, 131 (after RED-CHEEKED entry)
1047 PARROT, RED-SPECTACLED, **131**, *131*
1047 PARROT, RING-NECKED, *116*
1047 PARROT, TUCUMAN, **131**
1047 PARROT, VASA, **118** [→VASA-PARROT]
1047 PARROT, YELLOW-FACED, 119, **132**
1047 PARROT, YELLOW-LORED, **131**
1047 PARROT, YUCATAN, 131
1048 PARROTBILL, CRESTED, 646 (after CHINESE entry)
1048 PARROTBILL, EYEBROWED, 646
1048 PARROTBILL, ORANGE, *646*
1048 PARROTLET, AMAZONIAN, **128** (before BLACK-EARED entry)
1048 PARROTLET, SPECTACLED, **127**
1048 delete PARROTLET, TEPUI entry
1048 PARTRIDGE, BARE-THROATED, 16, 17

1048 PARTRIDGE, BOULTON'S, 16 (not BOLTON'S); sequence after BORNEAN
1048 PARTRIDGE, BUFF-THROATED, **11**
1048 PARTRIDGE, FORMOSAN, **16**
1048 PARTRIDGE, KINABALU, **17** (after JAVAN entry)
1048 PARTRIDGE, TAIWAN, 16
1048 *parva, Ficedula,* **527**, *527*
1048 *parvirostris, Tetrao,* 22 (not *Tetraogallus*)
1048 *parvus, Zimmerius,* 339 (after *Porphyrio* entry)
1049 *patachonica, Oidemia,* 32 (after *Pastor* entry)
1049 *patachonicus, Micropterus,* 32 (before *Tachyeres* entry)
1049 *pauliani, Otus,* 171 (after *patens* entry)
1049 *pavonina, Balearica,* **217**
1049 PEACOCK-PHEASANT, MALAYSIAN, *21*
1049 *pectoralis, Cuculus,* 97 (after *Coturnix* entry)
1049 PELICAN, PHILIPPINE, 315
1049 PENDULINE-TIT, EURASIAN, **566**, *566*
1049 PENDULINE-TIT, MASKED, 566 (after KAPOK entry)
1049 PENDULINE-TIT, WHITE-THROATED, *566*
1050 PENGUIN, BLACK-FOOTED, 319 (after BIG-CRESTED entry)
1050 PENGUIN, LITTLE, **319**, *319*
1050 PENGUIN, MACARONI, **319**, *319*
1050 PENGUIN, ROCKHOPPER, **319**, *319*
1050 PENGUIN, WHITE-FLIPPERED, *319*
1050 *peposaca, Netta,* **38** (not *peposacea*)
1050 *perplexus, Spilornis,* 273 (after *perousii* entry)
1050 *perrotii, Hylexetastes,* **412**, *412*
1050 *personata,* delete *Corythaixoides* entry
1050 *personatus, Corythaixoides,* **168** (after *Atlapetes* entry)
1050 *peruanum, Glaucidium,* **178** (after *peruana* entry)
1050 *petersoni, Otus, 173*
1050 PETREL, BONIN, **322**
1050 PETREL, CHATHAM, **321**, 323
1050 PETREL, CHATHAM ISLANDS, **321**, 323
1050 PETREL, COLLARED, **322**
1050 PETREL, COOK'S, **322**
1050 PETREL, DARK-RUMPED, *323*
1050 PETREL, FIJI, **321** (after DIVING entry)
1050 PETREL, GALAPAGOS, **323**
1050 PETREL, GOULD'S, **322**
1050 PETREL, HAWAIIAN, **323**
1050 PETREL, HERALD, **322**, *322*
1050 PETREL, MACGILLIVRAY'S, 321
1050 PETREL, MOTTLED, **322**
1051 PETREL, PHOENIX, **322**
1051 PETREL, PYCROFT'S, **322**
1051 PETREL, SNOW, 321 [→SNOW-PETREL]
1051 PETREL, STEJNEGER'S, **322**
1051 PETREL, TAHITI, **321**, *321*
1051 PETREL, TRINDADE, *322*
1051 *Petroicidae,* 444 (after *Petroica* entry)
1051 PETRONIA, ITALIAN YELLOW-THROATED, 672
1051 PEWEE, BOREAL, 352
1051 *phaeopygia, Pterodroma, 323*
1051 PHEASANT, HOOGERWERF'S, 19 (not HOOGERSWERF'S)
1051 PHEASANT, HORSFIELD'S, *19*
1051 PHEASANT, SALVADORI'S, **19**, *19*
1051 PHEASANT, after SWINHOE'S add "VIETNAMESE, **19**" and "VO QUY'S, 19"
1052 *Philesturnus, 505*
1052 *Philetairus,* **681** (not *Philetarius*)
1052 *Phragmacia,* 597 (after *Phormoplectes* entry)
1052 *Philydonyris, 436*
1052 *pica, Pica,* **467**, *467*